WILLIAM NAPIER

Major General Sir William Napier

HISTORY OF
THE WAR IN THE
PENINSULA

EDITED AND INTRODUCED BY
BRIAN CONNELL

LONDON
The Folio Society
1973

0·22656808 3

Second impression 1974
PRINTED IN GREAT BRITAIN
Printed by W & J Mackay Limited, Chatham

TO

THE DUKE OF WELLINGTON

THIS History I dedicate to your Grace, because I have served long enough under your command to know why the Soldiers of the Tenth Legion were attached to Cæsar.

W. F. P. NAPIER

Contents

Maps

Illustrations

*The publishers would like to thank the Victoria and Albert Museum for
permission to reproduce illustrations from Bertaux:* The Campaigns
of the Duke of Wellington, *Paris 1817: and the Cruikshank etching:
also the Trustees of the British Museum for Charles MacFarlane: A*

Memoir of the Duke of Wellington, *London 1813:* The Military Adventures of Johnny Newcombe, *by a Citizen of the World, London 1852:* Campaigns of the British Army in Portugal *by Henry L'Eveque, London 1812: and the portrait of Wellington by Goya. The portrait of Napier is reproduced from* Life of General Sir William Napier *by H. A. Bruce, London 1864.*

Introduction

No British military campaign in history has so caught the imagination of successive generations as the long struggle against Napoleon in Spain and Portugal. Of its commanders, Sir John Moore has become a legend familiar to every schoolboy. The Duke of Wellington stands almost above Marlborough as our most successful general. Its battle honours – Vimeiro, Bussaco, Badajoz, Ciudad Rodrigo, Salamanca and Vitoria grace regimental standards to this day. The war and its protagonists have provided the subject for countless books during the intervening decades. Yet the most full-blooded and authentic account, the six volumes of Sir William Napier's *History of the War in the Peninsula*, has been out of print since the nineteenth century and there has not even been a single volume abridgement these sixty years.

His majestic saga, worthy of Gibbon or Carlyle, celebrates a remarkable triumph of British arms, and if national pride tends to elevate its contribution to the downfall of Napoleon out of proportion to the gigantic struggle of Austria, Prussia and Russia against revolutionary France, the fact remains that Britain was the only implacable opponent of Napoleon and that the 'Spanish ulcer' as he described it, was one of the principal causes of his military collapse. The general insurrection of the Spanish people provided the pattern for the resurgence of national consciousness in his oft-defeated continental opponents that broke his political hegemony.

From 1794 to 1808, the several British governments under Pitt and his successors had been baffled by the power of France. All the continental coalitions they had financed and subsidized crumbled into military impotence. Their own army was frittered away in peripheral expeditions and gained only colonial successes. At sea their measures prevailed, largely due to the genius of Nelson, whose victory at Trafalgar in 1805 ensured that the French could no longer invade, but still opened no route for Britain to the coasts of Europe. Their sole weapon was maritime blockade to counter Napoleon's denial of the continental ports to British trade under his Berlin decrees. Napoleon reacted violently to this confinement, suborned his feeble Spanish ally to permit the passage of troops to Portugal to block this last inlet for British goods and then proceeded treacherously to the military subjugation of Spain. That violent and unpredictable nation rose in chaotic and disorganized revolt. Britain's opportunity had come.

Napier's account of the six years that followed is not only marvellously comprehensive, but of tremendous narrative power. No military historian has ever equalled the surging splendour of such descriptive passages as the advance of the British infantry at Albuera, the cavalry charge at Salamanca or the assault of Badajoz. His vignettes and asides are salty and authentic. Impartial his account is not, although it has some reputation for being so. He was that unlikely combination, a political radical in a highly conservative profession. He was vehemently critical of the politicians in power in London and had a considerable ideological admiration for Napoleon. His military hero was Sir John Moore, a general of liberal outlook, although he transferred his affections to Wellington, who was not. He is severe beyond reason with other British officers such as Beresford, who trained the Portuguese divisions, and fails to give others of high competence, like Hill, their due. He does scant justice to the Spanish guerrillas, none to the governing Junta and much injustice to the beset Portuguese. He developed an almost absurd cult of Marshal Soult, able general though he was. All this adds to, rather than detracts from the force of his narrative. His supreme value as a witness is that he was a participant, fighting with outstanding gallantry in the 43rd Regiment of the fabled Light Division from the Coruña campaign of Sir John Moore to Wellington's invasion of France. He declares his interest in his own Preface to the first edition of his work:

The Spaniards have boldly asserted, and the world has believed, the deliverance of the Peninsula to be the work of their hands. This claim, so untruthful, I combat. It is unjust to the fame of the British general, injurious to the glory of the British arms: military virtue is not the growth of a day, nor is there any nation so rich and populous, that, despising it, can rest secure. The imbecility of Charles IV., the vileness of Ferdinand, the corruption imputed to Godoy, were undoubtedly the proximate causes of the calamities which overwhelmed Spain; but the primary, the historical cause, was the despotism springing from the union of a superstitious court and a sanguinary priesthood, a despotism which suppressed knowledge, contracted the public mind, sapped the foundation of military and civil virtue, and prepared the way for invasion. No foreign potentate would have attempted to steal into the fortresses of a great kingdom, if the prying eyes and clamorous tongues of a free press had been ready to expose his projects, and a disciplined army present to avenge the insult: Spain, destitute of both, was first circumvented by the wiles, and then ravaged by the arms of Napoleon. She was deceived and fettered because the public voice was stifled; she was scourged and torn because her military institutions were decayed. When an English force took the field, the Spaniards ceased to act as principals in a contest carried on in the heart of their country, and involving their existence as an independent nation. They were self-sufficient and their pride was wounded by insult, they were superstitious and their religious feelings were roused to fanatic fury by an all-powerful clergy who feared to lose their own rich endowments, but after the first burst of indignation the cause of independence created little enthusiasm. Horrible barbarities were exercised on French soldiers thrown by sickness or the fortune of war into the power of the invaded, and this dreadful spirit of personal hatred was kept alive by the exactions and severe retaliations of the invader; but no great general exertion to drive the latter from the soil was made, at least none was sustained with steadfast courage in the field: manifestoes, decrees, lofty boasts, like a cloud of canvas covering a rotten hull, made a gallant appearance, but real strength and firmness could nowhere be found.

Strange indeed was the spectacle presented. Patriotism supporting a vile system of government, a popular assembly working to restore a despotic monarch, the higher classes seeking a foreign master, the lower armed in the cause of bigotry and misrule. The upstart leaders, secretly abhorring freedom though governing in her name, trembled at the democratic activity they excited; and while calling forth all the bad passions of the multitude repressed the patriotism that would regenerate as well as save: the country suffered the evils without enjoying the benefits of a revolution. Tumults and assassinations terrified and disgusted the sensible part of the community, a corrupt administration of the resources extinguished patriotism, neglect ruined the armies. The peasant-soldier, usually flying at the first onset, threw away his arms and went home; or, attracted by the licence of the partidas, *joined the banners of men, the most part originally robbers, who were as oppressive to the people as the enemy; and these* guerrilla *chiefs would in their turn have been quickly exterminated, had not the French, pressed by the British battalions, been compelled to keep in large masses: this was the secret of Spanish constancy. Copious supplies from England and the valour of the Anglo-Portuguese troops supported the war, and it was the gigantic vigour with which the Duke of Wellington resisted the fierceness of France, and sustained the weakness of three inefficient cabinets that delivered the Peninsula.*

Napier came of a military family. His father, Colonel George Napier, eldest son of the second marriage of the fifth Lord Napier of Merchiston, served in the American Revolutionary War, lost his first wife there from yellow fever, was invalided home and then married the enchanting Lady Sarah Bunbury, fourth daughter of the second Duke of Richmond. When young she captivated the youthful George III and even Horace Walpole was entranced with her. Two more of her five sons served in the Peninsula, Sir Charles James Napier of the 50th Regiment was captured at Coruña, served on Wellington's staff at Bussaco and became known as the conqueror of Scinde. Sir George Thomas Napier was a favourite of Sir John Moore, served in the 52nd Regiment and became Governor of the Cape of Good Hope. Lady Sarah, who had long been blind, graced London society until her eighty-eighth year and died in 1826, the last surviving great grand-daughter of Charles II.

All the Napiers were spectacularly handsome. Colonel George stood six feet two, with a faultless figure. William, born in 1785, was a six-footer and inherited the family good looks. High spirited and intelligent, they were an attractive clan, with entrée everywhere, and great favourites in society. The family home was in Celbridge, County Kildare, which father and sons defended vigorously during the insurrection of 1798. William attended the local grammar school, was commissioned in the Royal Irish Artillery in 1800 and then had a lieutenancy bought for him in the 'Blues' by his uncle, the Duke of Richmond.

In 1803, Sir John Moore, then forming his experimental Light Brigade at Shorncliffe, persuaded William to join, initially, the 52nd Regiment, and then obtained for him a captaincy in the 43rd. He first served under the then Sir Arthur Wellesley in the expedition against Copenhagen in 1807. In 1808, his regiment sailed to Spain as part of Sir John Moore's expeditionary force. During the retreat to Coruña he marched for several days with bare and bleeding feet, with only a jacket and a pair of linen trousers in the depth of winter, contracting a fever which permanently weakened his constitution. Sick with pleurisy during Wellington's Talavera campaign, he walked 48 miles to take part in the battle. He saved the Light Division in command of the rearguard on the River Coa in 1810 and took part with a wound in his hip at the Battle of Bussaco, when both of his brothers were hit. Wounded again during

Masséna's retreat, he contracted a fever before Badajoz and was invalided home on the express instructions of Wellington, who kept their mother personally informed of all her sons' vicissitudes. At the Battle of Salamanca he led the 43rd as regimental major in review order three miles across the hottest fire of the day. In the savage battles on the Nive during Wellington's invasion of France he was again twice wounded and invalided home once more.

He had married Caroline, daughter of General the Hon. Henry Fox and niece of the statesman. Illness prevented him rejoining his regiment until after the Battle of Waterloo and in 1819, lacking the money to purchase his regimental lieutenant-colonelcy, went on half-pay. He took a house in Sloane Street, London, and developed a genuine talent for painting and sculpture, working with and being much praised by Chantrey. He contributed articles on military subjects to the *Edinburgh Review* and other periodicals and in 1823, at the suggestion of Lord Langdale, decided to write a 'History of the Peninsular War'. Wellington gave him much verbal information and made him free of Joseph Bonaparte's correspondence captured at Vitoria. Langdale introduced him in Paris to Soult, who entrusted him with his archives and opened up other French sources to him, including the private military notes and instructions of Napoleon. Napier continued a familiar of many of his fellow officers, corresponded in detail with most of those who had held high command, and saw the official correspondence of Britain's diplomatic envoys in the Peninsula. Idiosyncratic as many of his comments and conclusions are, his marshalling of the facts is encyclopaedic.

In the autumn of 1826 Napier moved with his growing family to Battle House, Bramham, near Devizes. In 1826 the first volume appeared, to immediate acclaim, followed at regular intervals by the remaining five, the last in 1840. John Murray, the publisher, lost money on the first, and the rest were published at Napier's own expense. They soon eclipsed the rival versions of Captain Hamilton, Southey and Lord Londonderry and have remained unchallenged as a source book of immense verve and authenticity ever since.

His denigration of Beresford as a general, resulting from the inconclusive battle of Albuera, and his wholesale condemnation of Canning as Foreign Secretary and Perceval as Prime Minister involved him in years of acrimonious correspondence. Much truth lay on his side, although Wellington, who by training and family background understood the political scene, was never as damning in his complaints. What Napier's work did was to establish Wellington for all time as a national hero of superhuman stature. After his military triumphs, the Iron Duke became one of the most unpopular men in England for espousing reactionary policies as a cabinet and Prime Minister during the period that culminated in the Reform Bill of 1832. But by the time Queen Victoria came to the throne in 1837, the temper of the times had changed and Napier's panegyric elevated him to the position of trust and affection he was to hold until the end of his days.

Napier continued to be promoted in the army on the half-pay list – colonel in 1830, major-general in 1841 and lieutenant-general in 1851. He spent a period as Lieutenant-Governor of Guernsey and was one of the general officer pall-bearers at the funeral of the Duke of Wellington in 1852. He remained an insatiable controversialist all his life, defending the reputation of Sir John Moore, the conduct of his brother Charles in Scinde, pleading for the Chartists in 1839 and 1848, declining a seat in Parliament several times on the plea of poverty, but organizing a campaign in the House of Commons for compensation to the survivors of the *Birkenhead* troopship disaster.

Promoted general in 1859, he died the following year. His memorial statue stands in St Paul's Cathedral opposite that of his brother Charles, with the inscription 'Historian of the Peninsular War'.

Napier published a single-volume abridgement of the History in 1852, but it suffered from too much paraphrase of his own words, although I have adopted his basic pattern of concentrating on the 'English Battles and Sieges in the Peninsula'. The six original volumes contain the best part of a million words and even if the copious appendices, morning states of the armies, justificatory pieces and controversial correspondence are omitted, the narrative still totals some 750,000 words. To bring this down to a readable 150,000 I have discarded ruthlessly all the subsidiary campaigns, all but his essential railings against the British, Spanish and Portuguese governments whom he considered inimical to his military heroes and all the lengthy speculations of a military theorist about what might have or should not have been done in countless circumstances. I doubt if the full text has been read for pleasure for decades and it is time to restore the best of this pulsating masterpiece to a modern readership.

I have kept Napier's prose intact in chronological sections, with sufficient introductory links to set the scene, maintain continuity and give a sense of the underlying strategy involved. I have deliberately left in a full account of Sir John Moore's first campaign and Wellington's last in France, which get omitted in most other histories. Napier's eccentric Anglo-French spelling of Spanish place names has been put into modern form, but all his other splendid prejudices have been preserved.

BRIAN CONNELL

I

The Peninsula in Revolt
1808

In the autumn of 1807 Napoleon's power was at its zenith. He had crowned himself Emperor in 1804, defeated the Austrians and Russians at Austerlitz in 1805, the Prussians at Jena in 1806 and the Russians at Friedland in June 1807. Europe, from the Niemen to the Pyrenees and from the Baltic to the toe of Italy, acknowledged his supreme authority. The Emperor of Russia was his ally, as was the pathetic King Charles IV of Spain. There remained but one unconquered enemy, Britain, mistress of the seas, inviolate since Nelson's victory at Trafalgar in 1805.

Unable to strike at this threat to his hegemony, Napoleon had issued his Berlin decrees in 1806, ordering all continental ports to be closed to British ships and subjects. Blockade and counter-blockade ensued, with serious damage to trade on both sides, matched by the vast growth in smuggling to a Europe hungry for British manufactured goods.

Britain had but two friends in Europe, Sweden and Portugal. Napoleon left Sweden to be subdued by the Russians. In August 1807 he summoned the Portuguese to obey his decrees. They protested. Napoleon then browbeat the feeble Spanish government into signing the Treaty of Fontainebleau on 27 October for a joint invasion of Portugal. But on 19 October, General Junot had already crossed the Spanish frontier with 30,000 inferior French troops, who occupied Lisbon. The Portuguese Regency fled to Brazil.

All this was incidental to a grander design. By March 1808, Napoleon had poured 90,000 of his best soldiers, under senior marshals, into Spain. Charles IV was forced to abdicate in favour of his son Ferdinand, who in his turn was cast aside and supplanted by Napoleon's brother Joseph. The Spaniards, at first stupefied, rose in revolt in May. With the central administration in chaos, provincial 'juntas', hastily formed in Asturias and elsewhere, appealed to their country's nominal enemy, Britain, for aid.

The British government, admirable only in the constancy of its opposition to Napoleon, was devoid of military and strategic resource. For years, amphibious expeditions, too small and ill-equipped to do damage, had pricked at the periphery of continental Europe. In the spring of 1808 her one general of proven renown, Sir John Moore, had been sent on a foolish enterprise to the Baltic. A few thousand men were available to the Governor of Gibraltar, Sir Hew Dalrymple. At disposal in London, with a reputation gained in India, not a strong recommendation to the entrenched military hierarchy in the Horse Guards, was a major-general, aged 39, named Sir Arthur Wellesley.

NAPOLEON'S uninterrupted success for so many years had given him a moral influence doubling his actual force. Exciting at once, terror, admiration and hatred, he absorbed the attention of an astonished world, and, openly or secretly, all men acknowledged the power of his genius: the continent bowed before him, and in England absurd and virulent libels on his person and character constantly increasing, indicated the growth of secret fear. His invasion of Spain was at first viewed with anxiety rather than with the hope of arresting it; but when the full extent of the injustice became manifest, the public mind was vehemently excited; a sentiment of some extraordinary change being about to take place in the affairs of the world, prevailed among all classes of society; and when the Spanish people rose against the man feared by all, the admiration which energy and courage exact, even from the base and timid, became enthusiastic in a nation conscious of the same qualities.

The arrival of the Asturian deputies was, therefore, universally hailed as an auspicious event; their wishes were forestalled, their suggestions received with eagerness, their demands complied with; and the riches of England were so profusely tendered by the ministers, as to engender an incredible arrogance and extravagance with the patriots. There is a way of conferring a favour which appears like accepting one, and this secret being discovered by the English cabinet, the Spaniards soon demanded as a right what they had at first solicited as a boon. In politics it is a grievous fault to be too generous, gratitude in state affairs is a delusion, the appearance of disinterested kindness never deceives and should never be assumed.

The capture of the Spanish frigates in time of peace had placed Great Britain and Spain in a state of hostility without a declaration of war. The invasion of Napoleon produced a friendly alliance between them without a treaty; for the cessation of hostilities was not proclaimed until long after succours had been sent to the juntas. The ministers seemed, by their precipitate measures, to be more

afraid of losing the assistance of the Spaniards, than prepared to take
the lead in a contest, which could only be supported by the power
and riches of Great Britain. Instead of a statesman with rank and
capacity to establish the influence of England by judicious counsels
and applications of succour, a number of obscure and inexperienced
men were sent to various parts of the Peninsula, and were empowered to distribute money and supplies at discretion.

Selected principally because they spoke Spanish, few of them had
any knowledge of war beyond regimental duty, and there was no
controlling authority: each did what seemed good to him. The
Spanish generals willingly received men whose inexperience was a
recommendation, and whose friendship could advance their consequence. Their flattering confidential politeness diverted the attention of the agents from the true objects of their mission; they looked
not to the efficiency of the armies, but adopted the inflated language
and extravagant opinions of the chiefs, and by their reports, raised
erroneous notions as to the relative situations of the contending
forces. Some exceptions there were, but the ministers were better
pleased with the sanguine than the cautious, and made their own
wishes the measure of their judgment. Accordingly, enthusiasm,
numbers, courage and talent, were gratuitously found for every
occasion, and money, arms and clothing were demanded incessantly,
and supplied with profusion. The arms were however generally left
in their cases to rot or to fall into the hands of the enemy, and sometimes they were sold to foreign merchants; the clothing seldom
reached the soldier's back; the money always misapplied, was
sometimes embezzled by those who received it for the nation; more
often employed to forward the private views of the juntas to the
detriment of public affairs; and it is a fact that from the beginning
to the end of the war, an English musket was rarely to be seen in the
hands of a Spanish soldier.

But it is time to quit this subject, and trace the progress of
Junot's invasion of Portugal, by which the whole circle of operations
in the Peninsula will be completed. The reader can then take a
general view of the situation of all parties, at the moment when
Sir Arthur Wellesley, disembarking in the Mondego, commenced
those campaigns which have filled the world with his glory.

Peremptory orders forced Junot to advance from Salamanca at
an unfavourable season, when the roads were nearly impracticable,
and part of his troops still in the rear. He met the Spanish contin-
gent, destined to act under his orders, at Alcantara, the latter end
of November, 1807; but the march to that town nearly disorganized

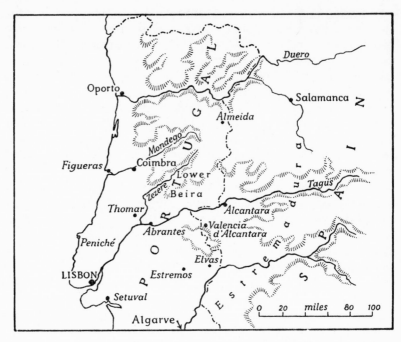

JUNOT'S INVASION OF PORTUGAL

his inexperienced army, and he could obtain no succours from the
Spanish authorities. Their repugnance, openly manifested, was so
embarrassing, that his chief officers, dismayed at the accumulating difficulties, would have had him discontinue his operations.
Junot was firm. He knew no English force had reached Lisbon. The
cowardice of the court there was notorious, and he commenced one
of those hardy enterprises which astound the mind by their success,
and leave the historian in doubt, whether to praise the happy daring
or stigmatize the rashness of the deed.

Without money, without transport, without ammunition sufficient for a general action, with an auxiliary force of Spaniards by no
means well disposed to aid him, Junot led a raw army through the
mountains of Portugal, on the most dangerous and difficult line by
which that country can be invaded. Ignorant of what was passing in
the interior, he knew not if he was to be opposed, nor what means
were prepared to resist him; but trusting to the inertness of the
Portuguese government, the rapidity of his movements, and the
renown of the French arms, he made his way through Lower Beira,
and suddenly appeared in the town of Abrantes, a fearful and

unexpected guest. There he obtained the first information of the true state of affairs. Lisbon was tranquil, the Portuguese fleet was ready to sail, the court still remained on shore. On hearing this, and, animated by the prospect of seizing the prince regent, he pressed forward, and reached Lisbon in time to see the fleet, having the royal family on board, clearing the mouth of the Tagus. One vessel dragged astern within reach of a battery, the French general himself fired a gun at her, and meeting, on his return to Lisbon, some Portuguese troops, he resolutely commanded them to form an escort for his person, and thus attended, passed through the streets of the capital.

Nature alone had opposed the progress of the invaders, yet such were the hardships endured, that of a column which numbered twenty-five thousand at Alcantara, two thousand tired grenadiers only entered Lisbon with their general. Fatigue, want, tempests, had scattered the remainder along two hundred miles of rugged mountains, inhabited by a warlike and ferocious peasantry, well acquainted with the strength of their fastnesses, and proud of successful defences made by their forefathers against former enemies. Lisbon itself contained three hundred thousand inhabitants and fourteen thousand regular troops; a powerful British fleet was at the mouth of the harbour, and the commander, Sidney Smith, urged the court to resist, offering to land his seamen and marines to aid in the defence of the town; his offers were declined, and the people, confounded by the strange scene and disgusted with the pusillanimous conduct of their rulers, evinced no desire to impede the march of events. Three weak battalions sufficed to impose a foreign yoke upon this great capital, and illustrated the truth of Napoleon's maxim: – '*In war the moral is to the physical force as three to one.*'

The prince regent, after having at the desire of the French government expelled the British residents, sent the British minister plenipotentiary away from his court, sequestered British property, and shut the ports of Portugal against British merchants; after having degraded himself and his nation by performing every submissive act which France could devise to insult his weakness, was still reluctant to forego the base tenure by which he hoped to hold his crown. Alternately swayed by fear and indolence, a miserable example of helpless folly, he lingered until the reception of a Moniteur dated the 13th of November, announced, in startling terms, that his reign was over! Lord Strangford, the British plenipotentiary, whose previous efforts to make the royal family emigrate had entirely failed, was then on board the squadron with the intention

of returning to England; but Sir Sidney threatened to bombard
Lisbon if the prince regent hesitated any longer, and thus urged on
both sides, he embarked with his whole court, and sailed for the
Brazils on the 29th of November, a few hours before Junot arrived.

As the treaty of Fontainebleau was unknown to the Portuguese,
the Spaniards were better received than the French. Indeed, the
treaty was little regarded by Junot, who soon proved that he held
Portugal as belonging entirely to France. When his stragglers had
come up, when the troops had recovered strength, and he knew a
reinforcement of five thousand had reached Salamanca, he assumed
paramount authority. He interfered with all the state departments,
gave Frenchmen all the lucrative offices, demanded a loan of two
hundred thousand pounds, and made his promises and protesta-
tions of amity frequent and loud in proportion to his encroachments.
At last being created Duke of Abrantes by Napoleon, he threw off
all disguise, suppressed the council of regency, seized the government and introduced beneficial reforms, but made the nation feel
that he was a conqueror. The flag and arms of Portugal were replaced by those of France, five thousand Portuguese soldiers were
incorporated with the French, and eight thousand sent away under
the Marquis of Alorna and Gomez Frere, two noblemen of greatest
reputation amongst the native officers. The rest of the troops were
disbanded.

An extraordinary contribution of four millions sterling was now
demanded by Napoleon, under the strange title of a 'State Ransom'.
This sum was exorbitant, and Junot prevailed on the emperor to
reduce it one half. He likewise, on his own authority, accepted the
forced loan, the confiscated English merchandise, the church plate
and the royal property, in part payment; yet the people were still
unable to raise the whole amount, for the court had carried the
greatest part of the church plate and bullion from the kingdom. It
had also drawn large sums of money from the people, under the pretext of defending the country, and with this treasure departed,
leaving the public functionaries, the army, private creditors, and
even domestic servants, unpaid. Discontent and misery prevailed,
yet the tranquillity of Lisbon during the first month was remarkable. The populace were submissive to a police, established under
the prince by the Count de Novion, a French emigrant, and continued by Junot. No European capital suffers so much as Lisbon
from the want of a good police, and the French general conferred
an unmixed benefit by giving full effect to Novion's plans. Yet so
deeply rooted is the prejudice for ancient customs, that no act gave

more offence than cleansing the streets and killing the wild dogs infesting them. A French sergeant who displayed zeal in destroying
those disgusting, dangerous animals, was assassinated.

During March and April, Junot's military system was completed. The arsenal of Lisbon contained abundance of naval and
military stores, and thousands of excellent workmen, who soon
renewed the artillery, the ammunition, the carriages and all the minor
equipments of the army. Two line-of-battle ships, three frigates and
seven lighter vessels of war were refitted, armed and employed to
defend the entrance of the Tagus and to awe the city. The army,
reinforced and better disciplined, well fed and clothed, had gained
confidence from success, and was become a fine body of robust men.

Including the French workmen and marines attached to it, the
army was above fifty thousand strong, nearly forty-five thousand
being fit for duty; that is to say, fifteen thousand five hundred Spaniards, five thousand Portuguese, and twenty-four thousand four
hundred French. Of these last, six thousand six hundred infantry
were distributed in Elvas, Almeida, Peniché, Abrantes and Setuval;
sixteen hundred were in the Algarves. Four hundred and fifty
cavalry were at Valencia d'Alcantara in Spanish Estremadura, and
three hundred and fifty held posts of communication from Lisbon to
Elvas, and from Almeida to Coimbra. Fifteen thousand of all arms
remained disposable.

Lisbon contained all the civil, military, naval, and greatest part
of the commercial establishments, the only fine harbour, two-
eighths of the population, and two-thirds of the riches of the whole
kingdom. It formed a centre, which was secured by the main body
of the French, while on the circumference strong posts gave support
to the operations of their moveable columns. The garrison of
Peniché secured the only harbour between the Tagus and the Mondego in which a large disembarkation of English troops could take
place, and the little fort of Figueras, held by a small garrison,
blocked the mouth of the last river. The division of Thomar secured
all the great lines of communication to the north-east, and in conjunction with the garrison of Abrantes, commanded both sides of the
Zezere. From Abrantes to Estremos, Elvas and Setuval, the lines
of communication were short, and through a country suitable for the
cavalry, which was all quartered on the south bank of the Tagus.
Thus, without breaking up the mass of the army, the harbours were
sealed against the English, and a large rich tract enclosed by posts,
so that any insurrection could be reached by a few marches and immediately crushed; the connexion between the right and left banks

of the Tagus at Lisbon was secured, the entrance defended by the refitted vessels of war, and a light squadron was prepared to communicate with South America. Nine Russian line-of-battle ships and a frigate, which, under the command of Admiral Siniavin, had taken refuge some time before from the English fleet, were of necessity engaged in the defence of the harbour, and formed an unwilling but not unimportant auxiliary force.

Such was Junot's military attitude in May. His political situation was not so favourable. His natural capacity was considerable but neither enlarged by study nor strengthened by mental discipline. Of intemperate habits, indolent in business, prompt and brave in action, quick to give offence, ready to forget an injury, he was at one moment a great man, the next below mediocrity. At all times he was unsuited to the task of conciliating and governing a people like the Portuguese, who, with passions as sudden and vehement as his own, retain a sense of injury or insult with incredible tenacity. He had many difficulties to encounter, and his duty towards France was in some instances incompatible with good policy towards Portugal. He was not, however, without resources for establishing a strong French interest, if he had possessed the ability and disposition to soothe a nation which had been as it were accidentally bowed to a foreign yoke.

Both the pride and poverty of the Portuguese, and the influence of ancient usages, interfered with Junot's policy. The monks, and most of the nobility, were inimical. All the activity of the expelled British factory, and the secret warfare of spies and writers in the pay of England, were directed to undermine his plans and render him and his nation odious; but he had possession of the government and capital, he had a fine army, he could offer novelty, so dear to the multitude, and he had the name and fame of Napoleon to assist him. The promises of power are always believed by the many, and there were abundance of grievances to remedy and wrongs to redress in Portugal. Among the best educated men, and in the universities, there existed a strong feeling against the Braganza family; and such an earnest desire for reformed institutions that steps were actually taken to have Prince Eugène declared King of Portugal: nor was this spirit extinguished at a much later date.

With these materials and the military vanity of the Portuguese to work upon, Junot might have established a powerful French interest. An active good government would soon have reconciled the people to the loss of an independence which had no wholesome breathing amidst the corrupt stagnation of the old system. But the arrogance of a conqueror, and the necessities of troops who were to be subsisted and paid by an impoverished people, gave rise to oppression, private abuses followed close upon public rapacity, and insolence left its sting to rankle in the wounds of the injured. The malignant humours broke out in quarrels and assassinations, severe punishments ensued, many of them unjust and barbarous, creating rage not terror, for the nation had not tried its strength in battle and would not believe it was weak. Meanwhile the ports were rigorously blockaded by the English fleet, and as the troubles of Spain interrupted the corn traffic, by which Portugal had been usually supplied, the unhappy people suffered under the triple pressure of famine, war-contributions and a foreign yoke. With all external ailment thus cut off, and a hungry army gnawing at its vitals, the nation could not remain tranquil; yet the first five months of Junot's government were, with the exception of a slight tumult at Lisbon when the arms of Portugal were taken down, undisturbed by commotion. Nevertheless the whole country was ripe for insurrection.

An abundant harvest gave Junot relief from his principal diffi-culty, but as one danger disappeared another presented itself. The Spanish insurrection excited the Portuguese; the neighbouring juntas communicated with the Spanish generals in Portugal; the capture of the French fleet in Cadiz became known; assassinations were multiplied; and the pope's nuncio fled on board the English fleet. English agents actively promoted this spirit, and the appearance of two English squadrons at different points of the coast having troops on board, alarmed the French, and augmented the impatient fierceness of the Portuguese, who discovered their hatred in various ways. Amongst other modes, an egg was exhibited in a church bearing an inscription intimating the speedy coming of Don Sebastian, who, like Arthur of romantic memory, is supposed to be hidden in a secret island, some day to re-appear and restore his country's ancient glory. The trick was turned against the contrivers. Other eggs prophesied unpatriotically: yet the belief of the Sebastianists lost nothing of its zeal. Many persons, not of the uneducated classes, were often observed upon the highest points of the hills, casting earnest looks towards the ocean in the hopes of descrying the island in which their long-lost hero was detained.   *   *   *

More than half a year had now elapsed since Napoleon first poured his forces into the Peninsula. Every moment of that time was marked by some extraordinary event, and a month had passed since a general and terrible explosion, shaking the unsteady structure of diplomacy to pieces, had left a clear space for the shock of arms. Yet the British cabinet was still unacquainted with the real state of public feeling in the Peninsula, and with the Spanish character; and with a disposable army of eighty thousand excellent troops, was totally unsettled in its plans, and unprepared for any vigorous effort. Agents were indeed despatched to every accessible province, the public treasure was scattered with heedless profusion, the din of preparation was heard in every department; but the bustle of confusion is easily mistaken for the activity of business, and time, removing the veil of official mystery covering those transactions, has exposed all their dull and meagre features: the treasure was squandered without judgment, the troops dispersed without meaning. Ten thousand soldiers exiled to Sweden; as many more, idly kept in Sicily, were degraded as the guards of a vicious court; Gibraltar was unnecessarily filled with fighting men; and Spencer wandered between Ceuta, Lisbon and Cadiz, seeking, like the knight of La Mancha, for a foe to combat.

A considerable force remained in England, but it was not ready for service; nine thousand men, collected at Cork, formed the only disposable army for immediate operations. The Grey and Grenville administration, so remarkable for unfortunate military enterprises, had assembled this handful of men with a view to permanent conquests in South America! Upon what principle of policy it is not necessary to inquire, but such was the intention; perhaps in imitation of the Roman senate, who sent troops to Spain when Hannibal was at the gates of the city. The Tory administration, relinquishing this scheme of conquest, directed Sir Arthur Wellesley to inform Miranda, the military adventurer of the day, not only that he must cease to expect assistance, but that all attempts to separate the colonies of Spain from the parent state would be discouraged by the English government. Thus the troops assembled at Cork became available, and Sir Arthur being appointed to command them, sailed on the 12th of July, to commence that long and bloody contest in the Peninsula which he was destined to terminate in such a glorious manner.

In recommending Portugal as the fittest field of action, the ministers were chiefly guided by the advice of the Asturian deputies, although Sir Hew Dalrymple's despatches gave more recent and extensive information than any supplied by those deputies. The latter left Spain at the commencement of the insurrection, were ill-informed of what was passing in their own province, ignorant of the state of other parts of the Peninsula, and of no capacity to advise in momentous affairs. But though Sir Arthur Wellesley was so vaguely instructed as to his military operations, he was expressly told the intention of the government was to enable Portugal and Spain to throw off the French yoke; and ample directions were given to him as to his future political conduct in the Peninsula. He was informed how to demean himself in any disputes arising between the insurgent nations, how to act with relation to the settlement of the supreme authority during the interregnum. He was directed to facilitate communications between the colonies and the mother country, and offer to arrange any differences between them. The terms upon which Great Britain would acquiesce in any negotiation between Spain and France were imparted to him; and finally he was empowered to recommend the establishment of a paper system in the Peninsula, as a good mode of raising money, and attaching the holders of it to the national cause! The Spaniards were not, however, sufficiently civilized to adopt this fine recommendation, and barbarously preferred gold to credit, at a time when no man's life, or faith, or wealth, or power, was worth a week's purchase.

Sir Hew was commanded to furnish Sir Arthur with every information which might be of use in the operations; and when the tenor of these instructions, and the great Indian reputation enjoyed by the latter, are considered, it is not to be doubted he was designed to lead the army of England. Yet, scarcely had he sailed when he was superseded. Not by one man whose fame and experience might have justified the act, but with a sweep, beyond mere vacillation, he was reduced to the fourth rank in that army, for the future governance of which he had, fifteen days before, received the most extended instructions. Sir Hew was now appointed to the chief command; and Sir John Moore, who had suddenly and unexpectedly returned from the Baltic, having by his firmness and address saved himself and his troops from the madness of the Swedish monarch, was, with marked disrespect, directed to place himself under the orders of Sir Harry Burrard, and proceeded to Portugal. Thus two men, comparatively unknown and unused to the command of armies, superseded the only generals in the British service whose talents and experience were indisputable. The secret springs of this proceeding are not so deep as to baffle investigation; but that task scarcely belongs to this history: it is sufficient to show the effects of envy, treachery and base cunning, without tracing those vices home to their possessors.

II

Vimeiro

Sir Arthur Wellesley was sufficiently ahead in his arrangements to fight and win his first engagement in the Peninsula before the dead hand of the two elderly thunderbolts of war who had been appointed to control him could descend. Junot, one of Napoleon's earliest military companions, was no administrator and his truculent and rapacious character soon began to alienate the Portuguese. The British expeditionary force landed when the French divisional generals, Loison, Laborde, Brennier and Kellerman, were somewhat dispersed to deal with threatening insurrection in the countryside. They concentrated swiftly, but Sir Arthur was too quick for them.

SIR ARTHUR WELLESLEY'S expedition sailed from Cork, he preceded it to Coruña, and on the 20th of July conferred with the Galician junta. They refused the aid of troops, but demanded arms and gold, and while the conference went on, an English frigate arrived with two hundred thousand pounds; then they desired to be rid of their guest, and recommended him to operate in the north of Portugal. They gave a false statement of the number of Spanish and Portuguese in arms near Oporto, promised to reinforce them with another division, and gave still more incorrect information of Junot's strength, and thus persuaded Sir Arthur not to land in Galicia, though it was at the mercy of Bessières, having neither men nor means to resist his progress.

Mr Charles Stuart, the British envoy to the junta, came with the general, and quickly penetrating the flimsy veil of Spanish enthusiasm, informed his government of the true state of affairs; but his despatches were unheeded, while the inflated reports of the subordinate civil and military agents were blazoned forth, and taken as sure guides. Sir Arthur proceeded to Oporto, where he found Colonel Browne, an intelligent officer employed to distribute succours, who told him no Spanish troops were in the north of Portugal, and the Portuguese force was upon the Mondego, to the south of which river the insurrection had spread. Eight thousand French were supposed to be in their front, and some great disaster was to be expected, because, 'with every good will in the people, their exertions were so shortlived, and with so little combination, there was no hope of their being able to resist the advances of the enemy'; in fact, only five thousand regulars and militia, half armed and associated with ten or twelve thousand peasants without any arms, were in the field. A large army was made out upon paper by the Bishop of Oporto, who proposed various plans of operation, which Sir Arthur was not inclined to adopt. After some discussion, the prelate agreed that the paper army should look to the defence of the Tras os Montes against Bessières, and the five thousand soldiers on the Mondego should be joined by the British.

[It was when he arrived] at the Mondego [that Sir Arthur] received official notice of Sir Hew Dalrymple's appointment and the sailing of Sir John Moore's troops, yet this mortifying intelligence did not relax his activity. He estimated Junot's force at sixteen or eighteen thousand men, a number, indeed, below the truth, yet sufficient to make the hardiest general pause before he disembarked with nine thousand, having no certainty that his fleet could remain even for a day in that dangerous offing – another officer also was to profit from success, while failure would ruin his own reputation with the English public, always ready to deride Indian generals.

It was difficult to find a place to land. The coast, from the Minho to the Tagus, save at a few points, is rugged and dangerous; all the river harbours have bars, and are difficult of access even for boats. With the slightest breeze from the seaboard, a terrible surf breaks along the whole coast; and when the south wind, which usually prevails from August to the winter months, blows, a more dangerous shore is not to be found in any part of the world.

Seventy miles northward of the Lisbon Rock, the small peninsula of Peniché offered the only safe and accessible bay adapted for a disembarkation; but the anchorage was within range of the fort, which contained a hundred guns and a garrison of a thousand men. The next best place was the Mondego river; there the little fort of Figueras, now occupied by English marines, secured a free entrance, and Sir Arthur adopted it. The landing commenced the 1st of August, and the weather was favourable, yet the operation was not completed before the 5th, and on that day, with singular good fortune, Spencer arrived [from Gibraltar]. The two corps, however, could only furnish twelve thousand three hundred men.

When the troops were on shore, the British general repaired to Montemor Velho, to confer with Don Bernardim Freire de Andrada, the Portuguese commander-in-chief, who proposed to unite all the troops, relinquish the coast, march into the heart of Beira, and commence an offensive campaign. He promised ample stores of provisions, but Sir Arthur placed no reliance on his promises. He gave Freire five thousand stand of arms with ammunition, refusing to separate from his ships; for seeing clearly the insurgents were unable to give any real assistance, he resolved to act with reference to the probability of their deserting him in danger. Irritated at this refusal, Freire reluctantly consented to join the British army, but pressed Sir Arthur to hasten to Leiria, lest a large magazine filled as he affirmed with provisions for the use of the British army, should fall into the enemy's hands; wherefore the advanced guard of the English army quitted the Mondego the 9th, taking the road to Leiria, and the main body followed the next day.

Upon the other side, Junot, who had received information of the English descent in the Mondego, as early as the 2nd, was embarrassed by the distance of his principal force, and the hostile disposition of the inhabitants of Lisbon. Exaggerated notions of the insurrection were entertained by himself and his principal officers. The anticipation of coming freedom was apparent in the wrathful looks and stubborn manners of the populace, superstition was at work to increase the hatred and the hopes of the multitude, and it was at this time the prophetic eggs, denouncing death to the French, and deliverance to the Portuguese, appeared. But less equivocal indications of approaching danger were to be drawn from the hesitations of Junot, who, wavering between his fear of an insurrection in Lisbon and his desire to check the immediate progress of the British army, exhibited a mind yielding to the pressure of events.

As the armies approached the Portuguese became alarmed; for, notwithstanding the language of their manifestos, and bombastic conversation, a conviction of French invincibility pervaded all ranks. The leaders, knowing their own deficiency, and incredulous of English courage, dreaded a battle, because defeat would render it hard to make terms, whereas, with five or six thousand men in arms, they could secure a capitulation. The Oporto junta, already aiming at supreme authority, foresaw also, that even with victory, it would serve their particular views to have an army untouched and disconnected with a foreign general. Freire, well instructed in the secret designs of this party, resolved not to advance beyond Leiria, but as a mask demanded provisions from the English, choosing to forget the magazine he had just monopolized, and the bishop's formal promise to feed the British troops.

This extraordinary demand, that an auxiliary army just landed should nourish the native soldiers instead of being itself fed by the people, was met by Sir Arthur Wellesley with a strong remonstrance. He had penetrated Freire's secret motives, yet, feeling the importance of a Portuguese force acting in conjunction with his own, he first appealed to his honour and patriotism, admonishing him that he would forfeit all pretension to either if he let the British fight without assistance. The appeal did not touch Bernardim, and he pretended a design to act independently by the line of the Tagus. Sir Arthur then changed from rebuke to conciliation, urging him not to risk his troops by an isolated march, but keep behind the English and await the result. The advice was agreeable to Freire, and Colonel Trant, a military agent, persuaded him to place fourteen hundred infantry, with two hundred and fifty cavalry, under the English general. This defection of the native force was, however, a serious evil. It shed an injurious moral influence, and deprived Sir Arthur of troops whose means of gaining intelligence and local knowledge might have compensated for his want of cavalry. Nevertheless, continuing his march, the advanced guard entered Caldas the 15th, on which day Junot reluctantly quitted Lisbon, with a reserve composed of two thousand infantry, six hundred cavalry, and ten pieces of artillery: he also took with him his grand parc of ammunition, and a military chest containing forty thousand pounds.

*   *   *

Early in the morning of the 17th, thirteen thousand four hundred and eighty allied infantry, four hundred and seventy cavalry, and eighteen guns, issued from Obidos, and soon afterwards broke into three distinct columns of battle.

The left, commanded by General Ferguson, was composed of his own and Bowes's brigade of infantry, reinforced by two hundred and fifty riflemen, forty cavalry, and six guns, forming a total of four thousand nine hundred combatants. He marched by the crests of the hills adjoining the Sierra de Baragueda, being destined to turn the right flank of Laborde's position, and oppose the efforts of Loison, if that general, who was supposed to be at Rio Mayor, should appear during the action.

The right, under Trant, composed of a thousand Portuguese infantry, and fifty horse of the same nation, moved by the village of St Amias, with the intention of turning the left flank of the French.

The centre, nine thousand strong with twelve guns, commanded by Sir Arthur in person, marched straight against the enemy by the

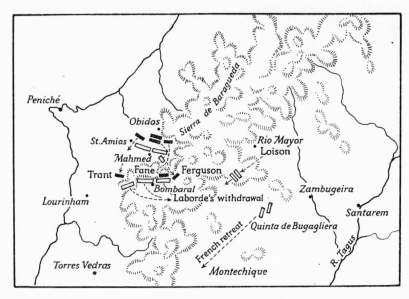

WELLESLEY MARCHES ON LISBON

village of Mahmed. It was composed of Hill's, Nightingale's, Catlin Crawfurd's and Fane's brigades of British infantry, four hundred cavalry, two hundred and fifty of which were Portuguese, accompanied by four hundred light troops of the same nation. As this column advanced, Fane's brigade, extending to its left, drove back the French skirmishers and connected Ferguson with the centre. Meanwhile the latter approached the elevated plain upon which Laborde was posted, and Hill, moving on the right of the main road, supported by the cavalry and covered by the fire of his light troops, pushed forward rapidly to the attack; on his left Nightingale displayed a line of infantry preceded by the fire of nine guns; Crawfurd's brigade and all the remaining pieces of artillery, formed a reserve. Fane's riflemen now crowned the nearest hills on the right flank of the French, the Portuguese troops showed the head of a column beyond St Amias on the enemy's left, and Ferguson was seen descending from the higher grounds in the rear of Fane: Laborde's position seemed desperate, but with the dexterity of a practised warrior he evaded the danger, and, covered by his cavalry, fell back to the heights of Zambugeira.

To dislodge him fresh dispositions were necessary. Trant continuing his march, was to turn his left; Ferguson and Fane united,

THE BATTLE OF VIMEIRO

were directed through the mountains to turn his right. Hill and
Nightingale advanced against the front, which was of singular
strength, and only to be approached by narrow paths winding
through deep ravines. A swarm of skirmishers, starting forward,
soon plunged into the passes, and spreading to the right and left,
won their way among the rocks and tangled evergreens that over-
spread the steep ascent. With greater difficulty the supporting
columns followed; their ranks were disordered in the confined
and rugged passes, the hollows echoed with a continued roll of
musketry, the shouts of the advancing soldiers were loudly answered
by the enemy, and the curling smoke, breaking out from the foliage
on the side of the mountain, marked the progress of the assailants,
and showed how stoutly the defence was maintained.

Anxiously watching for Loison, Laborde gradually slackened his
hold on the left, yet clung tenaciously to the right, still hoping to
be joined by that general, and the ardour of the 9th and 29th English
regiments favoured this skilful conduct. It was intended, they should
take the right-hand path of two leading up the same hollow, and
thus have come in upon Laborde's flank in conjunction with Trant's
column; but the left path led more directly to the enemy, the 29th
followed it, the 9th was close behind, and both regiments advanced
so vigorously, as to reach the plain above before the lateral movements of Trant and Ferguson could shake the credit of the position.
The right of the 29th arrived first at the top, under a heavy fire; ere
it could form Colonel Lake was killed, and some French companies,
which had been cut off on the right, gallantly broke through the
column, carrying with them a major and fifty or sixty other prisoners.
The head of the regiment, thus pressed, fell back, but rallied on
the left wing below the brow of the hill, and being joined by the 9th,
whose colonel, Stewart, also fell in this bitter fight, the whole
pushed forward again and regained the dangerous footing above.

Laborde, who brought every arm into action at the proper time
and place, endeavoured to destroy these regiments before they
could be succoured; he failed, yet gained time to rally his left wing
upon his centre and right. Now the 5th regiment, following the
right-hand path, arrived, the English were gathering thickly on the
heights, and Ferguson, who had at first taken an erroneous direction
towards the centre, recovered the true line and was rapidly passing
the French right. Laborde then retreated by alternate masses,
protecting his movements with short vigorous charges of cavalry,
and at Zambugeira attempted another stand; but the English bore
on too heavily and he fell back disputing the ground to the Quinta

de Bugagliera. There he halted until his detachments on the side
of Segura rejoined him, and then taking to the narrow pass of
Runa marched all night to gain the position of Montechique, leaving
three guns on the field of battle and the road to Torres Vedras open
for the victors. The loss of the French was six hundred killed and
wounded, among the latter Laborde himself. The British had two
lieutenant-colonels and nearly five hundred men killed, taken, or
wounded, and as not more than four thousand men were actually
engaged, this fight was very honourable to both sides.

A little after four o'clock the firing ceased, and Sir Arthur,
hearing Loison's division was at Bombaral, only five miles distant,
took a position for the night in an oblique line to that which he had
just forced; his left rested upon a height near the field of battle, his
right covered the road to Lourinham. Believing that Loison and
Laborde had effected their junction at the Quinta de Bugagliera,
and that both were retiring to Montechique, he resolved to march
the next morning to Torres Vedras, by which he would have secured
an entrance into the mountains. Before nightfall he heard that
Anstruther's and Acland's divisions, accompanied by a large fleet
of store ships, were off the coast, the dangerous nature of which
rendered it necessary to provide for their safety by a quick disembarkation. This changed his plans, and he resolved to seek some
convenient post, which being in advance of his present position
would likewise enable him to cover the landing of these reinforcements: the vigour of Laborde's defence had also its influence; before
an enemy so bold and skilful no precaution could be neglected with
impunity.

Estimating the French army at eighteen thousand men, Sir
Arthur judged that Junot could not bring more than fourteen thousand into the field; he designed, therefore, to strike the first blow,
and follow it up so as to prevent the enemy from rallying and
renewing the campaign upon the frontier. Hence the army was re-
organized during the 20th in eight brigades of infantry and four
squadrons of cavalry, and every preparation was made for the next
day's enterprise; but at that critical period of the campaign, the
ministerial arrangements which provided three commanders-in-chief
began to work. Sir Harry Burrard arrived in a frigate off the bay of
Maceira, and Sir Arthur, checked in the midst of his operations on
the eve of a decisive battle, repaired on board to report the situation
of affairs. He renewed his former recommendation relative to the
disposal of Sir John Moore's troops; but Burrard, having previously
resolved to bring the latter down to Maceira, forbade any offensive

movement until the whole army should be concentrated : whereupon
Sir Arthur returned to his camp.

Although somewhat vaguely defined as a position the ground
occupied by the army was strong. Vimeiro, situated in a valley
through which the little river of Maceira flows, contained the parc
and commissariat stores; the cavalry and the Portuguese were on
a small plain behind the village, in front of which was a rugged
height with a flat top, commanding all the ground to the southward
and eastward for a considerable distance. Upon this height Fane's
and Anstruther's infantry, with six guns, were posted. Fane's left
rested on a churchyard, blocking a road which led over the extremity
of the height to Vimeiro. Anstruther's troops were partly on Fane's
right, partly in reserve. A mountain, commencing at the coast,
swept in a half circle close behind the right of the Vimeiro hill, and
commanded, at rather long artillery range, all its upper surface.
The first, second, third, fourth and eighth brigades of infantry,
with eight guns, occupied this mountain, which was terminated on
the left by a deep ravine dividing it from another strong and narrow
range of heights over which the road from Vimeiro to Lourinham
passed. The right of these last heights also overtopped the hill in
front of Vimeiro; but the left, bending suddenly backward after the
form of a crook, returned to the coast and ended in a lofty cliff;
there was no water upon this ridge, wherefore only the fortieth
regiment and some piquets were placed there.

In the night of the 20th, about twelve o'clock, Sir Arthur was
aroused by a German officer of dragoons, who with some consterna-
tion reported that Junot, coming with twenty thousand men to
attack, was distant but one hour's march. Undisturbed by this inflated report, he merely sent out patrols, warned the piquets to be
alert, and before day-break had his troops, following the British
custom, under arms. The sun rose and no enemy appeared; but at
seven o'clock, a cloud of dust was observed beyond the nearest
hills, and at eight an advanced guard of horse was seen to crown the
heights to the southward, sending forward scouts on every side.
Scarcely had this body been descried, when a force of infantry,
preceded by other cavalry, was discovered moving along the road
from Torres Vedras to Lourinham with a rapid pace, and threatening to turn the left of the British position. Column after column
followed in order of battle. The French were evidently coming to
fight, but the right wing of the British was not menaced by this
movement, and the second, third, fourth and eighth brigades were
therefore directed to cross the valley behind the Vimeiro height and

take post where the fortieth regiment and the piquets stood. As they reached this ground, the second and third brigades were disposed in two lines perpendicular to the front shown by Fane and Anstruther, and the fourth and eighth were to have formed a third line, but ere the latter could reach the summit the battle had commenced. This flank movement was not seen by the enemy. A line of skirmishers, thrown out on the descent to the right, covered the flank of the two brigades, the cavalry was drawn up in the plain on the right of Vimeiro, and the fifth brigade and Portuguese were detached to the returning ridge of the crook, thus covering the extreme left and rear of the position. Hill remained with the first brigade on the mountain which the others had quitted, furnishing a support to the centre and a reserve to the whole; yet the ground between the armies was so wooded and broken, that after the French had passed the ridge where they had been first descried no correct view of their movements could be obtained; wherefore the British, being weak in cavalry, were forced to wait patiently until the columns of attack were close upon them.

Junot had quitted Torres Vedras the evening of the 20th, intending to fall on the English army at day-break, but the defile in his

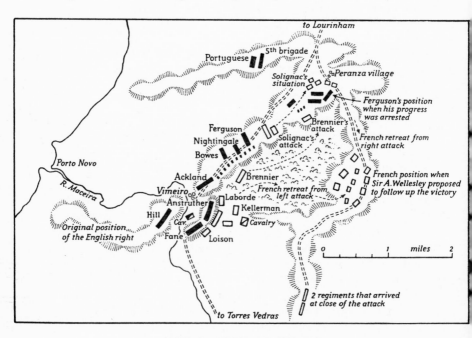

THE BATTLE OF VIMEIRO

front retarded the march and fatigued the troops. He found the
British order of battle presenting two faces of a triangle, the apex,
formed by the height in front of Vimeiro, well furnished; the left
face seemingly naked, for the piquets only could be seen, and the
march of the four brigades across the valley was hidden from him.
Concluding the principal force to be in the centre, he resolved to
form two connected attacks, the one against the apex, the other
against the left, which he thought an accessible ridge: but a deep
ravine, trenched as it were along the base, rendered it almost
impervious to an attack, except at the extremity, over which the
road from Torres Vedras to Lourinham passed. He had nearly fourteen thousand fighting men organized in four divisions. Three were
of infantry, one of cavalry, there were twenty-three pieces of very
small artillery, each division was composed of two brigades, and
at ten o'clock they commenced the Battle of Vimeiro.

Laborde marched with one brigade against the centre, Brennier
led another against the left, Loison followed at a short distance.
Kellerman moved with a reserve of grenadiers behind Loison; the
cavalry under Margaron, thirteen hundred, were, one part on the
right of Brennier, another in rear of the reserve; the artillery, distributed among the columns, opened its fire wherever the ground
was favourable. Laborde's and Brennier's attacks were to have been
simultaneous, but the latter, coming unexpectedly upon the ravine
before mentioned as protecting the English left, got entangled
among the rocks and water-courses; thus Laborde alone engaged
Fane and Anstruther, and under a heavy and destructive fire of
artillery which smote him front and flank; for the eighth brigade,
then in the act of mounting the heights where the left was posted,
seeing the advance of the French columns against the centre, halted,
and opened a battery against their right.

Junot perceiving this break of combination, ordered Loison to
support Laborde's attack with one brigade, and directed another
under Solignac to turn the ravine in which Brennier was entangled,
and so fall upon the left extremity of the English line; but Fane,
seeing Loison's advance, and having discretionary power over the
reserve artillery, directed Colonel Robe to bring it up, thus forming
with the divisional guns a powerful battery. Loison and Laborde
now formed one principal and two secondary columns of attack;
of the latter, one advanced against Anstruther's brigade, the other
endeavoured to penetrate by a road which passed between the
ravine and a church on the extreme left of Fane. The main column
under Laborde, preceded by a multitude of light troops, mounted

the face of the hill with great fury and loud cries, the English skirmishers were forced back upon the lines, and the French masses reached the summit, but shattered with the terrible fire of Robe's artillery, and breathless from their exertions. In this state, being first struck with musketry at the distance of half pistol shot, they were charged in front and flank by the fiftieth regiment, and overthrown.

Before this, the fifty-second and ninety-seventh regiments, of Anstruther's brigade, had repulsed the minor attack on that general's right, and he had detached the second battalion of the forty-third to the churchyard on Fane's left, where it was when Kellerman, reinforcing its opponents with a column of grenadiers, sent them on at a running pace. Those choice soldiers beat back the advanced companies of the forty-third, but to avoid Robe's artillery which ransacked their left, they dipped a little into the ravine on the right, and were immediately taken on the other flank by the guns of the fourth and eighth brigades. Then, when the narrowness of the way and the sweep of the round shot was crushing and disordering the French ranks, the forty-third, rallying in one mass, went furiously down upon the very head of the column, and with a short but fierce struggle drove it back in confusion. In this fight the British regiment suffered severely, and so close was the combat, that Patrick, sergeant-armourer of the forty-third, and a French soldier, were found dead, still grasping their muskets with the bayonets driven through each body from breast to back!

Now the French fell back along the whole front, and Colonel Taylor, riding out from the right of the central hill, led the few horsemen he commanded into the midst of the confused masses, scattering and sabreing them; but then Margaron, coming suddenly down to their support, slew Taylor and cut the half of his squadron to pieces, and Kellerman immediately threw his reserved grenadiers into a pine wood in advance to cover the retreat. All else was disorder. The woods and hollows were filled with wounded and straggling men, seven guns were lost, and the beaten masses retired towards the Lourinham road, in a direction nearly parallel to the British front, leaving the road from Vimeiro to Torres Vedras open.

Sir Arthur forbade pursuit, partly because Kellerman's grenadiers still held the pine wood flanking the line of retreat, partly because Margaron's horsemen, riding stiffly between the two armies, were not to be lightly meddled with. In this state, while Brennier was hampered in the ravine, Solignac, coming by the crest of the ridge above, encouraged Ferguson's brigade, which closed the left of the

English position. He expected to find a weak flank, but encountered a front of battle on a depth of three lines and protected by steep declivities on either side; a powerful artillery swept away his foremost ranks, and on his right, the fifth brigade and the Portuguese were seen marching by a distant ridge towards the Lourinham road, threatening his rear. Scarcely had he shown a front, when Ferguson, taking the lead, vigorously attacked, and the ground widening as the British advanced, the regiments of the second line running up in succession constantly increased the front; then the French, falling fast under the fire, drew back fighting until they reached the farthest declivity of the ridge. Their cavalry made several vain efforts to check the advancing troops, but Solignac was carried from the field severely wounded, and his retiring division, outflanked on its left, was cut off from the line of retreat and thrown into the low ground about the village of Peranza, where six guns were captured. Ferguson, leaving the eighty-second and seventy-first regiments to guard those pieces, continued to press the disordered columns, but at this moment Brennier, having at last cleared the ravine, came unexpectedly upon those two battalions and retook the artillery; his success was but momentary; the surprised troops rallied upon the higher ground, poured in a heavy fire of musketry, and returning to the charge with a shout, overthrew him and recovered the guns. Brennier himself was wounded and made prisoner, and Ferguson having completely separated the French brigades, would also have forced the greatest part of Solignac's to surrender, if an unexpected order had not obliged him to halt. The discomfited troops then re-formed under the protection of their cavalry with admirable quickness, and making an orderly retreat, were soon united to the broken brigades falling back from the attack on the centre.

Brennier being brought to Sir Arthur Wellesley the moment he was taken, eagerly demanded if Kellerman's reserve had yet charged; the English general quickly ascertained from the other prisoners that it had, and thus knew the enemy's attacks were exhausted, that no considerable body could be still hidden in the woods on his front and that the battle was won.

But Sir Harry Burrard, who was present during the action, though partly from delicacy and partly from approving Sir Arthur's arrangements he had not hitherto interfered, now assumed the chief command. From him the order arresting Ferguson's victorious career had emanated, and further offensive operations were forbidden, for he had resolved to wait in the position of Vimeiro until the arrival of Sir John Moore. The adjutant-general, Clinton, and Colonel George Murray the quarter-master-general, supported Sir Harry's views, and Sir Arthur's earnest representations could not alter their determination.

Burrard's decision was certainly erroneous, yet error is common in an art which at best is but a choice of difficulties. The circumstances of the moment were imposing enough to sway most generals. The French had failed in the attacks, yet rallied with surprising quickness under the protection of a strong and gallant cavalry. Sir Harry knew that the artillery carriages were so shaken as to be scarcely fit for service, the draft horses few and bad, the commissariat parc in the greatest confusion, and the hired Portuguese carmen making off with their carriages in all directions. The English cavalry was totally destroyed and Spencer had discovered a line of fresh troops on the ridge behind that occupied by the French army. Weighing all these things in his mind with the caution natural to age, Burrard refused to hazard the fortune of the day upon what he deemed a perilous throw; and Junot, who had displayed all that reckless courage to which he originally owed his elevation, was enabled by this unexpected cessation of the battle to re-form his broken army. Twelve hundred fresh men joined him at the close of the contest, and then, covered by his cavalry, he retreated with order and celerity until he regained the command of the pass of Torres Vedras, and at dark the relative position of the two armies was the same as on the evening before.

Sir Harry Burrard's control was soon over. Early on the morning of the 22nd, Sir Hew Dalrymple disembarked and assumed the chief command. Thus in the short space of twenty-four hours, during which a battle was fought, the army fell successively into the hands of three men, coming from the ocean with different views, habits and information, and without any previous opportunity of communing even by letter: and they were brought together at a moment when it was more than probable they must all disagree. For when Sir Hew was appointed to the command, Sir Arthur was privately recommended to him by the minister, as a person to be employed with more than usual confidence; and this unequivocal hint was backed with such an overbearing force by the previous reputation and recent exploits of the latter, that it could not fail to produce some want of cordiality. Sir Arthur could not do otherwise than take the lead in discussing affairs of which he had more than laid the foundation, and Sir Hew would have forfeited all claims to independence in his command, if he had not exercised the right of judging for himself between the conflicting opinions of his predecessors.

After receiving information upon the most important points, and taking a hasty view of the situation of the army – although the wounded were still upon the ground, and the wains of the commissariat employed to remove them – Sir Hew directed an advance on the 23rd. But, with Burrard, he thought the matter perilous, requiring the concentration of all the troops and means, wherefore he persisted in bringing Sir John Moore down to Maceira. Sir Arthur opposed this. The provisions on shore would not, he said, supply more than eight or nine days' consumption for the troops already at Vimeiro; the country could furnish no assistance; and the fleet was a precarious resource, because the first of the gales common at that season of the year, would certainly send it from the coast, if it did not destroy a great portion of it. Sir Hew however thought the separation of the troops more dangerous than the chance of distress from such events, and his position was embarrassing. The Bishop of Oporto had failed in his promise of assisting the troops with draft cattle – as indeed he did in all his promises – the artillery and commissariat were ill supplied with mules and horses; the cavalry was a nullity; and the enemy, with exception of his actual loss in killed and wounded, had suffered nothing from a defeat which did not deprive him of a single position necessary to his defence.

While weighing this state of affairs, he was informed that Kellerman, bearing a flag of truce and escorted by a strong body of cavalry, was at the outposts to demand a conference. This was very unexpected; but Junot after regaining Torres Vedras had occupied Mafra, and was preparing to fight again when he received intelligence that Lisbon was on the point of insurrection, whereupon he hastily sent a false account of the action to that city, together with a reinforcement for the garrison, and then consulted his generals as to further measures. It is an old and sound remark that 'a council of war never fights', and Kellerman's mission was the result of the above consultation. He demanded a cessation of arms, and proposed the basis of a convention to evacuate Portugal. Nothing could be more opportune, and Sir Hew readily accepted the proposal. He knew, from an intercepted plan of operations sketched by the chief of the French engineers, Colonel Vincent, that Junot possessed several strong positions in front of Lisbon; that a final retreat upon Almeida, or across the river upon Elvas, was considered a matter of course and easy of execution. Hence the proposed convention was an unexpected advantage offered in a moment of difficulty: the only subject of consideration was the nature of the articles proposed by Kellerman. Sir Hew, necessarily ignorant of many details, had recourse to Sir A. Wellesley, who, taking an enlarged view of the question, coincided as to the policy of a convention, by which a strong French army would be quietly got out of a country it had complete military possession of, a great moral effect in favour of the general cause produced, and an actual gain made of men and time for the further prosecution of the war in Spain.

III

Sir John Moore
1808—9

The Convention of Cintra, so-called, in defiance of logic, from the nearest town of any size, permitted Junot's army to leave Lisbon for France in British ships, carrying all their arms, belongings and booty. Its terms, as soon as they became known in London, caused a violent reaction, and the three general officers were recalled to face an inquiry. This, after a suitable delay, whitewashed all but Sir Harry Burrard, who, with Sir Hew Dalrymple, now disappears from this narrative. Sir Arthur Wellesley, nevertheless, remained under something of a cloud. The British army in the Peninsula came under the command of Sir John Moore, Napier's paladin, the military reformer of genius who had created the Light Division and sought to replace the lash by human understanding in the command of troops. On him fell the brunt of defying the full might of an outraged Napoleon.

THE CONVENTION of Cintra, followed by the establishment of a regency at Lisbon, disconcerted the plans of the bishop and junta of Oporto, and restored Portugal to comparative tranquillity. The simple-minded people would not heed the pernicious counsels of the factious prelate and his mischievous coadjutors, and what may be called the convulsive struggle of the war terminated. At first a remarkable similarity of feeling and mode of acting betrayed the common origin of the Spaniards and Portuguese; a wild impatience of foreign aggression, extravagant pride, vain boasting, passionate reckless resentment, were common to both. Soon, however, the finer marks of national character impressed by their different positions in the political world became visible. Spain, holding from time immemorial a high rank among the great powers, more often an oppressor than oppressed, haughtily rejected all advice; unconscious of her actual weakness and ignorance, and remembering only her former dignity, she assumed an attitude which would scarcely have suited the days of the emperor Charles V; whereas Portugal, always fearing the ambition of her powerful neighbour, and relying for safety as much upon her alliances as upon her own intrinsic strength, readily submitted to the direction of England. The turbulence of the first led to defeat and disaster; the docility and patience of the second were productive of the most beneficial results.

The national difference was not immediately perceptible. At this period the Portuguese were despised, while a splendid triumph was anticipated for the Spaniards. It was affirmed and believed, that, from every quarter enthusiastic multitudes of the latter were pressing forward to complete the destruction of a baffled and dispirited enemy; the vigour, the courage, the unmatched spring of Spanish patriotism was in every man's mouth; Napoleon's power and energy seemed weak in opposition. Few persons doubted the truth of such tales, and yet nothing could be more unsound, more eminently fallacious, than the generally entertained opinion of French weakness and Spanish strength. The resources of the former were unbounded, almost untouched; those of the latter were too slender even to support the weight of victory; in Spain the whole structure of society was shaken to pieces by the violence of an effort which merely awakened the slumbering strength of France.

Foresight, promptitude, arrangement, marked the proceedings of Napoleon; while with the Spaniards prudence was punished as treason, and personal interests everywhere springing up with incredible force wrestled against the public good. At a distance the insurrection appeared of towering proportions and mighty strength, when in truth it was a fantastic object, stained with blood and tottering from weakness. The helping hand of England alone was stretched forth for its support, all other assistance was denied; for the continental powers, although nourishing secret hopes of profit from the struggle, with calculating policy turned coldly from the patriots' cause. The English cabinet was indeed sanguine, and yet the ministers, while anticipating success in a preposterous manner, displayed little industry and less judgment in their preparations for the struggle; nor does it appear that the freedom of the Peninsula was much considered in their councils. They contemplated this astonishing insurrection as a mere military opening, through which Napoleon might be assailed, and they neglected, or rather feared, to look towards the great moral consequences of such a stupendous event – consequences which were indeed above their reach of policy: they were neither able nor willing to seize such a singularly propitious occasion for conferring a benefit upon mankind.

This opportunity for restoring the civil strength of a long degraded people by a direct recurrence to first principles, was, however, such as has seldom been granted to a sinking nation. Enthusiasm was aroused without the withering curse of faction; the multitude were ready to follow whoever chose to lead; the weight of ancient authority was, by a violent external shock, thrown off; the ruling power fell from the hands of the few, to be caught by the many, without the latter having thereby incurred the odium of rebellion or excited the malice of mortified grandeur. There was nothing to deter the cautious for there was nothing to pull down; the foundation of the social structure was already laid bare, and all the materials were at hand for building a noble monument of human genius and virtue: the architect alone was wanting. No anxiety to ameliorate the moral or physical condition of the people in the Peninsula was evinced by the ruling men of England; and if any existed amongst those of Spain, it evaporated in puerile abstract speculations. Napoleon indeed offered the blessing of regeneration in exchange for submission, but in that revolting form, and accompanied by the evils of war, it was rejected: in the clamorous pursuit of national independence, the independence of man was trampled under foot. The mass of the Spanish nation, blinded by personal hatred, thought only of revenge; the leaders, arrogant and incapable, neither sought nor wished for any higher motive of action. Without unity of design, and devoid of arrangement, their policy was mean and personal, their military efforts abortive, and a rude unscientific warfare disclosed at once the barbarous violence of the Spanish character and the utter decay of Spanish institutions.

The necessity for a single chief was admitted by all persons, but so stubborn were the tools of the provincial juntas in the assembly, that in despite of the British agent's efforts and the influence of the British cabinet, the generals were all confirmed in separate and independent commands. The miserable system of the Dutch deputies with Marlborough, and the revolutionary commissaries of France, were partially revived, and the English government was disregarded, though it had then supplied Spain with two hundred thousand muskets, clothing, ammunition, and sixteen millions of dollars [some £4 million]! Such ample succours rightly managed would have secured unlimited influence; but the gifts were made through one set of agents the demands through another; wherefore the first were taken as of right, the last unheeded. The resources of England were thus wasted without materially benefiting Spain; for though the armies were destitute, the central government had contracted a large debt and was without credit. Assuming however the insolence of conquerors dictating terms, rather than the language of grateful allies asking further assistance, it required from England an instant gift of ten millions of dollars, with stores sufficient to supply a well-governed army for years.

All the provincial juntas still retained full power within their respective districts. The central government feared them, but decreed, 1°. That their own persons were inviolable. 2°. That their president should, with the title of highness, receive 25,000 crowns a-year. 3°. That each deputy taking the title of excellency should have a salary of 5,000 crowns. 4°. That the collective body should be addressed as majesty. Then thinking themselves sufficiently confirmed they resolved to make a public entry to Madrid, and to conciliate the populace, declare a general amnesty, lower the duties on tobacco, and fling money to the crowd during the procession. Amidst this pomp and vanity the enemy was scarcely remembered, and public business totally neglected. This last evil extended to the lowest branches of administration; self-interest produced abundance of activity, but every department, almost every man, seemed struck with torpor when the public welfare was at stake, and withal, an astonishing presumption was common to the highest and the lowest.

The idea of failure never occurred, the government was content if the people believed its daily falsehoods about the French; and the public, equally presumptuous, was content to be so deceived. The soldiers were destitute even to nakedness, and their constancy cruelly abused. They were without arms or bread; the higher orders displayed cupidity, incapacity and disunion; the patriotic ardour was visibly abating with the lower classes; the rulers were grasping, improvident, untruthful and boasting; the enemy powerful; the government, cumbrous and ostentatious, was, to use Mr Stuart's words, 'neither calculated to inspire courage nor increase enthusiasm'.

This picture will be recognized by men who are yet living, and whose exertions were as incessant as unavailing to remedy the evils at the time; it will be recognized by the friends of that great man, Sir John Moore, the first victim to the folly and base intrigues of the day; it will be recognized by that general and army who afterwards won their way through Spain and found that to trust Spaniards in war was to lean against a broken reed. To others it may appear exaggerated, for without having seen it is difficult to believe the disorders which paralysed the enthusiasm of a whole people.

           *   *   *

Napoleon was chagrined but not dismayed at a resistance he had almost anticipated. He measured the efforts of Spain, calculated the power of foreign interference, and did not misjudge the value of English supplies. He foresaw the danger of suffering an insurrection of peasants to attain a regular form, to become disciplined troops, and to league with powerful nations. To defeat the raw levies was easy; but it was necessary to crush them, that dread of his invincible force might still pervade the world, and the influence of his genius remain unabated. He knew the constitution of Bayonne would contrast well with those chaotic governments, neither monarchical, nor popular, nor aristocratic, nor federal, thrown up by the Spanish revolution; but, before that could give him moral resources, it was essential to develop his military strength.

Imminent was the crisis. Watched by nations whose pride he had shocked without destroying their strength, if he bent all his force against the Peninsula, England might excite the continent to arms, and Russia and Austria might unite to raise fallen Prussia. The designs of Austria were covered, not hidden, by the usual artifices of her cunning rapacious cabinet. Subdued Prussia could not be supposed quiescent. Russia, more powerful perhaps from her defeats because more enlightened as to the cause, gave Napoleon most anxiety. He knew it would tax all his means to meet the hostility of that great empire, which would render his operations in Spain unsuitable to his fame. But with a long-sighted policy he had proposed an interview with the czar, intent to secure the friendship of that monarch, and not unsuccessfully did he strive at first. Indeed at this time he supported the weight of the political world, and every movement of his produced a convulsion. His strength was now taxed, yet confident in his unmatched genius, he sought only a moment of time, certain to make it victory. Meanwhile, sudden and strong of action as the dash of a cataract, he made one of those efforts which have stamped his age with the greatness of antiquity.

His armies were scattered over Europe. In Italy, in Dalmatia, on the Rhine, the Danube, the Elbe, in Prussia, Denmark, Poland, his legions were to be found; over that vast extent five hundred thousand disciplined men maintained the supremacy of France. From those bands he drew the imperial guards, the select soldiers of the warlike nation he governed, the terror of all other continental troops; these and the veterans of Jena, Austerlitz and Friedland, reduced in number but of confirmed hardihood, were marched towards Spain. A host of cavalry, unequalled for enterprise and knowledge of war, was also directed against that devoted land, and a long train of gallant soldiers followed, until two hundred thousand men, accustomed to battle, had penetrated the gloomy fastnesses of the western Pyrenees; while forty thousand of inferior reputation, drawn from the interior of France, from Naples, Tuscany, and Piedmont, assembled on the eastern ridges of those gigantic hills. The march of this multitude was incessant, and as his soldiers passed the capital, Napoleon, neglectful of nothing which could excite their courage and swell their military pride, addressed to them one of his nervous orations. In the tranquillity of peace it may seem inflated, but on the eve of battle a general should so speak.

'Soldiers! after triumphing on the banks of the Vistula and the Danube, you have passed with rapid steps through Germany. This day, without a moment of repose, I command you to traverse France. Soldiers! I have need of you. The hideous presence of the leopard contaminates the peninsula of Spain and Portugal: in terror he must fly before you. Let us bear our triumphal eagles to the pillars of Hercules; there also we have injuries to avenge. Soldiers! you have surpassed the renown of modern armies, but have you yet equalled the glory of those Romans, who in one and the same campaign were victorious upon the Rhine and the Euphrates, in Illyria, and upon the Tagus? A long peace, a lasting prosperity shall be the reward of your labours, but a real Frenchman could not, ought not to rest until the seas are free and open to all. Soldiers! All that you have done, all that you will do for the happiness of the French people and for my glory, shall be eternal in my heart!'

This said, he sent his army towards the frontiers of Spain, and himself hastened to meet the emperor Alexander at Erfurth. Their conference produced a treaty of alliance, offensive and defensive. Spain was by the one, with calm indifference, abandoned to the injustice of the other.

Upon the 18th of October Napoleon returned to Paris, secure of the present friendship and alliance of Russia, but uncertain of the moment when the stimulus of English subsidies would quicken the hostility of Austria into life. His peril was great, his preparations enormous. He called out two conscriptions. The first taken from the classes of 1806, 7, 8 and 9, furnished eighty thousand men arrived at maturity; these were destined to replace the veterans directed against Spain. The second, taken from the class of 1810, also produced eighty thousand, which were disposed of as reserves in the

HALF RATIONS

GOING SICK TO THE REAR

dépôts of France. The French troops left in Germany were concentrated on the side of Austria; Denmark was evacuated, and one hundred thousand soldiers were withdrawn from the Prussian states. The army of Italy, powerfully reinforced, was placed under Prince Eugène, assisted by Masséna. Murat, who had succeeded Joseph in the kingdom of Naples, was directed to assemble a Neapolitan army on the shores of Calabria and threaten Sicily. In fine, no measure of prudence was neglected by this wonderful man, to whom the time required by Austria for the preparation of a campaign, seemed sufficient for the subjection of the whole Peninsula.

The French legislative body was opened the 24th of October. The emperor, after giving a concise sketch of the political situation of Europe, touched upon Spain. 'In a few days I go,' said he, 'to put myself at the head of my armies, and with the aid of God to crown the king of Spain in Madrid! to plant my eagles on the towers of Lisbon!' Then quitting Paris he went to Bayonne.

*   *   *

Mr Canning's readiness to reject negotiation, and defy this stupendous power, would lead to the supposition, that on the side of Spain at least he was prepared for the encounter; yet no trace of a matured plan is to be found in the instructions to the generals commanding in Portugal previous to the 25th of September; nor was the project then adopted, one which discovered any adequate knowledge of the force of the enemy, or of the state of affairs: the conduct of the English cabinet relative to the Peninsula was scarcely superior to that of the central junta. Vague projects, or rather speculations, were communicated to the generals in Portugal, but in none was the strength of the enemy alluded to, in none was there a settled plan of operations: a strange delusion relative to Napoleon's power and intentions guided the English ministers.

It was the 6th of October before a despatch, containing the first determinate plan of campaign arrived at Lisbon. Thirty thousand infantry and five thousand cavalry were to be employed in the north of Spain. Of these ten thousand were to be embarked at the English ports, the remainder to be composed of regiments drafted from the army then in Portugal. Sir John Moore was to command, and was authorized to unite the whole by a voyage round the coast, or by a march through the interior. He chose the latter, 1°. because a voyage at that season of the year would have been tedious and precarious; 2°. because the intention of Sir Hew Dalrymple had been to enter Spain by Almeida, and the arrangements which that general had made were for such a march; 3°. because he was informed the province of Galicia would be scarcely able to equip the force coming from England under the command of Sir David Baird. He was however to take the field immediately, and fix upon some place, either in Galicia or on the borders of Leon, for concentrating the whole army; the specific plan of operations to be concerted afterwards with the Spanish generals. This was a shallow project. The Ebro was to be the theatre of war, and the head of the great French host coming from Germany was already in the passes of the Pyrenees; the local difficulties impeding the English general were of a nature to render that which was ill begun end worse, and that which was well arranged fail. To be first in the field is a great and decided advantage, yet here the plan of operations was not even arranged when the enemy's first blows were descending.

Sir John Moore had to organize an army of raw soldiers; and in a poor, unsettled country, just relieved from the pressure of a harsh and griping enemy, he was to procure the transport necessary for his stores, ammunition, and even the officers' baggage. With money and an experienced staff, such obstacles do not much embarrass a good general; but here, few of the subordinate officers had served a campaign, and the administrative departments, though zealous and willing, were new to a service where no energy can prevent the effects of inexperience from being severely felt. The roads were very bad, the rainy season, so baleful to troops, was at hand, it was essential to be quick, and gold which turneth the wheels of war was wanting. And this, at all times a great evil, was here most grievously felt; for the Portuguese, accustomed to fraud on the part of their own government and to forced contributions by the French, could not readily be persuaded that an army of foreigners, paying with promises only, might be trusted. Nor was this natural suspicion allayed by observing, that while the general and his troops were without money, the subordinate agents dispersed throughout the country were amply supplied. Sir David Baird, who was to land at Coruña, was likewise encompassed with difficulties: from Coruña to the nearest point where he could effect a junction with the forces marching from Lisbon was two hundred miles, and he also was without money.

No general-in-chief was appointed to command the Spanish armies, nor was Moore referred to any person with whom he could communicate at all, much less concert a plan of operations. He was unacquainted with the views of the Spanish government, and was alike uninformed of the numbers, composition and situation of the armies with which he was to contend. His own genius and twenty-five thousand pounds in the military chest, constituted his resources for a campaign which was to lead him far from the coast and all its means of supply. He was to unite his forces by a winter march of three hundred miles; another three hundred were to be passed before he reached the Ebro; he was to concert a plan of operations with generals, jealous, quarrelsome and independent, their positions extended from the northern sea-coast to Zaragoza, their men insubordinate, differing in customs, discipline, language and religion from the English, and despising all foreigners: and all this was to be accomplished in time to defeat an enemy already in the field, accustomed to great movements, and conducted by the most rapid and decided of men.

At this period also, the effects of that incredible folly and weakness, which marked all the proceedings of the central junta, were felt throughout Spain. In any other country its conduct would have been attributed to insanity. So apathetic with respect to the enemy as to be contemptible, so active in pursuit of self-interest as to become hateful; continually devising how to render itself at once despotic and popular, how to excite enthusiasm and check freedom of expression; how to enjoy the luxury of power without its labour, how to acquire great reputation without trouble, how to be indolent and victorious at the same moment. Fear prevented the members from removing to Madrid after every preparation had been made for a public entrance into that capital; they passed decrees repressing the liberty of the press on the ground of the deceptions practised upon the public, yet themselves never hesitated to deceive the British agents, the generals, the government and their own countrymen, by the most flagitious falsehoods upon every subject, whether of greater or less importance. They hedged their dignity with ridiculous and misplaced forms opposed to the vital principle of an insurrectional government, devoted their attention to abstract speculations, recalled the exiled Jesuits, and inundated the country with laboured state papers while the war was left uncared for. Every application of Mr Stuart, even for an order to expedite a common courier, was met by difficulties and delays; it was necessary to have recourse to the most painful solicitations to obtain the slightest attention: nor did that mode always succeed.

Sir John Moore strenuously grappled with the difficulties besetting him. He desired that troops who had a journey of six hundred miles to make previous to meeting the enemy, should not at the commencement be overwhelmed by the torrents of rain, which

in Portugal descend, at this period, with such violence as to destroy the shoes, ammunition and accoutrements, and render troops
almost unfit for service. The Spanish generals recommended that
his march should be by Almeida, Ciudad Rodrigo, Salamanca,
Valladolid and Burgos, and his magazines formed at one of the
latter towns. This advice coincided with previous preparations, and
the army was directed upon Almeida and Ciudad Rodrigo, the
artillery and cavalry to move by Alcantara. Almeida was to be the
place of arms, and reserve stores and provisions were directed
there; but want of money, the unsettled state of the country, and the
inexperience of the commissariat, rendered it difficult to procure the
means of transport even for the light baggage of the regiments,
although the quantity of the latter was so reduced as to create discontent. Nevertheless, Moore did not delay his march. He sent
agents to Madrid and other places to make contracts and raise
money; for the ministers, with a strange policy, gave the Spaniards
all their gold and left the English army to get it back in loans.

                    *   *   *

Napoleon now made dispositions indicating a vast plan of operations. Apparently he designed to invade Galicia, Andalusia and
Valencia by his lieutenants, and carry his arms to Lisbon in person.
Upon the 20th December, the sixth corps, the guards, and the
reserve, were assembled under his own immediate control. The first
corps was stationed at Toledo, and the light cavalry attached to it
scoured the roads leading to Andalusia even to the foot of the Sierra
Morena. The fourth corps was at Talavera, on the march towards
the frontier of Portugal. The second corps was on the Carrion river,
preparing to advance against Galicia. The eighth corps was broken
up; the divisions composing it were ordered to join the second, and
Junot repaired to the third corps, to supply the place of Moncey,
who was called to Madrid for a particular service – doubtless an
expedition against Valencia. The fifth corps, which had arrived at
Vitoria, was directed to reinforce the third, then employed against
Zaragoza. The seventh was always in Catalonia.

   Vast as this plan appears, it was not beyond the emperor's
means; for there were on his muster rolls more than three hundred
and thirty thousand fighting men, and sixty thousand horses; two
hundred pieces of field artillery followed the corps to battle, and as
many more remained in reserve. Of this monstrous army, two hundred and fifty-five thousand men and fifty thousand horses were
actually under arms with the eagles; thirty-two thousand were

detached or in garrisons, preserving tranquillity in the rear and guarding the communications of the active force; the remainder were in hospital; and so slight had been the resistance of the Spanish armies, that only nineteen hundred prisoners were to be deducted.

What was there to oppose this fearful array? What consistency or vigour in the councils? What numbers? What discipline and spirit in the armies of Spain? What enthusiasm among the people? What was the disposition, the means, what the activity of the allies of that country? The answers demonstrate that the deliverance of the Peninsula was due to other causes than the courage, the patriotism, or the constancy of the Spaniards. Spain was broken in strength and spirit except at a few places. Napoleon was in the centre of the country; he held the capital, the fortresses on the side of France, the command of the great lines of communication between the provinces; and on the military horizon no cloud was seen, save the heroic city of Zaragoza on the one side and a feeble British army on the other. Sooner or later he knew the former must fall, it was an affair of artillery calculation. The latter he supposed in full retreat for Portugal; but as the fourth corps was nearer to Lisbon than the British general, a hurried retreat alone could bring the latter in time to that capital; and no preparations for defence could be made sufficient to arrest the sixty thousand Frenchmen which he could carry there at the same moment. The subjugation of Spain appeared inevitable, but the genius and vigour of Sir J. Moore frustrated Napoleon's plans, the Austrian war drew the master spirit from the scene of contention, and then England put forth her vast resources under the fortunate direction of a general equal to the task of delivering the Peninsula, and it was delivered.

*   *   *

Sir John Moore participated at first in the universal belief that the nation was enthusiastic; and when he detected the exaggerations of the military agents and the incapacity of the Spanish generals and rulers, he still trusted the spirit of the people would compensate for all. Want of transport and supplies had caused the British to march in small and successive divisions, and it was the 23rd of November before the centre, consisting of twelve thousand infantry and a battery of six guns, was concentrated at Salamanca. Sir John Moore, though he had organized equipped and supplied his army, and marched four hundred miles in the space of six weeks, was too late in the field; the campaign was decided before the British entered Spain as an army.

It was the will of the people of England and the orders of the government that he should push forward to the assistance of the Spaniards; he had done so, without magazines and without money to form them, trusting to the official assurance of the minister that above a hundred thousand Spanish soldiers covered his march, that the people were enthusiastic and ready for any exertion to secure their own deliverance. He found them so supine and unprepared that the French cavalry, in parties as weak as twelve men, traversed the country and raised contributions without difficulty or opposition.

Napoleon's enormous force was unknown to Moore; but he knew it could not be less than eighty thousand fighting men, and that thirty thousand more were momentarily expected, and might have arrived. The only conclusion to be drawn from these facts was that the Spaniards were unable or unwilling to resist the enemy, and the British would have to support the contest alone. The first object was to unite the parcelled divisions of the English army.

Salamanca was five marches from Astorga, six from the Escorial; five days were required to bring the rear up to Salamanca, six to enable Hope to concentrate at the Escorial, sixteen to enable Baird to assemble at Astorga. Hence the English army could not under twenty days act in a body, and to advance in parcels would have been absurd. A retreat, though consonant to rule and to the minister's instructions which forbade any serious operation before the army was united, would have appeared ungenerous. Moore's high spirit rejected such a remedy for the false position his government had placed him in, and he adopted an enterprise such as none but great minds are capable of. He designed, if he could draw the extended wings of his army together in good time, to abandon all communication with Portugal, throw himself into the heart of Spain, defend the southern provinces, and trust to the effect which such an appeal to the patriotism and courage of the Spaniards would produce.

Napoleon was now in full career. He had raised a hurricane of war, and directing its fury as he pleased, his adversaries were obliged to conform their movements to his, the circumstances varied from hour to hour, and the determination of one moment was rendered useless in the next. The appearance of the French cavalry in the plains of Madrid had sent the junta headlong towards Badajoz; but the people of Madrid shut their gates, and displayed the outward signs of a resolution to imitate Zaragoza.

The fire essential to the salvation of the nation seemed to be kindling, and Moore hailed the appearance of an enthusiasm which

promised success to a just cause, and a brilliant career of glory to
himself. That the metropolis should thus abide the fury of the conqueror was a great event and full of promise, and the situation of
the army was likewise improved; Hope's junction was accomplished,
and as the attention of the French was turned towards Madrid,
there was no reason to doubt that Baird's junction could likewise
be effected. On the other hand, there was no certainty that the capital would remain firm when danger pressed, none that it would be
able to resist, none that the example would spread; yet without it
did so, nothing was gained, because it was only by an union of heart
and hand throughout the whole country that the great power of the
French could be successfully resisted.

In a matter so balanced, Moore, as might be expected from an
enterprising general, adopted the boldest and most generous side.
He ordered Baird, who, after destroying some stores, had fallen
back to Villa Franca, to concentrate his troops at Astorga, and
he himself prepared for an advance; but as he remained without
information as to the fate of Madrid, he sent Graham to obtain intelligence of what was passing. The Somosierra and Guadarrama

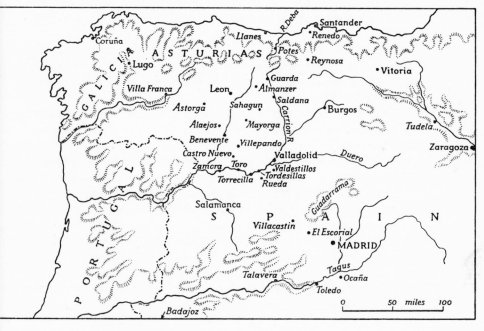

MOORE'S ADVANCE INTO SPAIN

were in the enemy's hands, wherefore no direct movement on Madrid could be made, nor indeed any operation on that side before the 12th, when Baird's rear would be closed up to Astorga. Moore knew Zaragoza was ready to stand a second siege, and he had in the first a guarantee for its obstinacy. The junta of Toledo had formally assured him that they would die on the ruins of the city, but never submit; and from several quarters he was told of new levies crowding up from the south. Upon these circumstances he conceived a daring enterprise stamped with the seal of genius, political and military.

He judged the French emperor more anxious to strike a blow against the English, than to overrun any particular province or get possession of any town in the Peninsula. He resolved therefore to throw himself upon the communications of the French army, hoping, if fortune was favourable, to inflict a severe loss upon the troops guarding them before aid could arrive. If Napoleon, suspending operations against the south, should detach largely, Madrid would thereby be succoured; if he did not detach largely the British could hold their ground. Moore knew well that great commander would most likely fall with his whole force upon those who menaced his line of communication; but to relieve Spain at a critical moment, and give time for the south to organize its defence and recover courage, he was willing to draw the enemy's whole power on himself. He saw the peril for his own army, knew that it must glide along the edge of a precipice, cross a gulf on a rotten plank; but he also knew the martial qualities of his soldiers, felt the pulsations of his own genius, and the object being worth the deed he dared essay it even against Napoleon.

Graham returned on the 9th, bringing intelligence that Madrid had capitulated. Mortifying as it was to find Madrid after so much boasting hold out but one day, the event itself did not destroy the ground of Moore's resolution to advance. It was so much lost, it diminished the hope of arousing the nation, and it increased the danger of the British army by letting loose a greater number of the enemy's troops; but as a diversion for the south it might still succeed, and as long as there was any hope the resolution of the English general was fixed to prove, that he would not abandon the cause even when the Spaniards were abandoning it themselves.

On the 11th of December the movement was commenced, but preparations for a retreat on Portugal were also continued, and Baird was ordered to form magazines at Benevente, Astorga, Villa Franca and Lugo, by which two lines of operation and greater freedom of action were obtained. Moore's first design was to march on

Valladolid to cover the arrival of his stores and ensure his junction with Baird, whose rear was still behind Astorga. In this view head-quarters were at Alaejos. The 13th, two brigades of infantry and Lord Paget's cavalry were at Toro, Hope was at Torrecilla, and Charles Stewart's horsemen were at Rueda, having the night before surprised there fifty infantry and thirty dragoons. The prisoners said the French believed the English army was retreating on Portugal, and an intercepted despatch from Berthier, disclosing the emperor's views, changed the direction of the march. It was addressed to Soult, and said Madrid was tranquil, the shops open, the public amusements going on as in profound peace. The fourth corps was at Talavera on the way to Badajoz, and this movement would force the English to retire on Portugal, if, contrary to the emperor's belief, they had not already done so. The fifth corps was on the march to Zaragoza, the eighth to Burgos. Soult was there-fore directed to drive the Spaniards into Galicia, to occupy Leon, Benevente and Zamora, and keep the flat country in subjection; for which purpose his two divisions of infantry, and the cavalry brigades of Franceschi and Debelle, were considered sufficient.

It is remarkable that this, the first correct information of the capitulation of Madrid, should have been thus acquired from the enemy, ten days after the event had taken place. Nor is it less curious, that while letters to Moore were filled with vivid descriptions of Spanish enthusiasm, Napoleon should have been so convinced of their passiveness, as to send this important despatch by an officer, who rode post without an escort and in safety, until his abusive language to the postmaster at Valdestillos created a tumult in which he lost his life. Captain Waters, an English officer sent to obtain intelligence, happening to arrive in that place, heard of the murder, and immediately purchased the despatch for twenty dollars; and this accidental information was the more valuable, as neither money nor patriotism had hitherto induced the Spaniards to bring any intelligence of the enemy's situation: each step the army had made was in the dark. It was now certain that Burgos was or would be strongly protected, and that Baird's line of march was unsafe if Soult, following these instructions, advanced. On the other hand, as the French were ignorant of the British movements, there was a chance to surprise and beat Soult before Napoleon could come to his succour. Wherefore Hope was ordered to pass the Duero at Tordesillas and direct his march upon Villepando; head-quarters were removed to Toro; and Valderas was given for the junction of Baird's division, the head of which was now at Benevente.

At Toro it was ascertained that the Spanish General Romana, although knowing of the British advance and pledged to support, was retiring to Galicia; nominally generalissimo, he had only a few thousand miserable soldiers, for the junta with great ingenuity contrived to have no general when they had an army, and no army when they had a general. Romana had rallied five thousand men at Renedo, in the valley of Cabernuigo, designing to hold on to the Asturias, but the vile conduct of the Asturian junta, joined to the terror created by the French victories, had completely subdued the spirit of the peasantry, and ruined the resources of that province. He complained that his men when checked for misconduct quitted their standards, and that any should have remained with the colours is to be admired; for among the sores of Spain there were none more cankered, more disgusting, than the venality, the injustice, the profligate corruption of the Asturian authorities. They openly divided the English subsidies, and defrauded not only the soldiers of their pay and equipments but the miserable peasants of their hire for work, doubling the wretchedness of poverty, and deriding the misery they occasioned by pompous declaration of their own virtue.

Head-quarters were at Castro Nuevo the 18th, and Moore informed Romana of his design against Soult, desiring his co-operation, and requesting he would, according to his own plan given to the British minister in London, reserve the Asturias for his line of communication and leave Galicia to the British. The latter were now in full march. Baird was at Benevente, Hope at Villepando, and the cavalry, scouring the country on the side of Valladolid had several successful skirmishes, the most remarkable being fought by Major Otway of the 18th Hussars, who captured Colonel Antignac and brought off more prisoners than his own party amounted to: the French could therefore be no longer ignorant of the movement, and the English general brought forward his columns rapidly. On the 20th the army was united, the cavalry at Melgar Abaxo, the infantry at Mayorga, both as much concentrated as the necessity of obtaining cover in a country devoid of fuel and deep with snow would permit. The weather was very severe, the marches long, but the men were robust, their discipline admirable, there were few stragglers, and the experience of one or two campaigns only was wanting to perfection. The number was small, nominally thirty-five thousand; but four regiments were still in Portugal, and three had been left by Baird at Lugo and Astorga; one thousand six hundred and eighty-seven were detached, four thousand were in hospital: the actual number present under arms on the 19th of December was only nineteen thousand and fifty-three infantry, two thousand two hundred and seventy-eight cavalry, one thousand three hundred and fifty-eight gunners; forming a total of twenty-three thousand five hundred and eighty-three men, with sixty pieces of artillery. They were organized in three divisions and a reserve of infantry, and there were two independent brigades of light troops. The cavalry was in one division, four batteries were attached to the infantry, two to the horsemen, and one was kept in reserve. Romana, who had been able to bring forward very few men, promised to march in two columns by Almanzer and Guarda, and sent some information of the enemy's position; but Moore thought little of his intelligence, when he found him even so late as the 19th, upon the faith of information from the junta, representing Madrid as still holding out; and when the advanced posts were already engaged at Sahagun, proposing an interview at Benevente to arrange the plan of operations.

On the French side, Soult was concentring his force on the Carrion. After his rapid and brilliant opening of the campaign, his corps remained on the defensive until the movements against Tudela and Madrid were completed; the order to recommence offensive operations was intercepted on the 12th, but on the 16th he heard of the English army. At that period Bonnet's division occupied Barquera de San Vincente and Potes on the Deba, watching some thousand Asturians whom Ballesteros had collected near Llanes; Merle's and Mermet's divisions were on the Carrion; Franceschi's dragoons at Valladolid, Debelle's at Sahagun. The whole furnished sixteen or seventeen thousand infantry and twelve hundred cavalry present under arms, of which only eleven thousand infantry and twelve hundred cavalry could be opposed to the British without uncovering the important post of Santander. Alarmed at this disparity of force, Soult required Mathieu Dumas, commandant at Burgos, to direct all the divisions and detachments passing through that town upon the Carrion, whatever might be their original destination. This was assented to by Dumas and approved by the emperor.

Moore designed to move during the night of the 23rd, so as to arrive at Carrion by daylight on the 24th, to force the bridge, and then ascending the river fall upon the main body, which his information led him to believe was still at Saldaña. This attack was however a secondary object, his attention was constantly directed towards Madrid. To beat the troops in his front would be a victory

of little value beyond the honour, because the third and fourth corps
were so near; the pith of the operation was to tempt the emperor
from Madrid, and his march from that capital was to be the signal
for a retreat which sooner or later was inevitable. In fine, to draw
Napoleon from the south was the design, and it behoved the man to
be alert who interposed between the lion and his prey.

On the 23rd Romana gave notice the French were in motion
from the side of Madrid, and in the night of the 23rd, the troops
being actually in march towards Carrion, this intelligence was
confirmed by the general's own spies; all of whose reports said
the whole French army was in movement to crush the English. The
fourth corps had been halted at Talavera, the fifth at Vitoria, the
eighth was closing up to reinforce the second, and the emperor in
person was marching towards the Guadarrama. The principal
object was thus attained. The siege of Zaragoza was delayed, the
southern provinces allowed to breathe, and it only remained to
prove, by a timely retreat, that this hazardous offensive operation
was not the result of improvident rashness, but the hardy enterprise of a great commander acting under peculiar circumstances. As
a mere military measure his judgment condemned it; as a political
one he thought it of doubtful advantage, because Spain was really
passive; but he desired to give the Spaniards an opportunity of
making one more struggle for independence. That was done. If they
could not or would not profit of the occasion, if their hearts were
faint or their hands feeble the shame and the loss were their own;
the British general had done enough, enough for honour, enough for
utility, more than enough for prudence: the madness of the times
required it. His army was already on the verge of destruction, the
enemy's force was hourly increasing in his front, the first symptoms
of a retreat would bring it headlong on, the emperor threatened
the line of communication with Galicia, and by the rapidity of his
march left no time for consideration.

After the first burst, by which he swept the northern provinces
and planted his standard on the banks of the Tagus, that monarch
had put all the resources of his subtle genius into activity, endeavouring to soften the public mind, and by engrafting benefits on
the terror his victories had created to gain over the people. But he
likewise gathered in his extended wings for a new flight, designed
to carry him over all the southern kingdoms of the Peninsula, and
give him the rocks of Lisbon as a resting-place for his eagles.
Madrid was tranquil; Toledo, notwithstanding her heroic promises
had never even shut her gates; one division of the first corps occu-

pied that town, another was at Ocaña, and the light cavalry scoured
the whole of La Mancha to the borders of Andalusia. The fourth
corps, with Milhaud's and Lasalle's horsemen, were at Talavera
preparing to march to Badajoz; and sixty thousand men with one
hundred and fifty guns and fifteen days' provisions in carts, were
reviewed at the gates of Madrid upon the 19th: three days afterwards they were in full march to intercept the line of Sir John
Moore's march.

Napoleon was informed of that general's advance on the 21st,
and in an instant the Spaniards, their juntas and their armies were
dismissed from his thoughts; his corps were arrested in their
different movements, ten thousand men were left to control the
capital, and on the evening of the 22nd fifty thousand men were at
the foot of the Guadarrama. A deep snow choked the passes, and
twelve hours of ineffectual toil left the advanced guards still on the
wrong side; the general commanding reported that the road was
impracticable, but Napoleon placing himself at the head of the
column, on foot and amidst storms of hail and drifting snow, led
his soldiers over the mountain. Many men and animals died during
the passage, which lasted two days, but the emperor, personally
urging on the troops with unceasing vehemence, reached Villa-
castin, fifty miles from Madrid on the 24th. The 26th he was at
Tordesillas with the guards and the divisions of Lapisse and Des-
soles; the dragoons of La Houssaye entered Valladolid the same
day, and Ney with the sixth corps was at Rio Seco.

From Tordesillas Napoleon wrote to Soult, concluding his
despatch thus: *'Our cavalry scouts are already at Benevente. If the
English pass to-day in their position they are lost: if they attack you
with all their force, retire one day's march; the farther they proceed the
better for us. If they retreat pursue them closely.'* Then, full of hope, he
hastened himself to Valderas, but had the mortification to learn he
was twelve hours too late. He had made a wonderful march, resting
neither day nor night, but the British were across the Esla! In fact
Soult was in full pursuit when this letter was written, for Moore,
well aware of his own situation, had given orders to retreat the
moment the intelligence of Napoleon's march from Madrid reached
him, and the heavy baggage was immediately moved to the rear,
while the reserve, the light brigades, and the cavalry remained at
Sahagun, the latter pushing patrols up to the enemy's lines, and
skirmishing to hide the retrograde march.

On the 24th, Hope, having two divisions, retired by the road
of Mayorga; Baird with another, by that of Valencia de San Juan,

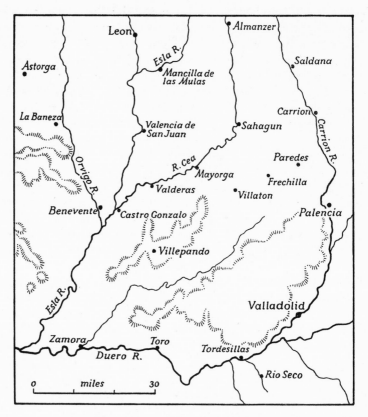

MOVEMENTS ALONG THE RIVER ESLA

where there was a ferry-boat to cross the Esla river; the Marquis of Romana undertook to guard the bridge of Mancilla. Lorge's dragoons arrived the same day at Frechilla, and the division of Laborde entered Paredes. The 25th Moore with the reserve and light brigades, followed Hope's column to Valderas; the 26th Baird passed the Esla at Valencia and took post on the other side, yet with some difficulty, for the boat was small, the fords deep and the river rising. The commander-in-chief approached the bridge of Castro Gonzalo early in the morning of the 26th, but the stores were a long time passing, a dense fog intercepted the view, and so nicely timed was the march, that the scouts of the imperial horsemen were already infesting the flank of the column, and even carried off some of the baggage.

The left bank of the river commanded the bridge, and General

Robert Craufurd remained with a brigade of infantry and two guns to protect the passage; for the cavalry was still watching Soult, who was now pressing forward in pursuit. Lord Paget, after passing Mayorga, had been intercepted by a strong body of horse belonging to the emperor's army. It was embattled on a swelling ground close to the road, the soil was deep and soaked with snow and rain, yet two squadrons of the tenth rode stiffly up to the summit, and notwithstanding the enemy's advantage of numbers and position, killed twenty and captured one hundred. This was a hardy action; but the English cavalry had been engaged more or less for twelve successive days, with such fortune and bravery that above five hundred prisoners had already fallen into their hands, and their leaders being excellent their confidence was unbounded. From Mayorga, Paget proceeded to Benevente, and Soult, with great judgment, pushed for Astorga by the road of Mancilla, whereupon Romana, leaving three thousand men and two guns to defend the bridge at the latter place, fell back to Leon. Thus Moore recovered by a critical march his communications with Galicia, and so far baffled the emperor: yet his position was neither safe nor tenable.

Moore, knowing the line of the Esla could not be maintained, resolved to remain no longer than was necessary to clear out his magazines at Benevente, and cover the march of his stores. But the road to Astorga by Leon was much shorter than that through Benevente, and as Romana was inclined to retreat to Galicia, Sir John requested him to maintain Leon as long as possible, and leave Galicia open for the English army. Romana assented to both requests, and as he had a great rabble, and a number of citizens and volunteers were willing and even eager to fight, the town might have made resistance. Moore hoped it would, and gave orders to break down the bridge at Castro Gonzalo in his own front, the moment the stragglers and baggage should have passed. Meantime the bad example of murmuring given by men of high rank had descended lower, many regimental officers neglected their duty, and what with dislike to a retreat, the severity of the weather, and the inexperience of the army, the previous fine discipline of the troops was broken down: disgraceful excesses had been committed at Valderas, and the general severely reproached the army for its evil deeds, appealing to the honour of the soldiers for amendment.

On the night of the 26th, the light cavalry of the imperial guard, riding close up to the bridge of Castro Gonzalo, captured some women and baggage, and endeavoured to surprise the post, which gave rise to a remarkable display of courage and discipline. John

Walton and Richard Jackson, private soldiers of the forty-third, were posted beyond the bridge, with orders that one should stand firm, the other fire and run back to the brow and give notice whether there were many enemies or few. Jackson fired but was overtaken and received twelve or fourteen sabre cuts in an instant; nevertheless, he came staggering on and gave the signal, while Walton, with equal resolution, stood his ground and wounded several of the assailants, who retired leaving him unhurt, but with his cap, knapsack, belts and musket cut in above twenty places, his bayonet bent double, bloody to the hilt and notched like a saw.

On the 27th, the cavalry and the stragglers being all over the river, Craufurd commenced destroying the bridge amidst torrents of rain and snow; half the troops worked, the other half kept the enemy at bay from the heights on the left bank, for the cavalry scouts of the imperial guard were spread over the plain. At ten o'clock at night a large party, following some wagons again endeavoured to pass the piquets and gallop down to the bridge; that failing, a few dismounted, and extending to the right and left commenced a skirmishing fire, while others remained ready to charge if the position of the troops, which they expected to ascertain by this scheme, should offer an opportunity. They failed, and this anxiety to interrupt the work induced Craufurd to destroy two arches instead of one, and blow up the connecting buttress; the masonry was so solid, that it was not until twelve o'clock in the night of the 28th that all preparations were completed, when the troops descended the heights on the left bank, and passing very silently by single files and over planks laid across the broken arches, gained the other side without loss: an instance of singular good fortune, for the night was dark and tempestuous, the river rising rapidly with a roaring noise, and the enemy close at hand. To have resisted an attack would have been impossible, but the retreat was undiscovered and the mine sprung with good effect.

Craufurd marched to Benevente where the cavalry and the reserve still remained. Here several thousand infantry slept in the upper part of an immense convent built round a square, and a frightful catastrophe was impending; for the lower galleries were thickly stowed with cavalry horses, there was but one entrance, and two officers of the forty-third coming from the bridge perceived on entering the convent, that a large window-shutter was on fire, that in a few moments the straw under the horses would ignite and six thousand men and animals must inevitably perish in the flames. One of them, Captain Lloyd, a man of great strength and activity, and of a presence of mind which never failed, made a sign of silence to his companion, and springing on to the nearest horse, ran along the backs of the others until he reached the blazing shutter, which he tore off its hinges and cast out of the window; then awakening a few men, he cleared the passage without any alarm, which in such a case would have been as destructive as the fire.

Two days' rest had been gained at Benevente, but little could be done to remove the stores, and the greatest part were destroyed. The army was and had been from the first without sufficient means of transport, the general had no money to procure it, and the ill-will and shuffling conduct of the juntas added infinitely to the difficulties. Hope and Fraser marching by Labaneza reached Astorga the 29th, where Baird joined them from Valencia de San Juan; on the same day the reserve and Craufurd's brigade quitted Benevente, but the cavalry remained in that town, having guards at the fords of the Esla. In this state of affairs General Lefebvre Desnouettes, leading the French advanced guard, came up to Castro Gonzalo and seeing only a few cavalry posts on the great plain, hastily concluded there was nothing to support them; wherefore crossing the river at day-break by a ford above the bridge, he advanced with six hundred horsemen of the imperial guard into the plain. The piquets under Loftus Otway retired fighting until joined by a part of the third German hussars, when the whole charged the leading French squadrons with some effect; C. Stewart then took the command, and the ground was obstinately disputed, yet the enemy advanced. At this moment the plain was covered with stragglers, baggage-mules and followers of the army, the town was filled with tumult, the distant piquets and vedettes were seen galloping in from the right and left, the French were pressing forward boldly, and every appearance indicated that the enemy's whole army was come up and passing the river.

Lord Paget ordered the tenth hussars to mount and form under the cover of some houses at the edge of the town, for he desired to draw the French, whose real situation he had detected at once, well into the plain before he attacked. In half an hour, he was ready and gave the signal; the tenth hussars galloped forward, the piquets already engaged closed together, and the whole charged. Quickly then the scene changed. The French fled at full speed towards the river, the British followed sabreing the hindmost until the French squadrons, without breaking their ranks, plunged into the stream and gained the opposite heights: there, like experienced soldiers, they wheeled, and seemed inclined to come forward a second time, but when two guns opened upon them they retired. During the pursuit in the plain, an officer was observed to separate from the main body and make towards another part of the river; he was followed by two men and refusing to stop, was wounded and brought in a prisoner. It was Lefebvre Desnouettes.

Although the imperial guards were outnumbered in the end, they were very superior at the commencement of this action, which was stiffly fought on both sides; for the British lost fifty men, and the French left fifty-five killed and wounded on the field, and seventy prisoners besides their general and other officers. Baron Larrey says seventy of those who recrossed the river were also wounded, making a total loss of two hundred excellent soldiers. Lord Paget maintained his posts on the Esla under an occasional cannonade until the evening, and then withdrew to La Baneza. Napoleon had now reached Valderas, Ney was at Villaton, Lapisse at Toro, and though the French troops were worn down with fatigue the emperor still urged them on; the Duke of Dalmatia, he said, would intercept the English at Astorga and their labours would be finally rewarded. Nevertheless, the destruction of the Castro Gonzalo bridge was so well accomplished that twenty-four hours were required to repair it, the fords were now impassable, and it was the 30th before Bessières could cross the river; but on that day he passed through Benevente with nine thousand cavalry, and bent his course towards La Baneza. Franceschi had meanwhile carried the bridge of Mancilla de las Mulas with a single charge of his light horsemen, and captured all the artillery and one half of the Spanish division left to protect it; Romana immediately abandoned Leon with many stores, and the 31st Soult entered that town without firing a shot, while Bessières entered La Baneza and pushed posts forward to the Puente d'Orvigo on one side, and the Puente de Valembre on the other: the rear of the English army was still in Astorga, the head-quarters having arrived there only the day before.

In the preceding month large stores had been gradually brought up to this town by Baird, and orders were given to destroy them after supplying the immediate wants of the army; but Romana, who would neither defend Leon nor Mancilla, had, contrary to his promises, pre-occupied Astorga with his fugitive army, and when the English divisions marched in, such a tumult and confusion arose, that no distribution could be made nor the destruction of the stores effected. This unexpected disorder was very detrimental to discipline, which the unwearied efforts of the general had partly restored;

the resources which he had depended on for the support of his soldiers thus became mischievous, and disorganized instead of nourishing them. He had the further vexation to hear Romana, the principal cause of this misfortune, proposing, with troops unable to resist a thousand light infantry, to recommence offensive operations on a plan in comparison with which the visions of Don Quixote were wisdom.

Napoleon entered Astorga the 1st of January 1809. Seventy thousand French infantry, ten thousand cavalry, and two hundred pieces of artillery, were after many days of incessant marching there united. The congregation of this mighty force, while it evinced the power and energy of the French monarch attested also the genius of the English general, who had found means to arrest the course of the conqueror, and draw him with the flower of his army to this remote and unimportant part of the Peninsula when its fairest provinces were prostrate beneath the strength of his hand. That Moore succoured Spain in her extremity and in her hour of weakness intercepted the blow descending to crush her, no man of candour can deny. For what troops, what preparations, what courage, what capacity was there in the south to have resisted even for an instant, the progress of a man, who, in ten days, and in the depth of winter crossing the snowy ridge of the Carpentinos, had traversed two hundred miles of hostile country, and transported fifty thousand men from Madrid to Astorga in a shorter time than a Spanish courier would have taken to travel the same distance!

This stupendous march was rendered fruitless by the quickness of his adversary; but Napoleon, though he had failed to destroy the English army, resolved, nevertheless, to cast it forth of the Peninsula. Being himself recalled to France by tidings that the Austrian storm was ready to burst, he fixed upon Soult to continue the pursuit. For this purpose three divisions of cavalry and three of infantry were added to that marshal's former command; yet of these last, the two commanded by Loison and Heudelet were several marches in the rear, and Bonnet's remained always in the Montaña de Santander. Hence the whole number immediately led to the pursuit was about twenty-five thousand men, of which four thousand two hundred were cavalry, composing the divisions of Lorges, La Houssaye, and Franceschi; fifty-four guns were with the columns, and Loison's and Heudelet's divisions followed by forced marches. But Soult was supported by Ney with the sixth corps, wanting its third division, yet mustering above sixteen thousand men under arms, the flower of the French army, and having thirty-seven pieces of artillery. Thus, including Laborde, Heudelet, and Loison's division nearly sixty thousand men and ninety-one guns were put on the track of the English army. The emperor returned to Valladolid, where he received the addresses of the notables and deputies from Madrid and other great towns and strove by promises and other means to win the good opinion of the public. Appointing Joseph his lieutenant-general, he allotted separate provinces for each 'corps d'armée', the imperial guard was to return to France, and himself departing on horseback with scarcely any escort, frustrated some designs, which the Spaniards had it is said formed against his person, by the astonishing speed of his journey.

IV

Coruña

SOULT, NOWISE inferior to any of his nation, if the emperor be excepted, followed Moore with a vigour indicating his desire to finish the campaign in a manner suitable to its opening at Gamonal. His main body followed the route of Foncevadon and Ponteferrada; a column took the road of Cambarros and Bembibre, and Franceschi entered the valley of the Syl, intending to move up that river and turn the position of Villa Franca del Bierzo. Thus Moore, after having twice baffled the emperor's combinations, was still pressed in his retreat with a fury that seemed to increase every moment. The separation of his light brigades, reluctantly adopted on the bad counsel of his quarter-master-general, Murray, had weakened the army by three thousand men. He however still possessed nineteen thousand of all arms, good soldiers to fight, and strong to march although shaken in discipline by the disorders at Valderas and Astorga; for his exertions to restore order and regularity were by many officers slightly seconded, and by some with scandalous levity disregarded. There was no choice but to retreat.

It was now only the fifteenth day since he had left Salamanca, and already the torrent of war, diverted from the south, was foaming among the rocks of Galicia. Nineteen thousand British troops posted in strong ground might have offered battle to very superior numbers; yet where was the use of merely fighting an enemy who had three hundred thousand men in Spain? Nothing could be gained, but he might by a quick retreat reach his ships unmolested, and carry his army from that narrow corner to the southern provinces, and renew the war under more favourable circumstances. It was by this combination of a fleet and army the greatest assistance could be given to Spain, and the strength of England become most formidable; a few days' sailing would carry the troops to Cadiz; six weeks' constant marching would not bring the French from Galicia to that neighbourhood. The northern provinces were broken, subdued in spirit, and possessed few resources; the southern provinces, rich and fertile, had scarcely seen an enemy, and there was the seat of government. Moore, reasoning thus, resolved to fall down to the coast and embark with as little delay as might be; but Vigo, Coruña and Ferrol were the principal harbours, and their relative advantages could only be determined by the reports of the engineers not yet received; and as those reports came in from day to day the line of retreat became subject to change.

When Soult took the command of the pursuing army, Hope's and Fraser's divisions were at Villa Franca, Baird's at Bembibre, the reserve and cavalry at Cambarros, six miles from Astorga. Behind Cambarros the mountains of Galicia rose abruptly, yet there was no position, because, after the first rise at the village of Rodrigatos, the ground continually descended to Calcabellos a small town four miles from Villa Franca; and the old road of Foncevadon and Ponteferrada, which turned the whole of this line, was choked with the advancing columns of the enemy. The reserve and the cavalry therefore marched during the night to Bembibre, and on their arrival Baird's division proceeded to Calcabellos; but in the immense wine-vaults of Bembibre hundreds of men remained inebriated, the followers of the army crowded the houses, and many of Romana's disbanded men were mixed with this heterogeneous mass of marauders, drunkards, muleteers, women and children: the weather was dreadful, and despite the utmost exertions of the general-in-chief, when the reserve marched the next morning, the number of those unfortunate wretches was not diminished. Moore, leaving a small guard with them, proceeded to Calcabellos, but scarcely had the reserve marched out when some French cavalry appeared and in a moment the road was filled with the miserable stragglers who came crowding after the troops, some with shrieks of distress and wild gestures, others with brutal exclamations. Some overcome with fear threw away their arms, others too stupidly intoxicated to fire reeled to and fro alike insensible to danger and disgrace, and the horsemen bearing at a gallop through the disorderly mob, cutting to the right and left as they passed, rode so close to the retiring column that it was forced to halt and check their audacity.

At Calcabellos the reserve took up a position, Baird marched to Herrerias, and Moore went on to Villa Franca; but in that town also great excesses had been committed by the preceding divisions; the magazines were plundered, the bakers driven from the ovens, the wine-stores forced, the commissaries prevented making the regular distributions; the doors of the houses were broken, and a scandalous insubordination then showed a discreditable relaxation of discipline by the officers. Moore arrested this disorder, caused one man taken in the act of plundering a magazine to be hanged in the market-place, and then issuing severe orders returned to Calcabellos.

A small but at this season of the year a deep stream, called the Guia, ran through that town, and was crossed by a stone bridge. On the Villa Franca side a lofty ridge, rough with vineyards and stone walls, was occupied by two thousand five hundred infantry, with a battery of six guns; four hundred riflemen, and a like number of cavalry, were posted on a hill two miles beyond the river, to watch the roads of Bembibre and Foncevadon. In this situation, on the 3rd of January, a little after noon, the French General Colbert approached with six or eight squadrons, but observing the ground behind Calcabellos so strongly occupied, demanded reinforcements. Soult believing the English did not mean to stand, ordered Colbert to charge without delay, and the latter, stung by the message, obeyed with precipitate fury. From one of those errors so frequent in war, the British cavalry, thinking a greater force was riding against them, retired at speed to Calcabellos, and the riflemen who had withdrawn when the French first came in sight, were just passing the bridge, when a crowd of staff-officers, the cavalry and the enemy, came in upon them in one mass: thirty or forty men were taken, and Colbert crossing the river charged on the spur up the road. The remainder of the riflemen had however thrown themselves into the vineyards, and when the enemy approached within a few yards, opened such a deadly fire, that the greatest number of the French horsemen were killed on the spot, and among the rest Colbert. His fine martial figure, his voice, his gestures and his great valour, had excited the admiration of the British, and a general feeling of sorrow was predominant when the gallant soldier fell. Some French voltigeurs [light troops] now crossed the river, and a few of the 52nd regiment descended from the upper part of the ridge to the assistance of the riflemen, whereupon a sharp skirmish commenced, in which two or three hundred men of both sides were killed or wounded. Towards the termination, Merle's infantry appeared on the hills and made a demonstration of crossing opposite to the left of the English position, but a battery checked this, night came on, and the combat ceased.

As the road from Villa Franca to Lugo led through a rugged country, the cavalry were sent on to the latter town, and during the night the French patrols breaking in upon the rifle piquets, wounded some men, yet were beaten back without being able to discover that the English had abandoned the position. This however was the case, and the reserve reached Herrerias, a distance of eighteen miles, on the morning of the 4th, Baird's division being then at Nogales, Hope's and Fraser's near Lugo.

At Herrerias, Moore, who constantly directed the movements of the rear-guard, received the first reports of the engineers relative to the harbours. Vigo, besides its greater distance, offered no position to cover the embarkation, but Coruña and Betanzos did. The march to Vigo was therefore abandoned, the ships were directed round to Coruña, and the general, who now deeply regretted the separation of his light brigades, sent forward instructions for the leading division to halt at Lugo, where he designed to rally the army and give battle if the enemy would accept it. These important orders were carried to Baird by Captain George Napier, aide-de-camp to the commander-in-chief, yet Sir David forwarded them by a private dragoon, who got drunk and lost the despatch; this blameable irregularity was ruinous to Fraser's troops, for in lieu of resting two days at Lugo, that general, unwitting of the order, pursued his toilsome journey towards Santiago de Compostela, and returning without food or rest lost more than four hundred stragglers.

On the 5th, the reserve, having by a forced march of thirty-six miles gained twelve hours' start of the enemy, reached Nogales, and there met a large convoy of English clothing, shoes and ammunition intended for Romana's army, yet moving towards the enemy – a circumstance characteristic of Spain. There was a bridge at Nogales which the engineers failed to destroy, and it was of little consequence, for the river was fordable above and below, and the general was unwilling, unless for some palpable advantage which seldom presented itself, to injure the communications of a country he was unable to serve: the bridges also were commonly very solidly constructed, and the arches having little span, could be rendered passable again in a shorter time than they could be destroyed. Moreover, the road was covered with baggage, sick men, women and plunderers, all of whom would have been thus sacrificed; the peasantry, although armed, did not molest the enemy, and fearing both sides alike carried their effects into the mountains, yet even there the villainous marauders followed them, and in some cases were killed – a just punishment for quitting their colours. Under the most favourable circumstances, the tail of a retreating force exhibits terrible scenes of distress, and on the road near Nogales the followers of the army were dying fast from cold and hunger. The soldiers, barefooted, harassed, and weakened by their excesses at Bembibre and Villa Franca, were dropping to the rear by hundreds, while broken carts, dead animals, and the piteous spectacle of women and children struggling or falling exhausted in the snow, completed a picture of war, which, like Janus, has a double face.

Franceschi, after turning Villa Franca, scoured the valley of the Syl, captured many Spanish prisoners and baggage, and now regained the line of march at Becerea. The French army, also, recovering their lost ground, passed Nogales towards evening, galling the rear-guard with a continual skirmish. Here it was that dollars to the amount of twenty-five thousand pounds were abandoned. This small sum was kept near head-quarters to answer sudden emergencies, and the bullocks drawing it being tired, the general, who could not save the money without risking an ill-timed action, had it rolled down the side of the mountain, where part of it was afterwards gathered by the enemy, part by the Galician peasants. When it was ordered to be rolled over the brink of the hill two guns and a battalion of infantry were actually engaged with the enemy for its protection, and some person in whose charge the treasure was, exclaiming, 'It is money!' the general replied, 'So are shot and shells.' Accidents also will happen in war. An officer of the guards had charge of the cars drawing this treasure; an officer of the line seeing the bullocks exhausted, pointed out where fresh and strong animals were to be found; but the escorting officer, either ignorant of or indifferent to his duty, took no notice of this recommendation, and continued his march with the exhausted cattle which occasioned the loss of the treasure.

Moore gave a severe yet just rebuke to the officers and soldiers for their previous want of discipline, at the same time announcing his intention to offer battle. It has been well said that a British army may be gleaned in a retreat but cannot be reaped; whatever may be their misery, the soldiers will always be found clean at review and ready at a fight: scarcely was this order issued, when the line of battle, so attenuated before, was filled with vigorous men, full of confidence and valour. Fifteen hundred had previously fallen in action or dropped to the rear, but as three fresh battalions, left by Baird when he first advanced from Astorga, had rejoined the army between Villa Franca and Lugo, nineteen thousand combatants were still under arms.

On the right the English ground was comparatively flat and partially protected by a bend of the Minho; the centre was amongst vineyards with low stone walls. The left, somewhat withheld, rested on the mountain supported and covered by the cavalry; for it was the intention of the general to engage deeply with his right and centre before he closed with his left wing, in which he had posted the flower of his troops : he thought thus to bring on a decisive battle, and trusted to the men's valour so to handle the enemy that he would be glad to let the army retreat unmolested. Other hope to re-embark the troops without loss there was none, save by stratagem; Soult, commanding soldiers habituated to war, might be tempted but could never be forced to engage in a decisive battle amongst those rugged mountains, where whole days might pass in skirmishing without any progress being made towards crippling an adversary.

It was mid-day before the French marshal arrived in person at the head of ten or twelve thousand men, and the remainder of his power followed in some disarray; for the marches had not been so easy but that many even of the oldest soldiers had dropped behind. As the columns came up, they formed in order of battle along a strong mountain ridge fronting the English. The latter were partly hidden by inequalities of the ground; Soult doubted if they were all before him, and taking four guns, and some squadrons commanded by Colonel Lallemande, he advanced towards the centre and opened a fire, which was immediately silenced by a reply from fifteen pieces : the marshal, thus convinced that something more than a rear-guard was in his front, retired. About an hour after, he made a feint on the right, and at the same time sent a column of infantry and five guns against the left. On that side the three regiments which had lately joined were drawn up, and the French, pushing the outposts hard, were gaining the advantage when Moore arrived, rallied the light troops, broke the adverse column, and treated it very roughly in the pursuit. The estimated loss of the French was between three and four hundred men.

It was now evident the British meant to give battle, and Soult hastening the march of Laborde's division which was still in the rear, requested Ney, then at Villa Franca, to detach a division of the sixth corps by the Val des Orres to Orense. Ney however, merely sent some troops into the valley of the Syl, and pushed his advanced posts in front as far as Nogales, Poyo and Dancos. At daybreak on the 8th the two armies were still embattled. On the French side, seventeen thousand infantry, four thousand cavalry, and fifty pieces of artillery were in line, yet Soult deferred the attack until the 9th. On the English part, sixteen thousand infantry, eighteen hundred cavalry, and forty pieces of artillery, impatiently awaited the assault, and blamed their adversary for delaying a contest which they ardently desired; but darkness fell without a shot being fired, and with it fell the English general's hope to engage his enemy on equal terms.

There was not bread for another day's consumption remaining in the stores at Lugo; the soldiers were in heart for fighting, but distressed by fatigue and bad weather; and each moment of delay increased privations that would soon have rendered them inefficient for a campaign in the south, the only point where their services could be effectual. For two whole days battle had been offered; this was sufficient to rally the troops, restore order, and preserve the reputation of the army. About Lugo there was strong ground, yet it did not cover Coruña, being turned by the road leading from Orense to Santiago de Compostela, which there was no reason to suppose the French would neglect: Soult pressed Ney to follow it. It was then impossible to remain, useless if it had been possible. The general adopted the third plan, and prepared to decamp in the night. He ordered the fires to be kept bright, and exhorted the troops to make a great exertion which he trusted would be the last required of them.

Immediately in rear of the position, the ground was intersected by stone walls and a number of intricate lanes; precautions were therefore taken to mark the right tracks by placing bundles of straw at certain distances; officers were appointed to guide the columns, and at ten o'clock the regiments silently quitted their ground and retired in excellent order. But a moody fortune pursued Moore throughout this campaign, baffling his prudence and thwarting his views, as if to prove the unyielding firmness of his mind. A terrible storm of wind and rain, mixed with sleet, commenced as the army broke up from the position; the marks were destroyed, the guides lost the true direction, only one of the divisions gained the main road, the other two were bewildered, and when daylight broke, the rear columns were still near to Lugo. The fatigue, the depression of mind occasioned by this misfortune, and the want of shoes, broke the order of the march, stragglers became numerous, and unfortunately Baird, thinking to relieve the men during a halt which took place in the night, desired the leading division to take refuge from the weather in some houses a little way off the road. Complete disorganization followed this imprudent act. From that moment it became impossible to make the soldiers keep their ranks, plunder succeeded, the example was infectious; and what with real suffering, and evil propensity encouraged by this error, the main body of the army, after having bivouacked for six hours in the rain, arrived at

Betanzos on the evening of the 9th in a state very discreditable to its discipline.

Sir John now assembled the army in one solid mass. The loss in the march from Lugo to Betanzos had been greater than that in all the former part of the retreat, added to all the losses in the advance and in the different actions. Fourteen or fifteen thousand infantry were however still in column, and by an orderly march to Coruña, demonstrated, that inattention and the want of experience in the officers was the true cause of the disorders, which had afflicted the army far more than the sword of the enemy or the rigour of the elements.

As the troops approached Coruña, the general's looks were earnestly directed towards the harbour, but an open expanse of water painfully convinced him, that to Fortune at least he was in no way beholden; contrary winds still detained the fleet at Vigo, and the last consuming exertion made by the army was rendered fruitless! The men were put into quarters, and their leader awaited the progress of events. The bridge of El Burgo was now destroyed, and so was that of Cambria, situated a few miles up the Mero river, but the engineer employed, mortified at the former failures, was so anxious that he remained too near the latter and was killed by the explosion. Meanwhile three divisions occupied the town and suburbs of Coruña, and the reserve was posted between the village of El Burgo and the road of Santiago de Compostela. For twelve days these hardy soldiers had covered the retreat, during which time they traversed eighty miles of road in two marches, passed several nights under arms in the snow of the mountains, were seven times engaged, and now took the outposts having fewer men missing from the ranks, including those who had fallen in battle, than any other division in the army: an admirable instance of the value of good discipline, and a manifest proof of the malignant injustice with which Moore has been accused of precipitating his retreat beyond the measure of human strength.

*   *   *

Coruña, although sufficiently strong to compel an enemy to break ground before it, was weakly fortified, and to the southward commanded by heights close to the walls. Moore caused the land front to be strengthened, and occupied the citadel; but he disarmed the sea face of the works, and the inhabitants cheerfully and honourably joined in the labour, although they were aware the army would finally embark, and they would incur the enemy's anger by taking part in the military operations. Such flashes of light from the dark cloud at this moment covering Spain may startle the reader, and make him doubt if the Spaniards could have been so insufficient to their own defence as represented. Yet the facts were as told, and it was such paradoxical indications of character that deceived the world at the time, and induced men to believe the reckless, daring defiance of the power of France, so loudly proclaimed by the patriots, would be strenuously supported. Of proverbially vivid imagination and quick resentments, the Spaniards feel and act individually rather than nationally, and during this war, what appeared constancy of purpose, was but a repetition of momentary fury generated like electric sparks by constant collision with the French, yet daily becoming fainter as custom reconciled the sufferers to those injuries and insults which are commonly the attendants of war. Procrastination and improvidence are their besetting sins. At this moment large magazines of arms and ammunition, which had been sent in the early part of the preceding year from England, were still in Coruña, unappropriated by a nation infested with three hundred thousand enemies, and having a hundred thousand soldiers unclothed and without weapons!

Three miles from the town were piled four thousand barrels of powder in a magazine built upon a hill, and a smaller quantity was collected in another storehouse some distance from the first. Both were fired on the 13th. The inferior one exploded with a terrible noise shaking all the houses in the town; and when the train reached the great store, there ensued a crash like the bursting forth of a volcano. The earth trembled for miles, the rocks were torn from their bases, the agitated waters of the harbour rolled the vessels as in a storm, a vast column of smoke and dust, with flames and sparks shooting out from its dark flanks, arose perpendicularly and slowly to a great height, where it burst, and then a shower of stones and fragments of all kinds descending with a roaring sound, killed many persons who had remained too near the spot: stillness, slightly interrupted by the lashing of the waves on the shore, succeeded, and the business of the war went on.

Now a painful measure was adopted; the ground in front of Coruña is impracticable for cavalry, the horses were generally foundered, it was impossible to embark them all in the face of an enemy, and a great number were reluctantly ordered to be shot; worn down and foot-broken, they would otherwise have been distributed among the French cavalry, or used as draught cattle until death relieved them from procrastinated suffering. But the very fact of their being so foundered was one of the results of inexperience; the cavalry had come out to Coruña without proper equipments, the horses were ruined, not for want of shoes, but want of hammers and nails to put them on!

Soon the French gathered on the Mero, and Moore sought a position of battle. A chain of rocky elevations, commencing on the sea-coast north-west of Coruña and ending on the Mero behind the village of El Burgo, offered a good line, which, covered by a branch of the Mero, would have forced the enemy to advance by the road of Compostela. But it was too extensive, and if not wholly occupied, the French could turn the right and move along a succession of hills to the very gates of Coruña: the English general was thus reduced to occupy an inferior range, enclosed as it were, and commanded by the first within cannon shot. Soult's army, exhausted by continual toil, could not concentrate before the 12th, but on that day the infantry took post opposite El Burgo, while La Houssaye's heavy cavalry lined the river as far as the ocean; Franceschi, crossing at the bridge of Celas, seven miles higher up, intercepted some stores coming from Santiago and made a few prisoners. The 14th, the bridges at El Burgo being rendered practicable for artillery, two divisions of infantry and one of cavalry passed the river, and to cover their march some guns opened on the English posts but were soon silenced by a superior fire. In the evening the transports from Vigo hove in sight; they entered the harbour in the night, and the dismounted cavalry, the sick, the best horses, and fifty pieces of artillery were embarked, six British and three Spanish guns worked by English gunners only, being kept on shore for action. On the 15th, Laborde's division arrived. Soult then occupied the greater ridge enclosing the British position, placing his right on the intersection of the roads leading to Santiago and Betanzos, his left on a rocky eminence overlooking both armies: his cavalry extended along the heights to their own left, and a slight skirmish took place in the valley below. The English piquets opposite the right of the French also engaged, and being galled by the fire of two guns, Colonel M'Kenzie of the fifth regiment, pushed out with some companies to seize the battery, whereupon a line of infantry, hitherto concealed by some stone walls, immediately arose, killed the colonel and drove his men back with loss.

In the night, Soult with great difficulty dragged eleven heavy guns to the rocks which closed the left of his line, and in the morning he formed his order of battle. Laborde's division was posted on the right, one half being on the high ground, the other on the descent towards the river. Merle's division was in the centre. Mermet's division formed the left. The position was covered on the right by the villages of Palavia Abaxo and Portosa, and in the centre by a wood. The left, secured by the rocks where the great battery was established, was twelve hundred yards from the right of the British line, and midway the little village of Elvina was held by the piquets of the fiftieth British regiment. The late arrival of the transports, the increasing force of the enemy, and the disadvantageous nature of the position, augmented the difficulty of embarking so much, that some generals now advised a negotiation for leave to regain the ships. There was little chance of this being granted, and there was no reason to try; the army had suffered, but not from defeat; its situation was perilous, yet far from desperate. Moore would not consent to remove the stamp of prudence and energy from his retreat by a proposal which would have given an appearance of timidity to his previous operations, as opposite to their real character as light is to darkness; his high spirit and clear judgment revolted at the idea, and he rejected the degrading advice without hesitation.

All the encumbrances being shipped on the morning of the 16th, it was intended to embark the fighting men in the coming night, and this difficult operation would probably have been happily effected; but a glorious event was destined to give a more graceful though melancholy termination to the campaign. About two o'clock a general movement of the French line gave notice of an approaching battle, and the British infantry, fourteen thousand five hundred strong, occupied their position. Baird's division on the right, and governed by the oblique direction of the ridge approached the enemy; Hope's division, forming the centre and left, although on strong ground abutting on the Mero, was of necessity withheld, so that the French battery on the rocks raked the whole line of battle. One of Baird's brigades was in column behind the right, and one of Hope's behind the left; Paget's reserve posted at the village of Airis, behind the centre, looked down the valley separating the right of the position from the hills occupied by the French cavalry. A battalion detached from the reserve kept these horsemen in check, and was itself connected with the main body by a chain of skirmishers extended across the valley. Fraser's division held the heights immediately before the gates of Coruña, watching the coast road, but it was also ready to succour any point.

These dispositions were dictated by the ground, which was very favourable to the enemy; for Franceschi's cavalry reached nearly

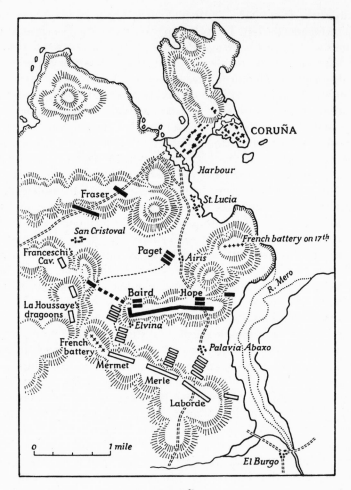

CORUÑA

to the village of San Cristoval, a mile beyond Baird's right, and
hence Moore was forced to weaken his front and keep Fraser's
division in reserve until Soult's attack should be completely un-
folded. There was however one advantage on the British side;
many thousand new English muskets, found in the Spanish stores,
were given to the troops in lieu of their rusty battered arms, and as
their ammunition was also fresh, their fire was far better sustained
than that of the enemy.

When Laborde's division arrived, the French force was not less
than twenty thousand men, and the Duke of Dalmatia made no idle

evolutions of display. Distributing his lighter guns along the front of his position, he opened a fire from the heavy battery on his left, and instantly descended the mountain with three columns covered by clouds of skirmishers. The British piquets were driven back in disorder, and the village of Elvina was carried by the first French column, which then divided and attempted to turn Baird's right by the valley, and break his front at the same time. The second column made against the English centre, and the third attacked Hope's left at the village of Palavia Abaxo. Soult's heavier guns over-matched the English six-pounders, and swept the position to the centre; but Moore observing that the enemy, according to his ex-pectations, did not show any body of infantry beyond that moving up the valley to outflank Baird's right, ordered Paget to carry the whole of the reserve to where the detached regiment was posted, and, as he had before arranged with him, turn the left of the French columns and menace the great battery. Fraser he ordered to support Paget, and then throwing back the fourth regiment, which formed the right of Baird's division, opened a heavy fire upon the flank of the troops penetrating up the valley, while the fiftieth and forty-second regiments met those breaking through Elvina. The ground about that village was intersected by stone walls and hollow roads, a severe scrambling fight ensued, the French were forced back with great loss, and the fiftieth regiment entering the village with the retiring mass, drove it, after a second struggle in the street, quite beyond the houses. Seeing this, the general ordered up a battalion of the guards to fill the void in the line made by the advance of those regiments, whereupon the forty-second, mistaking his intention, retired, with exception of the grenadiers, and at that moment the enemy, being reinforced, renewed the fight beyond the village.

Major Napier, the author's eldest brother, commanding the fiftieth, was wounded and taken prisoner. When the French renewed the attack on Elvina, he was somewhat in advance of that village, and alone, for the troops were scattered by the nature of the ground. Being hurt in the leg, he endeavoured to retire, but was overtaken, and thrown to the ground with five wounds; a French drummer rescued him, and when a soldier with whom he had been struggling made a second attempt to kill him, the drummer once more interfered. The morning after the battle Marshal Soult sent his own surgeon to Major Napier, and, with a kindness and con-sideration very uncommon, wrote to Napoleon, desiring that his prisoner might not be sent to France, which from the system of refusing exchanges would have ruined his professional prospects;

the drummer also received the cross of the legion of honour. When the second corps quitted Coruña, Marshal Soult recommended his prisoner to the attention of Marshal Ney. The latter, treating him rather with the kindness of a friend than the civility of an enemy, lodged him with the French consul, supplied him with money, gave him a general invitation to his house, and not only refrained from sending him to France, but when by a flag of truce he knew that Major Napier's mother was mourning for him as dead, he permitted him, and with him the few soldiers taken in the action, to go at once to England, merely exacting a promise that none should serve until exchanged. I would not have touched at all upon these private adventures, were it not that gratitude demands a public acknowledgment of such generosity, and that demand is rendered more imperative by the after misfortunes of Marshal Ney. That brave and noble-minded man's fate is but too well known! He who had fought five hundred battles for France, not one against her, was shot as a traitor! Could the bitterest enemy of the Bourbons have more strongly marked the difference between their interests and those of the nation!

Elvina then became the scene of another contest, which being observed by the commander-in-chief, he addressed a few animating words to the forty-second, and caused it to return to the attack. Paget had now descended into the valley, and the line of the skirmishers being thus supported vigorously checked the advance of the enemy's troops in that quarter, while the fourth regiment galled their flank; at the same time the centre and left of the army also became engaged, Baird was severely wounded, and a furious action ensued along the line, in the valley, and on the hills.

Sir John Moore, while earnestly watching the result of the fight about the village of Elvina, was struck on the left breast by a cannon shot; the shock threw him from his horse with violence; yet he rose again in a sitting posture, his countenance unchanged, and his steadfast eye still fixed upon the regiments engaged in his front, no sigh betraying a sensation of pain. In a few moments, when he saw the troops were gaining ground, his countenance brightened and he suffered himself to be taken to the rear. Then was seen the dreadful nature of his hurt. The shoulder was shattered to pieces, the arm hanging by a piece of skin, the ribs over the heart broken, and bared of flesh, the muscles of the breast torn into long stripes, interlaced by their recoil from the dragging of the shot. As the soldiers placed him in a blanket, his sword got entangled and the hilt entered the wound; Captain Hardinge, a staff officer, attempted to take it off, but the dying man stopped him, saying, '*It is as well as it is. I had rather it should go out of the field with me*', and in that manner, so becoming to a soldier, Moore was borne from the fight.

Notwithstanding this great disaster, the troops gained ground. The reserve, overthrowing everything in the valley, forced La Houssaye's dismounted dragoons to retire, and thus turning the enemy, approached the eminence upon which the great battery was posted. On the left, Colonel Nicholls, at the head of some companies of the fourteenth, carried Palavia Abaxo, which General Foy defended but feebly. In the centre, the obstinate dispute for Elvina terminated in favour of the British; and when the night set in, their line was considerably advanced beyond the original position of the morning, while the French were falling back in confusion. If Fraser's division had been brought into action along with the reserve, the enemy could hardly have escaped a signal overthrow; for the little ammunition Soult had been able to bring up was nearly exhausted, the river Mero was in full tide behind him, and the difficult communication by the bridge of El Burgo was alone open for a retreat. On the other hand, to fight in the dark was to tempt fortune; the French were still the most numerous, their ground strong, and their disorder facilitated the original plan of embarking during the night. Hope, upon whom the command had devolved, resolved therefore to ship the army, and so complete were the arrangements, that no confusion or difficulty occurred; the piquets kindled fires to cover the retreat, and were themselves withdrawn at daybreak to embark under the protection of Hill's brigade, which was in position under the ramparts of Coruña.

When morning dawned, the French, seeing the British position abandoned, pushed some battalions to the heights of San Lucia, and about midday opened a battery on the shipping in the harbour. This caused great confusion amongst the transports, several masters cut their cables, and four vessels went on shore, but the troops were rescued by the men of war's boats, the stranded vessels burned, and the fleet got out of harbour. Hill then embarked at the citadel, which was maintained by a rearguard under Beresford until the 18th, when the wounded being all on board, the troops likewise embarked, the inhabitants faithfully maintained the town meanwhile, and the fleet sailed for England. The loss of the British, never officially published, was estimated at eight hundred; of the French at three thousand. The latter is probably an exaggeration, yet it must have been great, for the English muskets were all new, the ammunition fresh; and whether from the peculiar construction of the muskets, the physical strength and coolness of the men, or all combined, the English fire is the most destructive known. The nature of the ground also barred artillery movements, and the French columns were exposed to grape, which they could not return because of the distance of their batteries.

Thus ended the retreat to Coruña, a transaction which has called forth as much of falsehood and malignity as servile and interested writers could offer to the unprincipled leaders of a base faction, but which posterity will regard as a genuine example of ability and patriotism. From the spot where he fell, the general was carried to the town by his soldiers; his blood flowed fast and the torture of the wound was great; yet the unshaken firmness of his mind made those about him, seeing the resolution of his countenance, express a hope of his recovery: he looked steadfastly at the injury for a moment, and said, '*No, I feel that to be impossible*'. Several times he caused his attendants to stop and turn round, that he might behold the field of battle; and when the firing indicated the advance of the British, he discovered his satisfaction and permitted the bearers to proceed. When brought to his lodgings, the surgeons examined his wound, there was no hope, the pain increased, he spoke with difficulty. At intervals he asked if the French were beaten, and addressing his old friend, Colonel Anderson, said, '*You know I always wished to die this way*'. Again he asked if the enemy were defeated, and being told they were, said, '*It is a great satisfaction to me to know we have beaten the French*'. His countenance continued firm, his thoughts clear, only once when he spoke of his mother he became agitated; but he often inquired after the safety of his friends and the officers of his staff, and he did not even in this moment forget to recommend those whose merit had given them claims to promotion. When life was just extinct, with an unsubdued spirit, as if anticipating the baseness of his posthumous calumniators, he exclaimed, '*I hope the people of England will be satisfied! I hope my country will do me justice!*' In a few minutes afterwards he died, and his corpse, wrapped in a military cloak, was interred by the officers of his staff in the citadel of Coruña. The guns of the enemy paid his funeral honours, and Soult with a noble feeling of respect for his valour raised a monument to his memory on the field of battle.

Thus ended the career of Sir John Moore, a man whose uncommon capacity was sustained by the purest virtue, and governed by a disinterested patriotism more in keeping with the primitive than the luxurious age of a great nation. His tall graceful person, his dark searching eyes, strongly defined forehead and singularly

expressive mouth, indicated a noble disposition and a refined understanding. The lofty sentiments of honour habitual to his mind, were
adorned by a subtle playful wit, which gave him in conversation an
ascendancy he always preserved by the decisive vigour of his
actions. He maintained the right with a vehemence bordering upon
fierceness, and every important transaction in which he was engaged
increased his reputation for talent, and confirmed his character as a
stern enemy to vice, a steadfast friend to merit, a just and faithful
servant of his country. The honest loved him, the dishonest feared
him. For while he lived he did not shun, but scorned and spurned
the base, and with characteristic propriety they spurned at him when
he was dead.

A soldier from his earliest youth, Moore thirsted for the honours
of his profession. He knew himself worthy to lead a British army,
and hailed the fortune which placed him at the head of the troops
destined for Spain. As the stream of time passed, the inspiring
hopes of triumph disappeared, but the austerer glory of suffering
remained, and with a firm heart he accepted that gift of a severe
fate. Confident in the strength of his genius, he disregarded the
clamours of presumptuous ignorance. Opposing sound military
views to the foolish projects so insolently thrust upon him, he
conducted his long and arduous retreat with sagacity, intelligence,
and fortitude; no insult disturbed, no falsehood deceived him, no
remonstrance shook his determination; fortune frowned without
subduing his constancy; death struck, but the spirit of the man
remained unbroken when his shattered body scarcely afforded it a
habitation. Having done all that was just towards others, he
remembered what was due to himself. Neither the shock of the
mortal blow, nor the lingering hours of acute pain which preceded
his dissolution, could quell the pride of his gallant heart, or lower
the dignified feeling with which, conscious of merit, he at the last
moment asserted his right to the gratitude of the country he had
served so truly. If glory be a distinction, for such a man death is
not a leveller!

The fleet steered home directly from Coruña, and a terrible storm
scattered it; many ships were wrecked, and the remainder driving
up the Channel were glad to put into any port. The soldiers thus
thrown on shore were spread from the Land's End to Dover. Their
haggard appearance, ragged clothing and dirty accoutrements,
things common enough in war, struck a people only used to the
daintiness of parade with surprise. The usual exaggerations of
men just escaped from perils and distresses, were increased by the

uncertainty in which all were as to the fate of their comrades. A deadly fever, the result of anxiety and of the sudden change from fatigue to the confinement of a ship, filled the hospitals at every port with officers and soldiers, and thus the miserable state of Sir John Moore's army became the topic of every letter, and the theme for every country newspaper along the coast. The nation, at that time unused to great operations, forgot that war is not a harmless game; and judging of the loss positively, instead of comparatively, was disposed to believe the calumnies of interested men, eager to cast a shade over one of the brightest characters that ever adorned the country. Those calumnies triumphed for a moment, but Moore's last appeal to his country for justice will be successful. Posterity, revering and cherishing his name, will visit such of his odious calumniators as are not too contemptible to be remembered, with a just and severe retribution; for thus it is that time freshens the beauty of virtue and withers the efforts of baseness.

V

Sir Arthur Wellesley Returns
1809

Britain was accustomed to disaster against Napoleon. In spite of the calamity of Sir John Moore's campaign, there was dawning comprehension in London that the Iberian peninsula offered a fair field for military operations, even of secondary magnitude. Austria was girding herself for another armed clash with Napoleon, in which she all but matched his power at the battles of Aspern and Wagram. Britain's contribution was as usual, lavish subsidies, together with a large and abortive expedition to the Scheldt, where Walcheren fever decimated most of the good soldiers they had left.

In Spain, Sir John Moore's incursion had prevented the French from taking over the whole country. The northern half was firmly under their control. King Joseph was installed in Madrid, almost without revenues, but with powers resented by the marshals – Soult, Ney and Victor – commanding in the field. They proved recalcitrant and, with the passage of time, each became less interested in co-operating with the other and more concerned with enriching himself in his own area of occupation. This was to prove the canker at the heart of the French military posture in Spain.

Some threadbare Spanish armies had survived the fearful drubbing they had received at the hands of the French, notably the troops under Generals Cuesta and Venegas in the south-west. The central government junta remained as hysterical and ineffective as ever.

Sir John Moore had considered the frontiers of Portugal indefensible. When the British government had recourse again to Sir Arthur Wellesley, he concurred, but gave as his opinion that if 20,000 British troops could be added to as many Portuguese levies, which had been brought up to a reasonable state of training and discipline by Marshal Beresford after Junot's ejection, the French would need to bring 100,000 men to bear, and they would not be able to concentrate as many. Marshal Soult had occupied Oporto after his victory at Coruña. Marshal Victor and King Joseph held the centre round Madrid. They offered alternative and widely separated targets. The British government decided to reinforce

*the troops left at Lisbon under Sir John Cradock and in April 1809 sent
out Sir Arthur Wellesley to supersede him.*

THIS UNEXPECTED arrival of a victorious commander
created the greatest enthusiasm; the regency nominated him
marshal-general, the people, always fond of novelty, hailed his
presence; and those persons, Portuguese and British, who blamed
Cradock's prudence, spoke largely of future operations: an un-
defined yet powerful sentiment that something great would soon be
achieved pervaded the public mind. Like Cradock, Sir Arthur felt
the necessity of covering Lisbon while Victor was on the Alemtejo
frontier, and he anxiously compared the enemy's resources with
his own. Neither concert nor communication could longer exist
between those marshals, and Soult's offensive strength was also
exhausted. He might establish himself in the provinces beyond the
Douro; he could not force his way to Lisbon, a distance of two hundred miles through a country tangled with flooded rivers, mountains and defiles. He could not hope, with twenty-four thousand
men, to beat a whole people in arms, assisted by an auxiliary army
of as high reputation, and nearly as numerous as his own; moreover discontent and conspiracy were in his camp, and of that Sir
Arthur was aware. Soult then did not menace the capital. Victor, at
the head of thirty thousand men, might march upon Lisbon,
through an open country; the only barrier being the Tagus, a river
fordable in almost all seasons. Such a movement, or the semblance
of it, would draw the British and native armies to that side; and then
Soult coming down to the Mondego, might from thence connect his
operations with Victor's by the line of the Zezere, or advance at
once on Lisbon as occasion offered.

Sir Arthur Wellesley's own military resources were:

1°. His central position.

2°. The British and German troops, twenty-six thousand, having
under arms, including sergeants, twenty-two thousand, with three
thousand seven hundred horses and mules; but in the British army
corporals and privates only are understood as present under arms;
whereas in the French army all military persons, officers, non-
commissioned officers, soldiers, drummers, combatants and non-
combatants, are included: a distinction to be borne in mind when
comparing the forces on each side.

3°. The Portuguese troops of the line, of which sixteen thousand
were organized and armed. Nearly all these troops were collected
between the Tagus and Mondego.

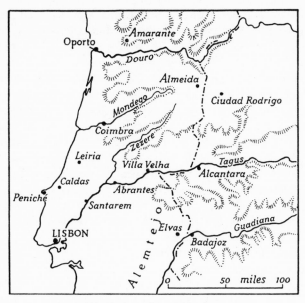

WELLESLEY'S POSITIONS

4°. The militia and *ordenanças* or insurgent force.

5°. The fortresses of Almeida, Ciudad Rodrigo, Elvas, Abrantes, Peniché and Badajoz.

6°. The English fleet, the Portuguese craft, and free use of the coast and river navigation for supplies.

7°. The co-operation of Cuesta, who had six thousand cavalry and thirty thousand infantry, of which twenty-five thousand were in front of Victor's posts.

His moral resources were the high courage of the English troops, personal popularity, the energy of an excited people, a favourable moment, the presentiment of victory, and a mind equal to the occasion. In a strategic view, to fall upon Victor was best; he was the most dangerous neighbour to Portugal, his defeat would be most detrimental to the French, most advantageous to the Spaniards; and the greatest body of troops could be brought to bear against him. But Soult held rich provinces, from whence the chief supply of cattle for the army was derived; he had the second city of the kingdom, and was there forming a French party; and the regency and people, troubled by the loss of Oporto, loudly demanded its recovery. To attack Victor, it was indispensable to concert with Cuesta; but he was ill disposed, and to insure his co-operation would have required time, which could be better employed in expelling Soult. For these reasons, Sir Arthur determined to fall upon the latter; intending, if successful, to organize a system of defence in the northern provinces, and then, in conjunction with Cuesta, turn against Victor, hoping thus to relieve Galicia more effectually than by following the French into that province.

Lisbon being the pivot of operations, time was the principal object to be gained. If Victor came fiercely on, he could not be stopped, but he might be impeded; his path could not be blocked, but it might be planted with thorns. To effect this, seven thousand Portuguese troops were directed upon Abrantes and Santarem, whither two British battalions and two regiments of cavalry, just disembarked, also marched; and they were joined by three other battalions drafted from the army at Leiria. A body of two thousand men, composed of a militia regiment and the Lusitanian legion, were placed under Colonel Mayne, with orders to defend the bridge of Alcantara, and if necessary to blow up the structure. The flying bridges at Villa Velha and Abrantes were removed, the garrison of the latter place reinforced, and Mackenzie took command of all the troops, Portuguese and British, thus distributed along the right bank of the Tagus. These precautions appeared sufficient, for there was a general disposition, and Sir Arthur was not exempt, to think the French weaker than they really were.

When these matters were arranged, the main body of the allies marched upon Coimbra, and four Portuguese battalions were incorporated in each British brigade. Beresford retained under his personal command only six thousand. The difficulty of bringing up forage and provisions was now somewhat lessened; but the land transport was still scanty; and the admiral, dreading the long shore navigation for large vessels, had no small craft to victual the troops by the coast. The magazines at Caldas were however partly filled, and twenty large country-boats loaded with provisions, the owners being induced by premiums, got safely into Peniché and the Mondego: in fine, the obstacles to a forward movement were great, but not insurmountable. Sir Arthur reached Coimbra the 2nd of May, and on the 5th concentrated there twenty-five thousand sabres and bayonets, of which nine thousand were Portuguese, three thousand Germans, the remainder British.

Soult immediately sent all the heavy artillery and baggage still in Oporto along the road of Amarante; and Mermet followed the same route as far as Vallonga and Baltar, having orders to secure the boats there and vigilantly patrol up the bank of the river. All the craft near Oporto were secured, guards were placed at different points, and the French marshal resolved to keep his ground during the 12th, that Lorge's dragoons and the smaller detachments might have time to concentrate at Amarante. Loison was again warned to hold the Tamega as he valued the safety of the army. Soult's attention was principally directed to the Douro below Oporto, because Franceschi's report led him to believe Hill's division had landed at Ovar from the ocean, and he expected the empty vessels would come round and effect a passage at the mouth of the river. Believing Loison to be holding Mezamfrio and Pezo de Ragoa, and having disposed three brigades between Oporto and Amarante, he thought his retreat secure; but the conspirators were busy, his orders were neglected and false reports of their execution made.

Before eight o'clock on the morning of the 12th, the British army was secretly concentrated behind the Serra convent height; but the Douro rolled between it and the French, and the latter had hitherto suffered no loss. They could in two marches gain the Tamega with a safe retreat to Bragança; and, in passing, might defeat Beresford whose force was ill-organized and unfit for battle. Sir Arthur had sent it to vex the French line of retreat by Villa Real, and thus induce Soult to take the less accessible road of Chaves and make for Galicia instead of Leon. That it could not do, unless the French were pressed by the main army, and Soult at Salamanca would be more formidable than at Oporto; and hence the safety of Beresford and the great object of the campaign alike demanded an immediate passage of the Douro. But how pass a river, deep, swift, more than three hundred yards wide, when ten thousand veterans lined the

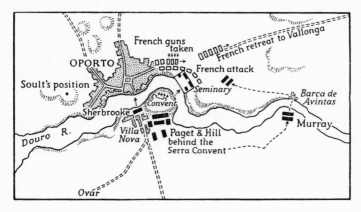

OPORTO

opposite bank? The Macedonian hero might have turned from it without shame!

The Serra rock, round which the Douro came with a sharp elbow, barred sight of the upper channel, and Soult thinking it secure took his station westward of the city, from whence he could see the lower channel to its mouth: but on the rock stood Sir Arthur, searching with an eagle's glance the river, the city and the country beyond. Horses and baggage were on the Vallonga road, the dust of columns in retreat, and no large force near the river; the guards were few and widely spread, the patrols not vigilant, and an auspicious negligence seemed to prevail. Suddenly a large building called the Seminary caught the English general's eye; it was isolated, with easy access to the river, and surrounded by a high wall extending to the water on either side, offering room for two battalions; and the only egress was by an iron gate opening on the Vallonga road. This structure commanded everything around, except one mound within cannon-shot but too pointed to hold a gun. There were no French posts near, and the direct line to the building across the river was hidden from the town by the Serra rock. Here then with a marvellous hardihood Sir Arthur resolved, if he could find but one boat, to force a passage in face of a veteran army and a renowned general.

Colonel Waters, a quick daring man, discovered a poor barber who had come over the river with a small skiff the previous night; and these two being joined by the prior of Amarante, who gallantly offered his services, crossed the water unperceived and returned in half an hour with three large barges. Meanwhile eighteen guns were placed in battery on the convent height, and General John Murray was sent with the German brigade, the 14th dragoons and two guns, three miles up the stream, to the Barca de Avintas, with orders to seek for boats and pass there if possible. When Waters came back with the barges, some English troops followed Murray in support, and others cautiously approached the river close under the Serra rock. It was then ten o'clock, the French were tranquil and unsuspicious, the British wondering and expectant, and Sir Arthur was told that one boat had reached the point of passage. 'Well let the men cross', was the reply, and on this simple order an officer with twenty-five men were in a quarter of an hour silently placed in the midst of the French army. The Seminary was thus gained, yet the French remained in Oporto. A second boat crossed, no hostile movement followed, no sound was heard, and a third boat passed higher up the river; but then tumultuous noise rolled through

Oporto, the drums beat to arms, shouts arose in all parts, and the people were seen vehemently gesticulating and making signals from their houses, while confused masses of troops, rushing out of the city by the higher streets and throwing out swarms of skirmishers, came furiously down against the Seminary. The British soldiers instantly crowded the river bank, Paget's and Hill's divisions at the point of passage, Sherbrooke's where the boat bridge had been cut away; but Paget himself, who had passed in the third boat and mounted the roof of the Seminary, fell there deeply wounded, whereupon Hill took his place. The musketry, sharp and voluble, augmented as the forces accumulated, and the French attack was eager and constant, their fire increased more rapidly, and their guns opened on the building, while the English guns from the Serra commanded the enclosure and swept the ground on the left so as to confine the assault to the iron gate front; but Murray did not appear, the struggle was violent, the moment critical, and Sir Arthur was only prevented crossing in person by the interference of those about him and the confidence he had in Hill.

In this state of affairs some citizens came over to Villa Nova with several great boats; and Sherbrooke's men were beginning to cross in large bodies, when a long loud shout in the town, and the waving of handkerchiefs from the windows, gave notice that the French had abandoned the lower city; at the same time Murray was descried coming down the right bank of the river. Three battalions were now in the Seminary, the attack slackened, and Hill advancing to the enclosure wall poured a destructive fire on the French columns, as they passed in haste and confusion along his front on the Vallonga road; five guns then came galloping out of the town, but, appalled by the terrible line of musketry from the enclosure, the drivers pulled up, and while thus hesitating a volley from behind stretched many artillerymen in the dust, and the rest dispersing left their guns in the road. This volley came from Sherbrooke's men, who had come through the town, and thus the passage being won the allies had the right bank of the Douro. Sherbrooke from the city now pressed the French rear, Hill from the Seminary sent a damaging fire on the flank of the retiring masses, and far on the right Murray menaced the line of retreat: the rear of the army was still passing the river, but the guns on the Serra rock searched the French columns from rear to front as they hurried onwards.

If Murray had fallen upon the disordered crowds their discomfiture would have been complete; but he suffered column after column to pass without even a cannon-shot, and seemed fearful lest

they should turn and push him into the river. General Charles
Stewart and Major Hervey, impatient of his timidity, charged with
two squadrons of dragoons, and riding over the enemy's rear-
guard as it was pushing through a narrow road to gain an open
space beyond, unhorsed Laborde and wounded Foy, yet on the
English side, Hervey lost an arm, and his gallant horsemen,
receiving no support from Murray, had to fight their way back with
loss. This finished the action, the French continued their retreat,
the British remained on the ground they had gained; the latter lost
twenty killed, a general and ninety-five men wounded; the former
had five hundred men killed and wounded, and five guns were taken.
A quantity of ammunition, and fifty guns, the carriages of which
had been burnt, were afterwards found in the arsenal, and several
hundred men were captured in the hospitals.

Napoleon's veterans were so experienced, so inured to warfare,
that no troops could more readily recover from a surprise. Before
they reached Vallonga they were again in order with a rear-guard;
and as a small garrison at the mouth of the Douro, guided by some
friendly Portuguese, also rejoined the army in the night, Soult,
believing Loison was still at Amarante, thought he had happily
escaped the danger. Sir Arthur Wellesley now brought over his
baggage, stores and the artillery, which occupied the 12th and 13th;
and though Murray's Germans pursued on the morning of the 13th,
they did not go more than two leagues on the road of Amarante.
This delay has been blamed. It is argued that an enemy once surprised should never be allowed to recover while a single regiment
could pursue. The reasons for halting were, that part of the army
was still on the left bank of the Douro, and the troops had outmarched provisions, baggage and ammunition; they had made
eighty miles of difficult country in four days, during three of which
they were constantly fighting, men and animals required rest, and
nothing was known of Beresford.

Next day the army marched in two columns towards the Minho,
the right by Barca de Trofa and Braga, the left by Ponte d'Ave and
Bacellos. Towards evening it was judged from the French move-
ments that Chaves and Montalegre, not Valença and Tuy, would be
their line of retreat; the left column was therefore directed on
Braga; and Beresford was ordered to move by Monterey upon
Villa del Rey if Soult should make for Montalegre. The 15th Sir
Arthur reached Braga; Murray was at Guimaraens on the right;
Beresford, anticipating his orders, was near Chaves, having sent
Silveira towards Salamonde to seize the passes of Ruivaens and

Melgasso. Soult's capture now appeared inevitable; yet he was already beyond the toils, having by a surprising effort extricated himself from perils as fearful as ever beset a general.

In retreating towards Amarante he had the Douro on his right hand, the Sierra de Catalina on his left, both reckoned impassable; and the narrow way between them was very rugged. Braga was beyond the Sierra, and from thence to Amarante, a road, practicable for guns, ran through Guimaraens; but it could only be reached through Amarante. Hence Soult's safety, while penetrating between the mountain and the river, depended upon Loison's holding the Tamega. That general had not corresponded for several days. Colonel Tholosé who had been sent the 12th to ascertain his situation found him at Amarante; yet neither that officer's remonstrances, nor the after intelligence that Soult was in full retreat for the Tamega, could prevent him marching on the 13th towards Guimaraens; he thus abandoned his commander and two-thirds of the army to what appeared certain destruction. This calamity was made known to Soult as he was passing the rugged bed of the Souza torrent. The weather was boisterous, the army, worn with fatigue, was dismayed, and voices were heard calling for a capitulation. But in that terrible crisis the marshal duke justified fortune for having raised him to such dignity. He had accidentally fallen from his horse, and his hip, formerly broken by a shot at the siege of Genoa, was severely injured; but neither pain, nor weakness of body, nor peril, could shake the firmness of his soul. A Spanish pedlar had told him of a path which, ascending the right bank of the Souza, led over the Sierra de Catalina to Guimaraens; wherefore, silencing the murmurs of treacherous officers and fearful foldiers, he destroyed his guns, abandoned the military chest and baggage, loaded the animals which carried them with sick men and musket ammunition, repassed the Souza, and followed his Spanish guide with a hardy resolution. The rain fell in torrents, the path such as might be expected in those wild regions, but with a fierce will he forced his troops over the mountain, gained Pombeira, and at Guimaraens found Loison's division. Lorge's dragoons also came from Braga, and thus almost beyond hope, the whole army was concentrated.

Soult's energy had been great, his sagacity was not less conspicuous. The slackness of pursuit after passing Vallonga, made him judge that Sir Arthur was pushing for Braga and would reach it first. A fighting retreat, and the loss of guns and baggage, would then ensue, which might fatally depress the soldiers' spirits. It would also favour the malcontents' views, and already one general,

apparently Loison, was urging a convention. Soult replied by destroying the guns, ammunition and baggage of the two divisions he
had reunited, and again took to the mountains on his right. In this
manner he reached Carvalho d'Este late in the evening of the 14th,
having gained a day's march in point of time. The next morning he
drew up the troops, twenty thousand, on the position he had occupied two months before at the battle of Braga; and by this imposing
spectacle on the scene of a recent victory aroused the sinking pride
of the French soldiers. It was a happy reach of generalship! Then
he re-organized his army and took the rear himself, giving the
advanced guard to Loison.

From Carvalho the French gained Salamonde, whence there
were two lines of retreat; the one through Ruivaens and Venda
Nova to Montalegre; the other shorter but more rugged, leading by
the Ponte Nova and Ponte Miserella into the road of Montalegre.
The scouts said the bridge of Ruivaens was broken, and defended
by twelve hundred Portuguese with artillery; and that another
party had been since the morning destroying the Ponte Nova on the
Cavado river. The destruction of the first bridge blocked the road
to Chaves, the second would, if completed, cut the French off from
Montalegre. The night was setting in, the soldiers harassed, barefooted and starving, the ammunition was injured by the rain, which
had never ceased since the 13th and was now increasing in violence accompanied with storms of wind; the British would fall upon
the rear in the morning; and if the Ponte Nova, where the guard
was weak, could not be secured, the hour of surrender was arrived.
In this extremity, Soult, addressing Major Dulong, an officer justly
reputed one of the most daring in the French ranks, said, 'I have
chosen you from the whole army to seize the Ponte Nova, which has
been cut by the enemy; select a hundred grenadiers and twenty-five
horsemen, endeavour to surprise the guards and secure the passage
of the bridge. If you succeed, say so, but send no other report,
your silence will suffice.' Thus exhorted, Dulong, favoured by the
storm, reached the bridge, killed the sentinel before any alarm was
given, and being followed by twelve grenadiers, crawled along a
narrow strip of masonry, the only part undestroyed. The Cavado was
flooded and roaring in its deep channel, and a grenadier fell into the
gulf, yet the waters were louder than his cry. Dulong and the others
surprised the nearest post, and then the main body rushed on, and
mounting the heights, shouting and firing, scared the peasantry,
who imagined the whole army was upon them. Thus the passage
was won.

THE PASSAGE OF THE DOURO

At four o'clock the bridge was repaired and the troops filed slowly over; but the road was cut in the side of a mountain, leaving an unfenced precipice on the left for several miles; and it was finally crossed by the Misarella torrent, which rolling down a gulf was to be crossed by the '*Saltador*' or leaper, a bridge with a single arch, so narrow that only three persons could walk abreast. This Saltador was not cut, but it was entrenched, and some hundred peasants occupied the rocks on the further side; yet the good soldier Dulong again saved the army; for when a first and second assault had failed he won the bridge by a third effort, in which he fell deeply wounded, but his men carried him forward and the head of the column poured over. It was full time, the English guns were thundering on the rear, and the Ponte Nova was choked with the dead.

Sir Arthur quitting Braga the 16th, had come about four o'clock upon Soult's rear guard at Salamonde, the right of which rested on a ravine, the left on a steep hill; this position was strong, but men momentarily expecting an order to retire seldom stand firmly. Some light troops turned the French left, Sherbrooke assailed them in front, and after one discharge they fled to the Ponte Nova in confusion, yet, as it was not on the direct line of retreat, they were for some time unperceived, and thus gained time to form a rear guard. When descried at last, the guns opened upon them sending man and horse crushed together over into the gulf, and the bridge and the rocks and the defile beyond were soon strewed with mangled bodies. This was the last calamity inflicted by the sword in a retreat signalized by many horrid and glorious actions. For the peasants in their fury tortured and mutilated the sick and straggling French, the troops in revenge shot the peasants, and the march of the army could be discovered from afar by the smoke of burning houses.

Soult reached Montalegre the 17th, without being followed, save by some cavalry, under Colonel Waters, who picked up a few stragglers. Sir Arthur halted at Ruivaens, seemingly without adequate cause, but the 18th renewed the pursuit, and at the Salas river found the enemy in force on the further bank: yet no action took place. Silveira had reached Montalegre from Chaves before this, but had put his men in quarters; and a Portuguese officer carrying orders for Beresford to move on Villa del Rey loitered on the road: this, coupled with Silveira's inactivity, broke the final combination for intercepting Soult, and though Beresford pushed on the 14th dragoons as far as Ginjo, Franceschi forced them to retire. Soult crossed the frontier the 19th at Allariz, and next day entered Orense without guns, stores, ammunition or baggage; his men, bowed with fatigue and misery, were mostly without shoes, many without accoutrements, some without muskets. He had quitted Orense seventy-six days before, with twenty-two thousand men, and three thousand five hundred had afterwards joined him from Tuy; he returned with nineteen thousand five hundred, having lost by the sword and sickness, by assassination and capture, six thousand good soldiers. Of this number, eighteen hundred were taken in hospitals at Viana and Braga, five hundred in Oporto, thirteen hundred in Chaves. A thousand were killed previous to the retreat, the remainder had been captured or perished within the last eight days. He had entered Portugal with fifty-eight pieces of artillery, he returned without a gun: yet his reputation as a stout and able soldier was nowise diminished.

VI

Talavera

With Portugal apparently secure, it was time for Sir Arthur Wellesley to challenge the French power in the interior of the Peninsula. He was being exhorted from London and Seville to march to the aid of his Spanish allies. What he had yet to appreciate was their military incompetence, their totally misleading boasts of strength and the savage factionalism of their generals. Blake and Venegas were creatures of the junta. Cuesta and Romana were its violent opponents. Their disarray was nearly to ruin Wellesley's army, faced now by two more marshals, Victor, Duke of Belluno, and old Jourdan. With them was Joseph, Napoleon's brother, the intrusive King of Spain himself.

THE SPANISH armies, numerous on paper, and the real amount considerable, were inadequate to the exigencies and the resources of the country. The regular forces, capable of taking the field in the south-eastern provinces, were about twenty thousand, of which ten thousand under Coupigny were watching Barcelona or rallying under Blake; the remainder were in Valencia, where Caro, Romana's brother, had taken the command. In the north-western provinces there were twenty-five thousand men, of which fifteen thousand were in Galicia, three or four thousand in the Asturias under Vorster and Ballesteros, the remainder under del Parque, who was directed to organize a new army in the neighbourhood of Ciudad Rodrigo. In Andalusia, or covering it, there were seventy thousand men. Of these, twenty-three thousand infantry and two thousand five hundred cavalry were assembled in the Morena near St Elena and Carolina, under Venegas; thirty-eight thousand, including seven thousand cavalry, were in Estremadura under Cuesta, who was nominally commander-in-chief of both armies.

The generals had lost nothing of their presumption, learnt nothing of war, and their mutual jealousies were as strong as ever. Cuesta, hating the junta, was feared and hated in return, and Venegas was placed at the head of the Carolina army as a counterpoise to him. Romana also was obnoxious to the junta, and in return, with more reason, the junta was despised and disliked by him. In Valencia and Murcia, generals and juntas appeared alike indifferent to the public welfare, satisfied if the war was kept from their own doors. In Catalonia there never was any unanimity. Blake had abandoned Romana in Galicia, and was Cuesta's enemy; for these reasons he was invested with supreme power in Valencia, Aragon and Catalonia. The armies of Cuesta and Venegas were hotbeds of petty factions. Sir Arthur advised the junta not to weaken but re-inforce Cuesta, not to assail the French in La Mancha or Estremadura, but to preserve a strict defensive in all quarters.

At this time the supreme junta was in dread of the old junta of Seville, and its folly, arrogance and neglect of the public weal furnished ample grounds for attack. After the battles of Medellin and Ciudad Real, the king had employed Joachim Sotelo, a Spanish minister in his service, to negotiate for the submission of the junta. The proposals were spurned, and in suitable terms, for dignified sentiments and lofty expressions were never wanting to the Span-iards; yet taken with their deeds, they were but a strong wind blowing shrivelled leaves. The junta failed not to make the nation remark their patriotism, and on every occasion loudly praised them-selves; they were however Spaniards of a different temper; men anxious to check the abuse of power, to lay bare ancient oppressions, and recur to first principles for present reforms and future govern-ment. They avowed the misrule which had led to the misfortunes of Spain; and knowing that national independence may co-exist with tyranny, yet is necessarily joined with civil and religious liberty, they desired to assemble the ancient Cortes and give the people assurance that independence was worth fighting for; and that their sufferings and exertions would lead to a sensible good instead of a mere choice between an old and new despotism.

They had issued a menacing proclamation, in which they endeav-oured to confound their political opponents with the spies and tools of the French; and having established a tribunal of public security, they caused it to publish an edict, in which all men who endeavoured to raise distrust of the junta, or who tried to overturn the govern-ment by popular commotions, or other means by the junta repro-bated, were declared guilty of high treason, undeserving the name of Spaniards, and sold to Napoleon: their punishment was to be death, and confiscation of property. Any person propagating rumours tending to weaken or soften the hatred of the people against the French, was instantly to be arrested and punished without remission, and rewards were offered for secret information upon these heads. This atrocious decree was not a dead letter. Many persons were seized, imprisoned and executed without trial or knowing their accusers. But the deepest stain upon the Spanish character, at this period, was the treatment experienced by prisoners of war; thousands, amongst them part of Dupont's troops who were only prisoners by a breach of faith, were sent to the Balearic Isles without any order being taken for their subsistence; and the junta when remonstrated with cast seven thousand ashore on the little desert rock of Cabrera. At Majorca numbers had been massacred by the inhabitants in the most cowardly and brutal manner, and those left on Cabrera suffered miseries scarcely to be described. The supply of food, always scanty, was often neglected altogether, there was but one spring on the rock, and it dried up in summer; clothes were never given save by English seamen, who from compassion assisted them when passing the island. Thus afflicted with hunger, thirst and nakedness they lived like wild beasts while they could live, but perished in such numbers that less than two thousand remained to tell the tale of this inhumanity: it was no slight disgrace to England that her government failed to interfere.

And what were the efforts made for the defence of the country by this barbarous junta, which, originally assembled to discuss the form of a central government, had unlawfully retained their delegated power and used it so shamefully? There was a Spanish fleet and sailors sufficient to man it in Cartagena, and there was another fleet with abundance of seamen in Cadiz. Lord Collingwood and others pressed the junta constantly to fit these vessels out and use them, or place them beyond the reach of the enemy; their remonstrances were unheeded, the sailors were mutinous for want of pay, and even of subsistence; yet the government would neither fit out the ships themselves, nor suffer the English seamen to do it for them. When Romana and the insurgents of Galicia were praying Cradock to give them a few stands of arms and five thousand pounds, the junta possessed many millions of money; and their magazines in Cadiz were bursting with the continually increasing quantity of stores and arms arriving from England, which were left to rot as they arrived, while from every quarter not yet subdued, the demand for these things was incessant. The fleet in Cadiz might have been at sea early in February; in a week it might have been at Vigo with money and succours of all kinds for the insurgents in Galicia; after which, by skilful operations along the coast from Vigo to St Sebastian, it might have occupied an enormous French force on that line of country. Instead of a fleet, the junta sent Colonel

Barios, an obscure person, to steal through by-ways, to take command of men who were not in want of such leaders, and to murder prisoners.

In like manner, the Cartagena fleet could have been employed on the Catalonian and French coasts. The junta's real means were enormous, but their warfare was one of virulent publications against the French, and the assembling of miserable peasants in masses, to starve for a while and then be cut to pieces by their experienced opponents.

It was at this period the *partidas* first commenced the *guerrilla*, or petty warfare, which has been so lauded, as if that had been the cause of Napoleon's discomfiture. Those bands were many, because every robber who feared a jail, or could break from one; every smuggler whose trade had been interrupted; every friar disliking the trammels of his convent; every idler who wished to avoid the ranks of the regular army, was to be found either as chief or associate in a *partida*. The French, although continually harassed by the cruel murder of isolated soldiers and camp followers, and sometimes by the loss of convoys and strong escorts, were never thwarted in any great object by these bands; but the necessity of providing subsistence and attaching men to his fortunes, forced the guerrilla chiefs generally to plunder his own countrymen; and one principal cause of the sudden growth of the *partidas* was the hope of intercepting the public and private plate, which under a decree of Joseph was being brought to Madrid; for he was driven to forced loans and to seize the property of suppressed convents and proscribed nobles, to maintain even the appearance of a court. This description will apply generally to the *partidas*, and *cuadrillas* as the bands formed of smugglers were called; yet there were some chiefs actuated by nobler motives, by revenge, by a gallant spirit and honest ambition, thinking thus to serve their country better than by joining the regular forces. Among the principal leaders may be placed Renovales and the two Minas in Navarre and Aragon; Porlier in the Asturias; Longa in Biscay; Juan Martin, called the *Empecinado,* who vexed the neighbourhood of Madrid; Julian Sanchez in the Gata and Salamanca country; Doctor Rovera, Perena and some others in Catalonia; the friar Nebot in Valencia; Julian Palarea, the *Medico,* between the Moreno and Toledo; the curate Merino, *El Principe,* and Saornil in Castille; the friar Sapia about Soria, Juan Abril near Segovia.

Renovales, a regular officer, raised the peasantry of the valleys between Pamplona and Zaragoza after the fall of the latter city, but was soon subdued. Juan Martin, Rovera, Julian Sanchez and the student Mina, discovered military talent, and Sanchez was a very bold and honest man. But Espoz y Mina, the uncle and successor of the student, outstripped his contemporaries in fame. He shed the blood of prisoners freely, yet rather from false principle and peculiar circumstances than from any real ferocity, for his natural disposition was manly and generous; he did not possess any peculiar military genius, but to a sound judgment, he added surprising energy and a constant spirit. By birth a peasant, he despised the higher orders of his own country, and never would suffer any *hidalgo* to join his band. From 1809 until the end of the war, he held the provinces bordering on the Ebro; and though often defeated and chased from place to place, he yet gradually increased his force until, in 1812, he was at the head of more than ten thousand men, regularly paid and supplied by different means, one of which was remarkable – he established a treaty with the French generals, by which everything but warlike stores, coming from France, had his safe conduct on paying a duty, which Mina appropriated to the subsistence of his followers: English succours were however his chief resource.

That the guerrilla system could never seriously affect the progress of the French, is proved by the constant attempts of the principal chiefs to introduce the customs of regular troops; and their success against the enemy was proportionate to their progress in discipline and organization. There were not less than fifty thousand of these irregular soldiers at one time in Spain; and so severely did they press upon the country, that if the English army had abandoned the contest, one of the surest means by which the French could have gained the good will of the nation would have been the extirpating of the *partidas*. Nevertheless this great unquestionable advantage was derived from them, and especially by the British; the French could never communicate with each other nor combine their movements except by the slow method of sending officers with strong escorts; whereas, their adversaries could correspond by post, and even by telegraph: an advantage equal to a reinforcement of fifty thousand men.

*   *   *

The real state of affairs in the Peninsula has been described; but it appeared with a somewhat different aspect to the English general; because false informations, egregious boasts and hollow promises, such as had been employed to mislead Sir John Moore, were renewed at this period, and the allied nations were influenced by a riotous rather than a reasonable confidence of victory. The English newspapers teemed with letters describing the enemy's misery and fears, nor was the camp free from these inflated feelings. Beresford was so credulous of French weakness as publicly to announce to the junta of Badajoz, that Soult's force, wandering and harassed by continual attacks, was reduced to eight or ten thousand distressed soldiers; nay Sir Arthur himself, swayed by the pertinacity of the tale-makers, the unhesitating assurances of the junta, perhaps also a little excited by a sense of his own great talents, was not free from the impression that the hour of complete triumph was come. He had not then, as he did afterwards to his cost, probed Spanish rulers and Spanish generals, who were alike importunate for offensive movements, and lavish in their promises of support. And the English general was eager enough to fight: for he had gallant troops, his foot was on the path of victory, and he felt that if the Duke of Belluno was not quickly disabled, the British army, threatened on both flanks, would, as in the case of Cradock, be compelled to take some defensive position near Lisbon, an object of suspicion and hatred to the Spanish and Portuguese people.

The French immediately protecting Madrid were only estimated at fifty thousand; confidential officers, sent to the head-quarters of Cuesta and Venegas, ascertained their respective armies to be thirty-eight thousand for the first, twenty-five thousand for the second; they were well armed and equipped, and the last certainly the best and most efficient army the Spaniards had yet brought into the field; and when Roche, the military agent, warned Sir Arthur that however well Cuesta's men looked, they were not to be trusted, his admonition was disregarded. The English force in Portugal amounted to thirty thousand men, exclusive of the sick; twenty-two thousand being under arms on the frontier, and eight thousand at Lisbon. Thus it appeared that a mass of ninety thousand regular troops could be brought to bear on fifty thousand; besides which, there were Wilson's legion, a thousand strong, and the Spanish *partidas* of the Guadalupe and Sierra de Bejar.

As the ridge of mountains separating the valley of the Tagus from Castille and Leon was impracticable for artillery, except at Baños and Perales, it was supposed the twenty thousand men under Beresford and del Parque would suffice to block those passes, and that Romana, moving by the Tras os Montes, would join del Parque: thus thirty thousand men, supported by two fortresses, would protect the flank of the British army in its march from Plasencia towards Madrid. But this calculation was false, Romana remained

ostentatiously idle at Coruña; Sir Arthur, never having seen the
Spanish troops in action, thought too well of them; and having no
experience of Spanish promises, trusted them too far, and mis-
judged the force and position of his adversaries. The arrival of the
sixth corps at Astorga and of the fifth at Valladolid was unknown
to him; the strength of Soult's corps, and the activity of its chief
were underrated: instead of fifteen or twenty thousand harassed
French troops without artillery, as he supposed, there were seventy
thousand fighting men well equipped behind the mountains!

Sir Arthur, though far from suspecting his real peril, finding two
corps d'armée were behind the mountains on his flank, took additional precautions. He warned Beresford to watch the French movements and look carefully to the pass of Perales; and as the pass of
Baños was also to be guarded, he applied to Cuesta. That general
reluctantly consented that two battalions from his army, and two
already quartered in Bejar on the other side of the pass, should unite
to defend it; and that del Parque should also send troops to the pass
of Perales. These measures would have sufficed against Soult if he
had been as crippled as he was supposed to be, but were futile
against his real power; and they became ridiculous when Cuesta
sent only six hundred men with twenty rounds of ammunition: but
this was part of a system which was now weighing heavily on the
English general.

Cuesta was always dreaded by the supreme junta; and when the
defeat at Belchite crushed Blake as a rival, the junta sought to make
Venegas a counterpoise, by increasing his army and giving him
the best troops. Still Cuesta was powerful, and to lessen him was a
common object with the junta. Cuesta's natural obstinacy and violence were exacerbated by these intrigues, in which he erroneously
thought Sir Arthur was concerned; and hence, when the latter came
to him at Mirabete on the 10th, and proposed that ten thousand
men should be detached to Avila and Segovia, Cuesta absolutely
refused, and would only give two battalions and a few cavalry to
reinforce Wilson, who was to act in the mountains on Victor's
right.

At Mirabete the discussion between Cuesta and the English
general lasted two days, but finally terminated in an agreement
that both generals should march on the 18th against Victor; and
that Venegas should push through La Mancha to Fuente Dueñas
and Villa Maurique on the upper Tagus. If Venegas' movement
drew Sebastiani to that side, he was to be held in play while the allied
armies defeated Victor; if Sebastiani disregarded it, Venegas was to

march on Madrid, while Sir Robert Wilson, reinforced with some Spanish battalions, was to menace that capital on the opposite quarter. But behind this fair plan foul intrigues were in activity which were to render it null. Previous to entering Spain, Sir Arthur had ascertained that the valleys of the Alagon and Arago, and those between Bejar and Ciudad Rodrigo, were capable of nourishing his army, and he had sent commissaries there to purchase mules and arrange with the alcaldes for the supply of the troops; he had obtained also warm assurances from the supreme junta that every needful article should be forthcoming, and their intendant-general, Lonzano de Torres, was at the British head-quarters with full powers. Relying upon these preparations, he crossed the frontier with scanty means of transport and without magazines; for Portugal could not furnish what was required, and the Portuguese peasants had an insuperable objection to quitting their own country.

From Castello Branco to Plasencia is but seven days' march, but that time was sufficient to prove the bad faith of the junta. Neither mules for transport, nor the promised help of the authorities, nor aid of any kind could be procured; and Lonzano de Torres, although to Sir Arthur he freely acknowledged the extent of the evil, the ill-will of the inhabitants and the shameful conduct of the supreme junta; afterwards, without shame, asserted that the British troops had always received and consumed double rations, and were in want of nothing. This assertion was repeated by Martin de Garay the Spanish secretary of state, the whole being a concerted plan to afford the junta a pretext for justifying their own and casting a slur upon the English general's conduct if any disasters should happen. Sir Arthur, seriously alarmed for the subsistence of his army, wrote upon the 16th to O'Donoghue, the chief of Cuesta's staff; he stated the distress of the troops, and intimated his resolution *not to proceed beyond the Alberche* unless his wants were immediately supplied. Faithful, however, to his agreement with Cuesta, he prepared to put his force in motion for that river.

On the 22nd, the allies moved forward in two columns, and Cuesta attacked the French rear guard near Gamonal with incredible ignorance, timidity and absurdity. Latour Maubourg, riding boldly on to the table land of Gamonal with only two thousand dragoons, forced Zayas to display the first Spanish line of fifteen thousand infantry and three thousand cavalry; nor would he have gone back at all if the red uniform of England had not been descried on his right, when supported by some infantry he regained the Alberche without loss. Six thousand Spanish horse and many batteries were close on his rear, yet they would not make even a partial charge, and by two o'clock the whole French army was concentrated. Ruffin's division on the left touched the Tagus and guarded the bridge over the Alberche, which was under the fire of fourteen guns; the heavy cavalry were in second line near the bridge, and the other divisions occupied higher ground on the right overlooking the surrounding country. Here they remained two days.

It was difficult to obtain information from the Spaniards by gentle means, and hence the French were usually better served than the British; the native generals never knew, nor cared to know anything about their enemy until they felt his blows; and up to this period Sir Arthur's best sources of information were the intercepted French letters. Victor had been in position without change of numbers since the 7th, yet the inhabitants of Talavera could not or would not say anything about his strength or situation; nor could either be discovered until Sir Arthur ascended the mountains south of the Tagus and from thence looked into the French position. The outline of an attack was then agreed upon, but when the details were to be arranged Cuesta went to bed! The British troops were in arms at three o'clock next morning, Cuesta's staff were not aroused until seven o'clock, and finally the old man objected to fighting that day. There was more than inertness in these proceedings. Victor was well assured the allies would not attack, he had corrupted some of the Spanish staff, and the result of the discussions between Sir Arthur and Cuesta at which only one officer on each side was present, became known to the enemy twenty-four hours afterwards; Cuesta himself was suspected of the treachery but apparently without reason.

In the course of the 23rd the Spanish outposts gave notice that the French were going to retreat, Cuesta then became willing to attack and proposed to examine the ground; he came in a coach with six horses, and when the rugged ground forced him to descend, he threw himself under a tree and went to sleep! Yet he was always ready to censure and thwart every plan of his great coadjutor. This time indeed he consented to fight, and the troops were put in motion early on the 24th; but Victor had been again duly informed, and withdrawing his troops from the upper Alberche, fell back in the night to Torrijos. Thus the first combination failed, and the enemy's forces were accumulating dangerously around the allies; for Venegas had not passed Damyel, the king was collecting his whole strength between Toledo and Talavera, and Soult was gathering a more formidable power behind the mountains of Bejar.

Sir Arthur knew not of this last danger or he would doubtless have returned at once to Plasencia, and secured his communications with Lisbon and with Beresford: but there were other powerful reasons to stop his advance.

Before he quitted Plasencia he had completed contracts with the alcaldes of the Vera de Plasencia, for two hundred and fifty thousand rations of forage and provisions, which, added to his previous collections, would have furnished supplies for ten or twelve days, a sufficient time to beat Victor and gain a fresh country. These rations had not been delivered, and his representations on the subject were by Cuesta and the junta disregarded; wherefore he gave both notice for the second time that he would not move beyond the Alberche, unless his wants were immediately supplied. This was unheeded, no means of transport had been provided for him, his troops were on half allowance, absolute famine approached, and when he demanded food he was answered with false excuses and false statements. Without food he could not move, but as his advance had been made in the exercise of his own discretion and without orders from his government, he had no room for hesitation and expressing warmly his discontent with the supreme junta, he then declared he would withdraw from Spain altogether. This state of affairs and Cuesta's folly justified his anger, but the faithless and perverse conduct of the junta, only partially known to him, exceeded even the measure of Cuesta's obdurate folly. After consenting to the general plea of operations, the junta concluded that the allies in the valley of the Tagus would suffice to overthrow Joseph, and secretly ordered Venegas not to fulfil his part; arguing with a stupid cunning that, keeping him safe, they would have a powerful force under one of their own creatures to maintain their power, while Cuesta's defeat if it happened would be to them a gain. Venegas obeyed these treacherous orders, and the welfare of millions was made the sport of men who, never tired of praising themselves, have been by English writers lauded for patriotism!

Sir Arthur Wellesley's declarations were lost on Cuesta. A French army was retreating before him, the Pyrenees rose on his sanguine view, and, resolving to be first in Madrid, he pushed forward, reckless alike of military precautions and the friendly warning of the English general, who vainly recommended him to communicate quickly with Venegas, and to beware how he let the enemy know he had separated from the British army. Heedless and headstrong, Cuesta crossed the Alberche, and not knowing by which road the French had retired, pursued them on both.

Victor had acted like an able commander when he fell back on Toledo instead of Madrid. Toledo was the strategic pivot upon which the French movements turned. It was only through that city Venegas could co-operate with the allies on the Alberche, and if the latter advanced to connect themselves with him Soult's operations rendered their destruction certain: every step forward was a stride towards ruin. The king knew Foy would on the 24th reach Soult, who being about Salamanca was only four marches from Plasencia and might be in the valley of the Tagus the 30th; hence to insure success the royal army needed only to keep the allies in check for four or five days. This plan Soult recommended, the king assented, and Marshal Jourdan strenuously supported it. Cuesta's folly, Venegas' duplicity, the separation of the allies, the distressed state of the English army, actually on the verge of famine, a circumstance not unknown to Victor, greatly facilitated this project; and did not preclude the king from punishing the Spanish army, scattered as it was, without order, discipline or plan. Cuesta had some perception of his danger on the 25th, and gave orders to retreat on the 26th. But the French, suddenly passing the Guadarama at two o'clock in the morning of that day, drove the Spanish cavalry out of Torrijos, and pursued them to Alcabon, where Zayas had drawn up four thousand infantry, two thousand horsemen and eight guns on a plain.

Zayas had his right on the road of Domingo Perez, his left on a chapel of the same name. Latour Maubourg's cavalry advanced in a parallel line against the position and a cannonade commenced; but when the head of the French cavalry appeared in sight the Spaniard's broke, and fled in disorder towards St Olalla, followed at full gallop by the horsemen, who pressed them sorely; the panic would then have spread through the whole army but for the courage of Albuquerque, who came up with a division of three thousand fresh cavalry, and held the enemy in play while Cuesta retreated in the greatest disorder towards the Alberche. At St Olalla the pursuit slackened, the main body halted, and the advanced guards, save a few cavalry-posts, did not pass El Bravo; no attempt was made to profit from the unconnected position of the allies – a gross and palpable error; for either by the sword or dispersion the Spaniards lost four thousand men, and such was their fear it required only a slight pursuit to cause a general rout. Albuquerque indeed showed front, but his efforts were unavailing, and the disorder continued to increase until Sherbrooke, marching out of Cazalegas, placed his divisions between the scared troops and the enemy. Still the

danger was imminent. There was no concert between the commanders, the ground on the left of the Alberche was unfavourable to a
retiring party, and as yet no position upon which the combined
forces could retire had been agreed upon. What then would have
been the consequence if the whole French army had borne down,
compact and strong, into the midst of the disordered masses!

Sir Arthur, seeing the confusion beyond the Alberche, knew that
a battle was at hand; and being persuaded that in a strong defensive position only could the Spaniards be brought to stand a shock,
besought Cuesta, while Sherbrooke's people could yet cover the
movement, to withdraw to Talavera, where there was ground
suited for defence. Cuesta's uncouth nature again broke forth. His
beaten army, dispirited, fatigued, bewildered, were clustering on a
narrow slip of low flat land between the Alberche, the Tagus and
the heights of Salinas; the first shot fired by the enemy must have
been the signal of dispersion; yet it was in vain Sir Arthur pointed
out this, and entreated him to avoid the fall of the rock thus trembling over head: he replied that his troops would be disheartened
by further retreat, that he would fight where he stood, and in
this mood passed the night. At daylight, the British general renewed his solicitations, at first fruitlessly, but when the enemy's
cavalry came in sight, and Sherbrooke prepared to retire, Cuesta
sullenly yielded, yet, addressing his staff with frantic pride, said,
'He had first made the Englishman go down on his knees'.

Now by virtue of his genius Sir Arthur assumed the command of
both armies. He left Mackenzie's division and a brigade of cavalry
to cover a retrograde movement, took a position six miles in the
rear, and recalled Wilson who had reached Naval Carnero on
the 25th, and would certainly have entered Madrid. Between the
Alberche and Talavera the country was a plain covered with olive
and cork trees; and nearly parallel with the Tagus at a distance of
two miles, a chain of round steep hills bounded this woody plain.
Beyond these hills, and separated from them by a deep and rugged
valley, something less than half a mile wide, was the mountain-
ridge which divides the Alberche from the Tietar; hence a line
drawn perpendicular to the Tagus would cross the first chain of
hills at the distance of two miles, and at two miles and a half would
fall on the mountains. Sir Arthur taking Talavera, which was built
close to the river, as his fixed point, placed the right of the Spaniards there, drawing them up in two lines, their left resting upon a
mound where a large field-redoubt was constructed, and behind
which a brigade of British light cavalry was posted. The front was

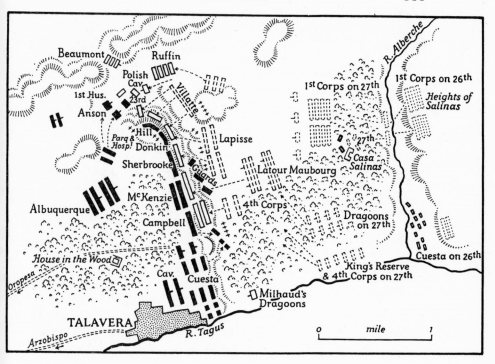

TALAVERA

covered by a convent, by ditches, mud walls, breast-works and felled trees; the Spanish cavalry was posted behind their infantry; and their rear was supported by a very large house in the wood, well placed, in case of defeat, to cover a retreat to the main roads leading from Talavera to Arzobispo and Oropesa. In this position they could not be attacked seriously, nor their disposition be even seen; thus one-half of the line of battle was rendered nearly impregnable, yet held by the worst troops.

This front was prolonged by the British infantry. Campbell's division formed in two lines touched Cuesta's left; Sherbrooke's division stood next to Campbell's, but arranged on one line only, because Mackenzie's division, destined to form the second line, was then near the Alberche. Hill's division should have closed the left of the British by taking post on the highest hill in the chain before mentioned as bounding the flat and woody country, yet from some cause unknown, the summit of this height was not immediately occupied. The whole line was two miles in length; the left rested on the ravine between the round hills and the mountain; the front was covered by a water-course, which commencing about the centre of the line became deep as it passed the left and was a chasm in the valley. Part of the British cavalry was with Mackenzie, part in the plain beyond the left, part behind the great redoubt at the junction of the allied troops. The British and Germans under arms were somewhat above nineteen thousand sabres and bayonets, with thirty guns. The Spaniards could only produce thirty-three or thirty-four thousand men, yet they had seventy guns. The combined army, therefore, offered battle with forty-four thousand infantry, ten thousand cavalry and a hundred pieces of artillery; the French came on with eighty guns, and including the king's guards nearly fifty thousand men, of which seven thousand were cavalry; but what a difference in the quality of the troops! The French were all hardy veterans, while the genuine soldiers of the allied army did not exceed nineteen thousand.

Joseph had put his army in motion before day-light the 27th. Latour Maubourg's cavalry led the march, Victor, Sebastiani and the royal guards and reserve followed in succession. At one o'clock Victor reached the heights of Salinas, from whence the dust of the allies, then taking up their positions could be seen, but their dispositions could not be made out because the forest masked them. Victor however, knowing the ground, guessed their true position, and the king following his advice directed Sebastiani against the allied right, the cavalry against the centre, and Victor himself against their left: the guards and the reserve supported Sebastiani. Two artillery roads led from the Alberche; one, the royal road to Talavera, was taken by the fourth corps and the reserve; the other, passing by the *Casa de Salinas*, led directly against the allies' extreme left and was taken by Victor, who to reach the Casa had to ford the Alberche and march two miles through the forest. A thick dust indicated the presence of Mackenzie's division and a brigade of cavalry near the Salinas, and no patrols had been sent out.

About three o'clock, Lapisse and Ruffin's divisions came so suddenly on that the British outposts were surprised and Sir Arthur, who was in the Casa, hardly escaped capture. The charge was hot, the English brigades were separated, and being principally young soldiers fired upon each other, and were driven in confusion from the forest to the plain. In the midst of this disorder the 45th, a stubborn old regiment, and some companies of the 60th rifles kept good array, and Sir Arthur in person restored the fight; the enemy was thus checked; but the division lost about four hundred infantry and, supported by two brigades of cavalry, hastily crossed the plain to regain the position. Mackenzie took post with one brigade behind the guards in the centre; Colonel Donkin finding the hill on the extreme left still unoccupied crowned it with the other brigade, and so accidentally filled the position: the cavalry formed in column behind the left.

Victor brought his artillery, his light cavalry and Villatte's infantry, to the Casa, and then issuing from the forest, rapidly crossed the plain and made up with a fine display close to the left of the allies, where he seized an isolated hill in front of Donkin and opened a heavy cannonade. About the same time the 4th corps and the reserve approached the allies' right, and sent their light cavalry forward to make Cuesta show his line of battle. The horsemen rode boldly up and commenced a pistol skirmish, whereupon the Spaniards made a general discharge of musketry and then, as if deprived of reason, ten thousand infantry and all the artillery broke and fled. The artillerymen carried off their horses, the infantry threw away their arms, the adjutant-general, O'Donoghue was foremost in flight, and even Cuesta himself went off slowly. The panic spread and the French charged, but Sir Arthur flanked the main road with some English squadrons, and the ditches on the opposite side rendered the ground impracticable for horsemen; the Spaniards who remained used their muskets with effect and the French finally retreated with some loss. Most of the runaways fled to Oropesa, saying the allies were defeated and the French in hot pursuit; thus the rear became a scene of incredible disorder; the commissaries went off with their animals, the pay-masters carried away their money-chests, the baggage was scattered, and the alarm spread far and wide. Nor is it to be concealed, that some English officers disgraced their uniform on this occasion. When Cuesta recovered himself, he sent many cavalry regiments to head the fugitives and drive them back, and part of the artillery and some thousands of the infantry were thus recovered during the night; yet in the next day's fight the Spanish army was less by six thousand men than it should have been, and the redoubt in the centre was silent for want of guns.

The hill on the left of the British was the key of the position. It was steep, rugged towards the French, and rendered more inaccessible by the ravine at the bottom, but towards the English side it was of smoother ascent. Victor seeing Donkin's brigade feeble and the high point of the hill unoccupied, conceived the design of seizing the latter by a sudden assault; the sun was sinking, yet the

twilight and the confusion amongst the Spaniards on the allies'
right appeared so favourable for this project, that without in-
forming the king he directed Ruffin's division to attack; Villatte
followed in support, and Lapisse was ordered to engage with the
Germans, as a diversion for Ruffin, yet not seriously. The assault
was quick and vigorous. Donkin repulsed the assailants in his front,
but others turning his left, gained the top of the hill. At this critical moment Hill was sent to his aid; it was nearly dark, and that
officer, while giving orders to the colonel of the 48th regiment, was
shot at by some troops from the highest point; thinking they were
stragglers from his own ranks firing at the enemy, he rode up
to them in company with his brigade-major, Fordyce, and in a
moment found himself in the midst of the French. Fordyce was killed,
and Hill's horse was wounded by a grenadier who roughly seized
the bridle also, but the general, spurring hard, broke the man's
hold, and galloping down met the 29th regiment, which he led up
with such a fierce charge the French could not sustain the shock.

Having thus happily recovered the summit, he brought up the
48th, and a battalion of detachments composed of Sir John Moore's
stragglers; and these in conjunction with the 29th and Donkin's
brigade presented an imposing mass. In time they came, for the
French troops repulsed were only a part of their ninth regiment
forming Ruffin's van; the other two regiments of his division had
got entangled in the ravine, and the attack had only subsided.
Lapisse also was in motion and soon opened his fire on the German
legion, while all the battalions of the 9th regiment, having re-
formed again, mounted the hill in mass. The fighting now became
vehement, and the opposing flashes of musketry seen in the darkness showed with what a resolute spirit the struggle was maintained; the combatants were scarcely twenty yards asunder and the
event seemed doubtful; yet soon the well-known shout of the
British soldier was heard above the din of arms, and the enemy's
broken troops were driven once more into the ravine below.
Lapisse, who had made some impression on the German legion, immediately abandoned his false attack, and the fighting of the 27th
ceased. The British lost eight hundred men, and the French about a
thousand. Then the bivouac fires blazed up on both sides, and the
French and British soldiers were quiet; but, at twelve o'clock, the
Spaniards on the right, hearing some horsemen moving, opened
a prodigious peal of musketry and artillery, which lasted for
twenty minutes without any object; and during the remainder of
the night, the whole line was frequently disturbed by their desul-

tory firing which killed several men and officers in the British lines.

Victor, having learned from the prisoners the exact position of the Spaniards, until then unknown, reported his own failure to the king, and proposed that a second attempt should be made next morning at daylight. Jourdan opposed this as a partial enterprise which could not lead to any great result; Victor was earnest for the trial, spoke of his intimate knowledge of the ground, won Joseph's assent, and immediately made the following dispositions for the attack. His own artillery being formed in one mass on a height corresponding to that on which the English left was posted, commanded the great valley on its right, could sweep heavily along the summit of the hill in front, and obliquely search the whole of the British line to the left as far as the redoubt between the allied armies. Ruffin's division was placed in advance, Villatte's in rear of this artillery; but the former kept one regiment close to the ravine. Lapisse occupied some low table land opposite to Sherbrooke's division, Latour Maubourg's cavalry formed a reserve to Lapisse, and Beaumont's cavalry formed a reserve to Ruffin. Hill's division was concentrated in their front, the English cavalry was massed behind the left, the parc of artillery and hospitals were established, under cover of the height, between the cavalry and Hill.

At daybreak Ruffin's troops, drawn up two regiments abreast and supported by a third in columns of battalions, went forth against the left of the British, some directly against the front, some by the valley on their right, thus embracing two sides of the hill. Their march was rapid and steady, they were followed by Villatte's division, and the assault was preceded by a burst of artillery which rattled round the height and swept away the English ranks by sections. The sharp chattering of the musketry succeeded, and then the French guns were pointed towards the British centre and right, while the grenadiers closed upon Hill and the height sparkled with fire. The inequalities of the ground broke the compact formation of the troops on both sides, and here and there small bodies were seen struggling for the mastery with all the virulence of a single combat; in some places the French grenadiers were overthrown at once, in others they would not be denied and reached the summit; but the English reserves were always ready to vindicate their ground, and no permanent footing was obtained. Still the conflict was maintained with singular obstinacy. Hill was wounded, and his men fell fast, yet the enemy suffered more, and gave back, step by step at first and slowly to cover the retreat of their wounded; yet finally, unable to sustain the increasing fury of the English, and having lost above fifteen hundred men in the space of forty minutes, the whole mass broke in disorder and returned to their own position covered by the renewed play of their powerful artillery.

To this destructive fire no adequate answer could be made, for the English guns were few and of small calibre; and when Sir Arthur desired a reinforcement from Cuesta, the latter sent him two pieces! yet those were serviceable, and the Spanish gunners fought them gallantly. The principal line of the enemy's retreat was by the great valley, and a favourable opportunity for a charge of horse occurred, but the English cavalry, having retired during the night for water and forage, were yet too distant to be of service. However, these repeated efforts of the French against the hill, and the appearance of some of their light troops on the mountain beyond the left, taught the English general that he should have prolonged his flank on that side; wherefore, obtaining Bassecour's division from Cuesta he placed it on the mountain and brought up a mass of his own cavalry behind the extreme left, with the leading squadrons looking into the valley: at the same time Albuquerque, discontented with Cuesta, came there with his horsemen, and thus a formidable mass, six lines deep, was presented in opposition.

Joseph now held a council with Jourdan and Victor upon the expediency of a general battle. Jourdan said, 'When the valley and the mountain were unoccupied on the 27th, the Spaniards should have been menaced to attract attention; then, in the night, the French army should have been silently placed in columns at the entrance of the valley ready to form in order of battle at day-break, perpendicular to the English position, and so have assailed that hill from whence Victor has been twice repulsed. That disposition would have forced the allies to change their front, and during their movement they might be attacked and beaten; it cannot now be attempted as the English general has occupied both valley and mountain. *The only prudent line is to go behind the Alberche and await Soult's operations on the English rear.*' Victor opposed this. He promised to carry the hill notwithstanding his former failures, provided Sebastiani would assail the centre and right at the same time, finishing his argument thus: '*If such a combination fails it is time to renounce war*'.

Joseph was embarrassed. He liked Jourdan's counsel, yet feared Victor would cause the emperor to believe a great opportunity had been lost; and while thus wavering, a despatch arrived from Soult, by which it appeared he could only reach Plasencia between the 2nd and 5th of August. A detachment from the army of Venegas had already appeared near Toledo, that general's advanced guard was approaching Aranjuez, and the king was troubled by the danger of Madrid, because the stores, reserve artillery and general hospitals of the whole army in Spain were deposited there: moreover, the tolls at the gates formed almost the only pecuniary resource of his court, so narrowly did Napoleon reduce the expenditure of the war. These considerations overpowered his judgment; adopting the worse counsel, he resolved to succour the capital, but first to try the chance of a battle. Indecision is a cancer in war, Joseph should have adhered to the plan arranged with Soult, the advantages were obvious, the success sure. The loss of Madrid was nothing in the scale, because it could only be temporary.

While the French generals were engaged in council, the men on both sides took some rest, and the English wounded were carried to the rear; but the soldiers were suffering from hunger, the regular service of provisions had ceased for several days, and a few ounces of wheat in the grain formed the whole subsistence of men who had fought and who were yet to fight so hardly. In the Spanish camp confusion and distrust prevailed, Cuesta inspired terror without confidence, and Albuquerque, from conviction or instigated by momentary anger, just as the French were coming on to the final attack, sent one of his staff to inform the English commander that Cuesta was betraying him. The aide-de-camp charged with this message delivered it to Donkin, who carried it to Sir Arthur. The latter, seated on the summit of the hill which had been so gallantly contested, was intently watching the movements of the advancing enemy; he listened to this somewhat startling message without so much as turning his head, and then drily answering – *'Very well, you may return to your brigade'*, continued his survey of the French. Donkin retired, filled with admiration of the imperturbable resolution and quick penetration of the man; but throughout that day, Sir Arthur's bearing was that of a general upon whose vigilance and intrepidity the fate of fifty thousand men depended.

Soon were the dispositions of the French completed. Ruffin on the extreme right, was destined to cross the valley, and moving by the foot of the mountain turn the British left. Villatte was to menace the hill with one brigade, and guard the valley with another; which being strengthened by a battalion of grenadiers, was to connect Ruffin's movement with the main attack.

Lapisse, supported by Latour Maubourg's dragoons and the king's reserve, was to pass the water-course in front of the English centre and fall with half his infantry upon Sherbrooke's division; while the other half, connecting its attack with Villatte's brigade, mounted the hill and made a third effort to master that important point.

Milhaud's dragoons were on the main road opposite Talavera, to keep the Spaniards in check; the rest of the heavy cavalry was brought into the centre behind Sebastiani, who was to assail the right of the British line. Part of the light cavalry supported Villatte's brigade in the valley, part remained in reserve, and a number of guns were distributed among the divisions, but the principal mass remained on the French hill with the reserve of light cavalry: there also Victor stationed himself to direct the movements of the first corps.

From nine o'clock in the morning until midday, the field of battle offered no appearance of hostility. The weather was intensely hot, and the troops on both sides mingled without fear or suspicion to quench their thirst at the little brook which divided the positions. Before one o'clock however, the French soldiers were seen to gather round the eagles, and the rolling of drums was heard along the whole line. Half an hour later, Joseph's guards, the reserve and the fourth corps were descried near the centre of the king's position marching to join the first corps; and soon the table-land and height on the French right, even to the valley, were covered with dark and lowering masses. At this moment, some hundreds of English soldiers, employed to carry the wounded to the rear, returned in one body, and were by the French supposed to be Wilson's corps joining the army; nevertheless, the Duke of Belluno gave the signal for battle, and eighty pieces of artillery immediately sent a tempest of bullets before the light troops, who came on with the swiftness and violence of a hail-storm, closely followed by the broad black columns in all the majesty of war.

Sir Arthur Wellesley from the summit of the hill on his left viewed the whole field of battle. He saw the fourth corps rushing forwards with the usual impetuosity of French soldiers, clearing the intersected ground in their front and falling upon Campbell's division with infinite fury; yet that general, assisted by Mackenzie's brigade and two Spanish battalions, withstood their utmost efforts. The British soldiers, putting the French skirmishers aside, met the advancing columns with loud shouts, broke their front, lapped their flanks with fire, and giving no respite pushed them back with a terrible carnage. Ten guns were taken, but as Campbell prudently resolved not to break his line by a pursuit, the French rallied on their supports and made head for another attack; then the British artillery and musketry played vehemently upon them, a Spanish cavalry regiment charged their flank, they retired in disorder, and the victory was secured in that quarter.

While this was passing on the English right, Villatte's division, preceded by the grenadiers and supported by two regiments of light cavalry, was seen advancing up the great valley against the left; and beyond Villatte, Ruffin was discovered marching towards the mountain. Sir Arthur ordered Anson's brigade of cavalry, composed of the 23rd light dragoons and the first German hussars, to charge the head of these columns. They went off at a canter, increasing their speed as they advanced and riding headlong against the enemy; but in a few moments, a hollow cleft which was not perceptible at a distance intervened, and at the same moment the French, throwing themselves into squares, opened their fire. Colonel Arentschild, commanding the hussars, an officer whom forty years' experience had made a master in his art, promptly reined up at the brink, exclaiming, in his broken phrase, '*I will not kill my young mans!*' The twenty-third found the chasm more practicable, the English blood is hot, and the regiment plunged down without a check, men and horses rolling over each other in dreadful confusion; yet the survivors, untamed, mounted the opposite bank by twos and threes; Colonel Seymour was severely wounded, but General Anson and Major Frederick Ponsonby, a hardy soldier, passing through the midst of Villatte's columns which were pouring in a fire from each side, fell with inexpressible violence upon a brigade of French chasseurs in the rear. The combat was then fierce, yet short, for Victor seeing the advance of the English, had detached his Polish lancers and Westphalia light-horse to the support of Villatte, and these fresh men coming up when the twenty-third, already overmatched, could scarcely hold up against the chasseurs, entirely broke them. Those who were not killed or taken, made for Bassecour's Spanish division and so escaped; yet with a loss of two hundred and seven men and officers, about half the number that went into action.

During this time the hill, the key of the position, was again attacked, and Lapisse, crossing the ravine, pressed hard upon the English centre; his artillery aided by the great battery on his right opened large gaps in Sherbrooke's ranks, and though the French came up to the British in the resolution to win, they were driven back in disorder. In the excitement of success the English guards followed with reckless ardour, but the French reserves of infantry and dragoons advanced, their repulsed men faced about, the batteries smote the guards in flank and front so heavily they drew back, and at the same time the Germans being sorely pressed got into confusion: Hill and Campbell stood fast on the extremities of the line, yet the British centre was absolutely broken, and fortune seemed to incline to the French. Suddenly the forty-eighth, led by Colonel Donellan, was descried advancing through the vast disordered masses, which seemed sufficient to carry it away bodily; but, wheeling back by companies, that regiment let the crowds pass through, and then resuming its proud and beautiful line fell on the flank of the victorious French columns, plying them with such a destructive musketry, and closing upon them with such a firm regular step that their offensive movement was checked. Then the guards and Germans rallied, a brigade of light cavalry came up at a trot, the artillery battered the French flanks without intermission, they wavered, lost their impulse, and the battle was restored.

In all actions there is one critical moment which will give the victory to the general who knows how to seize it. When the guards first made their rash charge, Sir Arthur, foreseeing the issue of it, had ordered the forty-eighth down from the hill, although a rough battle was going on there, and at the same time he directed Cotton's light cavalry to advance. These dispositions gained the day; the British became strongest at the decisive point; the French relaxed their efforts; the fire of the former grew hotter, and their ringing shouts – sure augury of success – were heard along the whole line. In the hands of a great general, Joseph's guards and the reserve might have restored the combat, but all combination was at an end on the king's side; the fourth corps, beaten on the French left with the loss of ten guns, was in confusion; the troops in the great valley on the French right, amazed at the furious charge of the twenty-third, and awed by the sight of four distinct lines of cavalry still in reserve, remained stationary; no impression had been made on the key hill, Lapisse was mortally wounded, his division had given way in the centre, and the whole army finally retired to the position from whence it had descended to the attack. This retrograde movement was covered by skirmishers and an augmented fire of artillery. The British, exhausted by toil and want of food and reduced to less than fourteen thousand sabres and bayonets, could not pursue; the Spanish army was incapable of any evolution, and about six o'clock all hostility ceased, each army holding the position of the morning. The battle was scarcely over when the dry grass and shrubs taking fire, a volume of flames passed with inconceivable rapidity across a part of the field, scorching in its course both the dead and the wounded.

Two British generals, Mackenzie and Langworth, thirty-one officers of inferior rank, and nearly eight hundred sergeants and soldiers were killed; three generals, a hundred and ninety-two officers, and more than three thousand seven hundred sergeants and privates wounded. Nine officers and nearly six hundred and fifty sergeants and soldiers were missing; making a total loss of more than six thousand two hundred, of which five thousand four hundred fell on the 28th. The French had above nine hundred, including two generals, killed; about six thousand three hundred wounded, and one hundred and fifty made prisoners; furnishing a total of seven thousand three hundred and eighty-nine men and officers, of which four thousand were of Victor's corps. Ten guns were taken by Campbell's division, seven were left in the woods by the French. The Spaniards returned about twelve hundred men killed and wounded, but their accuracy was much doubted.

The 29th, at day-break, the French army quitted its position, and before six o'clock was again in order of battle behind the Alberche. That day Robert Craufurd reached the English camp, with the forty-third, fifty-second and ninety-fifth regiments, and immediately took charge of the outposts. Those troops had been, after a march of twenty miles, hutted near Malpartida de Plasencia when the alarm caused by the Spanish fugitives spread to that part; Craufurd, fearing for the army, allowed only a few hours' rest, and then withdrawing about fifty of the weakest from the ranks, recommenced his march with a resolution not to halt until the field of battle was reached. As the brigade advanced crowds of the runaways were met with, not all Spaniards, but all propagating the vilest falsehoods: *'the army was defeated'* – *'Sir Arthur Wellesley was killed'* – *'the French army were only a few miles distant'*, nay, some, blinded by their fears, pretended to point out the enemy's advanced posts on the nearest hills. Indignant at this shameful scene, the troops hastened rather than slackened their impetuous pace, and leaving only seventeen stragglers behind, in twenty-six hours crossed the field of battle in a close and compact body; having in that time passed over sixty-two English miles in the hottest season of the year, each man carrying from fifty to sixty pounds weight upon his shoulders. Had the historian Gibbon known of such a march, he would have spared his sneer about the 'delicacy of modern soldiers!'

That the British infantry soldier is more robust than the soldier of any other nation can scarcely be doubted by those who, in 1815, observed his powerful frame, distinguished amidst the united armies of Europe; and notwithstanding his habitual excess in drinking, he sustains fatigue and wet and the extremes of cold and heat with incredible vigour. When completely disciplined, and three years are required to accomplish this, his port is lofty and his movements free, the whole world cannot produce a nobler specimen of military bearing: nor is the mind unworthy of the outward man. He does not indeed possess that presumptuous vivacity which would lead him to dictate to his commanders, or even to censure real errors, although he may perceive them; but he is observant and quick to comprehend his orders, full of resources under difficulties, calm and resolute in danger, and more than usually obedient and careful of his officers in moments of imminent peril. It has been asserted that his undeniable firmness in battle is the result of a phlegmatic constitution uninspired by moral feeling. Never was a more stupid calumny uttered! Napoleon's troops fought in bright fields where every helmet caught some beams of glory, but the British soldier conquered under the cold shade of aristocracy. No honours awaited his daring, no despatch gave his name to the applauses of his countrymen, his life of danger and hardship was uncheered by hope, his death unnoticed. Did his heart sink therefore? Did he not endure with surpassing fortitude the sorest of ills, sustain the most terrible assaults in battle unmoved, overthrow with incredible energy every opponent, and at all times prove that while no physical military qualification was wanting, the fount of honour was also full and fresh within him! The result of a hundred battles and the united testimony of impartial writers of different nations have given the first place amongst the European infantry to the British: but in a comparison between the troops of France and England, it would be unjust not to admit that the cavalry of the former stands higher in the estimation of the world.

VII

Bussaco

1810

Deserted by his Spanish allies, with Soult coming down from the north-west to bar his line of retreat, Sir Arthur only rescued his starving army by abandoning his wounded, crossing to the south bank of the Tagus and regaining Portugal by forced marches through Badajoz. He was created Viscount Wellington, the name by which he must now figure in this narrative, but he swore he would never again seek to act in conjunction with Spanish armies. But he appreciated, better than the historian Napier, the value of the guerrillas. First they ensured that his intelligence was always good and that of the French bad. Secondly, if one of the marshals concentrated his troops for offensive action, the country behind him rose in spontaneous insurrection. The French had 300,000 men in Spain. Wellington calculated correctly that little more than a quarter of that number could be brought against him at any given time in any given area.

The French made no attempt to penetrate Galicia again and Soult took his army south to carve out a fief for himself in Andalusia. The Spanish junta took refuge in Cadiz under the protection of the British navy. Napoleon reorganized his other commands and appointed his most formidable marshal, Masséna, to the 'Army of Portugal', which concentrated before Ciudad Rodrigo and Almeida before following Junot's route to Lisbon.

Wellington's army attempted to recuperate its strength on the southern borders of Portugal, but so many thousands became struck with 'Guadiana fever' that its cantonments were moved north of the Tagus again. Reinforcements arrived, the Portuguese were brought up to strength, and Wellington was in the happier position of having 18,000 British and 14,000 Portuguese under his immediate command, with another 20,000, mostly Portuguese, under General Hill to watch Soult in Estremadura. The pick of the army, perhaps the finest body of troops ever to wear British uniform, was the incomparable Light Division under General Robert Craufurd. They held the mountain frontier of Portugal.

CRAUFURD had commenced some remarkable operations beyond the Coa with the light division, composed of three regiments singularly fitted for difficult service. Long and carefully disciplined by Sir John Moore, they came to the field with such a knowledge of arms, that six years of warfare could not detect a flaw in their system, nor were they ever overmatched in courage or skill. With these soldiers much might be dared, but while the French were on the Agueda Craufurd might pass, yet could not keep beyond the Coa without cavalry; wherefore he invited Cole to take the line of that river in support while he advanced to the Agueda. Cole refused to quit Guarda, the key of all the positions, and Wellington approved of his decision; but the line of the Coa was essential to the succouring of Ciudad Rodrigo, and therefore Craufurd was reinforced with the German hussars, two battalions of Portuguese *caçadores* [light troops], and Ross's troop of horse artillery. Picton was also moved up to Pinhel, and he and Cole were to support the light division if called upon.

Craufurd having now four thousand men and six guns, about the middle of March [1810] lined the Agueda with his hussars from Escalhon on his own left to Navas Frias on his right, a distance of twenty-five miles. His infantry occupied the villages between Almeida and the lower Agueda; the artillery entered Fort Concepcion, and the *caçadores* were held in reserve. The French were then extended from San Felices back to Salamanca and Ledesma, and as they thus left the pass of Perales open, Carrera who was at Coria could also act in concert with Craufurd. The line of the Agueda was long, but from Navas Frias to the Douro it was rendered unfordable by heavy rains; and only four bridges crossed it on that extent. One was at Navas Frias, another a league below at Villar, one at Ciudad Rodrigo and one at San Felices, called the Barba del Puerco. The two first were distant and, the hussars being alert, the infantry were sure of time to concentrate around Almeida before an enemy could from thence reach them. Ciudad Rodrigo commanded its own bridge. That of San Felices was near, and the French troops close to it, but the channel of the river was so profound that a few rifle companies seemed sufficient to bar the passage. This disposition was good while the Agueda was flooded, but that river was capricious, often falling many feet in a night without apparent cause. When fordable, Craufurd concentrated his division, yet to do so safely required from the troops a promptitude and intelligence the like of which have seldom been known. Seven minutes sufficed to get under arms in the night, a quarter of an hour, night or day, to gather them in order of battle at the alarm posts, with baggage loaded and assembled at a convenient distance in the rear: and this not upon a concerted signal and as a trial, but all times certain, and for many months consecutively.

During one fight General Picton came up from Pinhel alone; Craufurd asked him for the support of the third division, he refused and they separated after a sharp altercation. Picton was wrong. Craufurd's situation was one of extreme danger; he could not re-tire, and Masséna might undoubtedly have thrown his reserves, by the bridge of Castello Bóm, upon the right flank of the division, and destroyed it between the Coa and the Pinhel rivers. Picton and Craufurd were, however, not formed by nature to act cordially to-gether. The stern countenance, robust frame, saturnine complexion, caustic speech, and austere demeanour of the first, promised little sympathy with the short thick figure, dark flashing eyes, quick movements and fiery temper of the second: nor did they often meet without a quarrel. Nevertheless, they had many points of re-semblance in their characters and fortunes. Both were inclined to harshness, and rigid in command; both prone to disobedience, yet

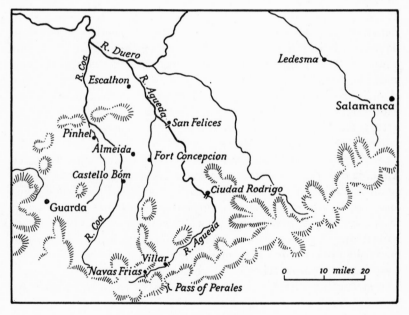

CIUDAD RODRIGO

exacting entire submission from inferiors. They were alike ambitious and craving of glory. Both possessed military talents, were enterprising and intrepid; yet neither were remarkable for skill in handling troops under fire. This they also had in common, that after distinguished services, they perished in arms, fighting gallantly; and being celebrated as generals of division while living, have since their death been injudiciously spoken of as rivalling their great leader in war.

That they were officers of mark and pretension is unquestionable. Craufurd more so than Picton, because the latter never had a separate command, and his opportunities were necessarily more circumscribed; but to compare either to Wellington displays ignorance of the men and of the art they professed. If they had even comprehended the profound military and political combinations he was then conducting, the one would have carefully avoided fighting on the Coa; the other, far from refusing, would have eagerly proffered his support.

*   *   *

Masséna's command extended from the banks of the Tagus to the Bay of Biscay, from Almeida to Burgos. His troops under arms exceeded one hundred and ten thousand men; but thirteen thousand were in the Asturias and the province of Santander, four thousand in the government of Valladolid, eight thousand under Serras at Zamora and Benevente, nineteen thousand under Drouet at Bayonne. This last named body entered Spain in August as the ninth corps, but though replaced at Bayonne by another reserve under Caffarelli, it did not join Masséna until long afterwards; his efficient troops were not more than seventy thousand, and as every man, combatant or non-combatant, is borne on the strength of a French army, only fifty-five thousand bayonets and eight thousand sabre-men were with the eagles.

Masséna's instructions were to convert Ciudad Rodrigo and Almeida into places of arms, and move on both sides of the Tagus against Lisbon in the beginning of September. But thinking his force too weak to act upon two lines at the same time, or trusting to the co-operation of Soult, he relinquished the Alemtejo, and looked only to the northern bank of the Tagus; and as Junot's march in 1807 warned him off the Sobreira mountains, his views were confined to the three roads of Belmonte, Celorico and Viseu. The strength of the position behind the Alva river was known to him, as were also the impediments to his descent from Covilhao upon Espinhal; but Alorna, Pamplona and the other Portuguese in the French camp asserted with singular ignorance that the road by Viseu to Coimbra along the right bank of the Mondego was easy, and no important position covered the latter town. The French general thus deceived, resolved suddenly to assemble all his forces, distribute thirteen days' bread, and rush in one mass down the right of the Mondego, not doubting to reach Coimbra before Hill could join Lord Wellington. In this view, the three corps were directed to concentrate on the 16th of September; Reynier's at Guarda, Ney's and the heavy cavalry at Maçal de Chao, Junot's at Pinhel. By this disposition all three roads were menaced, and the allies kept in suspense as to the ultimate object; Masséna thus hoped to gain one march, a great thing, seeing that from Coimbra he was not more than a hundred miles, whereas Hill's distance from that town was greater. To cover his real project and to keep Hill as long as possible at Sarzedas, he caused the town of Guarda to be seized on the 12th by a detachment, which however withdrew again as if it were only a continuation of former feints: meanwhile Reynier, having ascertained that Mortier was at Monasterio, menacing Estremadura, destroyed his boat-bridge at Alcantara, and marched rapidly towards Sabugal.

On the 13th the allies re-established their post at Guarda. On the 15th, it was again driven away by a considerable mass of the enemy and retired up the side of the Estrella; the cavalry in front of Celorico was also forced back in the centre, and the post at Trancoso chased towards Mongualde on the left. Wellington then felt assured the invasion was in serious progress, and having ascertained that the troops in Guarda were of Reynier's corps, despatched his final orders for Hill and Leith to concentrate on the Alva. On the 16th, Reynier descended from Guarda to the low parts bordering the Mondego, where he was joined by Ney's corps and Montbrun's cavalry, and the whole passed the river. Pushing through Celorico their horsemen drove back the cavalry posts of the allies to the village of Cortiço, but the first German hussars turned there and charged the leading squadrons making some prisoners. The road divaricated to Fornos on the right, to Gouvea on the left, and a French brigade advanced along the latter to cover the march of the main body towards Fornos, but this feint was soon discovered; for there is a custom, peculiar to the British army, of sending mounted officers, good riders, singly to observe the enemy's motions; they will penetrate through the midst of his cantonments, cross the line of his movement, and hover almost within musket-shot on the skirts of his columns to learn his numbers and the true direction of

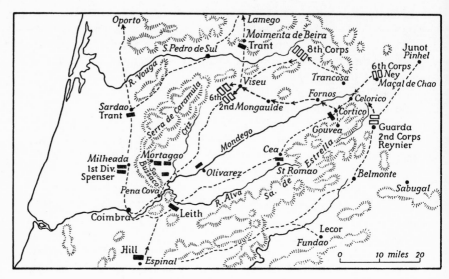

COIMBRA AND THE MONDEGO

his march. Colonel Waters, one of these exploring officers, being on the left of Reynier's troops this day, soon noticed the movement on Fornos and following with some German cavalry, made several prisoners and took the baggage of a general. The French operations being thus opened, Wellington made the first, third and fourth divisions march towards the Alva, withdrew the heavy cavalry from the front, and placed the light division at St Romao in the Estrella, to cover the head-quarters, which were transferred that night to Cea.

The 17th, the second and sixth corps passed the bridge of Fornos, and the advanced guard approached Mongualde. The eighth corps kept on the road leading towards Oporto, to observe ten thousand of the northern militia who under the command of Trant, J. Wilson and Miller, were collected to harass Masséna's right flank and rear. Trant was already at Moimenta de Beira in the defiles leading through the hills to Lamego, the *ordenança* [militia] were all in arms, the country on both sides of the Mondego laid waste, the mills destroyed, and the helpless part of the population hidden amongst the highest mountains.

On the 18th, the French advanced guard reached the deserted city of Viseu, and Pack's Portuguese brigade was sent across the Mondego at Fosdao to the Criz, while General Pakenham entered Coimbra with a brigade of the first division. On the 19th, Captain

THE BATTLE OF BUSSACO

Somers Cocks, a gallant and zealous officer who commanded the
cavalry post driven from Guarda, came down from the Estrella, and
following the enemy through Celorico ascertained that neither sick
men nor stores were left behind : hence it was evident that Masséna,
relinquishing his communications, had thrown his cavalry, infantry,
artillery, parcs, baggage and hospital waggons in one mass upon
the worst road in Portugal!

Wellington was in motion to cross the Mondego, when a false
report that the enemy was again on the left bank arrested the movement. The next day the truth became known, and the third, fourth
and light divisions, and the British cavalry, passed the river at Pena
Cova, Olivarez and other places. The light division marched to
Mortagao in support of Pack, the third and fourth entered the villages between the Sierra de Bussaco and Mortagao, the horsemen
occupied a plain between the light division and Pack's brigade. But
now the eighth corps pointed towards the valley of the Vouga, and
thus rendered it doubtful whether Masséna would not that way
gain the main road from Oporto to Coimbra. Spencer moved therefore with the first division upon Milheada, and Trant was directed
to join him by a march through San Pedro de Sul and Sardao. Meanwhile Leith arrived on the Alva, and Hill was only one march behind; for having discovered Reynier's movements on the 12th, and
hearing that the French boats on the Tagus had been destroyed, he
with ready decision, anticipating orders, sent his artillery by
Thomar, and marching rapidly with his troops by the military way
reached Espinal the evening of the 20th: there he was joined by
General Lecor, who with equal vigour and judgment had brought
the Portuguese brigade by long marches from Fundao. The 21st,
Hill reached the Alva and pushed his cavalry in observation beyond
that river; thus the whole of the allied army was united on the very
day the main body of the enemy entered Viseu: the French horsemen were indeed on the Criz, but the bridges had been destroyed by
Pack, and the project of surprising Coimbra was baffled.

Nor had Masséna escaped other evil consequences from his false
movement. Forced to repair the road from day to day for his artillery, it was twenty miles from Viseu on the 19th, and Trant formed
the hardy project of destroying it. Quitting Moimenta de Beira in
the night with a squadron of cavalry, two thousand militia and five
guns, he passed between the convoy and the army, and on the 20th
surprised a patrol of ten men, from whom he learned that the guns
were close at hand and Montbrun's cavalry in their rear. The enterprise was serious, but the defiles were narrow, and charging the

head of the escorting troops he took a hundred prisoners with some baggage. The convoy fell back, Trant followed, and such was the ruggedness of the defile that Montbrun's cavalry could never get to the front. The French were in disorder, and a resolute attack would have ruined them, when the militia became alarmed and unmanageable; the enemy then repulsed the Portuguese horsemen with a loss of twelve troopers, and Trant seeing nothing more could be effected returned to Moimenta de Beira and from thence marched to Lamego with his prisoners. Montbrun, ignorant of the number and quality of the assailants, fell back, and the artillery did not reach Viseu until the 23rd, whereby Masséna lost two most important days.

While Masséna remained at Viseu, Spencer held Milheada with the first division, observing the great road from Oporto; the light division was at Mortagao, watching the road from Viseu; the remainder of the army was in reserve ready to move to either side. But when the French advanced guard repaired the bridges over the Criz and passed that river, the first division was recalled, and the Sierra de Bussaco chosen for the position of battle. This mountain, eight miles in length, abuts with its right on the Mondego, while its left is connected with the Sierra de Caramula by a rugged country impervious to the march of an army. A road along the crest afforded an easy communication from right to left; and behind the ridge on the right, the ford of Pena Cova furnished a passage over the Mondego to the Alva. The face of Bussaco was steep, rough, and fit for defence; the artillery of the allies, placed on certain salient points could play along the front, and there was some ground on the summit suitable for a small body of cavalry. But neither guns nor horsemen on the French side had a field, and their infantry were to contend with every difficulty of approach and attack.

After passing the Criz, a table-land permitted Masséna to march with a wide order of battle to Mortagao; but from thence, a succession of ridges led to the Sierra Bussaco, which was separated from the last by a chasm, so profound the naked eye could hardly distinguish the movement of troops in the bottom, yet in parts so narrow that twelve-pounders could range across. From Mortagao four roads conducted to Coimbra. The first, unfrequented and narrow, crossed the Caramula to Boyalva, a village situated on the western slopes of that sierra, and from thence led to Sardao and Milheada. The other roads, penetrating through the rough ground in front, passed over the Sierra de Bussaco; one by a large convent, fronting the enemy's right and on the highest point; another on his left by a village called St Antonio de Cantara; the third, a branch from the second, being still more to his left, followed the Mondego to Pena Cova. When this formidable position was chosen, some officers expressed their fears that Masséna would not assail it. 'But if he does, I shall beat him', was the reply of the English general. He was however well assured the prince, whose advanced guard was already over the Criz, would attack. The second and sixth corps were massed behind that stream, and Massena was not likely, merely at the sight of a strong position, to make a retrograde movement and adopt a new line of operations by the Vouga, which would be exposed to Baccellar's militia: he was indeed anxious for a battle, but being still misled as to the topography, was convinced Wellington would retreat and embark.

General Pack having destroyed the bridges on the Criz fell back on the light division, but the French restored them the 23rd and drove the British cavalry into the hills behind Mortagao. Six or seven squadrons were retained there, the rest went to the low country about Milheada, from whence Spencer was recalled to Bussaco; Picton and Cole also took post on that position, the former at St Antonio de Cantara, the latter at the convent. The light division encamped in a pine wood, where happened one of those extraordinary panics attributed in ancient times to the influence of a god. No enemy was near, no alarm given, yet suddenly the troops, as if seized with a frenzy, started from sleep and dispersed in every direction; nor was there any possibility of allaying this strange terror until some persons called out that the enemy's cavalry were amongst them, when the soldiers mechanically run together, and the illusion was dissipated. On the 24th the French skirmished with the piquets, the division retired leisurely to some strong ground four miles in the rear, and towards evening some French cavalry, venturing too close, were charged by a squadron of the 14th and lost thirty men.

The French cavalry were gathering thickly, and three columns of infantry were descried on the table-land above Mortagao coming on all abreast with an impetuous pace, while behind them clouds of dust loading the atmosphere for miles, showed that the whole army had passed the Criz and was in march to attack. The horsemen were actually exchanging pistol-shots, when Wellington arrived and taking the command in person made the division retire, covered by the 52nd, the rifles and Ross's battery. It was a timely interference, for the French brought up guns and infantry so quickly, that all the skill of the general and the readiness of the troops could scarcely evade a disaster. Howbeit a series of rapid evolutions under a sharp cannonade placed the division in an hour safely on the Bussaco Sierra, and the opposite ridge was immediately crowned by the masses of the sixth corps, the French batteries opening while the English troops were yet ascending the position. Reynier, pursuing a Portuguese battalion, arrived about the same time at Antonio de Cantara in front of Picton, and before three o'clock forty thousand French infantry were embattled on the two points, their guns trying the range above, while the skirmishing clatter of musketry arose from the dark-wooded chasms beneath. Ney, whose military glance was sure, instantly perceived that the mountain, a crested not a table one, could hide no great reserves, that it was only half-occupied, and that the allies were moving with the disorder usual on the taking unknown ground. He wished therefore to attack, but Masséna was ten miles in rear, the officer sent to him waited two hours for an audience, and then returned with an order to attend the prince's arrival. Thus a great opportunity was lost, for Spencer was not up, Leith's troops, now called the 5th division, were only passing the Mondego, and Hill was still behind the Alva. Scarcely twenty-five thousand men were in the line, and with great intervals.

Next day Reynier and Ney wrote in concert to Masséna to urge an immediate attack; but he did not come up from Mortagao until twelve o'clock, bringing with him Junot's corps and the cavalry, which he formed as a reserve to connect Ney's and Reynier's troops; then, throwing out skirmishers along the whole front, he carefully examined the allies' position. It was no longer denuded. Hill, having crossed the Mondego, was athwart the road leading over the sierra to the Pena Cova ford; on his left Leith prolonged the line of defence, having the Lusitanian legion in reserve; Picton, supported by Champlemond's Portuguese brigade, was next to Leith; Spenser occupied the highest part of the ridge, between Picton and the convent. Cole was on the extreme left, covering a path leading to the flat country about Milheada. A regiment of heavy dragoons was in reserve on the summit of the sierra, and Pack's brigade and some other Portuguese troops were in front of Spencer half-way down the mountain. On their left, the light division, supported by a German brigade and the nineteenth Portuguese regiment of the line, occupied a spur jutting out nearly half a mile in front of but lower than the convent, the space between being scooped like the hollow of a wave before it breaks: the whole mountain side was covered with skirmishers, and fifty pieces of artillery were disposed upon the most salient points.

Ney was now averse to attack, but Masséna resolved to storm the ridge. Reynier, thinking he had only to deal with a rear-guard, encouraged the prince; and the latter, too confident in the valour of his army and his own fortune, directed the second and sixth corps to fall on the next day, each to its own front, while the eighth corps, the cavalry and the artillery remained in reserve. Towards dusk the light troops, dropping by twos and threes into the lowest parts of the valley, endeavoured to steal up the wooded dells and hollows, and establish themselves unseen close to the piquets of the light division; the riflemen and *caçadores* drove them back, but renewed attempts seemed to menace a night attack and excited all the vigilance of the troops. Yet only veterans tired of war could have slept while that serene sky glittered above, and the dark mountains were crowned with the innumerable bivouac fires of more than a hundred thousand warriors.

*   *   *

Before daybreak on the 29th, Ney planted three columns of attack opposite the convent, and Reynier planted two at Antonio de Cantara, those points being about three miles apart. Reynier's men, having easier ground to assail, were in the midst of the piquets and skirmishers of Picton's division almost as soon as they could be perceived in movement; and though the allies fought well, and six guns played along the ascent with grape, in less than half an hour the French were close upon the summit: so swiftly and with such astonishing power and resolution did they scale the mountain, overthrowing everything that opposed their progress. The right centre of the third division was forced back, the eighth Portuguese regiment broken, the hostile masses gained the highest part of the crest just between the third and the fifth divisions, and the leading battalions established themselves amongst the crowning rocks, while a confused mass in rear wheeled to the right, intending to sweep the summit of the sierra. At that moment Wellington caused two guns to open with grape upon their flank, a heavy musketry was poured into their front, and in a little time the eighty-eighth regiment and a wing of the forty-fifth charged so furiously that even fresh men could not have withstood the shock; the French, spent with their previous efforts, gave way, and both parties went mingled together down the mountain side with a mighty clamour and confusion, their track being marked with dead and dying even to the bottom of the valley.

Meanwhile those French battalions which had first gained the

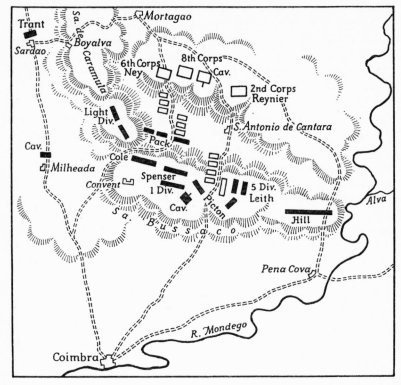

THE BATTLE OF BUSSACO

crest, were formed across the ridge with their right resting upon
a precipice overhanging the reserve side, and the position was in
fact gained if any reserve had been at hand; for the greatest part of
the third division, British and Portuguese, were fully engaged;
some of the French skirmishers were descending the back of the
position, and a misty cloud capped the summit, so that the hostile
mass, ensconced amongst the rocks, could only be seen by General
Leith. That officer, noticing the first impression made on Picton's
division, had moved with a brigade to his aid; he had two miles of
rugged ground to traverse on a narrow formation, but he was now
coming on rapidly, and directed the thirty-eighth regiment to turn
the French right flank while Colonel Cameron with the ninth
assailed their front. A precipice stopped the thirty-eighth, but
Cameron, hearing from a staff-officer the critical state of affairs,
formed line under a violent fire and, without returning a shot, ran
in upon and drove the French grenadiers from the rocks with

irresistible bravery; plying them with a destructive musketry as long as they could be reached, and yet with excellent discipline refraining from pursuit lest the crest of the position should be again lost: for the mountain was so rugged no general view could be taken. This secured the victory, for Hill's corps had now edged in towards the scene of action, Leith's second brigade had joined the first, and a great mass of fresh troops was thus concentrated, while Reynier had neither reserves nor guns to restore the fight.

Ney's attack had as little success. From the abutment of the mountain upon which the light division was stationed the lowest parts of the valley could be discerned, the ascent was steeper than where Reynier had attacked, and Craufurd in a happy mood of command made masterly dispositions. The table-land between him and the convent was sufficiently scooped to conceal the forty-third and fifty-second regiments drawn up in line; and a quarter of a mile behind them, on higher ground and close to the convent, the German infantry appeared to be the only solid line of resistance on this part of the position. In front of the British regiments, some rocks, over-hanging the descent, furnished natural embrasures in which Ross's guns were placed, and beyond them the riflemen and *caçadores* were planted as skirmishers, covering the slope of the mountain.

While it was still dark a straggling musketry was heard in the deep valley, and when the light broke, three heavy masses, detached from the sixth corps, were seen to enter the woods below and throw forward a profusion of skirmishers. One of these, under General Marchand, emerging from the dark chasm and following the main road, seemed intent to turn the right of the light division; a second under Loison made straight up the face of the mountain against the front, the third remained in reserve. Simon's brigade, leading Loison's attack, ascended with a wonderful alacrity, and though the light troops plied it unceasingly with musketry, and the artillery bullets swept through it from the first to the last section, its order was never disturbed nor its speed in the least abated. Ross's guns were worked with incredible quickness, yet their range was palpably contracted every round, the enemy's shot came sing-ing up in a sharper key, the English skirmishers, breathless and begrimed with powder, rushed over the edge of the ascent, the artillery drew back, and the victorious cries of the French were heard within a few yards of the summit.

Craufurd, standing alone on one of the rocks, had been intently watching the progress of this attack, and now with a shrill tone ordered the two regiments in reserve to charge! The next moment a horrid shout startled the French column and eighteen hundred British bayonets went sparkling over the brow of the hill. Yet so brave, so hardy were the leading French, that each man of the first section raised his musket and two officers and ten soldiers fell before them. Not a Frenchman had missed his mark! They could do no more. The head of their column was violently thrown back upon the rear, both flanks were overlapped at the same moment by the English wings, three terrible discharges at five yards' distance shattered the wavering mass, and a long trail of broken arms and bleeding carcasses marked the line of flight. The main body of the British now stood fast, but some companies pursued down the mountain, whereupon Ney threw forward his reserve division, and opening his guns from the opposite heights killed some of the pursuers: thus warned, they recovered their own ground, and the Germans were brought forward to the skirmish. During this fight a small flanking detachment, having passed round the right, rose near the convent and was gallantly charged and defeated by the nineteenth Portuguese regiment under colonel M'Bean.

Loison did not renew the action, but Marchand, having formed several small bodies, gained a pine wood half-way up the mountain on the right of the light division, and sent a cloud of skirmishers against the highest part; on that steep ascent however, Pack's men sufficed to hold them in check, and half a mile higher up Spencer showed a line of the footguards which forbad any hope of success. Craufurd's artillery also smote Marchand's people in the pine wood, and Ney, who was there in person, after sustaining this murderous cannonade for an hour, relinquished that attack also. The desultory fighting of the light troops then ceased, and at two o'clock parties from both armies were, under a momentary truce, mixed together carrying off wounded men. Towards evening a French company, with signal audacity, seized a village only a half-musket shot from the light division, and refused to retire, whereupon Craufurd turned twelve guns on the intruders and overwhelmed them with bullets for half an hour; but after paying the French captain this distinguished honour, recovered his temper, and sent a company of the forty-third down which cleared the village in a few minutes.

Meanwhile happened an affecting incident, contrasting strongly with the savage character of the preceding events. A poor orphan Portuguese girl, about seventeen and very handsome, was seen coming down the mountain, driving an ass loaded with all her property through the midst of the French army. She had abandoned her dwelling in obedience to the proclamation, and now passed over the field of battle with a childish simplicity, totally unconscious of her perilous situation, and scarcely understanding which were the hostile and which the friendly troops, for no man on either side was so brutal as to molest her.

The French were, notwithstanding their astonishing valour, repulsed in the manner to be expected from the strength of the ground and the bravery of the soldiers opposed to them; their loss was preposterously exaggerated at the time, but it was really great, one general, Grain-d'Orge, and eight hundred men were killed; Foy, Merle and Simon were wounded, and the last made prisoner. The whole loss might be about four thousand five hundred, while that of the allies was only thirteen hundred, because the French strove to win by audacity rather than by fire, and were exposed to grape all the time. Masséna then finding Bussaco impregnable, and seeing it could not be turned by the Mondego, because the allies might pass that river on a shorter line, held a council in which it was proposed to return to Spain; but at that moment a peasant told of a road leading from Mortagao over the Caramula ridge to Boyalva, and it was resolved to turn Wellington's left. To mask the movement, skirmishing was renewed the 28th so vigorously that a general battle was expected; but an ostentatious display of men, disappearance of baggage, and casting up of earth on the hill covering the road to Mortagao, plainly indicated some other design. Towards evening the French infantry were sensibly diminished, the cavalry were descried by the light division winding over the distant mountains towards the allies' left, and at that moment Wellington arrived from the right, and looked at the distant columns with great earnestness; he seemed uneasy, his countenance bore a fierce angry expression, and suddenly mounting his horse he rode away without speaking: one hour afterwards the whole army was in movement. Hill recrossing the Mondego retired by Espinal upon Thomar, the centre and left defiled in the night by narrow roads upon Milheada, the guns followed the convent road, and the light division furnished the rear-guard until the open country enabled the cavalry to take that duty.

Masséna's scouts reached Boyalva in the evening of the 28th, and it has been asserted that Trant's absence from Sardao enabled the French to execute their design. Trant was however at Sardao four miles from Boyalva at one o'clock the 28th; but having, under orders from Baccellar, moved from Lamego by the circuitous way of Oporto instead of the direct road by San Pedro da Sul, his numbers were reduced by fatigue and desertion to fifteen hundred, and his presence even at Boyalva, as Wellington had designed, would have produced no effect. As it was, the French cavalry pushed between him and the British horsemen, and drove him with loss behind the Vouga. Then Masséna's main body, clearing the defile of Boyalva, marched upon Coimbra, and the allies, crossing the Mondego near that city, commenced passing the defiles leading upon Condeixa and Pombal. The commissariat stores, previously removed from Pena Cova to Figueras, were embarked at Peniché, the light division and the cavalry remained on the right bank of the Mondego, and Baccellar was directed to bring down all the militia of the northern provinces upon the Vouga. The pernicious effect of the regency's folly and negligence was now manifest. Notwithstanding the proclamations, and the urgent and even menacing remonstrances of the English general, the regency had not caused the country behind the Mondego to be laid waste; while the enemy was stopped at Bussaco, only the richest inhabitants had quitted Coimbra. When the army retreated, that city was still populous; and when Masséna's approach left only the choice between flight and the death and infamy announced in the proclamation, so direful a scene of distress ensued that none could behold it without emotion. Mothers with children of all ages, the sick, the old, the bedridden, and even lunatics, went or were carried forth, the most part with little hope and less help, to journey for days in company with contending armies: fortunately for this unhappy multitude, the weather was fine and the roads firm or the greatest number must have perished in the most deplorable manner. And all this misery was of no avail, the object was not gained; the people fled, the provisions were left, and the mills were only partially and imperfectly ruined.

On the 1st of October, the allied outposts were driven from the hills north of Coimbra, but the French horsemen, entering the plain, suffered some loss from a cannonade. The British cavalry were in line on open ground, the disparity of numbers was not great, the opportunity fair; yet the English were withdrawn across the Mondego, and so unskilfully that the French cut down some troopers in the middle of the river and thus forced a combat in which fifty or sixty men fell. This scrambling affair caused the light division to march hastily through the city to gain the defiles of Condeixa which commence at the end of the bridge, and then all the inhabitants who had not quitted the place rushed out, driving before them a number of animals loaded with sick people and children. At the entrance to the bridge the press was great and the troops halted a

few moments under the prison; the jailer had fled with the keys, the
prisoners, crowding to the windows, endeavoured to tear down
the bars with their hands and even with their teeth, bellowing in
the most frantic manner, while the bitter lamentations of the multitude on the bridge increased, and the pistol shots of the cavalry
engaged at the ford below were distinctly heard. William Campbell, a staff officer, breaking the prison doors, soon freed the
wretched inmates, and the troops forced a passage over the bridge;
but at the other end, the defile, cut through high rocks, was so
crowded no effort could make way. A troop of French dragoons
which had passed the ford now came close upon the flank, and a single
regiment of infantry would have destroyed the division, wedged as
it was in a hollow way and unable to retreat, to advance, or break
out on either side. At last a passage was opened to the right, and
the road was cleared for the guns, yet it was dark before the troops
reached Condeixa, although the distance was less than eight miles.

That night the headquarters were at Redinha, the next day at
Leiria; the marches were therefore easy, and provisions were abundant, yet the usual disorders of a retreat had already commenced.
In Coimbra a quantity of harness and entrenching tools were
scattered in the streets; at Leiria, the magazines were plundered
by the troops and camp-followers; at Condeixa, a magazine of tents,
shoes, spirits and salt meat was destroyed or abandoned to the
enemy. And while the town was flowing with rum, the light division and Pack's Portuguese brigade, only a quarter of a mile distant,
had to slaughter their own bullocks, and received but half rations of
liquor! Wellington however arrested these growing disorders with
a strong hand. Three men taken in the fact were hanged at Leiria
for plundering, and some regiments more tainted than others were
forbidden to enter a village. This vigorous exercise of command,
aided by the fine weather and the enemy's inactivity, restored
regularity amongst the allies, while Masséna's conduct, the reverse
of the English general's, introduced the confusion of a retreat in the
pursuing army. At Coimbra, he permitted such waste that resources
were dissipated in a few days which would have supplied his troops
for two months under good arrangements; and during this
licentious delay the advantage gained by his dangerous flank march
to Boyalva was lost.

VIII

The Lines of Torres Vedras
1810–11

With the prudence and foresight that was to distinguish his whole career as a general, Wellington had calculated that his posture in the Peninsula might require an unassailable base, protected by topography and supplied by the Royal Navy, which could defy any deep incursion by the French into Portugal. Shortly after his return to Lisbon, he had ordered the construction of triple, unassailable lines of circumvallation before the Portuguese capital, anchored on the right by the River Tagus and the left by the Atlantic. Reviving an ancient Portuguese edict which would now be called a 'scorched earth policy', he decreed that the intervening country be laid waste, the crops destroyed and the population evacuated. To these Lines, of Torres Vedras, he now retired, unmolested, with his whole army.

Militarily, he was secure. Politically, his position was precarious. The British government failed to understand Wellington's strategic conceptions, feared a re-embarkation and, for a period, was readier with criticism than support. In Lisbon, the regency appointed when the Court had fled, endeavoured to assert its authority. One faction was pro-French and made secret overtures to Masséna. The former Bishop of Oporto, violent and mischievous as ever, had become patriarch and intrigued with the Souza faction. Their chief aim was to maintain the ascendancy of their fellow aristocrats from the north of Portugal and perpetuate the system of corruption in the administration and army by which they enriched themselves. Wellington, much beset, was obliged to take stern measures.

THE LINES OF Torres Vedras consisted of three distinct ranges of defence. The first, extending from Alhandra on the Tagus to the mouth of the Zizandre on the sea-coast, was, following the inflections of the hills, twenty-nine miles long. The second, traced at a distance, varying from six to ten miles, in rear of the first, stretched from Quintella on the Tagus to the mouth of the St Lorenza, being twenty-four miles in length. The third, intended to cover a forced embarkation, extended from Passo d'Arcos on the Tagus to the tower of Junquera on the coast. Here an outward line, constructed on an opening of three thousand yards, enclosed an entrenched camp, the latter being designed to cover an embarkation with fewer troops if such an operation should be delayed by bad weather. This second camp enclosed Fort St Julian, whose high ramparts and deep ditches defied an escalade, and were armed to enable a rear-guard to resist any force. From Passo d'Arcos to the nearest part of the second line was twenty-four miles; from the first line it was two marches, but the principal routes led through Lisbon, where means to retard the enemy were prepared.

Of these stupendous lines, the second, whether for strength or importance, was the principal; the others were appendages, the third a mere place of refuge. The first line was originally designed as an advanced work to stem the primary violence of the enemy and enable the army to take up its ground on the second line without hurry or pressure; but while Masséna remained inactive on the frontier, it acquired strength, which was now so much augmented by the rain that Wellington resolved to abide the attack there permanently.

These celebrated lines were great in conception and execution, more in keeping with ancient than modern military labours; and it is clear that the defence was not dependent, as some French writers suppose, upon the first line. If that had been stormed, the standard of Portuguese independence would still have floated securely amidst the rocks of the second line. But to occupy fifty miles of fortification, to man one hundred and fifty forts and work six hundred guns required many men, and numbers were not wanting. A great fleet in the Tagus, a superb body of marines sent out from England, the civic guards of Lisbon, the Portuguese heavy artillery corps, the militia and *ordenança* of Estremadura, furnished a powerful reserve to the regular army. The native gunners and the militia supplied all the garrisons of the forts on the second, and most of those on the first line; the British marines occupied the third line; the navy manned the gun-boats on the river, and aided in various ways the operation in the field. The recruits from the depôts, and the calling in of all the men on furlough, rendered the Portuguese army stronger than it had yet been, while the British troops, reinforced from Cadiz and England, and remarkably healthy, presented such a front as a general would desire to see in a dangerous crisis.

Masséna, surprised at the extent and strength of works which

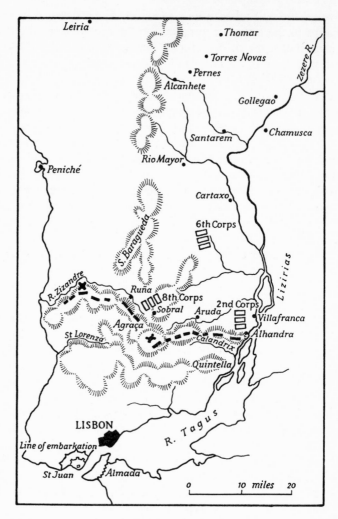

TORRES VEDRAS

he had only heard of five days before he came upon them, employed several days to examine their nature. The heights of Alhandra were inexpugnable; but the valleys of Calandrix and Aruda attracted his attention. By the former he could turn Alhandra and reach the weakest part of the second line; but the abattis and redoubts, hourly strengthening, gave little encouragement to attack there. The ground about Aruda did not give him a view of the troops, although he frequently skirmished to make Craufurd show his force; but that general, by occupying Aruda as an advanced post, had rendered it impossible to discover his true situation without a serious affair, and, in an incredibly short space of time, he secured his position in a manner worthy of admiration. Across the ravine on the left a loose stone wall sixteen feet thick and forty feet high was raised; across the great valley of Aruda a double line of abattis was drawn; not, as usual, of the limbs of trees, but of full-grown oaks and chesnuts, digged up with all their roots and branches, dragged by main force for several hundred yards, and then reset and crossed so that no human strength could break through. Breast-works, at convenient distances to defend this line of trees, were also cast up; and along the summits of the mountain, for a space of nearly three miles including the salient points, other stone walls, six feet high by four in thickness, with banquettes, were piled up! Romans never raised greater works in the time!

Monte Agraça and the upper Zizandre vale had no outworks; neither the Zibreira valley, nor the hills above Ruña had been fortified, and battle could be joined there on more equal terms; but the position was by nature strong, the rear supported by great forts, a powerful body of troops occupied the ground, and six battalions drawn from Hill's corps formed a reserve at Bucellas. Beyond Ruña, Masséna could not take a view; the Baragueda ridge and the forts of Torres Vedras stopped him. Convinced by this survey that the lines were not to be forced, he disposed his troops in permanent positions between Villa Franca and Sobral.

The war was now reduced to a blockade. Masséna only sought to feed his army until reinforcements reached it; Wellington endeavoured to starve the French before succour could arrive. The former spread his moveable columns in the rear to seek for provisions, and established magazines at Santarem. The latter drew down all the militia and *ordenança* of the north on the French rear, putting them in communication with the garrison of Peniché on one side, and on the other with the militia of Lower Beira: Carlos d'España also, crossing the Tagus, acted between Castello Branco and Abrantes. Thus the French were completely enclosed without any weakening of the regular army.

*   *   *

Masséna's invasion seriously affected the Portuguese finances, and the regency applied for an additional subsidy. Mr Stuart, seeing the extreme distress, directed the house of Sampayo to furnish provisions to the troops on the credit of the first subsidy; and he also made great exertions to feed the fugitive inhabitants, forty thousand of whom arrived before the 13th of October, and others were hourly coming in, destitute and starving. Corn at any price was sought for in Ireland, America and Egypt; and one thousand tons of government shipping were lent to merchants to fetch grain from Algiers. One commission of citizens was formed to facilitate the obtaining cattle and corn from the northern province; another to regulate the transport of provisions to the army and to push a trade with Spain through the Alemtejo. Small craft were sent up the Tagus to carry off the inhabitants and their stock from the islands and the left bank, and post-vessels were established along the coast to Oporto. Bullion and jewels were put on board the men-of-war, a proclamation was issued calling upon the people to be tranquil, and a strong police was established to enforce this object. Finally, to supply the deficiency of tonnage occasioned by sending transports in search of corn, an embargo was laid upon the port of Lisbon: this was protested against by the Americans, but an imperious necessity ruled.

All these measures were vehemently opposed by the patriarch and his faction; and that nothing might be wanting to show how entirely the fate of the Peninsula depended in that hour upon Wellington's firmness, the fears of the British cabinet, which had been increasing as the crisis approached, were now plainly disclosed. Their private letters contained hints at variance with their public despatches; they wished the general to abandon the country, yet threw the responsibility entirely upon him. They thought him rash, because they were unequal to the crisis; and having neither the modesty to resign, nor the manliness to continue the contest with vigour, cast their base policy with a view only to their own interests in case of failure. During the retreat from Beira, some officers of rank let their correspondence bear evidence of their own despondency; Spencer and Charles Stewart especially wrote so hopelessly to Lord Liverpool that he transmitted their letters to Wellington, and by earnestly demanding his opinion of their contents showed how deeply they had disturbed his own mind. Thus beset, the English general rose like a giant. Without noticing the arguments or forebodings in these letters, he took a calm historical review of the circumstances which had induced him to defend Portugal, and which he had before explained to the very minister he was addressing. He showed how, up to that period, his opinions had been justified by the results, and therefore he claimed confidence for the future; then tracing the probable course of coming events, he discussed his own and the enemy's designs with such sagacity that the subsequent course of the war never belied his anticipations.

THE LINES OF TORRES VEDRAS

The war had been hanging in even balance, and the weight of interested folly thus thrown in by the regency was beginning to sink the scale. Instead of performing its own duties, the government assumed that the war could be maintained on the frontier, and when it should have removed the people and food, urged impracticable military operations. When convicted of error by facts, it threw the task of driving the country upon the general, although he was necessarily ignorant of the names and places of abode of the officers and magistrates who were to execute it, and there was but one Portuguese agent at headquarters to give assistance in translating the necessary orders. When this was pointed out, they issued the orders, but made the execution referable to the general without his knowledge, well knowing he had no means of communicating with the provincial folks: the stopping of Masséna at Bussaco alone enabled the orders even to reach the country authorities. But the great object of the regency was to soothe and nourish the national indolence and throw the odium of rigorous measures on the British, and though Wellington reproached them for so doing, he never shrunk from that odium. Avowing himself the author of the wasting plan, he permitted the regency to shelter themselves under his name, but he would not tamely let them deprive him of the fruits; nor would he suffer them, shrinking as they did in the trial, to seek popularity at the expense of their country's safety.

Wellington's power in Portugal was confirmed, and his proceedings approved of. The subsidies were placed under Wellington's and Mr Stuart's control, Admiral Berkeley became a regent, and Portugal was thus reduced to the condition of a vassal state, which could never have been attempted, however necessary, if the people at large had not been willing to acquiesce. But firm in their attachment to independence, they submitted cheerfully to this temporary assumption of command, and fully justified the sagacity of the man who thus dared to grasp at the whole power of Portugal with one hand while he kept the power of France at bay with the other.

The strength of the works, defying attack, rendered it likely Masséna would finally operate by the left bank of the Tagus. This was to be dreaded. He could in the Alemtejo more easily subsist, more effectually operate to the injury of Lisbon, more securely retreat upon his own resources. Wellington had therefore repeatedly urged the regency to make the inhabitants carry off their herds and grain from that side, and from the numerous islands in the river, and above all things to destroy or remove every boat. To effect

these objects a commission had been appointed, but so many delays
and obstacles were interposed by the patriarch and his coadjutors,
that the commissioners did not leave Lisbon until the enemy was
close upon the river, both banks being then stocked with cattle and
corn, and forty large boats lying on the right side. The French
therefore entered the alluvial islands called the Lizirias, where they
obtained abundance of provisions; and while the regency thus provided for the enemy, they left the fortresses of Palmella, St Felippe
de Setuval and Abrantes with empty magazines. The supply of
grain coming from Spain was stopped, the chain of communication
was broken, the alarm spread to Lisbon, and there was no remedy
but to send General Fane, with some guns and Portuguese cavalry
which could be ill spared from the lines, to that side.

Fane destroyed all the boats he could find, hastened the removal
of provisions, and kept a strict watch upon the enemy's movements
as high as the mouth of the Zezere. But other embarrassments were
continually arising. The prisoners in Lisbon had accumulated so as
to become a serious inconvenience; for the English Admiralty, pretending alarm at a fever generated by the infamous treatment of the
prisoners, refused to let them be transported to England in vessels
of war, and no other ships could be had; thus the rights of humanity
and the good of the service, were alike disregarded; for had there
been real danger, Wellington would not have continually urged
the measure. About this time also, Admiral Berkeley admitted that
his elaborate report, made the year before, stating that the enemy
even though he should seize the heights of Almada could not injure
the fleet in the river, was erroneous: hence the engineers were
directed to construct lines on that side also, but it was in the
eleventh hour. And now also the native army showed the effects of
the regency's folly. The troops were so ill supplied that more than
once they would have disbanded had they not been succoured from
the British magazines. Ten thousand soldiers of the line deserted
between April and December, and of the militia two-thirds were
absent from their colours; for as no remonstrance could induce the
government to put the laws in force against delinquents, that which
was at first the effect of want became a habit: even when regularly
fed from the British stores within the lines the desertion was
alarmingly great.

Notwithstanding the mischiefs thus daily growing up, neither
the patriarch nor the principal ceased their opposition. The order
to fortify the heights of Almada caused a violent altercation.
Wellington complained of this opposition to the Portuguese prince

regent, which produced such a paroxysm of rage in the patriarch, that he personally insulted Mr Stuart, and vented his passion in the most indecent language. Soon after this, the state of the finances compelled the government to resort to the dangerous expedient of requisitions in kind for the feeding of the troops; and in that critical moment the patriarch, whose influence was from various causes very great, took occasion to declare that 'he would not suffer burthens to be laid upon the people which were evidently for no other purpose than to nourish the war in the heart of the kingdom'. But it was his and his coadjutor's criminal conduct that really nourished the war, for there were ample means to have carried off in time ten times the quantity of provisions left for the enemy. Masséna could not then have remained a week before the lines, and his retreat would have been attended with famine and disaster if the measures previously agreed to by the regency had been duly executed. The country about Thomar, Torres Novas, Gollegao and Santarem was absolutely untouched, the inhabitants remained, the mills were little injured and quickly repaired; and Wellington had the deep mortification to find his grand project frustrated by the very persons from whom he had a right to expect the most zealous support; there seemed nothing to prevent the Prince of Essling holding his positions until an overwhelming force should arrive from Spain. It is heart-breaking, exclaimed the British general – 'It is heartbreaking to contemplate the chance of failure from such obstinacy and folly.'

IX

Masséna Retreats

Time was on Wellington's side. The onset of winter, the jealousies between the French marshals, the long lines of communication harassed by guerrillas, rendered Masséna's position increasingly difficult. He recognized the impossibility of assaulting the Torres Vedras lines and retired 30 miles to Santarem to build hasty fortifications of his own from which he pretended to threaten Wellington. But his position was becoming untenable.

M ASSÉNA'S resolution to hold his ground was evident. Every advantageous point was occupied, the sentinels returned the fire of the skirmishers, strong reserves, some in arms, some cooking, were descried, the strokes of the hatchet and the fall of trees resounded in the woods clothing the Santarem hills, and the commencement of a triple line of abattis with the fresh earth of entrenchments were discernible. The demonstrations were renewed next day, yet soon ceased, and Hill was ordered to halt at Chamusca on the left bank of the Tagus. Craufurd, however, still thought a rear-guard only was at Santarem; his spirit was chafed, he seized a musket and, followed by a sergeant, advanced in the night along the causeway to commence a personal skirmish with the French piquet: he escaped from its fire miraculously and came back convinced that Masséna was not in flight.

Wellington was preparing forcibly to examine the French right on the 22nd, when Masséna, having ordered Reynier's baggage to return, directed Clausel to drive back the allies' posts near the town of Rio Mayor. This counter-stroke caused Spencer and Pack to be withdrawn to Cartaxo, and the light division also was held in readiness to retreat. In truth, Masséna was only to be assailed by holding Reynier in check at the Ponte Seca, while a powerful mass penetrated by Tremes and Pernes; but heavy rains rendered those roads impracticable, and the position of Santarem was maintained in quiet for several months. For this both generals have been censured, but it may be shown that they acted wisely and like great captains. Masséna, without any extreme dissemination, menaced several

points and commanded two distinct lines of retreat; but he had
other objects also in view; he expected detachments and convoys
from Castille, and the ninth corps, which had lately been placed
under his orders; his position, touching upon Leiria and the Zezere,
enabled him to give his hand to these reinforcements and convoys,
either by the line of the Mondego or that of Belmonte and the
Estrada Nova; and at the same time he could communicate with
troops coming from Andalusia. He was undoubtedly open to a
dangerous attack between Santarem and Alcanhete, but he thought
himself safe from such a decisive operation by an army composed
of three different nations and unpractised in great evolutions.
Guided by a long experience, he calculated upon moral causes with
confidence, and he who cannot do so is but half a general. Like a
great commander he counted likewise upon the political effect his
menacing attitude would produce. While he maintained Santarem,
he appeared to besiege Lisbon, and encouraged the disaffected, who
were expected to rise; and he prolonged the sufferings of the capital:
forty thousand persons are said to have died from privations within
the lines during the winter of 1810. He thus shook the English
influence in Portugal, and so obscured the future that few men had
sagacity to judge rightly. At this period also, the illness of George
the Third, reviving the question of a regency in England, had
strengthened the opposition in parliament, and Masséna's position
supported their arguments against the war. Wherefore he did right
to hold his ground: and if he committed errors early in the campaign, he now proved himself a daring, able, and pertinacious
commander.

On the English general's side the difficulties were so great that
a battle was equally to be desired and dreaded. Desired because
victory would silence opponents in England and Portugal, and
enable him to dictate to the ministers instead of struggling incessantly against their fears. It would relieve the misery of the Portuguese people from their horrible sufferings; and was also to be
desired, lest a second and a third army, now gathering in Castille
and in Andalusia, should reach Masséna and again shut up the allies
in their works. Dreaded, because a defeat or even a repulse would
have ruined the cause; for it was at this period the disputes relative
to the lines at Almada were most violent, and the slightest disaster
would have placed the patriarch at the head of a national party.
Dreaded, because of the regency discussion in England, as a serious
check would have caused the Whigs to triumph, and the troops
would have been withdrawn from Portugal. So powerful indeed

was the opposition, and so much did the ministers dread its cry for economy, that, forgetting the army in their keen love of place, they actually issued orders to discharge all the transport ships to save expense! In fine, the prime minister, Perceval, with that narrow cunning and selfish spirit which marked his whole public career, was, to use an expression of his own, starving the war in the Peninsula, despite Lord Wellington's energetic remonstrances from the field.

In this balanced state, it was essential that the battle should not be fought except on terms of advantage, and those terms were not to be had. Wellington, reinforced from Halifax and England, had indeed more than seventy thousand men under arms, and the enemy not more than fifty thousand; nevertheless, the latter could from the advantage of position bring more soldiers into the fight. The Portuguese army had in six months lost four thousand men by death, four thousand by discharges, and ten thousand by desertion. Thirty thousand recruits had come in, therefore the numbers were increased, but efficiency for great operations was diminished; and every department was neglected by a government which neither paid nor fed its soldiers. The Spanish auxiliaries, ill-governed and turbulent, quarrelled with the Portuguese, and their generals were not able in war nor amenable to better officers. The heights of Almada being naked, twelve thousand men were required on the left bank of the Tagus, and two British divisions were necessarily kept in the lines, because the French at Alcanhete were nearer to Torres Vedras than the allies were at Cartaxo. Reynier also might break out from Santarem during an attack on Pernes, wherefore ten thousand men were wanting to hold him in check; and thus the disposable troops, comprehending soldiers of three nations and many recruits, would have fallen short of forty-five thousand: but Masséna could bring nearly all his men to one point, because a few would have sufficed to watch the British division on the left of the Tagus and at Santarem.

Wellington's experience was not at this period equal to his adversary's; and the attack was to be made in a heavy difficult country, where the Alviella, the Almonda and other rivers, greatly swelled by incessant rain, furnished a succession of defensive lines to Masséna, and in case of defeat the means of carrying off two-thirds of his army. Victory might crown the attempt, but the stakes were unequal. If Masséna lost a third of his force, the ninth corps could have replaced it. If the allies failed, the lines were gone and with them the whole Peninsula. Wellington thought the relief of

the northern provinces, perhaps of Andalusia, would reward a victory; but those objects might be obtained without fighting, and
a battle would bring the greatest part of the French troops in Spain
upon him without bringing the Spaniards to his side. 'I cannot forget', he wrote to Lord Liverpool, 'that last year I brought upon
myself and General Cuesta not less than five corps d'armée, and
the king's guards and reserve, more than equal to a sixth corps;
and when Castille and the north of Spain was cleared of the enemy,
not a man was put in the field by those provinces, nor even one
raised!' These things considered, it was judged better to remain on
the defensive, to strengthen the lines, to forward the works at
Almada, to perfect the discipline of the Portuguese troops, to
improve the organization of the militia in rear of the enemy, and
to remedy the evils occasioned by the patriarch's faction.

*   *   *

The difficulty of communication was always a stumbling-block for
the French combinations in Spain. At this time Napoleon had remodelled the organization of his troops in a manner to give Masséna
great relief. The king's force was to be diminished, Soult's was to
be augmented; Drouet was to join Mortier with eleven thousand
of the ninth corps, the remainder of which was to be incorporated
in the divisions of the army of Portugal under Clausel and Foy.
Marmont was to supersede Ney with the sixth corps, Loison was
removed to the second corps, and Bessières was to send six thousand
men to Ciudad Rodrigo in support of General Claparède. Seven
thousand of the young guards were to occupy Zamora in observation of the Galicians, and the remainder were to be at Valladolid
with strong cavalry posts between to insure frequent intelligence
of what was passing in Portugal. These dispositions, at an earlier
period would have enabled Masséna to adopt any line of operations
without regard to his original base, and made his command easier
by removing captious subordinates; but they did not reach the
armies until a late period, and in the end of February the French
forces about Santarem being reduced to fifty thousand fighting men,
exclusive of Drouet's troops about Leiria, could no longer defend
their extended positions against Wellington's projected attack.
Hence when the Prince of Essling knew from the fidalgos [Portu-
guese notables affected to him] that the long-expected reinforcements from England had landed at Lisbon on the 2nd of March, he
commenced his retreat, and on the 6th all his positions were void.
   Masséna decided to gain the Mondego, but with intent to halt

behind it and reduce Oporto with a detachment. For he calculated
that the junction of the ninth corps and other troops from Leon
would raise his force to seventy thousand men, and enable him to
remain there until greater means were prepared for a renewed
advance against Lisbon by both banks of the Tagus, with an intermediate corps on the Zezere after the emperor's original scheme.
This design involved, as a preliminary step, a flank march, with
more than ten thousand sick men and all the army stores, under the
beard of an able adversary: yet this he effected like a great commander.

Commencing by the destruction of ammunition and all guns not
horsed, he passed his sick and baggage by degrees upon Thomar,
keeping only his fighting men in front and strongly indicating an
intention to pass the Zezere. But when the impediments had gained
two marches, Ney suddenly assembled the sixth corps and the
cavalry on the Lys near Leiria as if to advance against Torres
Vedras, thus holding Wellington in suspense while the second and
eighth corps, quitting Santarem, Tremes and Alcanhete in the night
of the 5th, fell back by Pernes upon Torres Novas and Thomar, and

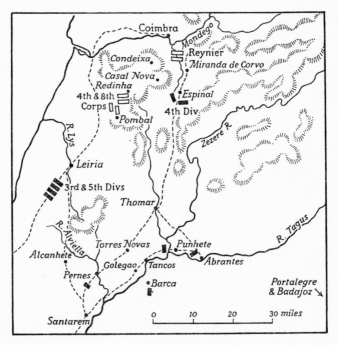

POMBAL

destroyed the bridges on the Alviella behind them. Next morning the boats were burnt at Punhete, and Loison retreated by the road of Espinal to cover the flank of the main line of retreat; he was followed by Reynier; but the rest of the army made rapid concentric marches towards a position in front of Pombal. The line of movement to the Mondego was thus secured, and four days gained; for Wellington, although knowing a retreat was in progress, could take no decided step lest he should open the lines to his adversary. Nevertheless he had made Beresford close towards Abrantes the 5th, and on the 6th, finding at daylight that the Santarem camp was abandoned, he followed Reynier with his own force.

Thomar seemed the French point of concentration, but as their boats were supposed to be still at Punhete, General Stewart was directed to cross the Tagus at Abrantes with the greatest part of Beresford's troops; the light division moved to Pernes where the broken bridge was rapidly restored, and the first, fourth and sixth divisions, with two brigades of cavalry, marched on Golegao. When it was found that Masséna had burned his boats, the Abrantes bridge was floated down the Tagus for Stewart to cross and move by the shortest line upon Thomar, and on that point also the divisions at Golegao were directed. The line of retreat being then clearly pronounced for the Mondego, the main body halted at Thomar, but the light division, the German hussars and the royal dragoons followed the 8th corps and took two hundred prisoners. During this march, in an obscure place among the hills, a large house was discovered filled with starving persons. Above thirty women and children were already dead, and sitting by the bodies were fifteen or sixteen living beings, of whom only one was a man, and all so enfeebled as to be unable to swallow the little food that could be offered to them. The youngest had fallen first, all the children were dead, none were emaciated, but the muscles of their faces were invariably drawn transversely, giving a laughing appearance unimaginably ghastly. The man seemed most eager for life, the women patient and resigned, and they had carefully covered and arranged the bodies of the dead!

While part of the army thus tracked the French, the third and fifth divisions moved from Torres Vedras upon Leiria, and the Abrantes' boats dropped down the river to Tancos to form a new bridge; that effected, the second and fourth divisions and some cavalry coming back from Thomar, recrossed the Tagus to succour Badajoz; and in that view also Beresford, who had remained at Barca, sent a brigade of cavalry to Portalegre.

Wellington, misled by a letter from Trant, by information obtained in Santarem, and by Masséna's first movements, thought on the 7th the retreat would be by Puente Murcella; on the 8th he trembled for Coimbra; but the 9th, the prince, instead of continuing his retrograde movement, concentrated the fourth and eighth corps and Montbrun's cavalry on a high table-land in front of Pombal, where the light division skirmished with the advanced posts, and in a cavalry fight the Germans took some prisoners. This was perplexing. To fight with advantage it would be necessary to bring up the troops destined to relieve Badajoz. To decline battle would be giving up Coimbra and the untouched country behind the Mondego to Oporto, and Masséna would retire as a conqueror. While thus embarrassed, Wellington received letters from Badajoz saying the place could hold out for a month, which decided the question; the fourth division and the heavy cavalry, then at Tancos on march for the Alemtejo, were recalled, General Nightingale was sent with a brigade of the first division and some horse by Espinal to follow Reynier, and the rest of the army closed concentrically upon Pombal. How dangerous a captain Masséna could be was here proved. He had maintained an army for nearly six months in a country supposed to be incapable of sustaining it for fifteen days, and carried it off with consummate skill. Moving the 4th, it was the 11th before sufficient troops could be assembled to fight him at Pombal; in these seven days he executed a very difficult operation, gained four marches, and organized his retreat; had rain fallen the first day, the allies could not have brought artillery by those bad roads; but he had before sent off or destroyed all his guns, except a few light pieces.

If the great error of relinquishing Coimbra be excepted, Masséna displayed infinite ability, but withal a harsh and ruthless spirit. The burning of Redinha, Condexia, Miranda de Corvo, and many villages on the route, covered his movements, and something may be attributed to the disorder of a forced retreat; but the town of Leiria and convent of Alcobaça, though out of the line, were given to the flames by express orders. The laws of war, rigorously interpreted, authorize such examples when the inhabitants take arms, yet it can only be justly done to overawe and not to revenge defeat: but every horror making war hideous attended this dreadful retreat! Distress, conflagration, death, in all modes! from wounds, from fatigue, from water, from the flames, from starvation: on every side of unlimited ferocity! I myself saw a peasant hounding on his dog to devour the dead and dying, and the spirit of cruelty once unchained smote even the brute creation; for on the 15th, Masséna, to diminish the encumbrances, ordered the destruction of some beasts of burthen, and the inhuman fellow charged with the execution ham-stringed five hundred asses and left them to starve. Being thus found by the British army, the mute yet deep expression of pain and grief visible in their looks wonderfully aroused the fury of the soldiers: and so little weight has reason with the multitude when opposed by a momentary sensation, that no quarter would have been given to any prisoner at that moment, and a humane feeling would have led to direct cruelty. The French have however been accused of crimes which they did not and could not commit; such as the driving of all women above ten years of age into their camp at Redinha, near which there were neither men nor women to be driven! The country was a desert! They have been also charged by the same writer with the mutilating of John the First's body in the convent of Batalha, during Masséna's retreat; whereas the body of that monarch had been wantonly pulled to pieces, and carried off by British officers during the retreat to the lines!

Masséna entered Portugal with sixty-five thousand men, and his reinforcements while at Santarem were about ten thousand; he repassed the frontier with forty-five thousand; the invasion therefore cost him thirty thousand men, of which fourteen thousand might have fallen by the sword or been taken. Not more than six thousand were lost during the retreat; but had Wellington, unrestrained by political considerations, attacked him vigorously at Redinha, Condeixa, Casal Nova and Miranda de Corvo, half the French army would have been destroyed, though with great loss to the assailants: a retreating army should fight as little as possible.

When the French reached the Agueda, their cavalry detachments, heavy artillery and convalescents, again augmented the army to more than fifty thousand men, but the fatigues of the retreat and the want of provisions would not suffer them to show a front to the allies; wherefore, drawing two hundred thousand rations from Rodrigo, they fell back to Salamanca, and Wellington invested Almeida. The light division then occupied Gallegos and Espeja, the rest of the army was disposed in villages on both sides of the Coa, and the headquarters were transferred to Villa Formosa, where Colonel Waters, who had been taken near Belmonte during the retreat, rejoined the army. He had refused his parole, and when carried to Ciudad Rodrigo, rashly consulted the Spaniard in whose house he was lodged about escaping; the man betrayed counsel, but his servant detesting the treachery secretly offered his own aid – Waters told him to get the rowels of his spurs sharpened, nothing more, for his design was one of open daring. He was placed under the guard of four *gens d'armes*, and when near Salamanca, the chief, who rode the only good horse of the party, alighted for a moment, whereupon Waters gave the spur to his own mare, a celebrated animal, and galloped off! It was an act of incredible resolution and hardihood, for he was on a wide plain, and before him and for miles behind him the road was covered with the French columns; his hat fell off, and thus marked he rode along the flank of the troops; some encouraged, others fired at him, and the *gens d'armes*, sword in hand, were always close at his heels. Suddenly he broke at full speed between two of the columns, gained a wooded hollow, and having thus baffled his pursuers, evaded the rear of the enemy's army and the third day reached head-quarters, where Lord Wellington, knowing his resolute, subtle character, had caused his baggage to be brought, observing that he would not be long absent!

*   *   *

On the 25th, Masséna reached Ciudad Rodrigo, and the 27th, his advanced guard felt the light division from Espeja to Marialva. Wellington arrived the 28th, and immediately concentrated the main body of the allies behind the Duas Casas river. The Azava was swollen and difficult to ford, and the enemy continued to feel the line of outposts until the 2nd of May, when, the waters having subsided, the French army came out of Ciudad Rodrigo, and the light division, after a slight skirmish of horse at Gallegos, commenced a retrograde movement, from that place and from Espeja, upon Fuentes de Oñoro. The country immediately in rear of those villages was wooded as far as the Duas Casas, but an open plain, separating the two lines of march, offered the enemy's powerful cavalry an opening to cut off the retreat; they neglected the opportunity, and the separated brigades remained unmolested in the woods bordering the plain until midnight, when they resumed their march and crossed the Duas Casas at Fuentes de Oñoro. That village had escaped injury during the previous warfare, although occupied alternately by French and English during a whole year. Every family was well known to the light division, and it was with deep regret and anger they found that the British troops preceding them had pillaged it, leaving only shells of houses, where three days before a friendly population had been living in comfort. This wanton and disgraceful act was felt so deeply throughout the army, that eight thousand dollars were afterwards collected for the poor despoiled people, yet the injury sunk deeper than the atonement.

Lord Wellington had resolved not to risk much for his blockade. Masséna he knew could bring down superior numbers; because the Portuguese troops continued to be so neglected by their government that they were starving under arms; the infantry abandoned their colours or dropped from exhaustion by thousands, the cavalry was entirely ruined, and a general dispersion was feared. Nevertheless, when the trial came, his warlike spirit would not let him go back; he could not indeed with only thirty-two thousand infantry, twelve hundred cavalry in bad condition and forty-two guns face Masséna on the plains beyond the Duas Casas; but he occupied a table-land between the Turones and Duas Casas, the left at Fort Concepcion, the centre opposite the village of Alameda, the right behind Fuentes de Oñoro. This line was five miles long, yet the Duas Casas, flowing in a deep ravine, covered his front; and the French dared not march by their right on Almeida because he would then have crossed the ravine at Alameda and Fuentes de Oñoro, and have fallen on their flank; hence, to cover the blockade, it sufficed to have the fifth division near Fort Concepcion, and the sixth opposite Alameda: the first and third divisions were concentrated in mass about cannon-shot behind Fuentes de Oñoro, where the table-land turned back on the Turones, becoming rocky and harsh as it approached that river.

Masséna came up three columns abreast. The cavalry, the sixth corps and Drouet's division threatened Fuentes de Oñoro; the eighth and second corps moved against Alameda and Fort Concepcion, menacing the allies' left; the light division, therefore, after passing the Duas Casas, reinforced the sixth division. Loison, without waiting for Masséna's orders, fell upon Fuentes de Oñoro, which was occupied by five battalions picked from the first and third divisions. Most of the houses were in the bottom of the ravine, but an old chapel and some buildings on a craggy eminence overhanging one end gave a prominent point for rallying. The low parts were vigorously defended, yet the violence of the attack, and the cannonade, made the British abandon the streets, and they could scarcely maintain the upper ground about the chapel. Colonel Williams, the commanding officer, fell badly wounded, and the fight was critical when the twenty-fourth, the seventy-first and the seventy-ninth regiments, marching down from the main position, charged roughly, and drove the French quite over the Duas Casas. During the night

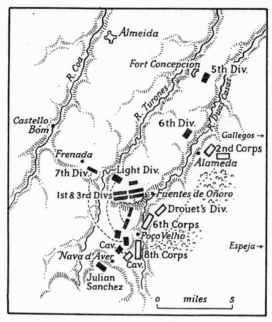

FUENTES DE OÑORO

the detachments were withdrawn, and the three succouring regiments were left in the village where two hundred and sixty of the
allies and somewhat more of the French had fallen.

On the 4th Masséna, accompanied by Bessières, who had brought
up fifteen hundred cavalry and a battery of the imperial guard,
examined all the line and made dispositions for the next day. His
design was to hold the left of the allies in check with the second
corps, and turn their right with the remainder of the army. Forty
thousand French infantry and five thousand horse, with thirty-six
pieces of artillery, were under arms; they had shown in the action
of the 3rd that their courage was not abated, and it was a very
audacious resolution to receive their battle.

It was Masséna's intention to commence the attack at day-break
on the 5th, but a delay of two hours occurred and all his movements
were descried. The eighth corps, withdrawn from Alameda, and
supported by all the French cavalry, was seen marching above the
village of Poço Velho, which with its swampy wood, was occupied
by Houstoun's left, his right being thrown back in the plain towards
Nava d'Aver. The sixth corps and Drouet's division took ground
to their own left, still keeping a division in front of Fuentes de

Oñoro, menacing that point; at this sight, the light division and the English horse hastened to the support of Houstoun, while the first and third divisions made a movement parallel to that of the sixth corps. The latter, however, drove the left wing of the seventh division from the village of Poço Velho, and it was fast gaining ground in the wood also when the riflemen of the light division arriving there restored the fight. The French cavalry then passed Poço Velho and commenced forming in order of battle on the plain, between the wood and the hill of Nava d'Aver where Julian Sanchez was posted. He immediately retired across the Turones, partly in fear, but more in anger, because his lieutenant, having foolishly ridden close up to the enemy making many violent gestures, was mistaken for a French officer and shot by a soldier of the guards before the action commenced.

Montbrun occupied himself with this weak *partida* for an hour, and when the guerrilla chief was gone, turned the right of the seventh division and charged the British cavalry which had moved up to its support; the combat was unequal, for by an abuse too common, so many men had been drawn from the ranks as orderlies to general officers and for other purposes, that not more than a thousand English troopers were in the field. The French therefore drove in all the cavalry outguards at the first shock, cut off Ramsay's battery of horse artillery, and came sweeping in upon the reserves of cavalry and upon the seventh division. Their leading squadrons, approaching in a disorderly manner, were partially checked by fire, but a great commotion was observed in their main body; men and horses were seen to close with confusion and tumult towards one point where a thick dust and loud cries, and the sparkling of blades and flashing of pistols, indicated some extraordinary occurrence. Suddenly the multitude became violently agitated, an English shout pealed high and clear, the mass was rent asunder, and Norman Ramsay burst forth sword in hand at the head of his battery; his horses, breathing fire, stretched like greyhounds along the plain, the guns bounded behind them like things of no weight, and the mounted gunners followed close, with heads bent low and pointed weapons, in desperate career. Captain Brotherton of the fourteenth dragoons, seeing this, instantly rode forth and with his squadron shocked the head of the pursuing troops, and General Charles Stewart, joining in the charge, took the French Colonel Lamotte, fighting hand to hand; but then the main body of the French came on strongly and the British cavalry retired behind the light division, which was immediately thrown into squares. The seventh division, which was more advanced, did the same, but the horsemen were upon them first, and some were cut down. The mass however stood firm, and the Chasseurs Britanniques, ranged behind a loose stone wall, poured such a fire that their foes recoiled and seemed bewildered.

While these brilliant actions were passing on the right, the French made progress in the wood of Poço Velho, and as the English divisions were separated and the right wing turned, it was evident the battle would soon be lost if the original concentrated position above Fuentes de Oñoro was not quickly regained. The seventh division were therefore ordered to cross the Turones and move down the left bank to Frenada, while the light division retired over the plain; the cavalry covered this movement; and the first and third divisions and the Portuguese were at the same time placed on the steppe of land before described, perpendicular to the ravine of Fuentes de Oñoro. General Craufurd, who had resumed the command of the light division, covered Houstoun's passage across the Turones, and then retired slowly over the plain in squares, followed by the French horsemen who continually outflanked but never dared to assail him; however, in approaching the new line, they sabred some of the foot guards under Colonel Hill, making that officer and fourteen men prisoners, and then continuing their course were repulsed by the forty-second regiment.

Many times Montbrun feigned to charge Craufurd's squares, but always he found them too dangerous to meddle with, and this crisis passed without a disaster, yet there was not during the whole war a more perilous hour. For Houstoun's division was separated from the position by the Turones, and the vast plain was covered with commissariat animals and camp-followers, with servants, led horses, baggage and country people, mixed with broken detachments and piquets returning from the woods, all in such confused concourse that the light division squares appeared but as specks; and close behind those surging masses were five thousand horsemen, trampling, bounding, shouting for the word to charge. Fifteen guns were up with the French cavalry, the eighth corps was in order of battle behind them, the woods on their right were filled with Loison's skirmishers; and if that general, pivoting upon Fuentes, had come forth with the sixth corps while Drouet assailed the village, and the cavalry had made a general charge, the loose crowds of noncombatants and broken troops would have been violently dashed against the first division, to intercept its fire and break its ranks, and the battle would have been lost. No such effort was made, the plain was soon cleared, the British cavalry took post behind the centre, and the light division formed a reserve on the right of the first division, having its riflemen amongst the rocks to connect it with Houstoun, who had reached Frenada and been there joined by Julian Sanchez. At sight of this new front, so deeply lined, the French stopped short and opened their guns, tearing the close masses of the allies; but twelve English guns soon replied so briskly that the violence of the French fire abated and their cavalry drew back out of range. A body of infantry then attempted to glide down the ravine of the Turones, but they were repulsed by the riflemen and the light companies of the guards, and the action on this side resolved itself into a cannonade.

Meanwhile a fierce battle was going on at Fuentes de Oñoro. There Drouet was to have carried the village when Montbrun's cavalry had turned the right of the line; he delayed his attack for two hours and thus marred the combination; but finally he assailed with such fierceness and vigour that the three British regiments, overmatched in numbers and unaccustomed to the desultory fighting of light troops, were pierced and divided. Two companies of the seventy-ninth were taken, Colonel Cameron of that regiment was mortally wounded, and the lower part of the village was lost: the upper part was however stiffly held and the rolling of musketry was incessant. Had the attack been made earlier, and all Drouet's division thrown frankly into the fight while the sixth corps moving through the wood closely turned the village, the passage must have been forced and the left of the new position out-flanked. But now Wellington, having all his reserves in hand, detached considerable masses to the support of the regiments in Fuentes; and as the French continued also to reinforce their troops, the whole of the sixth corps and part of Drouet's division were finally engaged. At one time the fighting was on the banks of the stream and amongst the lower houses, at another on the rugged heights and around the chapel, and some of the enemy's skirmishers penetrated completely through towards the main position; yet the village was never entirely abandoned by the defenders, and in one charge the seventy-first, seventy-ninth and eighty-eighth regiments, led by Colonel M'Kinnon, broke a heavy mass near the chapel and killed a great number of French. This fighting lasted until evening, when the lower part of the town was abandoned by both parties, the British remaining at the chapel and crags, the French retiring a cannon shot from the stream. After the action a brigade of the light division relieved the regiments in the village, a slight demonstration made by the second corps, near Fort Concepcion, was checked by a battalion of the Lusitanian legion, and both armies remained in observation. Fifteen hundred men and officers, of which three hundred were prisoners, constituted the loss of the allies. That of the enemy was estimated at five thousand, upon the erroneous supposition that four hundred dead were lying about Fuentes de Oñoro. All armies make rash estimates on such occasions. Having had charge to bury the carcases immediately about the village, I found only one hundred and thirty bodies, one-third being British.

X

Albuera

Masséna had fought his last campaign. Wellington always considered him his most skilful opponent, but he never again held active command, and was replaced by Marmont. The British general's name was beginning to echo round Europe. One by one, the great French captains had been checked – Junot, Soult, Victor and now Masséna. In Paris, Napoleon was embroiled in dynastic ambitions with his marriage to the Austrian Emperor's daughter, and never ventured to the Peninsula again. Wellington, still hopelessly outnumbered, had not yet been able to assert his strategic superiority. The British government, although Napier exaggerates their faults, had not yet grasped the full potentialities either of their general or his situation.

One door to Spain lay open with the French evacuation of the Portuguese frontier fortress of Almeida in the north. Another clanged shut in the south as the Spaniards surrendered Badajoz to Marshal Soult. To meet this threat Wellington divided his army to reinforce Beresford in Estremadura.

WHEN MARMONT had recovered the garrison of Almeida, he withdrew most of his forces to Salamanca. Wellington then placed the first, fifth, sixth and light divisions and the cavalry on the Azava, under Spencer, and directed the third and seventh divisions and the second German hussars upon Badajoz. On the 15th of May, hearing that Soult, hitherto reported by Beresford to be entirely on the defensive, was advancing at the head of a powerful army into Estremadura, he went in all haste to that province, but ere he could arrive a great battle had been fought with extraordinary fury.

While awaiting the adhesion of the Spanish generals, Beresford had fixed his headquarters at Almendralejos, but Latour Maubourg remained at Guadalcanal, and his parties foraged the most fertile tracts between the armies. To check them, Penne Villemur was reinforced with five squadrons, and Colonel Colborne was detached with a brigade of the second division, two Spanish guns and two squadrons of cavalry, to curb their inroads and give confidence to the people. Colborne, having a fine talent for war, by rapid marches and sudden changes, in concert with Villemur, confused the enemy's parties, intercepting several convoys and forced the French to quit Fuente Ovejuna, La Granja, Azuaga and many other frontier towns; and he imposed upon Latour Maubourg with so much address that the latter, imagining a great force was at hand, fell back to Constantino. Having cleared the country on that side, he made a singularly bold attempt to surprise the fortified post of Benalcazar. For riding on to the drawbridge with a few officers, in the grey of the morning, he summoned the commandant to surrender as a means of saving himself from the Spanish army which was close at hand and would give no quarter; the French officer was amazed at the appearance of the party, but too resolute to yield, and Colborne, perceiving the attempt had failed, galloped off under a few straggling shots, and then taking to the mountains, rejoined the army without any loss.

On the 5th of May William Stewart, having two squadrons of horse, six field-pieces and three brigades of infantry, had invested Badajoz on the left of the Guadiana; on the 7th the remainder of the infantry, reinforced by two thousand Spaniards under Carlos d'España, encamped in the woods near the fortress, Madden's Portuguese horse were in observation near Merida, and a troop of horse-artillery, coming from Lisbon, was attached to the English

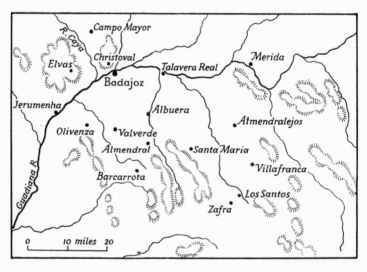

BADAJOZ

cavalry which remained near Los Santos and Zafra. The flying
bridge, moved from Jerumenha, was re-established near the mouth
of the Caya, yet was soon drawn back because, the right bank of the
Guadiana being still open, some French horse had come down the
river. On the 8th however, General Lumley invested Christoval
with a brigade of the second division, four light Spanish guns, the
seventeenth Portuguese infantry and two squadrons of horse drafted
from the garrison of Elvas. These troops did not arrive simultaneously at the point of assembly, which delayed the operation, and
sixty French dragoons moving under the fire of the place maintained
a sharp skirmish beyond the walls.

This was the first serious siege undertaken by the British in the
Peninsula and, to the discredit of the English government, no army
was ever worse provided for such an enterprise. The engineer
officers were zealous; and notwithstanding some defects in the constitution and customs of their corps, tending rather to make regimental than practical scientific officers, many of them were well
versed in the theory of their business: yet the ablest trembled at
their destitution in all things necessary to real service. Without a
corps of sappers and miners, without a private soldier who knew
how to carry on an approach under fire, they were compelled to
attack fortresses defended by the most warlike, practised and
scientific troops of the age; and the best officers and the finest soldiers sacrificed themselves in a lamentable manner, to compensate
for the negligence and incapacity of a government, always ready
to plunge the nation into war without the slightest care of what was
necessary to obtain success. The sieges carried on by the British
in Spain were a succession of butcheries, because the commonest
materials and means necessary for their art were denied to the engineers.

The chief engineer, Colonel Fletcher, proposed to breach the
castle, while batteries established on the right bank of the Guadiana
took the defence in reverse. False attacks against the Pardaleras
and Picurina were to be made by re-opening Soult's trenches; yet
it was necessary to reduce San Christoval before the batteries to
take the castle in reverse could be constructed, and Captain Squire
was directed to break ground there on the night of the 8th. The
moon shone bright, he was ill provided with tools, and exposed to a
destructive musketry from the fort, and to shot and shell from the
town; nevertheless he worked with great loss until the 10th, when
the French made a furious sally and carried the battery. They were
immediately driven back by the reserves, but the allies pursued too

far and, being taken in flank and front with grape, lost four hundred men. At this time five engineers had fallen and seven hundred officers and soldiers of the line had been inscribed upon the bloody list of victims offered to this Moloch, and only one small battery against an outwork was completed! On the 11th it opened, and before sunset the fire of the enemy had disabled four of its five guns and killed many more of the besiegers: nor could any other result be expected, because the concert essential to success in double operations, whether in sieges or the field, was totally neglected by Beresford. Squire's single work was exposed to the undivided fire of the fortress before the approaches against the castle were even commenced; and two distant batteries, which had been constructed at the false attacks, scarcely attracted the notice of the enemy. To check future sallies, a second battery was erected against the bridgehead, but this was also overmatched; and then Beresford, having received intelligence that the French army was in movement, arrested the progress of all the works. On the 12th, believing this information premature, he directed the trenches to be opened against the castle; yet the intelligence was true, and being confirmed at twelve o'clock in the night, the working parties were again drawn off and measures taken to raise the siege.

Marshal Soult had resolved to succour Badajoz the moment he heard of Beresford's appearance at Campo Mayor, and he rejoiced that the latter's tardiness gave Phillipon time to organize a good defence, and himself a respite to tranquillize Andalusia and arrange measures for resisting the allies in the Isla during his absence. With that object he had immediately commenced several additional fortifications in the city of Seville. He thus deceived Beresford, who believed that he was trembling for his own province. Nothing could be more fallacious. There were seventy thousand fighting men in Andalusia; and Drouet, who had quitted Masséna immediately after the battle of Fuentes de Oñoro, was likewise in march for that province by the way of Avila and Toledo, bringing with him eleven thousand men.

On the 10th of May, Soult quitted Seville with three thousand heavy dragoons, thirty guns and two strong brigades of infantry under the command of Werlé and Godinot. This force, drawn from the first and fourth corps and Dessolles' reserve, entered Olalla the 11th, and was there joined by Maransin. Godinot then marched by Constantino to reinforce the fifth corps, which was falling back from Guadalcanal in consequence of Colborne's operations. The 13th, a junction was effected with Latour Maubourg,

who assumed the command of the heavy cavalry, resigning the
fifth corps to Girard, who immediately advanced to Los Santos.
The 14th, Soult reached Villa Franca, and being then within thirty
miles of Badajoz, caused his heaviest guns to fire salvos during the
night, to give notice of his approach to the garrison. This expedient
failed, and the 15th, in the evening, the French army was concentrated at Santa Marta.

Beresford, perplexed by bad intelligence, did not raise the siege
until the night of the 12th, and then contrary to the earnest representations of the engineers, who promised to win the place in three
days. This promise was nought, and if it had been good Soult would
yet have surprised him in his trenches: his firmness therefore saved
the army, and his arrangements for carrying off the stores were
admirably executed. The artillery and platforms were removed in
the night of the 13th, and at twelve o'clock on the 15th, all the
guns and stores on the left bank were over the Guadiana, the
gabions and fascines burned, and the flying bridge removed. These
transactions were well masked by the fourth division, which in
concert with the Spaniards maintained the investment; it was only
by a sally on the rear-guard, in which the Portuguese piquets were
roughly treated, that the governor knew the siege was raised, and
of the cause he was still ignorant.

In a conference with the Spanish generals, held the 13th at Valverde, it was agreed to receive battle at Albuera. Ballesteros' and
Blake's corps being then united at Barcarrota, were falling back
upon Almendral, and Blake engaged to have them at Albuera before
twelve o'clock on the 15th. Badajoz was the centre of an arc, sweeping through Valverde, Albuera and Talavera Real, and Blake
undertook to watch the roads on the right, while Beresford and
Mendizabel watched those in the centre, and Madden those on the
left. The British being chiefly in the woods near Valverde could
reach Albuera by a half march, and no part of the arc was more than
four leagues from Badajoz. Soult on the 14th was at Los Santos
eight leagues distant, and Beresford, thinking he could not be forestalled on any point, kept the fourth division in the trenches. On the
14th Colborne came in, Madden retired to Talavera Real, Blake
reached Almendral, and the Anglo–Portuguese cavalry under
General Long fell back to Santa Marta, where they were joined by
Blake's dragoons.

In the morning of the 15th the Anglo-Portuguese army occupied
the left of the Albuera position, a ridge about four miles long,
having the Aroya Val de Sevilla in rear, and the Albuera river in

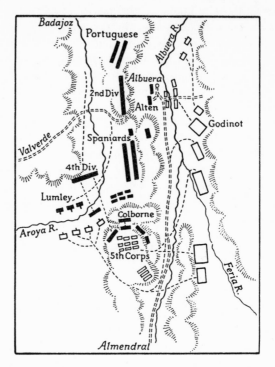

THE BATTLE OF ALBUERA

front. The right was prolonged towards Almendral, the left towards Badajoz, the ascent from the river was easy, and the ground
practicable for cavalry and artillery. In advance of the centre were
the bridge and village of Albuera, the former commanded by a
battery, the latter occupied by Alten's German brigade. Behind the
Germans, the second division under William Stewart formed one
line, the right on a commanding hill over which the Valverde road
passed, the left on the road of Badajoz, beyond which the order of
battle was continued, in two lines, by the Portuguese troops under
Hamilton and Collins. The right of the position, stronger, higher
and broader than any other part, was left for Blake's army; because
Beresford, thinking the hill on the Valverde road to be the key of
the position, as protecting his only line of retreat, was desirous to
secure it with the best troops. The fourth division and the infantry
of the fifth Spanish army were still before Badajoz; but Cole had
orders to send the seventeenth Portuguese regiment to Elvas, to
throw a Spanish battalion into Olivenza, to bring his second brigade,

which was before Christoval, over the Guadiana, by a ford above Badajoz, if practicable, and to be in readiness himself to march at the first notice.

In this posture of affairs, about three o'clock in the evening of the 15th, Beresford being at some distance on the left, the whole mass of the allied cavalry, closely followed by the French light horsemen, came in from Santa Marta, and finding no infantry beyond the Albuera in support, passed that river. Thus the wooded heights on the right bank were abandoned to the enemy, whose force and dispositions were thereby effectually concealed, and the strength of the allies' position was already sapped. Beresford immediately formed a temporary right wing with the cavalry and artillery, stretched his piquets along the road to Almendral, and sent officers to hasten Blake's movements; but that general, who had only a few miles of good road to march and had promised to be in line at noon, did not reach the ground before eleven at night, and his rear did not arrive before three in the morning of the 16th. Meanwhile, as the French army was now evidently in front, Cole and Madden were called up; the order failed to reach the latter, but Cole brought the infantry of the fifth army, two squadrons of Portuguese cavalry and two brigades of the fourth division into line between eight and nine o'clock; his third brigade, unable to pass the Guadiana above Badajoz, was in march by Jerumenha. The Spanish troops joined Blake on the right, the two brigades of the fourth division were drawn up in columns behind the second division, and the Portuguese squadrons were sent to reinforce Otway, whose horsemen, of the same nation, were pushed forwards in front of the left wing. The principal mass of the allied cavalry was concentrated behind the centre, and Beresford, dissatisfied with General Long, gave the command to General Lumley.

Thirty thousand infantry, more than two thousand cavalry and thirty-eight pieces of artillery, eighteen being nine-pounders, were in line, but the British infantry, the pith of battle, did not exceed seven thousand, and already Blake's arrogance was shaking Beresford's authority. Soult had forty guns, four thousand veteran cavalry and nineteen thousand chosen infantry, all of one discipline, animated by one spirit and amply compensated for their inferiority in number by their fine organization and their leader's capacity, which was immeasurably greater than his adversary's. He had examined the position without hindrance on the evening of the 15th, and hearing that the fourth division was left at Badajoz and Blake would not arrive before the 17th, resolved to attack next

morning, for he had detected the weakness of Beresford's dispositions. The hill in the centre, commanding the Valverde road, was
undoubtedly the key of the position if an attack was made parallel
to the front; but Soult saw that on the right a high rough broken
table-land trended back towards the Valverde road and looked into
the rear of Beresford's line. Hence, if he could suddenly place his
masses there, he might roll up the allies on their centre and push
them into the valley behind; the Valverde road could then be seized,
the retreat cut, and the strong French cavalry would complete the
victory.

Beresford's right and Soult's left approximated, being only
divided by a hill, about cannon-shot distance from either, which was
separated from the allies by the Albuera and from the French by a
rivulet called the Feria. This height, neglected by Beresford, was
ably made use of by Soult. During the night he placed behind it the
greatest part of the artillery under General Ruty, the fifth corps
under Girard, the heavy cavalry under Latour Maubourg, thus concentrating fifteen thousand men and thirty guns within ten minutes'
march of Beresford's right wing: yet that general could neither see
a man, nor draw a sound conclusion as to the real plan of attack.
The light cavalry, the brigades of Godinot and Werlé with ten
guns remained. They were placed in the woods near the confluence
of the Feria with the Albuera. Werlé was in reserve, Godinot was
to attack the bridge and village, to bear against the centre, attract
Beresford's attention, separate his wings, and double up his right
when the principal attack should be developed.

During the night and morning, sixteen thousand additional men
had come into line under Blake and Cole, but so defective were
Beresford's dispositions that Soult adhered to his first plan, and at
nine o'clock, just before Cole arrived, Godinot emerged from the
wood in one heavy column preceded by ten guns. Being flanked by
the light cavalry and followed by Werlé, he made for the bridge and
with a sharp cannonade and musketry endeavoured to force the
passage. At the same time General Briché led two hussar regiments
further down the river to observe Otway's horsemen, and the French
lancers passed the river above the bridge. The third dragoon guards
drove the lancers back to their own side, and Dickson's Portuguese
guns, opening from a rising ground above the village, ploughed
Godinot's column which crowded to the bridge though the river
was fordable above and below. Beresford, observing Werlé did not
follow closely, judged the chief effort would be on the right, and
therefore ordered Blake to form part of his first and all his second

line on the broad part of the hills at right angles to their actual
front. Then drawing the Portuguese infantry of the left wing to
the centre, he sent one brigade to support Alten at the bridge, and
directed Hamilton to hold the remainder in columns of battalions
as a general reserve. The thirteenth dragoons he posted near the
river, above the bridge, and sent the second division to support
Blake. The horse artillery, the cavalry under Lumley and the fourth
division also took ground to the right, and were posted, the horsemen and guns on a small plain behind the Aroya, the fourth division
in an oblique line half musket shot behind them. This done, Beresford galloped to Blake, for that general had refused to change his
front, and with great heat told Colonel Hardinge, the bearer of the
order, the real attack was at the village and bridge. A second time
he was entreated to obey, yet remained obstinate until Beresford
arrived in person, and then only assented because the enemy's
columns were actively menacing his flank: yielding to this evidence,
he changed his front, yet with such pedantic slowness that Beresford, impatient of his folly, took the direction in person.

Great was the confusion and the delay thus occasioned, and ere
the troops were completely formed the French were amongst them.
For scarcely had Godinot engaged Alten's brigade, when Werlé,
leaving only a battalion of grenadiers to support the former and
some squadrons to watch the thirteenth dragoons and connect the
attacks, countermarched with the remainder of his division and
rapidly gained the rear of the fifth corps as it was mounting the
hills on the right of the allies. The great mass of light cavalry also
quitted Godinot's column, crossed the river Albuera above the
bridge, ascended the left bank at a gallop, and sweeping round the
rear of the fifth corps joined Latour Maubourg's dragoons, who were
already facing Lumley's squadrons. Thus half an hour had sufficed
to render Beresford's position nearly desperate. Two-thirds of the
French were in compact order of battle perpendicular to his right,
and his army, composed of different nations, was making a disorderly
change of front. Vainly he tried to get the Spanish line advanced
to make room for the second division to support it; the French guns
opened, their infantry threw out a heavy musketry fire, and their
cavalry, outflanking the front and menacing different points, put the
Spaniards in disorder: they fell fast and went back.

Soult thought the whole army was yielding, he pushed forward
his columns, his reserves mounted the hill behind him, and General
Ruty placed all the French batteries in position; but then William
Stewart reached the foot of the height with a brigade of the second

division under Colborne, who, seeing the confusion above, desired
to form in order of battle previous to mounting; but Stewart, whose
boiling courage generally overlaid his judgment, led up in column
of companies, passed the Spanish right, and attempted to open a
line by succession of battalions as they arrived. The enemy's fire
was found too destructive to be borne passively, and the foremost
troops charged; but then heavy rain obscured the view, four regiments of French hussars and lancers galloped in from the right at
the moment of advancing, and two-thirds of the brigade went down:
the 31st regiment only, being on the left, formed square and resisted,
while the French horsemen, riding furiously about, trampled the
others and captured six guns. The tumult was great, a lancer fell
upon Beresford, who, being a man of great strength, put aside the
lance and cast him from his saddle; and then a shift of wind blowing
aside the smoke and mist, Lumley perceived the mischief from the
plain below, and sending four squadrons up against the straggling
lancers cut many of them off: Penne Villemur's Spanish cavalry was
also directed to charge the French horsemen in the plain, and they
galloped forwards until within a few yards of their foes but then
shamefully fled.

During this first unhappy effort of the second division, so great
was the disorder that the Spaniards in one part fired without
cessation, though the British troops were before them; in another
part, flying before the lancers, they would have broken through the
twenty-ninth, then advancing to succour Colborne, but with a stern
resolution that regiment smote friends and foes without distinction
in their onward progress. Meanwhile Beresford, finding the main
body of the Spaniards would not advance, seized an ensign by the
breast and bore him and his colours by main force to the front, yet
the troops did not follow, and the coward ran back when released
from the marshal's iron grasp. In this crisis the weather which had
ruined Colborne's brigade saved the day. Soult could not see the
whole field of battle, and kept his heavy columns inactive when the
decisive blow might have been struck. His cavalry indeed began to
hem in that of the allies, yet the fire of the horse-artillery enabled
Lumley, covered as he was by the bed of the Aroya and supported
by the fourth division, to check them on the plain; Colborne still
remained on the height with the thirty-first regiment, the British
artillery, under Julius Hartman, was coming fast into action, and
William Stewart, who had escaped the charge of the lancers, was
again mounting the hill with Houghton's brigade, which he brought
on with equal vehemence, but in a juster order of battle. The day

CHARGE OF THE POLISH LANCERS AT ALBUERA

then cleared and a dreadful fire poured into the thickest of the French columns convinced Soult that the fight was yet to be won.

Houghton's regiments reached the height under a heavy cannonade, and the twenty-ninth, after breaking through the fugitive Spaniards, was charged in flank by the French lancers; yet two companies, wheeling to the right, foiled this attack with a sharp fire, and then the third brigade of the second division came up on the left, and the Spanish troops under Zayas and Ballesteros at last moved forward. Hartman's artillery was now in full play, and the enemy's infantry recoiled, but soon recovering, renewed the fight with greater violence than before. The cannon on both sides discharged showers of grape at half range, the peals of musketry were incessant, often within pistol-shot, yet the close formation of the French embarrassed their battle, and the British line would not yield them an inch of ground or a moment of time to open their ranks. Their fighting was however fierce and dangerous. Stewart was twice wounded, Colonel Duckworth was slain, and the intrepid Houghton, having received many wounds without shrinking, fell and died in the very act of cheering on his men. Still the struggle continued with unabated fury. Colonel Inglis, twenty-two officers and more than four hundred men out of five hundred and seventy who had mounted the hill, fell in the fifty-seventh alone; the other regiments were scarcely better off, not one-third were standing in any: ammunition failed, and as the English fire slackened a French column was established in advance upon the right flank. The play of the guns checked them a moment, but in this dreadful crisis Beresford wavered! Destruction stared him in the face, his personal resources were exhausted, and the unhappy thought of a retreat rose in his agitated mind. He had before brought Hamilton's Portuguese into a situation to cover a retrograde movement; he now sent Alten orders to abandon the bridge and village of Albuera, and to take, with his Germans and the Portuguese artillery, a position to cover a retreat by the Valverde road. But while the commander was thus preparing to resign the contest, Colonel Hardinge had urged Cole to advance with the fourth division; and then riding to the third brigade of the second division, which, under the command of Colonel Abercrombie, had hitherto been only slightly engaged, directed him also to push forward into the fight. The die was thus cast, Beresford acquiesced, Alten received orders to retake the village, and this terrible battle was continued.

The fourth division was composed of two brigades: one of Portuguese under General Harvey; the other, under Sir William

Myers, consisting of the seventh and twenty-third regiments was called the fuzileer brigade: Harvey's Portuguese were immediately pushed in between Lumley's dragoons and the hill, where they were charged by some French cavalry, whom they beat off, and meantime Cole led his fuzileers up the contested height. At this time six guns were in the enemy's possession, the whole of Werlé's reserves were coming forward to reinforce the front column of the French, the remnant of Houghton's brigade could no longer maintain its ground, the field was heaped with carcasses, the lancers were riding furiously about the captured artillery on the upper parts of the hill, and behind all, Hamilton's Portuguese and Alten's Germans, now withdrawing from the bridge, seemed to be in full retreat. Soon however Cole's fuzileers, flanked by a battalion of the Lusitanian legion under Colonel Hawkshawe, mounted the hill, drove off the lancers, recovered five of the captured guns and one colour, and appeared on the right of Houghton's brigade, precisely as Abercrombie passed it on the left.

Such a gallant line, issuing from the midst of the smoke and rapidly separating itself from the confused and broken multitude, startled the enemy's masses, which were increasing and pressing onwards as to an assured victory; they wavered, hesitated, and then vomiting forth a storm of fire, hastily endeavoured to enlarge their front while a fearful discharge of grape from all their artillery whistled through the British ranks. Myers was killed, Cole and the three colonels, Ellis, Blakeney and Hawkshawe, fell wounded, and the fuzileer battalions, struck by the iron tempest, reeled and staggered like sinking ships; but suddenly and sternly recovering, they closed on their terrible enemies, and then was seen with what a strength and majesty the British soldier fights. In vain did Soult with voice and gesture animate his Frenchmen, in vain did the hardiest veterans break from the crowded columns and sacrifice their lives to gain time for the mass to open out on such a fair field; in vain did the mass itself bear up, and, fiercely striving, fire indiscriminately upon friends and foes, while the horsemen hovering on the flank threatened to charge the advancing line. Nothing could stop that astonishing infantry. No sudden burst of undisciplined valour, no nervous enthusiasm weakened the stability of their order, their flashing eyes were bent on the dark columns in their front, their measured tread shook the ground, their dreadful volleys swept away the head of every formation, their deafening shouts overpowered the dissonant cries that broke from all parts of the tumultuous crowd, as slowly and with a horrid carnage it was pushed by the incessant vigour of the attack to the farthest edge of the hill. In vain did the French reserves mix with the struggling multitude to sustain the fight, their efforts only increased the irremediable confusion, and the mighty mass, breaking off like a loosened cliff, went headlong down the steep: the rain flowed after in streams discoloured with blood, and eighteen hundred un- wounded men, the remnant of six thousand unconquerable British soldiers, stood triumphant on the fatal hill!

While the fuzileers were striving on the height, the cavalry and Harvey's brigade continually advanced, and Latour Maubourg's dragoons, being also battered by Lefebre's guns, retired before them; yet still they threatened the fuzileers with their right, and with their left prevented Lumley's horsemen from falling on the defeated infantry. Alten's Germans had now retaken the village with some loss, and Blake's first line, which had not been engaged, was directed to support them; Hamilton's and Collins's Portuguese, forming a mass of ten thousand fresh men, were brought up to support the fuzileers and Abercrombie's brigade, and at the same time Zayas, Ballesteros and España advanced. Nevertheless, so rapid was the execution of the fuzileers that the enemy's infantry were never attained by these reserves, which yet suffered severely; for Ruty got the French guns altogether and worked them with prodigious activity while the fifth corps still made head; and when the day was irrevocably lost, he regained the other side of the Albuera and protected the passage of the broken infantry.

Beresford was too hardly handled to pursue. He formed a fresh line with his Portuguese, parallel to the hill from whence Soult had advanced and where the French were now rallying with their usual celerity; the action still continued at the bridge, but Godinot's division and the connecting battalion of grenadiers were soon after- wards withdrawn, and all firing ceased before three o'clock. The serious fighting had endured four hours, and in that time nearly seven thousand of the allies and above eight thousand of their adversaries were struck down. Three French generals were wounded, two slain, and eight hundred soldiers so badly hurt as to be left on the field. On Beresford's side only two thousand Spaniards and six hundred Germans and Portuguese were killed or wounded; hence it is plain with what a resolution the pure British fought, for they had but eighteen hundred men left standing! The laurel is nobly won when the exhausted victor reels as he places it on his bleeding front.

The trophies of the French were five hundred unwounded

prisoners, a howitzer and several stand of colours. The British had nothing of that kind to boast of, but the horrid piles of carcasses within their lines told with dreadful éloquence who were the conquerors; and all that night the rain poured down, and the river and the hills and the woods resounded with the dismal clamour and groans of dying men. Beresford, compelled to place his Portuguese in the front line, was oppressed with the number of his wounded; they far exceeded the sound amongst the British soldiers, and when the piquets were posted few men remained to help the sufferers. In this cruel situation he sent Hardinge to demand assistance from Blake; but with him wrath and mortified pride were predominant, and he refused, saying it was customary with allied armies for each to take care of its own men. Morning came, and both armies kept their respective positions, the wounded still covering the field of battle, the hostile lines still menacing and dangerous. The greater number had fallen on the French side, the best soldiers on that of the allies; and the dark masses of Soult's powerful cavalry and artillery, covering all his front, seemed alone able to contend again for the victory. The right of the French also appeared to threaten the Badajoz road, and Beresford in gloom and doubt awaited another attack; but on the 17th, the third brigade of the fourth division came up by a forced march from Jerumenha, which enabled the second division to retake their former ground between the Valverde and the Badajoz roads, and on the 18th Soult retreated.

XI

Political Burdens

Napier considered his hero, Wellington, to be beset and thwarted by a combination of political villainy and incompetence in Britain, Spain and Portugal. His radical prejudices against his own government, and George Canning in particular, who held the post of Foreign Secretary from 1807–09, warped his judgment and caused violent controversy when his work was published. Wellington, although often exasperated, could deal with politicians and his position was greatly strengthened by the appointment of one brother, Lord Wellesley, to the Cabinet and another, Henry, as envoy to the Spanish junta. The tide of the war was about to turn, with Napoleon drawing many good troops back from Spain in preparation for his invasion of Russia. In spite of his political difficulties and continuing numerical inferiority, Wellington was ready to pounce.

IT WAS CLEAR that merely to defend Portugal with enormous loss of treasure and of blood would be a ruinous policy; and to redeem the Peninsula, the Spaniards must be brought to act more reasonably. The national character and the extreme ignorance of public business, military and civil, which distinguished the generals and statesmen, rendered this a very difficult task: yet Wellington, finding the English power weak to control, its influence as weak to sway the councils of Spain, hoped by industry, patience and the glory of his successes to acquire a personal ascendancy which would enable him to direct the resources of the whole Peninsula towards a common object. The difficulty of attaining that ascendancy can, however, only be made clear by a review of the intercourse between the British government and the Spanish authorities, from the first bursting out of the insurrection to the period now treated of: a review which will disclose the utter unfitness of Mr Canning to conduct great affairs. For heaping treasure, stores, arms, flattery, upon those who were unable to bear the latter or use the former beneficially, he neglected all persons who were capable of forwarding the cause. And neither in the choice of his agents, nor in his instructions to them, nor in his estimation of the value of events, did he discover wisdom or diligence, although he covered his misconduct at the moment by his glittering oratory.

When the Spanish deputies first applied for the assistance of England, Mr Charles Stuart, who was the only regular diplomatist sent to Spain, carried to Coruña such a sum as made up with previous subsidies one million of dollars for Galicia alone. The deputies from Asturias had demanded five millions of dollars, and one was paid in part of their demand; but when this was known, two millions more were demanded for Galicia and not refused: yet the first point in Mr Canning's instructions to Mr Stuart was, '*to enter into no political engagements*'. Mr Duff, consul at Cadiz, also carried out a million of dollars for Andalusia, the junta asked for three or four millions more, and the demands of Portugal although less extravagant were very great; thus above sixteen millions of dollars were craved, and more than four millions, including the gift to Portugal, had been sent. The remainder was not denied, and the amount of arms and stores given may be estimated by the fact that eighty-two pieces of artillery, ninety-six thousand muskets, eight hundred thousand flints, six millions and a half of ball-cartridges, seven thousand five hundred barrels of powder and thirty thousand swords and belts had been sent to Coruña and Cadiz. The supply to the Asturians was in proportion, but Mr Canning's instructions to Mr Duff and other agents were still the same. '*His majesty had no desire to annex any conditions to the pecuniary assistance which he furnished to Spain.*'

Mr Canning said he considered the amount of money as nothing! yet he acknowledged specie was so scarce that it was only by a direct and secret understanding with the former government of Spain, under the connivance of France, that any considerable amount of dollars had been collected in England. 'Each province of Spain', he said, 'had made its own particular application, and the whole occasioned a call for specie such as had never before been made upon England at any period of its existence. There was a rivalry between the provinces with reference to the amount of sums demanded which rendered the greatest caution necessary. And the more so that the deputies were incompetent to furnish either information or advice upon the state of affairs in Spain', yet Mr Duff was commanded, by the man representing these astounding things to the junta of Seville, '*to avoid any appearance of a desire to overrate the merit and value of the exertions then making by Great Britain in favour of the Spanish nation, or to lay the grounds for restraining or limiting those exertions within any other bounds than those which were prescribed by the limits of the actual means of the country'*. In proof of Mr Canning's sincerity upon this head, he afterwards sent them two millions of dollars by Mr Frere, while the British army was without any funds at all! Moreover the supplies, so recklessly granted, being transmitted through subordinates and irresponsible persons, were absurdly and unequally distributed.

This obsequious extravagance produced the utmost arrogance on the part of the Spanish leaders, who treated the English minister's humble policy with the insolence it courted. When Mr Stuart reached Madrid, after the establishment of the supreme junta, that body, raising its demands upon England in proportion to its superior importance, required in the most peremptory language additional succours so enormous as to startle even the prodigality of the English government. Ten millions of dollars instantly, five hundred thousand yards of cloth, four million yards of linen for shirts and for the hospitals, three hundred thousand pair of shoes, thirty thousand pair of boots, twelve million of cartridges, two hundred thousand muskets, twelve thousand pair of pistols, fifty thousand swords, one hundred thousand arobas of flour, besides salt meat and fish! These were their demands, and when Mr Stuart's remonstrance compelled them to alter the insulting language of their note, they insisted the more strenuously upon having the succours, observing that England had as yet only done enough to set their force afloat, and that she might *naturally expect demands like the present to follow the first*. They desired also that the money should be furnished at once by bills on the British treasury, and at the same time required the confiscation of Godoy's property in the English funds!

Such was Mr Canning's opening policy. The sequel was worthy of the commencement. His proceedings with respect to the Erfurt proposals for peace, his injudicious choice of Mr Frere, his leaving of Mr Stuart without instructions for three months at the most critical period of the insurrection, and his management of affairs in Portugal and at Cadiz during Sir John Cradock's command, have been already noticed: and that he was not misled by any curious accordance in the reports of his agents is certain, for he was early and constantly informed of the real state of affairs by Mr Stuart. That gentleman was the accredited diplomatist, and in all important points his reports were very exactly corroborated by the letters of Sir John Moore, and by the running course of events; yet Mr Canning neither acted upon them nor published them, although he received all the idle vaunting accounts of subordinate civil and military agents with complacency, and published them with ostentation: thus encouraging the misrepresentations of ignorant men, increasing the arrogance of the Spaniards, deceiving the English nation, and as far as he was able misleading the English general.

Mr Stuart reached Coruña in July 1808, and on the 22nd of that month informed Mr Canning that the reports of successes in the south were not to be depended upon, seeing they increased exactly in proportion to the difficulty of communicating with the alleged scenes of action, and with the dearth of events, or the recurrence of disasters in the northern parts. He also assured him the numbers of the Spanish armies within his knowledge were by no means so great as they were represented. On the 26th of July he gave a detailed history of the Galician insurrection, by which he plainly showed that every species of violence, disorder, intrigue and deceit were to be expected from the leading people, that the junta's object was to separate Galicia from Spain, that so inappropriate was the affected delicacy of abstaining from conditions while furnishing succours, that the junta of Galicia was only kept in power by the countenance of England, evinced in her lavish supplies and by the residence of her envoy at Coruña. The interference of British naval officers to quell a political tumult had been asked for and had been successful; Mr Stuart had been entreated to meddle in the appointments of the governing members and in other contests for power which were daily taking place. In fine, the folly, peculation, waste and improvidence characterizing Spanish proceedings were by Mr Stuart forcibly laid before Mr Canning without altering the latter's egregious policy, or even attracting his notice: he even intimated to the ambitious junta of Seville that England would acknowledge its supremacy if the other provinces would consent, thus offering a premium for anarchy.

Mr Stuart was kept in a corner of the Peninsula whence he could not communicate freely with any other province, and where his presence materially contributed to cherish the project of separating Galicia; and this without a pretence, because there was a British admiral and consul, and a military mission at Coruña, all capable of transmitting local intelligence. Indeed, so little did Mr Canning care to receive his envoy's reports, that the packet conveying his despatches was ordered to touch at Gijon to receive the consul's letters, which caused the delay of a week when every moment was big with important events: a delay not to be remedied by the admiral on the station, because he had not even been officially informed that Mr Stuart was an accredited person! And when the latter, looking to the public interest, proceeded on his own responsibility to Madrid and finally to Andalusia, he found the evils springing from Mr Canning's inconsiderate conduct everywhere equally prominent. In the capital the supreme junta regarded England as a bonded debtor; and the influence of her diplomatist at Seville may be estimated from the following note written by Mr Stuart to Mr Frere upon the subject of permitting British troops to enter Cadiz. 'The junta refuse to admit General Mackenzie's detachment; you tell me it is merely from alarm respecting the disposition of the inhabitants of Seville and Cadiz. I am not aware of the feelings which prevail in Seville, but with respect to this town, whatever the navy or the English travellers may assert to the contrary, I am perfectly convinced there exists only a wish to receive them, and general regret and surprise at their continuance on board.'

Nor was the mischief confined to Spain. Frere, apparently tired of the presence of a man whose energy and talent were a continued reflection upon his own imbecile diplomacy, ordered Mr Stuart either to join Cuesta's army or to go by Trieste to Vienna; he chose the latter, because there was not even a subordinate political agent there, although this was the critical period which preceded the Austrian declaration of war against France in 1809. He was without formal powers as an envoy, yet his knowledge of the affairs of Spain, and his intimate personal acquaintance with many of the leading statesmen at Vienna, enabled him at once to send home the most exact information of the proceedings, the wants, the wishes and intentions of the Austrian government in respect to the impending war. But that great diversion for Spain, which with infinite pains had been brought to maturity by Count Stadien, was on the point of being abandoned because of Mr Canning's conduct. He had sent no minister to Vienna, and while he was lavishing millions upon the Spaniards without conditions, refused in the most haughty and repulsive terms the prayers of Austria for a subsidy, or even a loan, without which she could not pass her own frontier. When Mr Stuart suggested the resource of borrowing some of the twenty-five millions of dollars which were then accumulated at Cadiz, it was rejected because Mr Frere said it would alarm the Spaniards. Thus, the aid of a great empire with four hundred thousand good troops, was in a manner rejected in favour of a few miserable self-elected juntas in the Peninsula, while one-half the succours which they received and misused would have sent the whole Austrian nation headlong upon France; for all their landwehr was in arms, and where the emperor had only calculated upon one hundred and fifty battalions, three hundred had come forward voluntarily, besides the Hungarian insurrection. In this way Mr Canning proved his narrow capacity for business, and how little he knew either the strength of France, the value of Austria, the weakness of Spain or the true interests of England; although he had not scrupled, by petulant answers to the proposals of Erfurt, to confirm a war which he was so incapable of conducting. Instead of improving this great occasion, he angrily recalled Mr Stuart for having proceeded to Vienna without permission; the breach of form was with him of higher importance than the success of the object. Yet it is capable of proof that Mr Stuart's presence would have made the Austrians slower to negotiate after the battle of Wagram; and the Walcheren expedition [the abortive British landing in Holland north of the Scheldt, in which 40,000 troops were decimated by fever] would have been turned towards Germany, where a great northern confederation was ready to oppose France. The Prussian cabinet, in defiance of the king, or rather of the queen whose fears influenced the king's resolutions, only waited for that expedition to declare war, and it seems certain Russia would also have adopted that side.

The misfortunes of Moore's campaign, the folly and arrogance of the Spaniards, the loss of a British army in Walcheren, the exhausting England of troops and specie when she most needed both; finally the throwing Austria entirely into the hands of France, may be distinctly traced to Mr Canning's incapacity as a statesman. But through the whole of the Napoleonic war he was the evil genius of the Peninsula. He gave misplaced military power to Mr Villiers' legation in Portugal while he neglected the political affairs in that country; he sent Lord Strangford to Rio Janeiro whence all manner of mischief flowed; and when Mr Stuart succeeded Villiers at Lisbon, Mr Canning insisted upon having the enormous mass of intelligence received from different parts of the Peninsula translated before it was sent home – an act of undisguised indolence, which retarded the real business of the embassy, prevented important information from being transmitted rapidly, and exposed the secrets of the hour to the activity of the enemy's emissaries at Lisbon. In after times, when Napoleon returned from Elba and Mr Canning was by a notorious abuse of ministerial power sent ambassador to Lisbon, he complained that no archives of former embassies remained, and compelled Mr Stuart, then minister plenipotentiary at the Hague, to employ several hundred soldiers copying papers relating to the previous war, to be sent at great public expense to Lisbon, where they were to be seen in 1826 unpacked!

And while this folly was passing, the interests of Europe in general were neglected, and the particular welfare of Portugal seriously injured by another display of official importance still more culpable. It had been arranged that a Portuguese auxiliary force was to have joined the Duke of Wellington's army previous to the battle of Waterloo, and to have this agreement executed was the only business of importance which Mr Canning had to transact during his embassy. Marshal Beresford, well acquainted with the character of the Portuguese regency, had assembled fifteen thousand men, the flower of the old troops, perfectly equipped, with artillery baggage and all things needful to take the field: the ships were ready, the men willing to embark, and the marshal told the English ambassador that he had only to give the order and in a few hours the whole would be on board, warning him at the same time that in no other way could the thing be effected. This summary proceeding did not give Mr Canning an opportunity to record his own talents for negotiation, and he replied that it must be done by diplomacy; the Souza faction eagerly seized the opportunity of displaying their talents in the same line, they beat Mr Canning at his own weapons and, as Beresford had foreseen, no troops were embarked at all. Wellington was thus deprived of important reinforcements, the Portuguese were deprived of the advantage of supporting their army for several years on the resources of France, and of their share of the contributions from that country. Last and worst, those veterans of the Peninsula war, the strength of the country, were sent to the Brazils, where they all perished by disease or by the sword in the obscure wars of Don Pedro! If such errors may be redeemed, by an eloquence always used in defence of public corruption, and a wit that made human sufferings its sport, Mr Canning was an English statesman and wisdom has little to do with the affairs of nations.

When the issue of the Walcheren expedition caused a change of ministry, Lord Wellesley obtained the foreign office. Mr Henry Wellesley then replaced Mr Frere at Cadiz, and he and Mr Stuart received orders to demand guarantees for the due application of the British succours; those succours were more sparingly granted, and the envoys were directed to interfere with advice and remonstrances in all the proceedings of the respective governments to which they were accredited. Mr Stuart was even desired to meddle with the internal administration of the Portuguese nation; the

exertions and sacrifices of Great Britain, far from being kept out of
sight, were magnified, and the system adopted was in everything
a contrast to that of Mr Canning. But there was in England a
powerful, and as recent events have proved an unprincipled parliamentary opposition, and two parties in the cabinet. The one headed
by Lord Wellesley, who was anxious to push the war vigorously
in the Peninsula without much regard to the ultimate pressure upon
the people of his own country; the other headed by Mr Perceval
who sought only to maintain himself in power. Narrow, harsh,
factious and illiberal in everything relating to public matters, this
man's career was one of unmixed evil. His bigotry taught him to
oppress Ireland, but his religion did not deter him from passing a
law to prevent the introduction of medicines into France during a
pestilence; he lived by faction; he had neither the wisdom to support,
nor the manliness to put an end to the war in the Peninsula; and
his crooked contemptible policy was shown by withholding what was
necessary to sustain the contest and throwing on the general the
responsibility of failure.

With all the fears of little minds, he and his coadjutors awaited
the result of Wellington's operations in 1810. They affected to
dread his rashness, yet could give no reasonable ground for their
alarm; and their private letters were at variance with their public
instructions that they might be prepared for either event. They
deprived him without notice of his command over the troops at
Cadiz; they gave Graham power to furnish pecuniary succours to
the Spaniards at that place, which threw another difficulty in the
way of obtaining money for Portugal; and when Wellington complained of the attention paid to the unfounded apprehension of some
superior officers more immediately about him, he was plainly told
that those officers were better generals than himself. At the same
time he was with a pitiful economy ordered to dismiss the transports on which the safety of the army depended in the event of
failure! Between these factions there was a constant struggle, and
Wellington's successes in the field only furthered the views of
Perceval, because they furnished ground for asserting that due
support had been given to him. Such a result is to be always appre-
hended by English commanders. The slightest movement in war
requires a great effort, and is attended with many vexations which
the general feels acutely and unceasingly; the politician, believing
in no difficulties because he feels none, neglects the supplies, charges
disaster on the general and covers his misdeeds with words. The
inefficient state of the cabinet under both Canning and Perceval

may however be judged of by the following extracts, the writers of which as it is easy to perceive were in official situations.

'I hope by next mail will be sent something more satisfactory and useful than we have yet done in the way of instructions. But I am afraid the late O. P. riots have occupied all the thoughts of our great men here, so as to make them, or at least some of them, forget more distant but not less interesting concerns.'

'With respect to the evils you allude to as arising from the inefficiency of the Portuguese government, the people here are by no means so satisfied of their existence as you who are on the spot. Here we judge only of the results, the details we read over, but being unable to remedy, forget them the next day; and in the meantime, be the tools you have to work with good or bad, so it is that you have produced results so far beyond the most sanguine expectations entertained here by all who have not been in Portugal within the last eight months, that none inquire the causes which prevented more being done in a shorter time; of which indeed there seems to have been a great probability, if the government could have stepped forward at an earlier period with one hand in their pockets, and in the other strong energetic declarations of the indispensable necessity of a change of measures and principles in the government.'

'I have done everything in my power to get people here to attend to their real interests in Portugal, and I have clamoured for money! money! money! in every office to which I have had access. To all my clamour and all my arguments I have invariably received the same answer, *'that the thing is impossible'*. The prince himself certainly appears to be *à la hauteur des circonstances*, and has expressed his determination to make every exertion to promote the good cause in the Peninsula. Lord Wellesley has a perfect comprehension of the subject in its fullest extent, and is fully aware of the several measures which Great Britain ought and could adopt. But such is the state of parties and such the condition of the present government that I really despair of witnessing any decided and adequate effort on our part to save the Peninsula. The present feeling appears to be that we have done mighty things, and all that is in our power, that the rest must be left to all-bounteous Providence, and that if we do not succeed we must console ourselves by the reflection that Providence has not been so propitious to us as we deserved. This feeling you must allow is wonderfully moral and Christian-like, but still nothing will be done until we have a more vigorous military system, and a ministry capable of directing the resources of the nation to something nobler than a war of descents and embarkations.'

A more perfect picture of an imbecile administration could scarcely be exhibited, and it was not wonderful that Lord Wellington, oppressed with the folly of the Peninsula governments, should have often resolved to relinquish a contest that was one of constant risks, difficulties and cares, when he had no better support from England.

*   *   *

Having now brought the story of the war to that period, when, after many changes of fortune, the chances had become more equal and the fate of the Peninsula thrown between the contending powers, a prize for the readiest and boldest warrior, I would, ere it is shown how Wellington seized it, recall to the reader's recollection the previous vicissitudes of the contest. How, when the first or insurrectional epoch of the war had terminated successfully for the Spaniards, Napoleon vehemently broke and dispersed their armies and drove the British auxiliaries to embark at Coruña. How the war with Austria and the inactivity of Joseph rendered the emperor's victories unavailing and revived the confidence of the Spaniards. How Sir A. Wellesley, victorious on the Douro, marched into Spain, and though compelled by the great force of the enemy combined with Spanish bad faith to retreat, as Moore from the same causes had retreated, his advance had freed Galicia as Moore's advance had previously saved Andalusia. How the Peninsulars, owing to the exertions of their allies, still possessed the Asturias, Galicia, Portugal, Andalusia, Murcia, Valencia and Catalonia, and every important harbour and fortress except Santander, Santoña, Barcelona and San Sebastian.

How Wellington, appreciating the advantages which an invaded people possess in their numerous lines of operation, counselled the Spaniards and forced the Portuguese to adopt a defensive war; and with the more reason that England, abounding beyond all nations in military resources and invincible as a naval power, could form with her ships a secure exterior floating base or line of dépôts round the Peninsula, and was ready to employ her armies as well as her squadrons in the struggle. How the Spaniards, unheeding these admonitions, sought great battles and in a few months lost the Asturias, Andalusia, Estremadura, Aragon and the best fortresses of Catalonia, and were again laid prostrate and helpless before the enemy. How the victorious French armies moving onwards in swelling pride dashed against the rocks of Lisbon, and then receded, broken and refluent, until the English general once more stood a conqueror on the frontier of Spain. Had he then retaken

Badajoz and Rodrigo he would have gloriously finished the fourth
or defensive epoch of the war; but being baffled partly by skill,
partly by fortune, factiously opposed by the Portuguese regency,
thwarted by the Spanish government, only half supported by his
own cabinet, and pestered by the follies of all three, he was reduced
to seeming inactivity while the French added Tarragona and the
rich kingdom of Valencia to their conquests.

Up to this period the invasion, although diversified by occasional
disasters on the part of the invaders, had been progressive. The
tide, sometimes flowing sometimes ebbing, still gained upon the
land, and if the Spaniards partially arrested its progress it was
because England urged their labour and renovated their strength;
but no firm barrier, no solid dike had been opposed save by the
British general in Portugal; and even there the foundation of his
work, sapped by the trickling waters of folly and intrigue, was
sliding away. By what surprising efforts of courage and judgment he
secured it, shall now be shown; but as the field operations were
always more influenced by political considerations than military principles it is necessary again to show the state of all parties to the war.

France, abounding in riches and power, was absolute mistress
of Europe from the Pyrenees to the Vistula; but Napoleon, pursuing
his system of continental exclusion, was hurrying on to a new war
so vast that even his power was strained to meet it. The Peninsula
already felt relief from this cause. The dread of his arrival ceased
to influence the operations of the allied army in Portugal, and many
able French officers were recalled; it was known that the Poles and
imperial guards were to be withdrawn, and hence the scale of offensive projects was necessarily contracted. Conscripts and young
soldiers instead of veterans, and in diminished numbers, were now
to be expected; and in the French army there was an oppressive
sense of the enormous exertions required to bring two such mighty
wars to a happy conclusion. The Peninsulars were cheered by seeing
so powerful a monarch as the czar rise in opposition to Napoleon,
and the English general's anticipations of a northern war, which
was the great basis of his calculations, were realized. He had not
indeed been strong enough hitherto to meet eighty thousand French
in battle and there were more than three hundred thousand in Spain;
but hope rose when he saw the great warrior of the age turn personally from the contest in the Peninsula to carry to another point
four hundred thousand veterans whose might seemed sufficient to
subdue the world.

One immediate beneficial effect of this impending war was to restore Joseph's authority over the French armies in Spain; for when the emperor was distant the supreme control could only be given to the king, though it revived, and with greater virulence, former jealousies and bickering. And as Joseph was obstinate in his policy, and the pride of the French generals was not lessened, pretexts for disputes were never wanting and their mischievous nature may be gathered from one example. In November the king, pressed for money, sold the magazines of corn collected near Toledo for the army of Portugal and without which the latter could not exist; Marmont, regardless of the political scandal, immediately sent troops to recover the magazines by force and desired the purchasers to reclaim their money from the monarch!

Cadiz was in 1811 the focus of all disorder. The government, weak and dishonest, used many pitiful arts to extract money from England: no subterfuge was too mean. When Blake was going to Estremadura, previous to the battle of Albuera, Bardaxi entreated the British envoy to grant a loan or a gift, without which Blake, he said, could not move; Mr Wellesley refused because a large debt was already due to the legation, and the next morning a Spanish ship of war from America landed a million and a half of dollars! In July the regency and the Cortes were without influence, the former was held in universal merited contempt; and notwithstanding the vast sums received, every service was famished while the treasury was declared empty and there was no probability of any further remittances from America. The temper of the public was soured towards England, the press openly assailed the British character, and all things tended so evidently towards anarchy that Mr Wellesley declared 'Spanish affairs to be then worse than they had been at any previous period of the war'.

At first the Cortes had been swayed by priests and lawyers who cherished the inquisition and opposed all free institutions; now it was chiefly led by a liberal or rather democratic party averse to the British influence, and in August a new constitution opposed to the aristocratic principle was promulgated. That many sound abstract principles of government were clearly and vigorously laid down in the scheme of the constitution cannot be denied; the complicated oppressions of the feudal system were swept away with a bold and just hand. But of what avail, as regarded the war, was the enunciation of principles which were never attempted to be reduced to practice! What encouragement was it to the soldier to be told he was a free man fighting for a constitution as well as for national independence, when he saw the authors of that constitution corruptly revelling in wealth which should have clothed and armed and fed him! What was nominal equality to him when he saw incapacity rewarded, crimes and treachery unpunished in the rich, the poor and patriotic oppressed! He laughed to scorn those who could find time to form the constitution of a great empire but could not find time or honesty to cherish the men who were to defend it!

Many grievous reports of misfortune and treachery, some true some false, were soon spread by the enemies of democracy; and at the most critical period of the war in Valencia they excited a popular commotion to sweep away the Cortes. There was withal a strong disposition in the great to submit to the invader, because the remaining estates of the nobility being chiefly in Valencia they were willing to save their last resources at the cost of national independence. The monks and friars, furious at the suppression of the inquisition, were the chief plotters everywhere.

In November the public cry for a new regency became general, and it was backed by the English plenipotentiary. Nevertheless the matter was deferred upon divers pretexts, the democratic party gained strength in the Cortes, and the anti-British feeling appeared more widely diffused than it really was, because some time elapsed before the church and aristocratic party discovered that the secret policy of England was the same as their own. It was so however, even to the upholding of the inquisition which it was ridiculously asserted had become objectionable only in name; as if the framework of tyranny existing, there could ever be wanting the will to fill it up. Necessity alone induced the British cabinet to put on a smooth countenance towards the Cortes; and the negotiation for mediation was used by the Spaniards merely as a ground for demanding loans, subsidies and succours in kind, which they used in fitting out new expeditions against the revolted colonists, the complaints of the British legation being quite disregarded.

Mr Wellesley, seeing fatal consequences to the war must ensue if a stop was not put to the misconduct of the regency, sent Mr Vaughan, secretary of legation, to acquaint the British cabinet with the facts and solicit a more firm and decided course of policy. He desired to have the subsidies settled by treaty that the people of Spain might really know what England had done and was still doing for them; for on every occasion, arms, clothing, ammunition, loans, provisions, guns, stores, and even workmen and funds to form foundries, were obtained wasted and embezzled; the people knew nothing of this extravagant generosity, and the receivers and masters were heaping calumnies on the donors.

On the 21st of January, 1812, after a secret discussion of twenty-four hours, a new regency of five members, two being Americans, was proclaimed. They were the Duke of Infantado then in England, Henry O'Donnel, Admiral Villarvicencio, Joachim de Mosquera, and Ignacios de Ribas. Each was to have the presidency by rotation for six months, and they commenced beneficially. O'Donnel, being friendly to the British alliance, proposed a military feast to restore harmony between the English and Spanish officers; he made many changes in the department of war and finances, consulted the British generals, disbanded several bad regiments and incorporated the men with other battalions; he also reduced many inefficient and malignant colonels, and striking off from the pay lists all unemployed and absent officers they were found to be five thousand in number!

But all this activity was simply to obtain an English loan! Failing of that, the old disputes broke out, the democratic spirit gained strength in the Cortes, the anti-English party augmented, the press abounded in libels impugning the good faith of the British nation, especially with respect to Ceuta, for which however there was some plausible ground of suspicion, because the acquisition of that fortress had actually been proposed to Lord Liverpool. The new regency, as violent as their predecessors with respect to America, disregarded the mediation and, having secretly organized in Galicia an expedition against the colonies, supplied it with artillery furnished from England for the French war, and then, under another pretence, demanded money of the British minister to forward this iniquitous folly.

The political state of Portugal in October 1811 was such that all evils were aggravated. The return of the royal family was put off, and the military reform which Beresford was at Lisbon to effect thwarted or retarded by the regency. Mr Stuart indeed forced a repair of the bridges and roads in Beira, and the partial supply of the fortresses; and though opposed by Redondo, for the first time he made the regency substitute a military chest and commissariat instead of the old 'Junta de Viveres'. Forjas and Redondo then disputed for the custody of the new chest; and when Mr Stuart explained to the one that the intent being to separate the money of the army from that of the civil departments, his claims were incompatible with such an object, and to the other that the conduct of his own department was already more than he could manage, both were offended. This new source of disorder was only partially closed by withholding the subsidy until they yielded.

Great malversations in the revenue were also discovered; and a plan to enforce an impartial exaction of the 'decima', which was drawn up by Nogueira at the desire of Wellington, was so ill-received by those whose illegal exemptions it attacked, that the Souzas immediately placed themselves at the head of the objectors out of doors. Nogueira then modified it, but the Souzas still opposed, and as Wellington, judging the modification to be an evasion of the principle, would not recede from the first plan, a permanent dispute and a permanent evil were thus established by that pernicious faction. In fine, not the Souzas only but the whole regency, thinking the war was virtually decided in their favour, were intent to drive the British away by disgusting the general.

*   *   *

On these things the reader should reflect. They are the proofs that English steel, English gold, English genius, English influence, fought and won the battle of Spanish independence; and this is not said as a matter of boast, although it was very glorious! but as a useful lesson of experience. On the other hand, the prodigious strength of France under Napoleon, that strength which could at once fight England and Austria and aim at the conquest of the Peninsula and the reduction of Russia at the same moment of time, and all with good hope of success, creates amazement! Let it not be said the emperor's efforts in the war of Spain were feeble, for if the insurrectional epoch which was unexpected and accidental be set aside, the grandeur of his efforts will be found answerable to his gigantic reputation. In 1809 the French army was gradually de-creased by losses and drafts for the Austrian war from three hundred and thirty-five thousand to two hundred and twenty-six thousand. But in 1810 it was again raised to three hundred and sixty-nine thousand, and fluctuated between that number and three hundred and thirty thousand until August, 1811, when it was again raised to three hundred and seventy-two thousand men with fifty-two thousand horses! And yet there are writers who assert that Napoleon neglected the war in Spain! But so great is the natural strength of that country, that had the firmness of the nation in battle and its wisdom in council been commensurate with its constancy in resist-ance, even this power, backed by the four hundred thousand men who marched to Russia, would scarcely have sufficed to subdue it. But weak in fight and steeped in folly, the Spaniards would have been trampled in the dust but for the man whose great combinations are now to be related.

The nicety, quickness, prudence and audacity of Wellington's operations cannot however be justly estimated without an exact knowledge of his political, local and moral position. His political difficulties have been described, his moral situation was simply that of a man who felt that all depended upon himself, and that he must by rapid and unexpected strokes effect in the field what his brother could not effect in the cabinet while the power of the Perceval faction was prevalent in England.

His own troops were not in good plight. He had indeed received reinforcements, but the infantry had served at Walcheren and exposure to night air or even slight hardships threw them by hundreds into the hospital, while the new regiments of cavalry, inexperienced and not acclimated, were found, men and horses, so unfit for duty that he sent them to the rear. The pay of the army was three months in arrear, the supplies, brought up with difficulty, were very scanty – half and quarter rations were often served, sometimes the troops were without any bread for three days consecutively, and their clothing was so patched that scarcely a regiment could be known by its uniform. Chopped straw, the only forage, was very scarce, the regimental animals were dying of hunger, corn was rarely distributed save to the generals and staff, and even the horses of the artillery and the old cavalry suffered; the very mules of the commissariat were pinched and the muleteers eight months in arrears of pay. The cantonments about the Coa and Agueda were unhealthy from the rains, twenty thousand men were in hospital and, deduction made for other drains, only fifty-four thousand of both nations, including garrisons and posts of communication, were under arms. To finish the picture, a sulky apathy in the Portuguese regency was becoming more hurtful than the former active opposition. Yet these distresses Wellington with surprising subtlety turned to the advantage of his present designs; for the enemy were aware of the misery in the army and their imagination magnified it; and as the allied troops were scattered for relief from the Gata mountains to the Douro, from the Agueda to the Mondego immediately after the battering-train entered Almeida, both armies concluded that the guns were to arm that fortress as a cover to the extended country quarters which necessity had forced upon the British general. Not even the engineers employed in the preparations knew more than that a siege or the simulation of a siege was in contemplation; but when it was to be attempted, or that it would be attempted at all, none knew – even the quarter-master general, Murray, was suffered to go home on leave with the full persuasion that no operation would take place before spring.

THE TAKING OF CIUDAD RODRIGO

In the new cantonments abundance of provisions and dry weather, for in Beira the first rains generally subside during December, stopped the sickness and restored three thousand men to the ranks; and the privations had in no manner weakened the moral courage of the troops. The old regiments were incredibly hardy and experienced in all things necessary to sustain their strength and efficacy; the staff was well practised; and Lord Fitzroy Somerset, military secretary, had established such an intercourse between the head-quarters and the battalion chiefs, that the latter had, so to speak, direct communication with the general-in-chief upon all the business of their regiments, a privilege which stimulated the enthusiasm and zeal of all. For the regimental commanders being generally very young men, the distinctions of rank were not rigidly enforced, and the merit of each officer was consequently better known and more earnestly supported when promotion and honours were to be obtained. By this method Lord Fitzroy acquired an exact knowledge of the moral state of each regiment, rendered his own office important and gracious with the army, and with such discretion and judgment that the military hierarchy was in no manner weakened: all the daring young men were excited and, being unacquainted with the political difficulties of their general, anticipated noble triumphs which were happily realized.

The favourable moment for action so long watched for by Wellington came at last. An imperial decree had again remodelled the French armies. That of Aragon was directed to give up four divisions to form a new corps under Reille, called the *'army of the Ebro'*, its head-quarters to be at Lerida. The army of the south was recomposed in six divisions of infantry and three of cavalry, exclusive of the garrison of Badajoz. Marshal Victor returned to France discontented, for he was one of those whose reputation had been abated by this war, and his divisions were given to Conroux, Barrois, Villatte, Laval, Drouet, Daricau, Peyremont, Ligeon and the younger Soult. The reserve of Monthion was broken up, and the army of the north, destined to maintain the great communications with France and to reduce the partidas on that line, was ordered to occupy the districts round Santander, Sebastian, Burgos and Pamplona, and to communicate by the left with the new army of the Ebro; it was also exceedingly reduced in numbers, for the imperial guards, seventeen thousand strong, being required for the Russian war marched in December to France. All the Polish battalions, the skeletons of the cavalry regiments and several thousand choice men destined to fill the ranks of the old guard were drafted, so that not

less than forty thousand of the best soldiers were withdrawn, and
the maimed and worn-out men being sent to France at the same
time, the force in the Peninsula was diminished by sixty thousand
men.

The head-quarters of the army of the north arrived at Burgos in
January, and a division was immediately sent to drive Mendizabel
from the Montaña de Santander. But as this arrangement weakened
the grand line of communication with France, Marmont was ordered
to abandon the valley of the Tagus and fix his head-quarters at
Valladolid or Salamanca. Ciudad Rodrigo, the sixth and seventh
governments, and the Asturias, were also placed under his authority, by which Souham and Bonnet's division, forming together
about eighteen thousand men, were added to his army, but the
former general returned to France. These two divisions were however extended for the sake of supplies from the Asturias to Toledo,
and as Montbrun was then near Valencia and Soult's attention distracted between Tarifa and Hill's pursuit of Drouet, the French
were employed over an immense tract of country. Marmont also,
deceived by the seemingly careless winter attitude of the allies, left
Rodrigo unprotected and Wellington instantly jumped with both
feet on the devoted fortress.

XII

Ciudad Rodrigo and Badajoz
1812

Two formidable fortresses had to be reduced before Wellington could break into Spain. Ciudad Rodrigo on the northern frontier with Portugal and Badajoz on the southern. He was short of both time and equipment for such enterprises, being woefully deficient in heavy siege guns and the means to transport them. Hazarding all, on New Year's Day 1812, he moved first against the northern bastion.

THIRTY-FIVE thousand men, cavalry included, were disposable for the siege of Ciudad Rodrigo. When the place was closely examined, it was found that two convents which flanked and strengthened the bad Spanish entrenchments round the suburbs had been fortified; and on the greater Teson an enclosed and palisadoed redoubt, called Francisco, was constructed and supported by two guns and a howitzer placed on the flat roof of a convent having the same name. All the ground was rocky except on the Tesons, and though the ramparts were there better covered by out works and could fire more heavily on the trenches, it was, following the English general's views, most assailable, because elsewhere the batteries must have been placed on the edge of the counterscarp before they could see low enough to breach: this would have been a tedious process, whereas the smaller Teson furnished the means of striking over the crest of the glacis at once, and a deep gulley offered cover for the miners. It was therefore resolved to storm fort Francisco, form a lodgment there, open the first parallel along the greater Teson, place thirty-three pieces in counter-batteries to ruin the defences, and drive the besieged from the convent of Francisco. Afterwards, working forward by the sap, it was proposed to construct breaching batteries on the lesser Teson and blow in the counterscarp, while seven guns, battering a weak turret on the left, opened a second breach with a view to turn any retrenchment behind the principal breach.

Four British divisions and Pack's Portuguese laboured in the

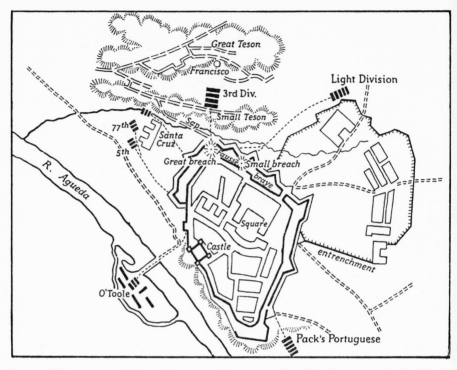

THE SIEGE OF CIUDAD RODRIGO

siege; but on the right bank of the Agueda there was neither fuel
nor cover and the troops therefore kept their quarters on the hither
bank, having, although a severe frost and fall of snow had set in, to
ford the river each day by divisions in succession, carrying their
provisions cooked. To obviate the difficulty of obtaining country
transport, the English general had previously constructed eight
hundred carts drawn by horses, which were now his surest depen-
dence for bringing up ammunition; and so many delays were anticipated from the irregularity of the native carters and muleteers and
the chances of weather, that he calculated upon an operation of
twenty-four days. Yet he hoped to steal this time from his adversaries, sure, even if he failed, that the clash of his arms would again
draw their scattered troops to that quarter as tinkling bells draw
swarming bees to an empty hive.

On the 8th the light division and Pack's Portuguese forded the
Agueda three miles above the fortress, and making a circuit took
post beyond the great Teson, where they remained quiet during the

day, and as there was no regular investment the enemy did not think the siege was commenced. But in the evening the troops stood to their arms, and Colonel Colborne, now commanding the fifty-second, having assembled two companies from each of the British regiments of the light division, stormed the redoubt of Francisco; this he did with so much fury that the assailants appeared to be at one and the same time in the ditch, mounting the parapets, fighting on the top of the rampart and forcing the gorge of the redoubt where the explosion of one of the French shells had burst the gate open. Of the defenders a few were killed, not many, and the remainder, forty in number, were made prisoners. When the post was thus taken with the loss of only twenty-four men and officers, Elder's *caça-dores* were set to labour on the right of it because the fort itself was instantly covered with shot and shells from the town; this tempest continued through the night, but at daybreak the parallel, six hundred yards in length, was sunk three feet deep, the communication over the Teson was completed, and the siege advanced several days by this well-managed assault.

The 9th, the first division took the trenches in hand, the place was encircled by posts to prevent any external communication, and at night twelve hundred workmen commenced three counter-batteries for eleven guns each, under a heavy fire of shells and grape. Before daylight the labourers were under cover, and a ditch was also sunk in the front to provide earth for the batteries, which were made eighteen feet thick at top to resist the very powerful artillery of the place.

On the 10th the fourth division relieved the trenches and a thousand men laboured, but in great peril, for the besieged had a super-abundance of ammunition and did not spare it. In the night the communication from the parallel to the batteries was opened, and on the 11th the third division undertook the siege. That day the magazines in the batteries were excavated and the approaches widened; but the enemy's fire was destructive, and the shells came so fast into the ditch in front of the batteries that the troops were withdrawn and the earth raised from the inside. Great damage was also sustained from salvoes of shells with long fuzees, whose simultaneous explosion cut away the parapets in a strange manner; and in the night the French brought a howitzer to the garden of the convent of Francisco with which they killed many men and wounded others.

On the 12th the light division resumed work, the riflemen, profiting from a thick fog, covered themselves in pits which they digged in front of the trenches and from thence picked off the enemy's gunners; yet the weather was so cold and the besieged shot so briskly that little progress was made. The 13th the same causes impeded the labourers of the first division. Scarcity of transport also balked the operations. One-third only of the native carts had arrived and the drivers of those present were very indolent; much of the twenty-four pound ammunition was still at Villa de Ponte, and intelligence arrived that Marmont was collecting his forces to succour the place. In this difficulty, it was resolved to hasten the siege by opening a breach with the counter-batteries, which were not quite six hundred yards from the curtain, and then to storm the place without blowing in the counterscarp: in other words to overstep the rules of science and sacrifice life rather than time, for the capricious Agueda might in one night flood and enable a small French force to relieve the place. The whole army was therefore brought up from the distant quarters and posted in the villages on the Coa ready to cross the Agueda and give battle.

In the night of the 13th the batteries were armed with twenty-eight guns, the second parallel and the approaches were continued by the flying sap, and the Santa Cruz convent was surprised by the Germans of the first division, which secured the right flank of the trenches. The 14th, the enemy, who had observed that the men in the trenches always went off in a disorderly manner on the approach of the relief, made a sally and overturned the gabions of the sap; they even penetrated to the parallel, and were upon the point of entering the batteries when a few of the workmen getting together checked them until a support arrived and the guns were saved. This affair, coupled with the death of the engineer on duty and the heavy fire from the town, delayed the opening of the breaching-batteries; yet at half-past four in the evening twenty-five heavy guns battered the 'fausse braye' and rampart, and two pieces were directed against the convent of Francisco. Then was beheld a spectacle at once fearful and sublime. The enemy replied to the assailants' fire with more than fifty pieces, the bellowing of eighty large guns shook the ground far and wide, the smoke rested in heavy volumes upon the battlements of the place or curled in light wreaths about the numerous spires, the shells, hissing through the air, seemed fiery serpents leaping from the darkness, the walls crashed to the stroke of the bullet, and the distant mountains faintly returning the sound appeared to mourn over the falling city. And when night put an end to this turmoil the quick clatter of musketry was heard like the pattering of hail after a peal of thunder, for the fortieth regiment then carried the convent of Francisco by storm and established itself in the suburb.

Next day the ramparts were again battered and fell so fast it was judged expedient to commence the small breach at the turret, wherefore in the night five more guns were mounted. At daylight the besiegers' batteries recommenced, but at eight o'clock a thick fog compelled them to desist; nevertheless the small breach had been opened and the place was summoned but without effect. At night the parallel on the lower Teson was extended and a sharp musketry was directed from thence against the great breach; the breaching-battery as originally projected was also commenced, and the riflemen of the light division continued from their pits to pick off the enemy's gunners.

On the 17th the fire on both sides was very heavy, and though the wall of the place was beaten down in large cantles several of the besiegers' guns were dismounted, their batteries injured, many men killed, General Borthwick commandant of artillery wounded, the sap entirely ruined, and the riflemen in the pits overpowered with grape; yet towards evening the latter recovered the upper hand and the French could only fire from the more distant embrasures. In the night the battery intended for the lesser breach was armed and that on the lower Teson raised so as to afford cover in the day-time.

On the 18th the besiegers' fire was resumed with great violence, the turret was shaken at the small breach, the large breach became practicable in the middle, and the enemy commenced retrenching it. The sap made no progress, the superintending engineer was badly wounded, and a twenty-four pounder having bursted in the batteries killed several men. In the night the battery on the lower Teson was improved, and a field-piece and howitzer being placed there kept up a constant fire on the great breach to destroy the French retrenchments. On the 19th both breaches became practicable, Major Sturgeon closely examined the place and a plan of attack was formed on his report; the assault was then ordered and the battering-guns were turned against the artillery of the ramparts.

All the troops reached their posts without seeming to attract the attention of the enemy, but before the signal was given, and while Wellington, who in person had been pointing out the lesser breach to Major Napier, was still at the convent of Francisco, the attack on the right commenced and was instantly taken up along the whole line. Then the space between the troops and the ditch was at once covered with soldiers and ravaged by a tempest of grape from the ramparts. The storming parties of the third division jumped out of

the parallel when the first shout arose, but so rapid had been the
movements on their right, that before they could reach the ditch, the
fifth, seventy-seventh and ninety-fourth regiments had already
scoured the fausse braye, and were pushing up the great breach
amidst the bursting of shells, the whistling of grape and muskets and
the shrill cries of the French, who were driven fighting behind the
retrenchments. There they rallied, and aided by the musketry from
the houses made hard battle for their post; none would go back on
either side, and yet the British could not get forward, and men and
officers falling in heaps choked up the passage, which from minute
to minute was raked with grape from two guns flanking the top
of the breach at the distance of a few yards: thus striving, and
trampling alike upon the dead and the wounded, these brave men
maintained the combat.

On the left, the stormers of the light division, who had three
hundred yards of ground to clear, would not wait for the hay-bags,
but with extraordinary swiftness running to the crest of the glacis
jumped down the scarp, a depth of eleven feet, and rushed up the
fausse braye under a smashing discharge of grape and musketry.
The ditch was dark and intricate, the forlorn hope [the spearhead of
volunteers] inclined towards the left, the stormers went straight to
the breach which was so narrow at the top that a gun placed across
nearly barred the opening; there they were rejoined by the forlorn
hope and the whole body rushed up, but the head of the mass,
crushed together as the ascent narrowed, staggered under the fire,
and with the instinct of self-preservation snapped their own muskets
though they had not been allowed to load. Major Napier struck by
a grape-shot fell at this moment with a shattered arm, but he called
aloud on his men to use their bayonets, and all the unwounded
officers simultaneously sprung to the front; thus the required impulse was given and with a furious shout the breach was carried.
Then the supporting regiments coming up in sections abreast gained
the rampart, the fifty-second wheeled to the left, the forty-third to
the right, and the place was won.

During this contest, which lasted only a few minutes on the
breach, the fighting at the great breach had continued with unabated
violence: but when the stormers and the forty-third came pouring
along the rampart towards that quarter the French wavered, three
of their expense magazines exploded at the same moment, and then
the third division with a mighty effort broke through the retrenchments. The garrison fought indeed for a moment in the streets, yet
finally fled to the castle, where Lieutenant Gurwood, who though

severely wounded in the head had entered amongst the foremost at the lesser breach, received the governor's sword.

Now into the streets plunged the assailants from all quarters, and at the other side of the town Pack's Portuguese and the reserves meeting no resistance had entered. Throwing off the restraints of discipline the troops committed frightful excesses; the town was fired in three or four places, the soldiers menaced their officers and shot each other; many were killed in the market-place, intoxication soon increased the tumult, and at last, the fury rising to absolute madness, a fire was wilfully lighted in the middle of the great magazine, by which the town would have been blown to atoms but for the energetic courage of some officers and a few soldiers who still preserved their senses. Three hundred French had fallen, fifteen hundred were made prisoners, and the immense stores of ammunition, with one hundred and fifty pieces of artillery, including the battering-train of Marmont's army, were captured. The allies lost twelve hundred men and ninety officers in the siege, of which six hundred and fifty and sixty officers were slain or hurt at the breaches. Generals Craufurd and Mackinnon, the former a person of great ability, were killed, and with them died many gallant men; amongst others, a captain of the forty-fifth, of whom it has been felicitously said that 'three generals and seventy other officers had fallen, yet the soldiers fresh from the strife only talked of Hardyman'. General Vandeleur, leading the light division after Craufurd fell, was badly wounded, so was Colonel Colborne and a crowd of inferior rank; and unhappily the slaughter did not end with the battle, for the next day, as the prisoners and their escort were marching out by the breach, an accidental explosion took place and numbers of both were blown into air.

To recompense an exploit so boldly undertaken and so gloriously finished, Lord Wellington was created Duke of Ciudad Rodrigo by the Spaniards, Earl of Wellington by the English, Marquis of Torres Vedras by the Portuguese; but it is to be remarked that the prince regent of Portugal had previous to that period displayed great ingratitude in the conferring of honours upon the British officers.

*   *   *

Wellington had sent Colquhoun Grant, a celebrated scouting officer, to watch Marmont, and that gentleman, in whom the utmost daring was so mixed with subtlety of genius and both so tempered by discretion it is hard to say which quality predominated, very rapidly executed his mission. Attended by Leon, a Spanish peasant of fidelity and quickness of apprehension who had been his companion on many occasions of the same nature, he arrived in the Salamancan district, passed the Tormes in the night, and remained in uniform, for he never assumed any disguise, three days in the midst of the French camp. He obtained exact information of Marmont's object and more especially of his preparations of provisions and scaling-ladders, notes of which he sent to head-quarters from hour to hour by Spanish agents. On the third night some peasants brought him a general order addressed to the French regiments, saying the notorious Grant being within the circle of their cantonments the soldiers were to use their utmost exertions to secure him, for which purpose also guards were placed as it were in a circle round the army. Nothing daunted, he consulted with the peasants and before daylight next morning entered the village of Huerta close to a ford on the Tormes and six miles from Salamanca. A battalion was in Huerta, and beyond the river cavalry vedettes were posted, two of which constantly patrolled backward and forward for the space of three hundred yards, meeting always at the ford. When day broke the French assembled on their alarm-post, and at that moment Grant was secretly brought opposite the ford, he and his horse being hidden by the gable of a house from the infantry while the peasants standing on loose stones and spreading their large cloaks covered him from the cavalry. There he calmly waited until the vedettes were separated the full extent of their beat, when he dashed through the ford between them and receiving their fire without damage reached a wood where the pursuit was baffled: Leon being in his native dress met with no interruption and soon rejoined him.

He had before this ascertained that means to storm Rodrigo were prepared, and the French officers openly talked of that operation; but to test that project, to ascertain Marmont's real force, and to discover if he was not really going by Perales to the Tagus, Grant now placed himself on a wooded hill near Tamames where the road branched off to Perales and to Rodrigo. There lying perdue until the French passed by in march, he noted every battalion and gun, and finding all moved towards Rodrigo he entered Tamames and discovered they had left the greatest part of their scaling-ladders behind, thus showing the intention to storm was not real: this it was which allayed Wellington's fears for that fortress.

When Marmont passed the Coa in this expedition, Grant preceded him with intent to discover if his further march would be by Guarda upon Coimbra, or by Sabugal upon Castello Branco; for to reach the latter it was necessary to descend from a very high ridge or rather succession of ridges, by a pass at the lower mouth of which stands Penamacor. Upon one of the inferior ridges in the pass this persevering officer placed himself, thinking the dwarf oaks with which the hills were covered would effectually secure him from discovery; but from the higher ridge the French detected his movements with their glasses; and Leon, whose lynx-eyes were always on the watch, soon called out, *the French! the French!* and pointed to the rear whence some dragoons came galloping up. Grant and his follower darted into the wood for a little space and then suddenly wheeling rode off in a different direction, but at every turn new enemies appeared, and at last the hunted men, dismounting, fled on foot through the thickest of the low oaks until they were again met by infantry detached in small parties down the sides of the pass and directed in their chase by the waving of the French officers' hats on the ridge above.

Leon fell exhausted and the barbarians who first came up killed him in despite of his companion's entreaties. Grant they carried without injury to Marmont, who with apparent kindness invited him to dinner. The conversation turned upon the prisoner's exploits, and the French marshal said that he had been long on the watch, knew all his haunts, his disguises, and that only the night before he had slept in the French head-quarters, with other adventures which had not happened, for this Grant never used any disguise. But there was another Grant, also remarkable in his way, who used to remain for months in the French quarters using all manner of disguises, and the similarity of names caused the actions of both to be attributed to one, which is the only palliative for Marmont's subsequent conduct. Treating his prisoner with apparent kindness, he exacted from him an especial parole that he would not consent to be released by the partidas while on his journey through Spain to France: this secured his captive, for Wellington offered two thousand dollars to any guerrilla chief who should rescue him. The exaction of such a parole was a tacit compliment to the man; but Marmont sent a letter with the escort to the governor of Bayonne, in which, still labouring under the error that there was only one Grant, he designated his captive as a dangerous spy who had done infinite mischief to the French army, and whom he had not executed on the spot out of respect to something resembling an uniform which he wore: but he desired that at Bayonne he should be placed in irons and sent up to Paris.

This proceeding was too little in accord with French honour to be supported, and before the Spanish frontier was passed, Grant, it matters not how, was made acquainted with the contents of the letter. Now the custom at Bayonne in ordinary cases was for the prisoner to wait on the authorities and receive a passport to travel to Verdun, which was duly accomplished, the delivery of the fatal letter being by certain means delayed. Grant then with sagacious boldness resolved not to escape towards the Pyrenees, thinking he would naturally be pursued in that direction; he thought if the governor of Bayonne did not recapture him at once, he would for his own security suppress the letter in hopes the matter would be no further thought of; wherefore on the instant he inquired at the hotels if any French officer was going to Paris, and finding that Souham, then on his return from Spain, was so bent, he boldly introduced himself and asked permission to join his party. The other readily assented, and while travelling, he very often rallied his companion about his adventures, little thinking he was then an instrument in forwarding the most dangerous and adroit of them all.

In passing through Orleans, Grant by a species of intuition discovered an English agent, and from him received a recommendation to another secret agent in Paris whose assistance would be necessary to his final escape; for he looked upon Marmont's double dealing and the expressed design to take away his life as equivalent to a discharge of his parole, which was moreover only given with respect to Spain. When he arrived at Paris he took leave of Souham, opened an intercourse with the Parisian agent, from whom he obtained money, and by his advice avoided appearing before the police to have his passport examined. He took a lodging in a very public street, frequented the coffee-houses and visited the theatres without fear, because the secret agent, who had been long established and was intimately connected with the police, had ascertained that no inquiry about his escape had been set on foot.

When some weeks had elapsed, the agent told him a passport was ready for one Jonathan Buck, an American who had died suddenly on the day it was to have been claimed. Boldly demanding this passport he departed for the mouth of the Loire, because certain reasons, not necessary to mention, led him to expect more assistance there than at any other port. There however new difficulties awaited him and were overcome by fresh exertions of his surprising talent which fortune seemed to delight in aiding. He took a passage for America in a ship of that nation, but its departure being unexpectedly delayed, he frankly explained his true situation to the captain, who desired him to assume the character of a discontented seaman, and giving him a sailor's dress and forty dollars sent him to lodge the money in the American consul's hands as a pledge that he would prosecute the captain for ill-usage when he reached the United States. This being the custom on such occasions, the consul gave him a certificate which enabled him to pass from port to port as a discharged sailor seeking a ship. Thus provided, he prevailed upon a boatman by a promise of ten Napoleons, to row him in the night towards a small island where English vessels watered unmolested, and in return permitted the few inhabitants to fish and traffic without interruption. The boat sailed, the masts of the British ships were dimly seen on the other side of the island and the termination of his toils appeared at hand, when the boatman from fear or malice suddenly returned to port. Some men would then have striven in desperation to force fortune and so have perished, the spirits of others would have sunk in despair, for the money promised was all he had and the boatman, notwithstanding his breach of contract, demanded the whole: with inexpressible coolness and resolution, Grant gave him one Napoleon and a rebuke for his misconduct – he threatened reference to the police but was no match in subtlety for his opponent, who told him plainly that he would then denounce him as aiding the escape of a prisoner of war and would adduce the great price of his boat as a proof of his guilt!

A few days after Grant engaged an old fisherman who faithfully performed his bargain, but there were no English vessels near the island; however the fisherman cast his nets and caught some fish with which he sailed towards the southward, where he had heard there was an English ship of war. In a few hours they obtained a glimpse of her and were steering that way, when a shot from a coast-battery brought them to, and a boat with soldiers put off to board them. The fisherman called Grant his son, and the soldiers were only sent to warn them not to pass the battery because the English vessel they were in search of was on the coast. The old man, expecting this, bribed the soldiers with his fish, assuring them he must go with his son or they would starve, and that he was so well acquainted with the coast he could always escape the enemy. His prayers and presents prevailed, he was desired to wait under the battery till night and then depart; but under pretence of arranging his escape from the English vessel he made the soldiers point out her bearings so exactly that when darkness fell he run her straight on board and the intrepid Grant stood in safety on the quarter-deck.

When he reached England he obtained permission to choose a French officer of equal rank with himself to send to France, that no doubt might remain about the propriety of his escape. Great was his astonishment to find in the first prison he visited the old fisher-man and his real son, who had meanwhile been captured notwith-standing a protection given to them for their services; but Grant's generosity and benevolence were as remarkable as the qualities of his understanding; he soon obtained their release, sent them with a sum of money to France, returned to the Peninsula, and within four months from the date of his first capture was again on the Tormes, watching Marmont's army! Other strange incidents of his life could be told, were it not more fitting to quit a digression already too wide; yet I was unwilling to pass unnoticed this adventure of that generous, spirited and gentle-minded man, who having served his country nobly and ably in every climate died not long since exhausted by the continual hardships he had endured.

*   *   *

Having shown the prudence of Wellington with respect to the cam-paign generally, it remains to consider the siege of Badajoz, which has so often been adduced in evidence that not skill but fortune plumed his ambitious wing; a proceeding indeed most consonant to the nature of man; for it is hard to avow inferiority by attributing an action so stupendous to superior genius alone. A scientific exam-ination would be misplaced in a general history, but to notice leading points involving the general conception will not be irrelevant. The choice of the line of attack, justified by the English engineers as that requiring least expenditure of means and time, has by the French engineers been censured. Colonel Lamarre affirms that the front next the castle was the one least susceptible of defence; because it had neither ravelin nor ditch to protect it, had fewer flanks, and offered no facility of retrenching behind it: a view confirmed by Phillipon, who being the best judge of his own weak points, did for many days think it was the true object of the allies' approaches. But Lamarre advances a far more interesting question, when he says Badajoz might have been taken by escalade and storm the first night of the siege with less difficulty than on the 7th of April. Then, he says, the defences were not so complete, the garrison was less prepared, and surprise would have availed somewhat – whereas at the second period the breaches were the strongest part of the town, and as no other advantage had been gained by the besiegers the chances were in favour of the first period.

So sensible was the English general of Phillipon's firmness and the courage of his garrison that he spared them the affront of a summons, yet, seeing the breach strongly entrenched and the

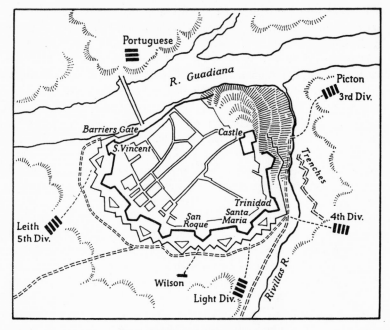

THE SIEGE OF BADAJOZ

enemy's flank fire still powerful, he would not in this dread crisis trust his fortune to a single effort. Eighteen thousand daring soldiers burned for the signal, and he, unwilling to lose the service of one, gave to each division a task such as few generals would have the hardihood even to contemplate. For on the right Picton was to file out of the trenches, cross the Rivillas river, and scale the castle walls, eighteen to twenty-four feet in height, furnished with all means of destruction and so narrow at top the defenders could easily reach and overturn the ladders. On the left Leith was to make a false attack on the Pardaleras, but a real assault on the distant bastion of San Vincente, where the glacis was mined, the ditch deep, the scarp thirty feet high, and the parapet garnished with bold troops provided each with three loaded muskets that the first fire might be quick and deadly.

In the centre, the fourth and light divisions under Colville and Andrew Barnard were to march against the breaches. They were furnished like the third and fifth divisions with ladders and axes, and preceded by storming parties of five hundred men each with their respective forlorn hopes: the light division was to assault the bastion of Santa Maria, the fourth division to assault the Trinidad and the curtain, and the columns were divided into storming and firing parties, the former to enter the ditch, the latter to keep the crest of the glacis.

At first, only one brigade of the third division was destined to attack the castle, but just before the hour of assault a sergeant of sappers deserted from the French and reported that there was but one communication from the castle into the town, wherefore the whole division was directed to assail in mass. To aid these great attacks General Power's Portuguese were to make a feint from the other side of the Guadiana, and Major Wilson of the forty-eighth was to storm the San Roque with the guards of the trenches; this general outline was filled up with many nice arrangements, some of which were followed, others disregarded, for it is seldom all things are attended to in a desperate fight. Nor was the enemy idle. While it was yet twilight some French cavalry issued from the Pardaleras, escorting an officer who endeavoured to look into the trenches with a view to ascertain if an assault was intended; but the piquet on that side jumped up, and firing as it ran drove him and his escort back into the works: then darkness fell and silently the troops awaited the signal.

Dry but clouded was the night, the air thick with watery exhalations from the rivers, the ramparts and the trenches unusually still; yet a low murmur pervaded the latter, and in the former lights were seen to flit here and there while the deep voices of the sentinels at times proclaimed that all was well in Badajoz. The French, confiding in Phillipon's direful skill, watched from their lofty station the approach of enemies whom they had twice before baffled, and now hoped to drive a third time blasted and ruined from the walls. The British, standing in deep columns, were as eager to meet that fiery destruction as the others were to pour it down, and both were alike terrible for their strength, their discipline and the passions awakened in their resolute hearts. Former failures there were to avenge, and on both sides leaders who furnished no excuse for weakness in the hour of trial. The possession of Badajoz had become a point of personal honour with the soldiers of each nation, but the desire for glory with the British was dashed by a hatred of the citizens on an old grudge; and recent toil and hardship with much spilling of blood had made many incredibly savage; for these things render the noble-minded indeed averse to cruelty but harden the vulgar spirit: numbers also, like Caesar's centurion who could not forget the plunder of Avaricum, were heated with the recollection of Ciudad Rodrigo and thirsted for spoil. Thus every spirit

THE SIEGE OF BADAJOZ

found a cause of excitement, the wondrous power of discipline bound the whole together as with a band of iron, and in the pride of arms none doubted their might to bear down every obstacle that man could oppose to their fury.

At ten o'clock, the castle, the San Roque, the breaches, the Pardaleras, the distant bastion of San Vincente and the bridgehead on the other side of the Guadiana were to have been simultaneously assailed, and it was hoped the strength of the enemy would shrivel within that fiery girdle. But many are the disappointments of war. An unforeseen accident delayed the attack of the fifth division, and a lighted carcass thrown from the castle, falling close to the third division discovered their array and compelled them to anticipate the signal by half an hour. Then, everything being suddenly disturbed, the double columns of the fourth and light divisions also moved silently and swiftly against the breaches, and the guard of the trenches rushing forward with a shout encompassed the San Roque with fire and broke in so violently that scarcely any resistance was made. But a sudden blaze of light and the rattling of musketry indicated the commencement of a more vehement combat at the castle. There General Kempt, for Picton hurt by a fall in the camp and expecting no change in the hour was not present, there Kempt, I say, led the third division. Having passed the Rivillas in single files by a narrow bridge under a terrible musketry, he had reformed and, running up a rugged hill, reached the foot of the castle where he fell severely wounded, and as he was carried back to the trenches met Picton who was hastening to take the command. Meanwhile the troops, spreading along the front, had reared their heavy ladders, some against the lofty castle some against the adjoining front on the left, and with incredible courage ascended amidst showers of heavy stones, logs of wood and bursting shells rolled off the parapet, while from the flanks the enemy plied his musketry with fearful rapidity, and in front with pikes and bayonets stabbed the leading assailants or pushed the ladders from the walls: and all this was attended with deafening shouts and the crash of breaking ladders, and the shrieks of crushed soldiers answering to the sullen stroke of the falling weights.

Still swarming round the remaining ladders those undaunted veterans strove who should first climb, until all being overturned the French shouted victory, and the British, baffled but untamed, fell back a few paces and took shelter under the rugged edge of the hill. There the broken ranks were somewhat re-formed, and the heroic Ridge, springing forward, seized a ladder and calling with stentorian voice on his men to follow, once more raised it against the castle, yet to the right of the former attack where the wall was lower and an embrasure offered some facility. A second ladder was soon placed alongside of the first by the grenadier officer, Canch, and the next instant he and Ridge were on the rampart, the shouting troops pressed after them, the garrison amazed and in a manner surprised were driven fighting through the double gate into the town, and the castle was won. A reinforcement from the French reserve then came up, a sharp action followed, both sides fired through the gate and the enemy retired, but Ridge fell, and no man died that night with more glory – yet many died, and there was much glory.

All this time the tumult at the breaches was such as if the very earth had been rent asunder and its central fires bursting upwards uncontrolled. The two divisions had reached the glacis just as the firing at the castle commenced, and the flash of a single musket discharged from the covered way as a signal showed them that the French were ready: yet no stir was heard and darkness covered the breaches. Some haypacks were thrown, some ladders placed, and the forlorn hopes and storming parties of the light division, five hundred in all, descended into the ditch without opposition; but then a bright flame shooting upwards displayed all the terrors of the scene. The ramparts crowded with dark figures and glittering arms were on one side, on the other the red columns of the British, deep and broad, were coming on like streams of burning lava; it was the touch of the magician's wand, for a crash of thunder followed and with incredible violence the storming parties were dashed to pieces by the explosion of hundreds of shells and powder-barrels.

For an instant the light division stood on the brink of the ditch amazed at the terrific sight, but then with a shout that matched even the sound of the explosion the men flew down the ladders, or disdaining their aid leaped reckless of the depth into the gulf below – and at the same moment, amidst a blaze of musketry that dazzled the eyes, the fourth division came running in and descended with a like fury. There were only five ladders for the two columns which were close together, and a deep cut made in the bottom of the ditch as far as the counter-guard of the Trinidad was filled with water from the inundation; into that watery snare the head of the fourth division fell, and it is said above a hundred of the fuzileers, the men of Albuera, were there smothered. Those who followed checked not, but, as if such a disaster had been expected, turned to the left and thus came upon the face of the unfinished ravelin, which being rough and broken was mistaken for the breach and instantly covered with men: yet a wide and deep chasm was still between them and the ramparts from whence came a deadly fire wasting their ranks. Thus baffled, they also commenced a rapid discharge of musketry and disorder ensued; for the men of the light division, whose conducting engineer had been disabled early and whose flank was confined by an unfinished ditch intended to cut off the bastion of Santa Maria, rushed towards the breaches of the curtain and the Trinidad, which were indeed before them, but which the fourth division had been destined to storm. Great was the confusion, for the ravelin was quite crowded with men of both divisions, and while some continued to fire others jumped down and ran towards the breach: many also passed between the ravelin and the counter-guard of the Trinidad, the two divisions got mixed, the reserves, which should have remained at the quarries, also came pouring in until the ditch was quite filled, the rear still crowding forward and all cheering vehemently. The enemy's shouts were also loud and terrible, and the bursting of shells and of grenades, the roaring of guns from the flanks, answered by the iron howitzers from the battery of the parallel, the heavy roll and horrid explosion of the powder-barrels, the whizzing flight of the blazing splinters, the loud exhortations of the officers and the continual clatter of the muskets made a maddening din.

Now a multitude bounded up the great breach as if driven by a whirlwind, but across the top glittered a range of sword-blades, sharp-pointed, keen-edged on both sides and firmly fixed in ponderous beams chained together and set deep in the ruins; and for ten feet in front the ascent was covered with loose planks studded with sharp iron points, on which feet being set, the planks moved and the unhappy soldiers falling forward on the spikes rolled down upon the ranks behind. Then the Frenchmen, shouting at the success of their stratagem and leaping forward, plied their shot with terrible rapidity, for every man had several muskets and each musket in addition to its ordinary charge contained a small cylinder of wood stuck full of wooden slugs, which scattered like hail when they were discharged. Once and again the assailants rushed up the breaches, but always the sword-blades, immoveable and impassable, stopped their charge, and the hissing shells and thundering powder-barrels exploded unceasingly. Hundreds of men had fallen, hundreds more were dropping, still the heroic officers called aloud for new trials, and sometimes followed by many sometimes by a few, ascended the ruins; and so furious were the men themselves that in one of these charges the rear strove to push the foremost on to the sword-blades, willing even to make a bridge of their writhing bodies, but the others frustrated the attempt by dropping down: and men fell so far from the shot, it was hard to know who went down voluntarily who were stricken, and many stooped unhurt that never rose again. Vain also would it have been to break through the sword-blades, for the trench and parapet behind the breach were finished, and the assailants crowded into even a narrower space than the ditch was, would still have been separated from their enemies and the slaughter would have continued.

At the beginning of this dreadful conflict, Andrew Barnard had with prodigious efforts separated his division from the other and preserved some degree of military array; but now the tumult was such no command could be heard distinctly except by those close at hand, and the mutilated carcases heaped on each other and the wounded struggling to avoid being trampled upon broke the formations: order was impossible! Officers of all ranks, followed more or less numerously by the men, were seen to start out as if struck by sudden madness and rush into the breach, which yawning and glittering with steel seemed like the mouth of a huge dragon belching forth smoke and flame. In one of these attempts Colonel Macleod of the forty-third, a young man whose feeble body would have been quite unfit for war if it had not been sustained by an unconquerable spirit, was killed; wherever his voice was heard his soldiers had gathered, and with such a strong resolution did he lead them up the fatal ruins, that when one behind him in falling plunged a bayonet into his back, he complained not but continuing his course was shot dead within a yard of the sword-blades. Yet there was no want of gallant leaders or desperate followers until two hours passed in these vain efforts had convinced the troops the breach of the Trinidad was impregnable; and as the opening in the curtain, although less strong, was retired and the approach to it impeded by deep holes and cuts made in the ditch, the soldiers did not much notice it after the partial failure of one attack which had been made early. Gathering in dark groups and leaning on their muskets they looked up with sullen desperation at the Trinidad, while the enemy stepping out on the ramparts and aiming their shots by the light of the fire-balls which they threw over, asked as their victims fell, *'Why they did not come into Badajoz?'*

In this dreadful situation, while the dead were lying in heaps and others continually falling, the wounded crawling about to get some shelter from the merciless shower above, and withal a sickening stench from the burnt flesh of the slain, Captain Nicholas of the engineers was observed by Lieutenant Shaw of the forty-third making incredible efforts to force his way with a few men into the Santa Maria bastion. Shaw immediately collected fifty soldiers of all regiments and joined him, and although there was a deep cut along the foot of that breach also, it was instantly passed and these two young officers led their gallant band with a rush up the ruins; but when they had gained two-thirds of the ascent a concentrated fire of musketry and grape dashed nearly the whole dead to the earth: Nicholas was mortally wounded and the intrepid Shaw stood alone! With inexpressible coolness he looked at his watch, and saying it was too late to carry the breaches rejoined the masses at the other attack. After this no further effort was made at any point, and the troops remained passive but unflinching beneath the enemy's shot which streamed without intermission; for of the riflemen on the glacis, many leaping early into the ditch had joined in the assault, and the rest, raked by a crossfire of grape from the distant bastions, baffled in their aim by the smoke and flames from the explosions and too few in number, entirely failed to quell the French musketry.

About midnight, when two thousand brave men had fallen, Wellington, who was on a height close to the quarries, ordered the remainder to retire and re-form for a second assault; he had heard the castle was taken, but thinking the enemy would still resist in the town was resolved to assail the breaches again. This retreat from the ditch was not effected without further carnage and confusion, the French fire never slackened, a cry arose that the enemy was making a sally from the distant flanks, and there was a rush towards the ladders. Then the groans and lamentations of the wounded who could not move and expected to be slain increased, and many officers who had not heard of the order, endeavoured to stop the soldiers from going back: some would even have removed the ladders but were unable to break the crowd.

All this time Picton was lying close in the castle, and either from fear of risking the loss of a point which ensured the capture of the place, or that the egress was too difficult, made no attempt to drive away the enemy from the breaches. On the other side however the fifth division had commenced the false attack on the Pardaleras, and on the right of the Guadiana, the Portuguese were sharply engaged at the bridge: thus the town was girdled with fire, for Walker's brigade, having passed on during the feint on the Pardaleras, was escalading the distant bastion of San Vincente.

His troops had advanced along the banks of the river and reached the French guard-house at the barrier-gate undiscovered, the ripple of the waters smothering the sound of their footsteps; but just then the explosion at the breaches took place, the moon shone out, the French sentinels discovering the columns fired, and the British soldiers springing forward under a sharp musketry began to hew down the wooden barrier at the covered way. The Portuguese, panic-stricken, threw down the scaling ladders, the others snatched them up again and forcing the barrier jumped into the ditch; but the guilding engineer officer was killed, there was a *cunette* [strong-point] which embarrassed the column, and the ladders proved too short for the walls which were generally above thirty feet high. The fire of the enemy was deadly, a small mine was sprung beneath the soldiers' feet, beams of wood and live shells were rolled over on their heads, showers of grape from the flank swept the ditch, and man after man dropped dead from the ladders.

Fortunately some of the defenders had been called away to aid in recovering the castle, the ramparts were not entirely manned, and the assailants discovering a corner of the bastion where the scarp was only twenty feet high placed three ladders there under an embrasure which had no gun and was only stopped with a gabion. Some men got up with difficulty, for the ladders were still too short, and the first man who gained the top was pushed up by his comrades and drew others after him until many had won the summit; and though the French shot heavily against them from both flanks and from a house in front, their numbers augmented rapidly and half the fourth regiment entered the town itself to dislodge the French from the houses, while the others pushed along the rampart towards the breach and by dint of hard fighting successively won three bastions.

In the last of these combats Walker, leaping forward sword in hand at the moment when one of the enemy's cannoneers was discharging a gun, was covered with so many wounds it was wonderful that he could survive, and some of the soldiers immediately after, perceiving a lighted match on the ground, cried out a mine! At that word, such is the power of imagination, those troops who had not been stopped by the strong barrier, the deep ditch, the high walls and the deadly fire of the enemy, staggered back appalled by a chimera of their own raising; and in this disorder a French reserve under General Veillande drove on them with a firm and rapid charge, pitching some men over the walls, killing others outright, and cleansing the ramparts even to the San Vincente. There however Leith had placed Colonel Nugent with a battalion of the thirty-eighth as a reserve, and when the French came up, shouting and slaying all before them, this battalion, two hundred strong, arose and with one close volley destroyed them; then the panic ceased, the soldiers rallied, and in compact order once more charged along the walls towards the breaches: but the French, although turned on both flanks and abandoned by fortune, did not yet yield. Meanwhile the portion of the fourth regiment which had entered the town was strangely situated. For the streets were empty and brilliantly illuminated and no person was seen, yet a low buzz and whispers were heard around, lattices were now and then gently opened, and from time to time shots were fired from underneath the doors of the houses by the Spaniards, while the troops with bugles sounding advanced towards the great square of the town. In their progress they captured several mules going with ammunition to the breaches; yet the square itself was as empty and silent as the streets, and the houses as bright with lamps: a terrible enchantment seemed to be in operation, they saw only an illumination and heard only low whispering around them while the tumult at the breaches was like the crashing thunder. Plainly however the fight was there raging, and hence, quitting the square, they attempted to take the garrison in reverse by attacking the ramparts from the town-side, but they were received with a rolling musketry, driven back with loss, and resumed their movement through the streets. At last the breaches were abandoned by the French, other parties entered, desultory combats took place, Veillande and Phillipon, who was wounded, seeing all ruined, passed the bridge with a few hundred soldiers and entered San Christoval, which was surrendered next morning upon summons to Lord Fitzroy Somerset: for that officer had with great readiness pushed through the town to the drawbridge ere the French had time to organize further resistance. But even in the moment of ruin the night before, this noble governor had sent some horsemen out from the fort to carry the news to Soult, and they reached him in time to prevent a greater misfortune.

Now commenced that wild and desperate wickedness which tarnished the lustre of the soldier's heroism. All indeed were not alike, hundreds risked and many lost their lives in striving to stop the violence, but madness generally prevailed, and as the worst men were leaders here, all the dreadful passions of human nature were displayed. Shameless rapacity, brutal intemperance, savage lust, cruelty and murder, shrieks and piteous lamentations, groans, shouts, imprecations, the hissing of fires bursting from the houses, the crashing of doors and windows, and the reports of muskets used in violence, resounded for two days and nights in the streets of Badajoz! On the third, when the city was sacked, when the soldiers were exhausted by their own excesses, the tumult rather subsided than was quelled: the wounded men were then looked to, the dead disposed of!

Five thousand men and officers fell in this siege, and of these, including seven hundred Portuguese, three thousand five hundred had been stricken in the assault, sixty officers and more than seven hundred men being slain on the spot. The five generals, Kempt, Harvey, Bowes, Colville and Picton were wounded, the first four severely; six hundred men and officers fell in the escalade of San Vincente, as many at the castle, and more than two thousand at the breaches, each division there losing twelve hundred! And how deadly the breach strife was may be gathered from this: the forty-third and fifty-second regiments of the light division lost more men than the seven regiments of the third division engaged at the castle!

Let it be considered that this frightful carnage took place in a space of less than a hundred yards square; that the slain died not all suddenly nor by one manner of death – that some perished by steel, some by shot, some by water, that some were crushed and mangled by heavy weights, some trampled upon, some dashed to atoms by the fiery explosions; that for hours this destruction was endured without shrinking and the town was won at last. Let these things be considered and it must be admitted a British army bears with it an awful power. And false would it be to say the French were feeble men, the garrison stood and fought manfully and with good discipline, behaving worthily: shame there was none on any side. Yet who shall do justice to the bravery of the British soldiers! the noble emulation of the officers! Who shall measure out the glory of Ridge, of Macleod, of Nicholas, of O'Hare of the ninety-fifth, who perished on the breach at the head of the stormers, and with him nearly all the volunteers for that desperate service! Who shall describe the springing valour of that Portuguese grenadier who was killed the foremost man at the Santa Maria? Or the martial fury of that desperate rifleman, who, in his resolution to win, thrust himself beneath the chained sword-blades and there suffered the enemy to dash his head to pieces with the ends of their muskets! Who can sufficiently honour the intrepidity of Walker, of Shaw, of Canch, or the hardiness of Ferguson of the forty-third, who having in former assaults received two deep wounds was here, his former hurts still open, leading the stormers of his regiment, the third time a volunteer, the third time wounded! Nor would I be understood to select these as pre-eminent many and signal were the other examples of unbounded devotion, some known, some that will never be known; for in such a tumult much passes unobserved, and often the observers fell themselves ere they could bear testimony to what they saw: but no age, no nation ever sent forth braver troops to battle than those who stormed Badajoz.

When the extent of the night's havoc was made known to Lord Wellington, the firmness of his nature gave way for a moment, and the pride of conquest yielded to a passionate burst of grief for the loss of his gallant soldiers.

XIII

Salamanca

Two roads to Spain now lay open, against Soult in Andalusia and Marmont in the north. Wellington never diverged from his main strategy. The natural lines of communication in the Iberian peninsula run east and west with the main rivers. Only the central table-land provides routes from north to south. Soult could be held in check by the reliable Hill, who had replaced Beresford, at Merida, south of the Tagus, and the Mediterranean flanks could be harassed by amphibious expeditions. If the northern route to France could be forced, the French armies in the south and east would have to withdraw or be cut off. During the spring and early summer of 1812 Wellington and Marmont sparred and skirmished, marched and counter-marched, along the valley of the river Douro and its tributaries. The armies were well matched in skill, numbers and manoeuvrability. But it was the Fabian warrior Wellington who, after initial reverses in the vicinity, found the moment to strike, at Salamanca.

THE FRENCH army, from its peculiar organization could, while the ground harvest lasted, operate without any regard to lines of communication; it had supports on all sides and procured its food everywhere; the troops were taught to reap the standing corn and grind it themselves if their cavalry could not seize flour in the villages. This organization, approaching the ancient Roman military perfection, gave them great advantages; it baffled the irregular and threw the regular force of the allies entirely upon the defensive; for if their flanks were turned, a retreat only could save the communications, but the French offered no point for retaliation. Wherefore, with a force composed of four different nations, Wellington was to execute difficult evolutions in an open country, his chances of success being to arise only from the casual errors of his adversary, who was an able general, knew the country perfectly, and led an army, brave, excellently disciplined and of one nation: the game would have been quite unequal if the English had not been so strong in cavalry.

The country was like the open down of England, with here and there water-gulleys, dry hollows and bold naked heads of land; and behind the most prominent of these last, on the other side of the Trabancos, lay the whole French army. Cotton, seeing only horsemen, advanced with his cavalry towards the river, but cautiously, by his right, along some high table-land and his troops were lost to the view of the infantry, for the morning fog was thick on the stream and nothing could be descried beyond. Soon however the deep tones of the artillery shook the ground, the sharp ring of musketry was heard in the mist, and the forty-third regiment passed hastily through Castrejon to support the advancing cavalry; for besides the ravine which separated the fourth from the light division, there was another ravine with a marshy bottom between the latter and the cavalry, and the village of Castrejon was the only good point of passage.

Now the cannonade became heavy and the spectacle surprisingly beautiful. The lighter smoke and mist curling up in fantastic pillars formed a huge and glittering dome tinged of many colours by the rising sun; and through the grosser vapour below the restless horsemen were seen or lost as the fume thickened from the rapid play of the guns, while the high bluff head of land beyond the Trabancos, covered with French troops, appeared by an optical deception close at hand, dilated to the size of a mountain and crowned with gigantic soldiers who were continually breaking off and sliding down into the fight. Suddenly a dismounted cavalry officer stalked from the midst of the smoke towards the line of infantry with a gait peculiarly rigid, and he appeared to hold a bloody handkerchief to his heart; but that which seemed a cloth was a broad and dreadful wound, a bullet had entirely effaced the flesh from his left shoulder and from his breast, and had carried away part of his ribs, his heart was bared and its movement plainly discerned. It was a piteous and yet a noble sight, for his countenance though ghastly was firm, his step scarcely indicated weakness and his voice never faltered: this unyielding man's name was Williams. He died a short distance from the field of battle, and it was said in the arms of his son, a youth of fourteen who had followed his father to the Peninsula in hopes of obtaining a commission, for they were not affluent.

Cotton maintained this exposed position with skill and resolution from daylight until seven o'clock, at which time Wellington arrived in company with Beresford and proceeded to examine the enemy's movements. At this moment some French horsemen, not many, broke suddenly away from the head-land beyond the Trabancos and came galloping on as if deserting, but soon with headlong course

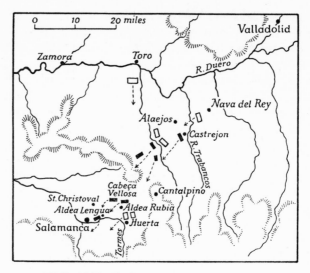

THE ADVANCE UPON SALAMANCA

they mounted the table-land on which Cotton's left was posted and drove a whole line of cavalry skirmishers back in confusion. The English reserves on that side then advanced from Alaejos, and these furious swordsmen, scattered by their own charge, were in turn driven back or cut down; yet thirty or forty, led by a noble officer, brought up their right shoulders and came over the edge of the table-land, above the hollow which separated the British wings, at the instant when Wellington and Beresford arrived on the same slope. Infantry piquets were in the bottom, and higher up near the French were two guns covered by a squadron of light cavalry disposed in perfect order. When the French officer first saw this squadron he reined in his horse with difficulty, his troopers gathered in a confused body round him seemingly as lost men, and the British instantly charged; but with a shout the gallant Frenchmen soused down upon the squadron and the latter, turning, galloped through the guns; then the whole mass, friends and enemies, went like a whirlwind to the bottom, carrying away Lord Wellington and Beresford, who with drawn swords and some difficulty got clear of the tumult. The French horsemen, when quite exhausted, were attacked by a reserve squadron and most of them were killed, but their indomitable leader, when assailed by three enemies at once, struck one dead from his horse, and with surprising exertions saved himself from the other two, though they rode hewing at him for a quarter of a mile.

At Cantalpino it became evident that the allies were outflanked, and all this time Marmont had so skilfully managed his troops that he furnished no opportunity even for a partial attack. Wellington therefore fell off a little and made towards the heights of Cabeça Vellosa and Aldea Rubia, intending to halt there while the sixth division and Alten's cavalry, forcing their march, seized Aldea Lengua and secured the position of Christoval. But he made no effort to seize the ford of Huerta, because his own march had been long and as the French had passed over nearly twice as much ground he thought they would not attempt to reach the Tormes that day. However, when night approached, although his second line had got possession of the heights of Vellosa, his first line was heaped up without much order in the low ground between that place and Hornillos, the French army crowned all the summit of the opposite hills, and their fires, stretching in a half circle from Villaruela to Babila Fuente, showed that they commanded the ford of Huerta: they could even have attacked the allies with great advantage had there been light for the battle. The English general then ordered fires to be made, and under cover of the smoke filed the troops off in succession with celerity towards Vellosa and Aldea Rubia, but during the movement the Portuguese cavalry coming in from the front were mistaken for French and lost some men by cannon-shot ere they were recognized.

Wellington was deeply disquieted at the unexpected result of this day's operations, which had been entirely to the advantage of the French. Marmont had shown himself perfectly acquainted with the country, he had outflanked and outmarched the allies and gained the command of the Tormes; and as his junction with the king's army was thus secured he might fight or wait for reinforcements or continue his operations as it seemed good to himself. But the scope of Wellington's campaign was hourly being more restricted. His reasons for avoiding a battle except at advantage were stronger than before, because Caffarelli's cavalry was now known to be in march and the army of the centre was on the point of taking the field; hence though he should fight and gain a victory, unless it was decisive his object would not be advanced. That object was to deliver the Peninsula, which could only be done by a long course of solid operations incompatible with sudden and rash strokes un-authorized by anything but hope; wherefore yielding to the force of circumstances he prepared to return to Portugal and abide his time. Nevertheless that steadfast temper which then prevented him from seizing an adventitious chance, would not now let him yield to fortune more than she could ravish from him: he still hoped to give the lion's stroke, and resolved to cover Salamanca and the communication with Ciudad Rodrigo to the last moment. A letter stating his inability to hold his ground was however sent to Castaños, but was intercepted by Marmont, who thereupon exultingly pushed forwards with so little regard to the king's movements, that Joseph imagined the letter a subtlety of Wellington's to draw the French general into a premature battle.

*   *   *

Marmont then passed the Tormes by the fords between Alba and Huerta, and moving up the valley of Machacon encamped behind Calvariza Arriba, at the edge of a forest which extended from the river to that place. Wellington also passed the Tormes in the course of the evening by the bridges and by the fords of Santa Marta and Aldea Lengua; but the third division and d'Urban's cavalry remained on the right bank and entrenched themselves at Cabrerizos lest the French who had left a division on the heights of Babila Fuente should re-cross the Tormes in the night and overwhelm them. It was late when the light division descended the rough side of the Aldea Lengua mountain to cross the river, and the night came suddenly down with more than common darkness, for a storm, that common precursor of a battle in the Peninsula, was at hand. Torrents of rain deepened the ford, the water foamed and dashed with increasing violence, the thunder was frequent and deafening, the lightning passed in sheets of fire close over the column or played upon the points of the bayonets, and a flash falling amongst the fifth dragoon guards near Santa Marta killed many men and horses; hundreds of frightened animals then breaking loose from their piquet ropes and galloping wildly about were supposed to be the enemy's cavalry charging in the darkness, and indeed some of their patrols were at hand. But to a military eye there was nothing more imposing than the close and beautiful order in which the soldiers of that noble light division were seen by the fiery gleams to step from the river to the bank and pursue their march amidst this astounding turmoil, defying alike the storm and the enemy.

Wellington's left rested in the low ground on the Tormes near Santa Marta, having a cavalry post in front towards Calvariza de Abaxa. The right wing extended along a range of heights which ended also in low ground half a mile from the village of Arapiles, this line, perpendicular to the course of the Tormes from Huerta to Salamanca, covered that city. But Marmont extending his left along the edge of the forest still menaced the line of communication with Ciudad Rodrigo; and in the night advice came that General Chauvel, with two thousand of Caffarelli's northern horsemen and twenty guns, had reached Pollos on July 20th and would surely be up the 22nd or 23rd. A final retreat was rendered imperative by this accession of cavalry, and Wellington, to avoid the action of the latter while retiring, resolved unless the enemy should commit some flagrant error by attacking him to go back to Portugal before Chauvel arrived. But at daybreak Marmont, who had called his troops from Babila Fuente over the Tormes by the ford of Encina, brought Bonnet's and Maucune's divisions up from the forest and occupied Calvariza de Arriba; he also took possession of a wooded height close to the allies on which was an old chapel called Nuestra Señora de la Pena, thus showing his resolution to force on a battle.

At a little distance from the French left and close to the English right, were two isolated hills called the *Arapiles* or *Hermanitos*, about half cannon-shot from each other. Steep and savagely rugged they were, and had the French general gained them he could have formed across Wellington's right and compelled him to fight on bad ground with his back to the Tormes. They were however neglected by the English until Colonel Waters, observing French troops stealing towards them, told Beresford, who treated it lightly; then he told Wellington, who instantly sent the seventh *caçadores* to seize the most distant. Now ensued a combat similar to that between Cæsar and Afranius at Lerida, for the French, seeing the *caçadores* approaching, broke their own ranks, and running to the encounter gained the first Hermanito and kept it, but were repulsed from the second; at the same time a detachment from the seventh division, flanked by a squadron of German hussars under Victor Alten, assailed the Señora de la Pena height and won back half of it, yet the French kept the other half and Alten was wounded.

This dispute for the Hermanitos rendered a retreat difficult to the allies during daylight; for though the rock gained by the English was like a fortress in the way of the French army, Marmont, by extending his left and gathering a force behind his own Hermanito, could still frame a dangerous battle and pounce upon the allies during their movement. Wellington therefore extended his right into the low ground and placed the light companies of the guards in the village of Arapiles, while the fourth division, with exception of the twenty-seventh regiment which remained on the Hermanito, took post on a gentle ridge behind the village. The fifth and sixth divisions were massed on the internal slope of the English Hermanito where a great scoop in the ground hid them from the enemy; but a sharp cannonade was exchanged from the tops of those hills, on whose crowning rocks the contending generals stood like ravenous vultures watching for their quarry.

This new position had breaks and hollows which concealed most of the troops, and those exposed to view seemed and were indeed pointing towards the Rodrigo road in retreat; the dust of the commissariat and baggage retiring could be seen for miles and, save the proximity of the armies, nothing indicated an approaching battle. This could not last long. About twelve o'clock, Marmont, fearing that his menacing position on the Hermanito would induce Wellington to assail it in force, hastily brought up Foy's and Ferey's divisions in support, placing the first with some guns on a wooded height lying between the Hermanitos and the Señora de la Pena; the second, reinforced with Boyer's dragoons, he posted behind Foy on the Calvariza ridge. His fear was not ill founded. Wellington, thinking he could not retreat safely by day without holding both the hills, had actually ordered the seventh division to attack when Marmont's disposition induced him to stop lest he should thus bring on a battle disadvantageously: he preferred waiting on events, certain that by night he could retire, and thinking Marmont's rash vanity might lead him to assail the position of the allies.

He was not mistaken. Although the French division coming from Babila Fuente had not yet come out of the forest, the French marshal, fearing the allies would retreat before he could form his order of battle, suddenly directed Maucune with two divisions, covered by fifty guns and supported by the light cavalry, to move by their left and menace the Rodrigo road, designing if his adversary moved in opposition to fall on him by the village of Arapiles with six divisions of infantry and Boyer's dragoons, who were taking fresh ground to their left of the French Hermanito, leaving only one regiment of cavalry on Foy's right. The positions of the two armies now embraced an oval basin formed by ridges enclosing it like an amphitheatre, the Hermanitos being the door-posts. It was about a mile and a half broad from north to south, and more than two miles long from east to west. On the northern and western ridges stood the allies, their line running from Wellington's Hermanito by Las Torres towards Aldea Tejada. The eastern side was held by the French, and their left under Maucune was moving along the southern ridges; but his march was wide and loose, there was a long interval between him and the troops about the Hermanitos, and the divisions destined to fill this gap were still in the forest. The mass

THE BATTLE OF SALAMANCA

of artillery covering this march was however very imposing, and
it opened its fire grandly, taking ground to its left by guns in
succession as the infantry moved on; and these last marched eagerly,
continually contracting their distance from the allies and bringing
up their left shoulders as if to envelop Wellington's position and
embrace it with fire. At this time also Bonnet's troops, one regiment
of which held the French Hermanito, carried the village of Arapiles,
and though driven from part of it again maintained a fierce struggle.

Marmont's first arrangements had occupied several hours without giving positive indication of his designs, and Wellington,
ceasing to watch him, had retired from the Hermanito, and was
lying down when, about three o'clock, a report came that the
French left was rapidly pointing towards the Ciudad Rodrigo road.
Starting up, he repaired to the high ground and observed their
movements for some time with a stern contentment, for their left
wing was then entirely separated from the centre; the fault was
flagrant and he fixed it with the stroke of a thunder-bolt. A few
orders issued from his lips like the incantations of a wizard, and
suddenly the dark mass of troops which covered the English Hermanito seemed agitated by some mighty spirit; rushing violently
down the interior slope of the mountain they entered the great
basin amidst a storm of bullets which appeared to shear away the

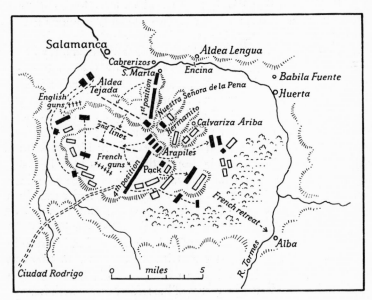

SALAMANCA

whole surface of the earth over which they were moving. The fifth division instantly formed on the right of the fourth, connecting the latter with Bradford's Portuguese, who hastened forward at the same time from the right of the army, and then Le Marchant's cavalry galloping up on the right of Bradford closed this front of battle. The sixth and seventh divisions, flanked on the right by Anson's light cavalry, were ranged on a second line, now prolonged by the Spanish troops in the direction of the third division, which, reinforced by Arentschild's German hussars and d'Urban's Portuguese horsemen, closed the extreme right at Aldea Tejada. A reserve composed of the light divisions, Pack's Portuguese, Bock's and Alten's cavalry, remained in heavy masses on the highest ground behind all.

When this grand disposition was completed, the third division and its attendant horsemen, the whole formed in four columns and flanked on the left by twelve guns, received orders to cross the enemy's line of march. The remainder of the first line, including the main body of the cavalry, was directed to advance whenever the attack of the third division should be developed; and as the fourth division must in this forward movement necessarily lend its flank to the enemy's troops stationed on the French Hermanito, Pack's brigade was commanded to assail that rock the moment the left of the British line should pass it. Thus, after long coiling and winding like angry serpents, the armies suddenly fastened together in deadly strife.

Marmont, from the French Hermanito, saw the country beneath him suddenly covered with enemies when he was in the act of making a complicated evolution, and when by the rash advance of his left his troops were separated into three parts, each too great a distance to assist the other and those nearest the enemy neither strong enough to hold their ground nor knowing what they had to encounter. The third division was however still hidden from him by the western heights, and he hoped the tempest of bullets under which the British line was moving in the basin beneath would check it until he could bring up his reserve divisions, and assail by the Arapiles village and the English Hermanito. But this his only resource was weak; the village was well disputed, the English Hermanito offered a strong bastion of defence, and behind it stood the reserve, twelve thousand strong with thirty guns. In this crisis, despatching officer after officer to hasten up his troops from the forest, others to stop the progress of his left wing, he with fierce and sanguine expectation still looked for victory until he saw Pakenham

with the third division shoot like a meteor across Maucune's path;
then pride and hope alike died with him, and desperately he was
hurrying in person to that fatal point when an exploding shell
stretched him on the earth with a broken arm and two deep wounds
in his side – confusion ensued, and his troops, distracted by ill-
judged orders and counter-orders, knew not where to move, who
to fight, or who to avoid.

It was about five o'clock when Pakenham fell on Maucune's first
division under Thomières, who had then just reached an isolated
open hill at the extremity of the southern range of heights, expecting to see the allies in full retreat to the Rodrigo road closely
followed by Marmont from the Hermanitos. The counter-stroke
was terrible! Two batteries of artillery placed on the summit of the
western heights suddenly took his troops in flank, Pakenham's
mass of infantry supported by cavalry and guns was bearing full
on his front, and two-thirds of his own division, lengthened out
and unconnected, were still behind in a wood where they could hear
but could not see the storm which was bursting: from the chief to
the lowest soldier all felt they were lost, and in an instant Pakenham, the most frank and gallant of men, commenced the battle.
Forming lines as they marched, his columns pressed to the fight,
while the French gunners, standing up manfully, sent showers of
grape into the approaching masses and a crowd of light troops
poured in their musketry, under cover of which the main body strove
to open a front of battle. But bearing onwards with the might of a
giant, Pakenham broke the half-formed lines into fragments and
sent the whole in confusion upon the supporting columns: one only
officer, standing alone with unyielding spirit, fired the last gun at
the distance of a few yards, and whether he lived or died could not
be seen for the smoke.

Some French squadrons now fell on the flank of the third division; the fifth regiment repulsed a part, and the remainder were
charged by d'Urban and Arentschild's horsemen; in the tumult the
Oporto regiment under Major Watson assailed a square of infantry
unsuccessfully, for Watson fell wounded and his men retired. Meanwhile Pakenham continuing his tempestuous course found the remainder of Thomières' division very imperfectly arrayed on the
wooded heights behind the first hill, offering two fronts; the one
opposed to the third division and its attendant horsemen, the other
to the fifth division, Bradford's Portuguese and the great masses
of cavalry and artillery which were now moving across the basin.
At this time Bonnet's troops had been repulsed from the Arapiles

village, and were in turn assailed by the fourth division; but the French still kept their menacing position at the Hermanito, for Clausel's division had arrived from the forest, and the connexion between the centre and left was in some measure restored. Two divisions of infantry and Boyer's dragoons were indeed still in march from Calvariza, Thomirères was killed, Bonnet, who had succeeded Marmont, was disabled, and hence more confusion; but the chief command had devolved on Clausel and he was of a capacity equal to the crisis. The scene was however terrible. He saw the fourth and fifth divisions and Bradford's brigade hotly engaged and steadily gaining ground, Le Marchant's heavy cavalry, Anson's light dragoons, and Bull's troop of artillery advancing at a trot on Pakenham's left, and on that general's right d'Urban's horsemen overlapping the disordered masses of his left wing. Half an hour only had elapsed since the battle commenced and already the French had lost their commander and two other generals, and their left turned and thrown into confusion was enveloped. And though Clausel's own division reinforced Maucune and a front was spread along the southern heights of the basin, the array was loose, it was in lines, in columns, in squares, without unity; a powerful sun played in the men's eyes, and the light soil, stirred up and driven by a breeze from the west, came mingled with smoke full upon them in such stifling clouds, that scarcely able to breathe and unable to see they delivered their fire at random.

In this oppressed state, while Pakenham was pressing their left with a conquering violence, while the fifth division was wasting their ranks with fire, the interval between those divisions was suddenly filled with a whirling cloud of dust which moved swiftly forward carrying within it the trampling sound of a charging multitude; it passed the left of the third division in a chaotic mass, but then opening, Anson's light cavalry and Le Marchant's heavy horsemen were seen to break forth at full speed, and the next moment twelve hundred French infantry were trampled down with a terrible clamour and disturbance. Bewildered and blinded, they cast away their arms and crowded through the intervals of the squadrons, stooping and crying out for quarter, while the dragoons, big men and on big horses, rode onwards, smiting with their long glittering swords in uncontrollable power, and the third division following at speed, shouted as the French lines fell in succession before this dreadful charge.

Nor were these valiant horsemen yet exhausted. Le Marchant and many other officers had fallen, but Cotton and all his staff were

at their head, and with ranks confused and blended in one mass
they still galloped on against a fresh column from whence a stream
of fire emptied a hundred saddles, but with fine courage and might
they broke through this the strongest body yet encountered, and
Lord Edward Somerset, with a happy perseverance continuing the
charge at the head of one squadron, captured five guns. The left was
thus entirely broken, two thousand prisoners were taken, the French
light cavalry forsook that part of the field, and the three divisions
under Maucune no longer existed as a military body. Anson's
cavalry had suffered little in the charge, and now passing quite over
the ridge were joined by d'Urban's horsemen and took the place
of Le Marchant's exhausted men. United with the third and fifth
divisions and the guns, they formed one formidable line more than
a mile in advance of where Pakenham had commenced the battle,
and that impetuous officer with unmitigable fury was still pressing
forward spreading terror and confusion.

While these signal events, which occupied about forty minutes,
were passing on the allies' right, a terrible battle raged also
in the centre. For the fourth division, moving in a line with
the fifth and under the same cannonade, had driven Bonnet's
troops step by step back to the south-eastern part of the basin,
where they got mixed with the disordered masses of Maucune's
and Clausel's divisions then retreating before Pakenham and the
cavalry; and the French Hermanito being thus apparently isolated
was assailed by Pack's Portuguese about the time of Le Marchant's
charge. The French front of battle was now however fully developed
and connected, for Foy had commenced a distant cannonade against
the British reserves, while on his left Pack was mounting the
Hermanito; further on Bonnet's troops were still strongly fighting,
and the broken troops of the left wing were rallying upon them.
Clausel had indeed made a surprising effort beyond all men's expectations, and a great change was already visible. Drawing Ferey's
division from Calvariza, he had placed it in the centre behind
Bonnet's troops, and at the same time united there the light cavalry,
Boyer's dragoons and the two divisions so long expected from the
forest. By this able disposition he offered a mass for the broken left
wing to rally upon, and made Sarrut's, Brennier's and Ferey's unbroken divisions, supported by the whole of the cavalry, cover the
line of retreat to Alba de Tormes, while another division was in mass
close behind Marmont's Hermanito, and Foy remained untouched
on the right. It was a great stroke, but not content with restoring
an order of battle and saving his retreat, Clausel attempted to stem

the tide of victory in the very fulness of its strength and roughness. His hopes were founded on Pack's failure, for that officer having ascended the French Hermanito in one column was within thirty paces of the top and believed himself victorious, when suddenly the hidden French reserves leaped forward from the rocks upon his front and left flank, there was a thick cloud of smoke, a shout, a stream of fire, and then the side of the hill was covered with the killed, the wounded and the flying Portuguese: they were scoffed at for the failure, but unjustly, no troops could have withstood that crash upon such steep ground, and the propriety of attacking the hill at all seems questionable. The result went nigh to shake the whole battle. For the fourth division had just then reached the southern ridge of the basin, and one of the best regiments in the service was actually on the summit, when twelve hundred fresh adversaries arrayed on the reverse slope charged up hill; the British fire was straggling and ineffectual, the soldiers being breathless and disordered by the previous fighting, and the French, who came up resolutely and without firing, won the crest: they were even pursuing, when two regiments placed in line below checked them with a destructive volley.

This vigorous counter-blow happening simultaneously with Pack's defeat, permitted Clausel, no longer fearing for the Hermanito, to menace the left flank and rear of the fourth division, but the fortieth regiment wheeling about with a rough charge cleared the rear and the French did not engage more deeply in that quarter. Ferey however pressed the front of the division, Brennier did the same by the first line of the fifth division, and Boyer's dragoons came on at a trot; the allies were outflanked, overmatched, lost ground, and fiercely the French followed and the fight once more raged in the basin below. Cole had fallen deeply wounded, Leith had the same fortune, but Beresford promptly drew Spry's Portuguese brigade from the second line of the fifth division and thus flanked the advancing columns of the enemy; yet he also fell desperately wounded, and then Boyer's dragoons came freely into action because Anson's cavalry had been checked by a heavy fire of artillery. The crisis of the battle had now arrived, and victory was for the general who had the strongest reserves in hand.

Wellington, who was seen that day at every point precisely when his presence was most required, brought the sixth division up from the second line, and its charge, vehement and sustained, was successful, but the struggle was not slight; Hulse's brigade on the left went down by hundreds, and the sixty-first and eleventh regiments won their way through such a fire as British soldiers only can sustain. Some of Boyer's dragoons also, breaking in between the fifth and sixth divisions, slew many men and disordered the fifty-third, yet that brave regiment lost no ground, nor did Clausel's impetuous counter-attack avail at any point after the first burst. The allies retook the southern ridge, the French General Menné was severely and Ferey mortally wounded, Clausel himself was hurt, and when Boyer's reserve of horse came on at a canter for a redeeming charge they were broken by the fire of Hulse's noble brigade. Then the changing current of battle once more set for the British. Pakenham continued to outflank the French left, the Hermanito was abandoned, Foy retired from the ridge of Calvariza, and the allied host, righting itself like a gallant ship after a sudden gust, again bore onwards in blood and gloom. For though the air purified by the storm of the night was peculiarly clear, one vast cloud of smoke and dust rolled along the basin and within it was the battle with all its sights and sounds of terror.

When the English general had restored the fight in the centre he directed the first division to push between Foy and the rest of the French army, which would have rendered it impossible for the latter to rally or escape; but this order was not executed, and Foy's division and that which had just descended from the French Hermanito were skilfully used by Clausel to protect the retreat. The first, posted on undulating ground and flanked by some squadrons of dragoons, covered the roads to the fords of Huerta and Encina – the second, now added to Maucune's command and reinforced with fifteen guns, was placed on a steep ridge in front of the forest covering the road to Alba de Tormes, and behind this ridge the rest of the army, then falling back in disorder before the third, fifth and sixth divisions, took refuge. Wellington immediately sent the light division, formed in two lines and flanked by some squadrons of dragoons, against Foy, supporting it with the first division in columns, and flanking that again on the right with two brigades of the fourth division which he had drawn off from the centre when the sixth division restored the fight: the seventh division and the Spaniards followed in reserve, the country was covered with troops and a new army seemed to have risen out of the earth.

Foy, throwing out a cloud of skirmishers, retired slowly by wings, turning and firing heavily from every rise of ground upon the light division, which marched steadily forward without returning a shot save by its skirmishers, and for two miles this march continued under musketry, which was occasionally thickened by a cannonade, yet very few men were lost, the French aim being baffled by the twilight and by the even order and rapid gliding of the lines. The French General Desgraviers was however killed, and the flanking brigades from the fourth division having now penetrated between Maucune and Foy, it seemed difficult for the latter to extricate his troops from the action; nevertheless he did it and with great dexterity. For having increased his skirmishers on the last defensible ridge, along the foot of which ran a marshy stream, he redoubled his fire of musketry and made a menacing demonstration with his horsemen just as the darkness fell, where- upon the British guns immediately opened, a squadron of dragoons galloped forwards from the left, the infantry crossing the marshy stream with an impetuous pace gained the summit of the hill and a rough shock seemed at hand; but the main body of the French had gone into the thick forest on their own left during the firing, and the skirmishers fled swiftly after, covered by the smoke and by the darkness.

Maucune was maintaining meanwhile a noble battle. He was outflanked and outnumbered, but the safety of the French army depended on his courage; he knew it, and Pakenham, marking his bold demeanour, advised Clinton who was immediately in his front not to assail him until the third division should have turned his left. Nevertheless the sixth division was plunged afresh into action and under great disadvantage; for after being kept by its commander a long time close under Maucune's batteries, which ploughed heavily through the ranks, it was suddenly directed by a staff officer to attack the hill. Assisted by a brigade of the fourth division the troops then rushed up, but in the darkness of the night the fire showed from afar how the battle went. On the side of the British a sheet of flame was seen, sometimes advancing with an even front sometimes pricking forth in spear heads, now falling back in waving lines and anon darting upwards in one vast pyramid, the apex of which often approached yet never gained the actual summit of the mountain – the French musketry in opposition, rapid as light- ning, sparkled along the brow of the height with unvarying fulness, and with what destructive effects the dark gaps and changing shapes of the adverse fire showed too plainly. But when Pakenham had again turned the enemy's left and Foy's division had glided into the forest, Maucune's task was completed, the effulgent crest of the ridge became black and silent and the whole French army vanished as it were in the darkness.

During this combat Wellington, who was with the leading regiment of the light division, turned towards the ford of Huerta, leaving the forest to his right; for he thought the Spanish garrison was still in the castle of Alba de Tormes and that the enemy must of necessity be found in a confused mass at the fords. It was for this final stroke that he had so skilfully strengthened his left wing, nor was he disabused of his error by marching through standing corn where no enemy could have preceded him, nor by Foy's retreat into the forest, because it pointed at first towards the fords of Encina and Gonzalo which that general might be endeavouring to gain, and the right wing of the allies would find him there: a squadron of French dragoons also, bursting from the woods in front of the advancing troops soon after dark, fired their pistols and then passed at full gallop towards the ford of Huerta, thus indicating great confusion in the defeated army and confirming the notion that its final retreat would be in that direction. Had the castle of Alba been held the French could not have carried off a third of their army – nor would they have been in much better plight if Carlos d'España, who soon discovered his error in withdrawing the garrison, had informed Wellington of the fact; but he suppressed it, and dishonourably suffered the colonel who had only obeyed his orders to be censured. The left wing therefore continued their march to the ford without meeting any enemy, and the night being far spent were there halted; the right wing, exhausted by long fighting, had ceased to pursue after the action with Maucune, and thus the French gained Alba unmolested; but the action did not terminate without two remarkable accidents. While riding close behind the forty-third regiment, Wellington was struck in the thigh by a musket-ball which first passed through his holster. Afterwards, when the night piquets had been set at Huerta, Sir Stapleton Cotton, who had gone to the ford and returned a different road, was shot through the arm by a Portuguese sentinel whose challenge he had disregarded. These were the last events of this famous battle, in which the skill of the general was worthily seconded by troops whose ardour may be appreciated by the following anecdotes.

Captain Brotherton of the fourteenth dragoons, fighting on the 18th at the Guarena amongst the foremost as he was always wont to do, had a sword thrust through his side, yet he was again on horseback the 22nd and, being denied leave to remain in that condition with his own regiment, secretly joined Pack's Portuguese in an undress, and was again hurt in the unfortunate charge at the Hermanito. Such were the officers. A man of the forty-third, one by no means distinguished above his comrades, was shot through the middle of the thigh and lost his shoes in passing the marshy stream, but refusing to quit the fight, limped under fire in rear of his regiment, and with naked feet and streaming with blood from his wound marched for several miles over a country covered with sharp flints. Such were the soldiers, and the devotion of a woman was not wanting to the illustration of this great day.

The wife of Colonel Dalbiac, an English lady of a gentle disposition and possessing a very delicate frame, had braved the dangers and endured the privations of two campaigns with that patient fortitude which belongs only to her sex. In this battle, forgetful of everything but the strong affection which had so long supported her, she rode deep amidst the enemy's fire, trembling, yet irresistibly impelled forwards by feelings more imperious than horror, more piercing than the fear of death.

Clausel carried his army clear off without further loss, and with such celerity that his head-quarters were that night at Flores de Avila forty miles from the field of battle. After remaining a few hours there he crossed the Zapardiel and would have halted the 24th, but the allied cavalry entered Cisla and his march was then continued to Arevalo. This was a wonderful retreat, and the line was chosen with judgment, for Wellington naturally expected the French army would have made for Tordesillas instead of the Adaja. The pursuit was however somewhat slack. The British left wing, being quite fresh, could have ascended the Tormes on the night of the battle and reached the Almar before daylight, or passing at Huerta have marched by Ventosa to Peneranda; but the vigorous following of a beaten enemy was not a prominent characteristic of Lord Wellington's warfare.

Valladolid was occupied by the allies amidst the rejoicings of the inhabitants, and eight hundred sick and wounded men were captured there with seventeen pieces of artillery and large stores. Three hundred other prisoners were taken by the guerrilla chief Martinez, and a large convoy on its way to Soult was forced to retrograde to Burgos. The left wing of the allies then pursued the enemy up the Arlanza, while the right wing moving against the king reached Cuellar the 1st of August. On the same day the garrison of Tordesillas surrendered to the Galicians, and Joseph, having first dismantled the castle of Segovia and raised a contribution of money and church plate, retreated through the Puerta de Guadarrama, leaving a rear-guard of cavalry which escaped by the Ildefonso pass on the approach of the allied horsemen. Thus the army of the centre was irrevocably separated from the army of Portugal, the operations against the latter were terminated, and new combinations were made conformable to the altered state of affairs.

Wellington, seeing that the king had crossed the Tagus in retreat, entered Madrid, a very memorable event were it only from the affecting circumstances attending it. He, a foreigner, marching at the head of a foreign army, was met and welcomed to the capital of Spain by the whole remaining population. The multitude who before that hour had never seen him came forth to hail his approach, not with feigned enthusiasm, not with acclamations, extorted by the fear of a conqueror's power, nor yet excited by the natural proneness of human nature to laud the successful, for there was no tumultuous exultation; famine was amongst them and long-endured misery had subdued their spirits; but with tears and every other sign of deep emotion they crowded around his horse, hung upon his stirrups, touched his clothes, and throwing themselves upon the earth blessed him aloud as the friend of Spain. His triumph was as pure and glorious as it was uncommon, and he felt it to be so.

Madrid was however still disturbed by the presence of the enemy. The Retiro contained enormous stores, twenty thousand stand of arms, more than one hundred and eighty pieces of artillery, and the eagles of two French regiments; it had a garrison of two thousand fighting men besides invalids and followers, but its inherent weakness was soon made manifest. The works consisted of an interior fort called La China, with an exterior entrenchment; but the fort was too small, the entrenchment, too large, and easily deprived of water. In the lodgings of a French officer also was found an order directing the commandant to confine his real defence to the fort; and accordingly, in the night of the 13th, he abandoned the entrenchment and next day accepted honourable terms, because La China was so contracted and filled with combustible buildings that his fine troops would with only a little firing have been smothered in the ruins; yet they were so dissatisfied that many broke their arms and their commander was like to have fallen a victim to their wrath. They were immediately sent to Portugal, and French writers with too much truth assert that the escort basely robbed and murdered many of the prisoners. This disgraceful action was perpetrated on the frontier of Portugal by the Spanish garrison of Ciudad Rodrigo; the British troops, who furnished no escorts after the first day's march from Madrid, are guiltless, and Lord Wellington made strenuous but unsuccessful efforts to have the Spanish criminals punished.

Napoleon had notice of Marmont's defeat as early as the 2nd of

September, a week before the great battle of Borodino; the news was carried by Fabvier, who made the journey from Valladolid in one course and, having fought on the 22nd of July at the Arapiles, was wounded on the heights of Moskowa the 7th of September! Marmont, suffering alike in body and in mind, had excused himself with so little strength or clearness, that the emperor, contemptuously remarking that the despatch contained more complicated stuffing than a clock, desired his war minister to demand why Marmont had delivered battle without the orders of the king? Why he had not made his operations subservient to the general plan of the campaign? Why he broke from defensive into offensive operations before the army of the centre joined him? Why he would not even wait two days for Chauvel's cavalry which he knew were close at hand? 'From personal vanity,' said the emperor with seeming sternness, 'the Duke of Ragusa has sacrificed the interests of his country and the good of my service, he is guilty of the crime of insubordination and is the author of all this misfortune.'

XIV

Retreat from Burgos

Wellington had scattered the French armies in central Spain, but his situation remained precarious. As soon as his enemies had time to regroup and concentrate, he would be in danger. In spite of his victories in battle, which had emblazoned his fame throughout Europe, some weariness of spirit descended on him at this time. Created an earl after Ciudad Rodrigo and a marquess after Salamanca, a grandee of Spain and commander-in-chief of all the allied forces, his military control flagged. Pursuing Clausel and King Joseph up the great road to France, he invested the fortress of Burgos. But still sickened by the slaughter of his best men at Ciudad Rodrigo and Badajoz, he pressed the siege half-heartedly. By the end of September, the French armies were gathering once more and Wellington was obliged to seek the safe haven of Portugal again, just as Napoleon was beginning his retreat from Moscow.

ALL THE HOSPITALS in the rear were crowded. Salamanca, in which there were six thousand sick and wounded besides French prisoners, was the abode of misery. The soldiers endured much during the first two or three days after the battle, and the inferior officers' sufferings were still more heavy and protracted. They had no money and many sold their horses and other property to sustain life; some actually died of want, and though Wellington, hearing of this, gave orders they should be supplied from the purveyor's stores in the same manner as the soldiers, the relief came late. It is a common yet erroneous notion, that the English system of hospitals in the Peninsula was admirable and the French hospitals neglected. Strenuous and unceasing exertions were made by Wellington and the chiefs of the medical staff to form good hospital establishments, but the want of money, and still more the want of previous institutions, foiled their utmost efforts. Now there was no point of warfare which more engaged Napoleon's attention than the care of his sick and wounded; and he being monarch as well as general, furnished his hospitals with all things requisite, even with luxuries. Under his fostering care also, Larrey, justly celebrated were it for this alone, organized the establishment called the hospital '*Ambulance*'; that is to say waggons of a peculiar construction, well horsed and served by men trained and incorporated as soldiers, who being rewarded for their courage and devotion like other soldiers were always at hand, and whether in action or on a march, ready to pick up, to salve and to carry off wounded men. The astonishing rapidity with which the fallen French soldiers disappeared from a field of battle attested the excellence of this institution.

In the British army, the carrying off the wounded depended partly upon the casual assistance of a weak waggon train very badly disciplined, furnishing only three waggons to a division and not originally appropriated to that service; partly upon the spare commissariat animals, but principally upon the resources of the country whether of bullock carts, mules or donkeys, and hence the most doleful scenes after a battle or when an hospital was to be evacuated. The increasing numbers of the sick and wounded as the war enlarged pressed on the limited number of regular medical officers, and Wellington complained that when he demanded more the military medical board in London neglected his demands and thwarted his arrangements. Shoals of hospital mates and students were indeed sent out, and they arrived for the most part ignorant alike of war and their own profession; while a heterogeneous mass of purveyors and their subordinates, acting without any military organization or effectual superintendence, baffled the exertions of those medical officers, and they were many, whose experience, zeal and talents would, with a good institution to work upon, have rendered this branch of the service most distinguished. Nay, many even of the well-educated surgeons sent out were for some time of little use, for superior professional skill is of little value in comparison of experience in military organization; where one soldier dies from the want of a delicate operation, hundreds perish from the absence of military arrangement. War tries the strength of the military frame-work; it is in peace the frame-work itself must be formed, otherwise barbarians would be the leading soldiers of the world. A perfect army can only be made by civil institutions, and those, rightly considered, would tend to confine the horrors of war to the field of battle, which would be the next best thing to the perfection of civilization that would prevent war altogether.

The army was many months in arrears, those officers who went to the rear sick suffered the most cruel privations, those who remained in Madrid, tempted by the pleasures of the capital, obtained some dollars at an exorbitant premium from a money-broker; and it was grievously suspected that his means resulted from the nefarious proceedings of an under commissary: the soldiers, equally tempted and having no such resource, plundered the stores of the Retiro. In fine, discipline became relaxed throughout the army, and the troops kept in the field were gloomy, envying those who remained at Madrid.

The city exhibited a sad mixture of luxury and desolation. When it was first entered, a violent and cruel unjust persecution of those who were called '*Afrancesados*' was commenced, and continued until the English general interfered, and as an example made no distinction in his invitations to the palace feasts. Truly it was not necessary to increase the sufferings of the miserable people, for though the markets were full of provisions there was no money wherewith to buy; and though the houses were full of rich furniture there were neither purchasers nor lenders; even noble families secretly sought charity that they might live. At night, the groans and stifled cries of famishing people were heard, and every morning emaciated dead bodies, cast into the streets, showed why those cries had ceased. The calm resignation with which these terrible sufferings were borne was a distinctive mark of the national character; not many begged, none complained, there was no violence, no reproaches, very few thefts; the allies lost a few animals, nothing more, and these were generally thought to be taken by robbers from the country. But with this patient endurance of calamity the Madrileños discovered a deep and unaffected gratitude for kindness received at the hands of the British officers who contributed, not much for they had it not, but enough of money to form soup charities by which hundreds were succoured. It was in the third division the example was set, and by the forty-fifth regiment, and it was not the least of the many honourable distinctions those brave men have earned.

Wellington, desirous of sheltering his troops from the extreme heat, had sent four divisions and the cavalry to the Escorial and St Ildefonso, from whence they could join Hill by the valley of the Tagus, or Clinton by Arevalo; but when he knew the king's retreat upon Valencia was decided, that Soult had abandoned Cordoba and Clinton was falling back before Clausel, he ordered the first, fifth and seventh divisions, Pack's and Bradford's Portuguese brigades, Ponsonby's light horsemen and the heavy German cavalry, to move rapidly upon Arevalo, and on the first of September quitted Madrid himself to take the command. Yet his army had been so diminished by sickness that only twenty-one thousand men, including three thousand cavalry, were assembled in that town. He could scarcely feed the Portuguese soldiers, who were also very ill equipped, and their government, instead of transmitting money and stores, endeavoured to throw off the burthen by an ingenious device. For having always a running account with the Spanish government, they now made a treaty by which the Spaniards were to feed the Portuguese troops and check off the expense on the national account, which was then in favour of the Portuguese; that is, the soldiers were to starve under the sanction of this treaty, because the Spaniards could not feed their own men and would not, if they could, have fed the Portuguese. Neither could the latter take provisions from the country, because Wellington demanded the resources of the valleys of the Duero and Pisuerga for the English soldiers, as a set-off against the money advanced by Sir Henry Wellesley to the Spanish regency at Cadiz. To stop this shameful expedient he refused payment of the subsidy from the chest of aids, whereupon the old discontents and disputes revived and acquired new force, the regency became intractable and the whole military system of Portugal was like to fall to pieces.

The retreat from Burgos was commenced on the night of the 21st of October by a measure of great nicety and boldness; for the road, divaricating at Gamonal, led to the bridge of Villaton on the one hand and the bridge of Burgos on the other, and Wellington chose

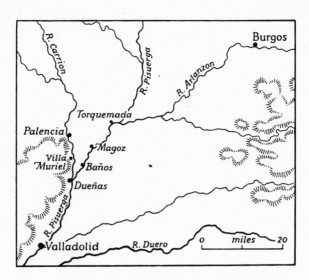

THE RETREAT FROM BURGOS

THE DUKE OF WELLINGTON

the latter, as being the shortest, though it passed the Arlanzan river close under the guns of the castle. The army quitted the position after dark, the artillery-wheels were muffled with straw, and defiled over the bridge of Burgos with such silence and celerity that Dubreton, watchful and suspicious as he was, knew nothing of their march until the partidas, failing in nerve, commenced galloping; then he poured a destructive fire down, but soon lost the range.

The usual concomitants of an English retreat were exhibited at Torquemada, where the great wine-vaults were invaded and it is said twelve thousand men were at one time in a state of helpless inebriety. In this crisis the English general, who had now retreated some fifty miles, seeing the enemy so hot and menacing in pursuit, resolved to check his course because, the means of transport being scanty and the weather bad, the convoys of sick and wounded were still on the wrong side of the Duero. Wherefore, having by a short march crossed the Carrion at its confluence with the Pisuerga, he halted behind it, and was there fortunately joined by a regiment of the guards and by detachments coming from Coruña. His position, extending from Villa Muriel to Dueñas below the meeting of the waters, was strong, being along a range of hills, lofty yet descending with an easy sweep to the Carrion which covered his left, while the Pisuerga secured his right wing. A detachment was employed to destroy the bridge of Baños on the Pisuerga, a battalion of the royals was sent to aid the Spaniards in destroying the bridges at Palencia; and some houses and convents beyond the rivers furnished good posts, behind which the bridges of Muriel and San Isidro on the Carrion and that of Dueñas on the Pisuerga could be broken.

Souham, excited by his success, cannonaded the rear-guard at Torquemada, passed the Pisuerga, directed Foy's division upon Palencia, and sent Maucune with an advanced-guard against the bridges of Baños, Isidro and Muriel; but he halted himself at Magoz; and if fame does not lie, because the number of French drunkards at Torquemada were even more numerous than those of the British army.

Hill had a discretionary power to retire by the valley of the Tagus or the Guadarrama; a position in the former taken on the flank of the enemy would have prevented the king from passing the Guadarrama and at the same time have covered Lisbon; a retreat by the Guadarrama exposed Lisbon; but thinking the valley of the Tagus in that advanced season would not support the French army, and knowing Wellington to be pressed by superior forces, he chose the Guadarrama. This movement uncovered the magazines, so negligently left along the line of communication to Badajoz; the enemy could have sent men to seize them; nor were the removal and destruction of the stores in Madrid effected without disorders of a singular nature. The municipality demanded all the provision remaining there, as if for the enemy, and when refused excited a mob to attack the magazines; firing even took place and the fourth division was called in to restore order. Some wheat being finally given to the poorest of the people, Madrid was abandoned, and it was affecting to see the earnest and true friendship of the population. Men women and children, crowding around the troops, bewailed their departure, and moving with them in one vast mass for more than two miles left their houses empty when the French cavalry scouts were at the gates on the other side. This emotion was distinct from political feeling, because there was a very strong French party in Madrid, and among the causes of wailing, the return of the plundering and cruel partidas unchecked by the presence of the British was very loudly proclaimed. The Madrileños have been stigmatized as a savage and faithless people, the British army found them patient, gentle, generous and loyal. Nor is this fact to be disputed because of the riot which occurred in the destruction of the magazines; for the provisions had been obtained by requisition from the country around Madrid under an agreement with the Spanish government to pay at the end of the war; and it was natural for the people, excited as they were by the authorities, to endeavour to get their own flour back rather than have it destroyed when they were starving.

Joseph, thinking to prevent the junction of the allies, had gained Arevalo by the Segovia road the 5th, Souham's scouts were met with at Medina del Campo the 8th, and for the first time since he had quitted Valencia the king obtained news of the army of Portugal. One hundred thousand combatants, twelve thousand being cavalry with a hundred and thirty pieces of artillery, were thus assembled on those plains over which, three months before, Marmont had marched with so much confidence to his own destruction. Soult, then expelled from Andalusia by Marmont's defeat, was now, after having made half the circuit of the Peninsula, come to drive into Portugal that very army whose victory had driven him from the south; and as Wellington had foreseen and foretold, the recovery of Andalusia, politically important and useful as it was, proved injurious to himself; it had concentrated a mighty power to escape from which both skill and fortune were necessary; and the

Spanish armies, let loose by this union of all the French troops, kept aloof, or coming to aid were found a burthen.

On the 7th Hill passed the Tormes at Alba and mined the bridge, the light division and Long's cavalry remaining on the right bank during the night. Wellington held San Christoval, and the king, even at this late period, was doubtful if Ballesteros's troops had or had not joined the allied army at Avila. Wellington also was uncertain of the king's numbers, but designed to maintain the Tormes permanently and give his troops repose. He had retreated two hundred miles, and Hill had retired the same distance besides his march from Estremadura. Skerrett had come from Cadiz, and all required rest, for the soldiers, especially those who besieged Burgos, had been in the field with scarcely an interval of repose since January; the infantry were barefooted, their equipments spoiled, the cavalry weak, the horses out of condition, the discipline of all failing. The excesses committed on the Burgos line have been shown, and during the first day's march from the Tagus, five hundred of the rear-guard under Cole, chiefly of one regiment, finding the inhabitants had fled according to custom whichever side was approaching, broke open the houses, plundered and got drunk: a multitude were left in the cellars of Valdemoro and two hundred and fifty fell into the hands of the enemy. The rest of the retreat being unmolested was made with more regularity, but the excesses still committed furnished glaring evidence that the moral conduct of a general cannot be fairly judged by following in the wake of a retreating army. There was no want of provisions, no hardships to exasperate the men, and yet the author of this history counted on the first day's march from Madrid seventeen bodies of murdered peasants; by whom killed, or for what, whether by English or Germans, by Spaniards or Portuguese, in dispute, in robbery or in wanton villainy was unknown; but their bodies were in the ditches, and a shallow observer might thence have drawn foul and false conclusions against the English general and nation.

Another notable thing was the discontent of the veteran troops with the staff officers. The assembling of the sick men at the place and time prescribed to form the convoys was punctually attended to by the regimental officers – not so by the others, nor by the commissaries who had charge to provide the means of transport – hence delay and great suffering to the sick, and the wearing out of healthy men's strength by waiting with their knapsacks on for the negligent. When the light division was left on the right bank of the Tormes to cover the passage at Alba, a prudent order that all baggage or other impediments should pass rapidly over the narrow bridge at that place without halting on the enemy's side, was, by those charged with the execution, so rigorously interpreted as to deprive the troops of their ration bullocks and flour mules at the very moment of distribution; and the tired soldiers, thus absurdly denied food, had the further mortification to see a string of commissariat carts deliberately passing their post many hours afterwards. All regimental officers know that discontent thus created is most hurtful to discipline, and it is in these particulars the value of a good and experienced staff is found.

However, while desirous to fight, the English general looked also to retreat; he sending his sick to the rear, brought up small magazines from Rodrigo to intermediate points, caused the surplus ammunition at Salamanca to be destroyed by small explosions, and delivered large stores of clothing, arms and equipments to the Spaniards, who were thus completely furnished; but in an hour after they were selling their accoutrement under his own windows! Salamanca presented indeed an extraordinary scene, and the Spaniards, civil and military, evinced hatred of the British. Daily did they attempt or perpetrate murder, and one act of peculiar atrocity merits notice. A horse led by an English soldier being frightened backed against a Spanish officer commanding at a gate, he caused the soldier to be dragged into his guard-house and there bayoneted him in cold blood; and no redress could be had for this or other crimes, save by counter-violence which was not long withheld. A Spanish officer while wantonly stabbing at a rifleman was shot dead by the latter; and a British volunteer slew a Spanish officer at the head of his own regiment in a sword-fight, the troops of both nations looking on.

The civil authorities, not less savage, were more insolent than the military, treating every English person with an intolerable arrogance. Even the Prince of Orange was like to have lost his life; for upon remonstrating about quarters with the sitting junta, they ordered one of their guards to kill him; and he would have been killed had not Lieutenant Steele of the forty-third, a bold athletic person, felled the man before he could stab; yet both the prince and his defender were forced to fly from the soldier's comrades.

The allied army was united in the position of the Arapiles, and it was still hoped the French would give battle there; but the first division was placed at Aldea Tejada on the Junguen stream, to secure that passage in case of retreat to Ciudad Rodrigo. Drouet, finding the bridge of Alba broken and the castle occupied, had meantime crossed at Galisancho and taken post on the ridge of Señora de Utiera; and Soult, who had commenced fortifying Mozarbes, extended his left at the same time to the height of Señora de la Buena near the Rodrigo road; yet slowly, for the ground was heavy and the many sources of the Junguen and Valmusa being filled by rain impeded his march. This evolution was nearly the same as that practised by Marmont, but it was on a wider circle, by a second range of heights enclosing as it were those by which the Duke of Ragusa moved and beyond the reach of such a sudden attack and catastrophe. The result in each case was remarkable. Marmont closing with a short quick turn, a falcon striking at an eagle, received a buffet that broke his pinions and spoiled his flight. Soult, a wary kite, sailing slowly and with a wide wheel to seize a helpless prey lost it altogether.

About two o'clock, Wellington, too weak to attack and seeing the French cavalry pointing to the Ciudad Rodrigo road, thought the king wished to establish a fortified head of cantonments at Mozarbes and then operate against the allies' communication with Rodrigo; wherefore, suddenly casting his army into three columns, he crossed the Junguen, and then covering his left flank with his cavalry and guns, defiled in order of battle before the enemy at little more than cannon-shot. With a wonderful boldness and facility, and good fortune also for there was a thick fog and a heavy rain which rendered the bye-ways and fields by which the enemy moved nearly impassable while the allies had the use of the high roads, he carried his whole army in one mass quite round the French left: thus he gained the Valmusa river and halted at night in rear of those who had been threatening him in front a few hours before. This exploit, foretold by Jourdan, was certainly surprising, but it was not creditable to the generalship on either side; for first it may be asked why the English commander, having somewhat carelessly suffered Soult to pass the Tormes and turn his position, waited so long on the Arapiles as to render this dangerous movement necessary – a movement which bad roads, bad weather and want of vigour on the other side rendered possible and no more.

It has been said the drawback to Soult's genius is want of promptness in seizing the decisive moment. It is a great thing to fight a great battle, and against such a general as Wellington and such troops as the British; a man may well be excused if he thinks twice ere he puts his life and fame, and the lives and fame of thousands of his countrymen, the weal or woe of nations, upon the hazard of an event which may be decided by the existence of a ditch five feet wide, or the single blunder of a single fool, or the confusion of a coward, or by any other circumstance however trivial. It is no mean consideration, that the praise or the hatred of nations, universal glory, or universal, perhaps eternal contempt waits on an action the object of which may be more safely gained by other means, for in war there is infinite variety. And here Soult certainly vacillated after passing the Tormes, purposely perhaps to avoid an action; holding it unwise in the disjointed state of French affairs and when without any fixed base or reserves in case of defeat to fight a decisive battle. Nor is this prudence blameable, for though he who would be great in war must be daring, to set all upon one throw belongs only to an irresponsible chief, not to a lieutenant whose task is but a portion of the general plan; neither is it wise in monarch or general to fight when all may be lost by defeat, unless all may be won by victory. The king, more unfettered than Soult, desired a battle, and with an army so good and numerous the latter's prudence seems misplaced; he should have grappled with his enemy, for once engaged at any point the allies could not have retreated, and there were ninety thousand good men to fight less than seventy thousand.

On the 16th of November the allies retired by the three roads which lead across the Matilla stream through Tamames, San Munos and Martin del Rio; the light division and the cavalry closed the rear, and the country was a forest penetrable in all directions. The troops bivouacked in the evening behind the Matilla stream and the march was only twelve miles, yet the stragglers were numerous for the soldiers meeting with vast herds of swine quitted their colours by hundreds to shoot them, and such a rolling musketry echoed through the forest it was thought the French were attacking. It was in vain the staff officers endeavoured to stop this disgraceful practice, which had indeed commenced the evening before; in vain that two offenders were hanged; the hungry soldiers still broke from the columns, the property of whole districts was swept away in a few hours, and the army was in some degree placed at the mercy of the enemy.

The success and long confirmed reputation of Wellington could not protect him from the vanity and presumption of subordinate officers. The allusion fixes here. Knowing the direct road was impassable, he ordered the movement by another road longer and apparently more difficult; this seemed so extraordinary to some general officers that, after consulting together, they deemed their commander unfit to conduct the army and led their troops by what appeared to them the fittest line of retreat! He had before daylight placed himself at an important point on his own road, and waited impatiently for the arrival of the leading division until dawn; then suspecting what had happened he galloped to the other road and found the would-be commanders stopped by water. The insubordination and the danger to the army were alike glaring, yet the practical rebuke was so severe and well timed, the humiliation so complete and so deeply felt, that with one proud sarcastic observation, indicating contempt more than anger, he led back the troops and drew off all his forces safely. Some confusion and great danger still attended the operation, for even on his road one water-gully was so deep that the light division, bringing up the rear, could only pass it man by man over a felled tree, and it was fortunate that Soult, unable to feed his troops, stopped on the Huebra and only sent some cavalry to Tamames. The retreat was unmolested, but whether from necessity or negligence in the subordinates, many wounded men, most of them hurt by cannon-shot, were left behind, the enemy never passed the Huebra and the miserable creatures perished by a horrible and lingering death.

The marshy plains now to be passed exhausted the strength of the tired soldiers, thousands straggled, the depredations on the herds of swine were repeated, and the temper of the army generally prognosticated the greatest misfortunes if the retreat should be continued. This was however the last day of trial, the weather cleared up, some hills afforded dry bivouacs and fuel, the distribution of good rations restored the strength and spirits of the men, and the next day Rodrigo and the neighbouring villages were occupied in tranquillity. The cavalry was then sent out to the forest, and being aided by Julian Sanchez' partidas, brought in from a thousand to fifteen hundred stragglers who must otherwise have perished. During these events Joseph occupied Salamanca, but Colonel Miranda, the Spanish officer left at Alba de Tormes, held that place until the 27th and then carried off his garrison in the night.

Thus ended the retreat from Burgos. The French gathered a good spoil of baggage but the loss of the allies in men cannot be exactly determined, because no Spanish returns were ever seen. An approximation may however be easily made. According to the muster-rolls, about a thousand Anglo-Portuguese were killed, wounded and missing between the 21st and 29th of October, the period of their crossing the Duero, but this only refers to loss in action; Hill's loss between the Tagus and the Tormes was, including stragglers, four hundred, and the defence of Alba de Tormes cost one hundred. If the Spanish regulars and partidas marching with the two armies be reckoned to have lost a thousand, which considering their want of discipline is not exaggerated, the whole loss previous to the French passage of the Tormes will amount perhaps to three thousand men. But the loss between the Tormes and the Agueda was certainly greater, for nearly three hundred were killed and wounded at the Huebra; many stragglers died in the woods, and Jourdan said the prisoners, Spanish, Portuguese and English, brought into Salamanca up to the 20th November were three thousand five hundred and twenty. The whole loss of the double retreat cannot therefore be set down at less then nine thousand, including the loss in the siege.

*   *   *

When the campaign terminated, Wellington, exasperated by the conduct of the army and the many crossings he had experienced during the campaign, gave vent to his indignation in a circular letter addressed to the superior officers, which, being ill-received by the army at the time has been frequently referred to since with angry denunciations of its injustice. In substance it declared, 'that discipline had deteriorated during the campaign *in a greater degree than he had ever witnessed or ever read of in any army*, and this without any disaster, any unusual privation or hardship save that of inclement weather, that the officers had lost all command over their men, and excesses, outrages of all kinds and inexcusable losses had occurred, that no army had ever made shorter marches in retreat or had longer rests, no army had ever been so little pressed by a pursuing enemy, and this unhappy state of affairs was to be traced to the habitual neglect of duty by the regimental officers.'

These severe reproaches were partially unjust, and the statements on which they were founded were in some particulars inaccurate, especially as regarded the retreat from Salamanca. The marches, though short as to distance after quitting the Tormes, were long as to time; and it is the time an English soldier bears his burthen, for like the ancient Roman he carries the load of an ass, that crushes his strength. Some regiments had come from Cadiz without halting, and as long garrison duty had weakened their bodies, their constitutions and inexperience were too heavily taxed. The line of march from Salamanca was through a flooded clayey country, not much easier to the allies than the marshes of the Arnus were to Hannibal's army; and mounted officers, as that great man well knew when he placed the Carthaginian cavalry to keep up the

Gallic rear, never judge correctly of a foot-soldier's exertions: they measure his strength by their horses' powers. On this occasion the troops, stepping ankle-deep in clay, mid-leg in water, lost their shoes and with strained sinews heavily made their way, and withal they had but two rations in five days. Their general thought otherwise. He knew not that the commissariat stores which he had ordered up did not arrive regularly because of the extreme fatigue of the animals who carried them; and those that did arrive were not available for the troops, because, as the rear of an army and especially a retreating army is at once the birth-place and the recipient of false reports, the subordinate commissaries and conductors of the temporary dépôts were alarmed with rumours that the enemy's cavalry had carried off or destroyed the field-stores: the soldiers were actually feeding on acorns when supposed to have good rations!

The destruction of the swine may be thus in some measure palliated, but there is neither palliation nor excuse to be offered for the excesses and outrages committed on the inhabitants, nor for many officers' habitual inattention to their duty. Intolerable disorders had marked the retreat, and great part of the sufferings arose from these and previous disorders; for it is too common with soldiers to break up the arrangements of their general by want of discipline, and then complain of the misery which those arrangements were designed to obviate. Nevertheless this circular was not strictly just, because it excepted none from blame, though in conversation Wellington admitted the reproach did not apply to the light division nor to the guards. With respect to the former indeed the proof of its discipline was easy, though so much had not been said; for how could those troops be upbraided who held together so closely with their colours that, exclusive of the killed in action, they did not leave thirty men behind. Never did the extraordinary vigour and excellence of their discipline merit praise more than in this retreat. But it seems to be a drawback to the greatness of Lord Wellington's character, that while capable of repressing insubordination by firmness or dexterity as the case may require; capable also of magnanimously disregarding or dangerously resenting injuries, his praises and his censures are yet bestowed indiscriminately, or so directed as to acquire partisans and personal friends rather than the attachment of the multitude. He did not make the hard-working military crowd feel that their honest unobtrusive exertions were appreciated. In this he differs not from many other great generals and statesmen, but he thereby failed to influence masses, and his genius falls short of that sublime flight by which Hannibal in ancient and Napoleon in modern times commanded the admiration of the world. But it is only by such great men that he can be measured, nor will any slight examination of his exploits suffice to convey a true notion of his intellectual power and resources. Let this campaign be taken as an example.

It has been by English writers called his easy and triumphant march to Madrid, yet nothing happened according to the original plan; the operations were one continual struggle to overcome obstacles occasioned by the enemy's numbers, the insubordination of the troops, the slowness, incapacity and unfaithful conduct of the Spanish commanders, the want of money and the active folly of the different governments. For first the design was to menace the French in Spain so as to bring their forces from other parts, and then retire into Portugal, again to issue forth when want should cause them to disperse. Wellington was not without hope indeed to strike a decisive blow, yet he was content if the occasion came not to wear out the French by continual marching, and trusted the frequent opportunities thus given to the Spaniards would finally urge them to a general effort. But he found his enemy from the first too powerful for him, even without drawing succour from distant parts, and he would have fallen back at once were it not for Marmont's rashness. Nor would the victory of the Arapiles itself have produced any proportionate effect but for the errors of the king, and his rejection of Soult's advice. These errors caused the evacuation of Andalusia, but only to concentrate an overwhelming force with which the French finally drove the victors back to Portugal.

Such then were the various military events of the year 1812, and the English general taking a view of the whole, judged that however anxious the French might be to invade Portugal, they would be content during the winter to gather provisions and wait for reinforcements from France wherewith to strike a decisive blow at his army. But those reinforcements never came. Napoleon, unconquered of man, had been vanquished by the elements. The fires and the snows of Moscow combined had shattered his strength, and in confessed madness, nations and rulers rejoiced that an enterprise, at once the grandest, the most provident, the most beneficial ever attempted by a warrior-statesman, had been foiled – they rejoiced that Napoleon had failed to re-establish unhappy Poland as a barrier against the most formidable and brutal, the most swinish tyranny that has ever menaced and disgraced European civilization.

XV

The Turn of the Tide
1812–13

Recovering quickly from his retreat, Wellington rebuilt his army to its highest strength, half of them British and the remainder Portuguese and Spanish, the latter, equipped and regularly fed under his command, at last acquiring military qualities. The whole population of Spain now awaited his third advance, but the French, although reduced, were still powerful. Wellington kept his plans to himself to achieve total surprise. He had decided on the most daring strategy of all, possible only with troops restored in morale and confident of their ability – to outflank the French successively along the traditional invasion route by forcing the mountain line to their north.

WHEN WELLINGTON took winter-quarters, the French occupied a line stretching from Valencia to the foot of the Galician mountains. Suchet on the extreme left was opposed by the allies at Alicante, Soult, commanding the centre, had his head-quarters at Toledo, having a detachment near the Sierra Morena watching Del Parque, and two others in the valley of the Tagus. Of these last one was at Talavera, one on the Tietar; the first observed Morillo and Penne Villemur, who from Estremadura menaced the bridges on the Tagus; the second watched Hill at Coria. From the Tietar the French communicated by the Gredos mountains with Avila, where Foy's division of the army of Portugal was posted; partly for the sake of food, partly to watch Bejar and the upper Tormes, because the allies, possessing the pass of Bejar, might have suddenly united north of the mountains and breaking the French line have fallen on Madrid. On the right of Foy, Reille's army occupied Salamanca, Ledesma and Alba on the lower Tormes; Valladolid Toro, and Tordesillas on the Duero; Benevente, Leon and other points on the Esla. Behind the right of this great line Caffarelli's army had retaken its old positions, and the army of the centre was fixed as before in and around Madrid; its operations being bounded north of the Tagus by the mountains which invest that capital, and south of that river by the districts of Aranjuez, Tarancon and Cuenca.

Joseph issued a royal regulation marking the extent of country which each army was to forage, and ordered a certain and consider-able revenue to be collected by the civil authorities for the support of his court. The subsistence of the French armies was thus made secondary to the revenue of the crown, and soldiers in a time of insurrectional war were to obey Spanish civilians; an absurdity heightened by the peculiarly active, vigorous and prompt military method of the French, as contrasted with the dilatory, improvident promise-breaking and visionary system of the Spaniards. Hence, scarcely was the royal regulation issued when the generals broke through it in a variety of ways, and the king as usual became in-volved in very acrimonious disputes. If he ordered one to detach troops in aid of another, he was told he should rather send additional troops to the first. If he reprimanded a general for raising contri-butions contrary to the regulations, he was answered that the soldiers must be fed; and always the authority of the prefects and intendants was disregarded in pursuance of Napoleon's orders. For that monarch continually reminded his brother that as the war was carried on by the French armies their interests were paramount; that the king of Spain could have no authority over them and must never use his military authority as lieutenant of the empire in aid of his kingly views, for with those the French soldiers could have nothing to do — their welfare could not be confided to Spanish ministers whose capacity was by no means apparent, and whose fidelity was not certain.

In reply Joseph again pleaded his duties towards his subjects, and his sentiments, explained with feeling and great beneficence of design, were worthy of all praise abstractedly; but totally inappli-cable, because the Spaniards were not his subjects; they were his inveterate enemies and it was impossible to unite the vigour of war with the benevolence of a paternal monarch. All his policy was vitiated by this fundamental error, which arose from inability to view any subject largely, for his military operations had a like defect; and though he was acute, courageous and industrious in details, he never grasped the whole at once. Men of this character, conscious of labour and good intentions, are commonly obstinate; but their qualities, useful under the direction of an able chief, lead to mischief when they become chiefs themselves; for in matters of great moment, and in war especially, it is not the actual but the comparative importance of operations which should determine the choice of measures; and when all are important, judgment of the highest kind is required, judgment which no man ever possessed more largely than Napoleon and which Joseph did not possess at all. He neither comprehended his brother nor would accept advice from those whose capacity approached that of the emperor. When every general complained of insufficient means, instead of combining their forces to press in mass against the decisive point, he disputed with each and demanded additional succours for all; at the same time repeating and urging his own schemes upon Napoleon whose intellect was so immeasurably greater than his own. The insurrection in the northern provinces he treated as a political question. Nor was his judgment truer with respect to time. He proposed, if a continuation of the Russian war should prevent the emperor from sending more men to Spain, to make Burgos the royal residence, to transport there the archives and all that constituted a capital; then to have the provinces behind the Ebro, Catalonia excepted, governed by himself through the medium of his Spanish ministers and as a country at peace, while those beyond the Ebro should be given up to the generals as a country at war.

In this state, his civil administration would, he said, remedy the evils inflicted by the armies, would conciliate the people by keeping all the Spanish families and authorities in safety and comfort, would draw all those who favoured his cause from all parts of Spain, and would encourage that attachment to his person which he believed many Spaniards to entertain. And while he declared the violence and injustice of the French armies to be the sole cause of the protracted resistance of the Spaniards, a declaration false in fact, the violence being only one of many causes, he continually urged the necessity of beating the English before pacifying the people. As if it were possible, off-hand, to beat Wellington and his veterans, embedded as they were in the strong country of Portugal, while British fleets with troops and succours of all kinds, hovering on both flanks of the French, were feeding and sustaining the insurrection of the Spaniards in their rear. Napoleon was willing enough to drive the English from the Peninsula and tranquillize the people by a regular government; but with profound knowledge of war, of politics and of human nature, he judged the first could only be done by a methodical combination, in unison with that rule of art which prescribes the establishment and security of the base of operations, security which could not be obtained if the benevolent visions of the king were to supersede military vigour. He laughed in scorn when his brother assured him that the Peninsulars, with all their fiery passions, their fanaticism and their ignorance, would receive an equable government as a benefit from the hands of an intrusive monarch before they had lost all hope of resistance by arms.

*   *   *

While the French power was being disorganized in the manner just related, Wellington re-organized the allied army with greater strength than before. Large reinforcements, especially of cavalry, had come out from England, the efficiency of the Portuguese was restored in a surprising manner, and discipline had been vindicated in both services with a rough but salutary hand. Rank had not screened offenders; some had been arrested, some tried, some dismissed for breach of duty; the negligent were terrified, the zealous encouraged; every department was reformed, and it was full time. Confidential officers commissioned to detect abuses in the general hospitals and dépôts, those asylums for malingerers, discovered and drove so many skulkers to their duty that the second division alone recovered six hundred bayonets in one month; and this scouring was rendered more efficient by the establishment of permanent and ambulatory regimental hospitals; a wise measure founded on a principle which cannot be too widely extended; for as the character of a battalion depends on its fitness for service, a moral force will always bear upon the execution of orders under regimental control which it is in vain to look for elsewhere.

The Duero had been rendered navigable as high as Castillo de Alva above the confluence of the Agueda; a pontoon-train of thirty-five pieces had been formed; carts of a peculiar construction had been built to repair the great loss of mules during the retreat from Burgos; and a recruit of these animals was also obtained by emissaries, who purchased them with English merchandise even at Madrid under the beard of the enemy, and when Clausel was unable for want of transport to fill the magazines of Burgos! The ponderous iron camp-kettles of the soldiers had been laid aside for lighter vessels carried by men, the mules being destined to carry tents instead; it is however doubtful if these tents were really useful in wet weather, because when soaked they became too heavy for the animal and seldom arrived in time at the end of a march: their greatest advantage was when the soldiers halted for a few days. Many other changes and improvements had taken place, and the Anglo-Portuguese troops, conscious of a superior organization, were more proudly confident than ever, while the French were again depressed by intelligence of the defection of the Prussians, following on the disasters in Russia. Nor had the English general failed to amend the condition of those Spanish troops which the Cortes had placed at his disposal. By a strict and jealous watch over the application of the subsidy he kept them clothed and fed during the winter, and now had several powerful bodies fit to act in conjunction with his own forces.

Thus prepared, he was anxious to strike, anxious to forestall the effects of his Portuguese political difficulties as well as to keep pace with Napoleon's efforts in Germany, and his army was ready to take the field in April; but he could not concentrate before the green forage was fit for use and deferred the execution of his plan until May. It was a wide plan. The relative strength for battle was no longer in favour of the French; their force had been reduced by losses in the secondary warfare, and by drafts since Wellington's retreat, from two hundred and sixty to two hundred and thirty thousand. Of the last number thirty thousand were in hospital, and only one hundred and ninety-seven thousand men, including the reserve at Bayonne, were present with the eagles. Sixty-eight thousand, including sick, were in Aragon, Catalonia and Valencia; the remainder, with the exception of the ten thousand left at Madrid, were distributed on the northern line of communication from the Tormes to Bayonne: it has been shown how scattered and how occupied.

Wellington was somewhat thwarted by the Duke of York, with whom he was not on very cordial terms; instead of receiving remounts for the cavalry, four of his regiments were withdrawn because of their loss of horses, leaving him weaker by twelve hundred than he ought to have been. But he had prepared two hundred thousand allied troops for the campaign; and on each flank there was a British fleet, now a very effective aid because the French lines of retreat ran parallel to and near the sea-coast on each side of Spain, and every port opened by the advance of the allies would form a dépôt for subsistence.

The campaign of 1812 had shown how strong the French lines of defence were, especially on the Duero, which they had since entrenched in different parts, and most of the bridges over it had been destroyed in the retreat. But it was not advisable to operate in the central provinces of Spain. The country there was exhausted, the lines of supply would be longer and more exposed, the army further removed from the sea, the Galicians could not be easily brought down to co-operate, the services of the northern partidas would not be so advantageous, and the ultimate result would be

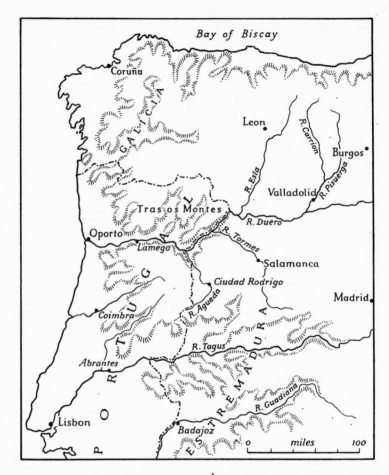

WELLINGTON'S PLANS

less decisive than operations against the great line of communication with France. Wherefore on the northern line the operations
were to run, and those defences which could scarcely be forced
were to be evaded. Wellington proposed to operate with his left
ascending the right of the Duero to the Esla, crossing that river to
unite with the Galicians, while the rest of the army advancing from
the Agueda should force the passage of the Tormes. By this combination, which he hoped to effect so suddenly that the king should
not have time to concentrate in opposition, the front of the allies
would be changed to their right, the Duero and Carrion turned and

the enemy thrown in confusion over the Pisuerga. Then moving forward in mass, the English general could fight or turn any position taken by the king; gaining at each step more force by the junction of the Spanish irregulars until he reached the insurgents of Biscay; gaining also new communications with the fleet, and consequently new dépôts at every port opened.

In the first movement the army would be divided into three parts, each too weak to meet the whole French force; and the Tras os Montes operation, upon the nice execution of which the whole depended, would be in a difficult mountainous country. Hence exact and extensive combinations were essential to success, but failure would not be dangerous because each corps had a strong country to retire upon; the worst effect would be loss of time and the opening of other operations, when the harvest would allow the French to act in masses. The problem was to be solved by hiding the project and gaining time for the Tras os Montes march; and to do this, minor combinations and resources for keeping the French armies scattered and employed were to be freely used. In that view, the bridge equipage was secretly prepared in Abrantes, and the bullock carts to draw it came from Spain by Lamego. The improved navigation of the Duero seemed more conducive to subsist a movement by the right, and yet furnished large boats by which to pass the left over that river; the wide-spread cantonments permitted changes of quarters under pretence of sickness, and thus the troops were gradually closed upon the Duero without suspicion. Hill and the Spaniards in Estremadura and Andalusia always menaced the valley of the Tagus, and contributed to draw attention from the true point; but more than any other thing the vigorous excitement of and sustenance of the northern insurrection occupied the enemy, scattered his forces, and rendered the success of the project nearly certain.

The Spanish troops in Estremadura were to join those forces on the Agueda which were destined to make the passage of the Tormes; and the Galicians were to come down on the Esla to unite with the Tras os Montes corps. Thus seventy thousand Anglo-Portuguese, eight thousand Spaniards from Estremadura, and twelve thousand Galicians, in all ninety thousand fighting men, would be suddenly placed on a new front and marching abreast would drive the surprised and separated masses of the enemy refluent to the Pyrenees. A grand design and grandly it was executed! For high in heart and strong of hand, Wellington's veterans marched to the encounter, the glories of twelve victories played about their bayonets, and he, their leader, was so proud and confident that in passing the stream which marks the frontier of Spain, he rose in his stirrups and waving his hand cried out 'Farewell Portugal!'

*   *   *

Napoleon had early and clearly fixed the king's authority as generalissimo, and forbad him to exercise his monarchical authority towards the French armies, yet Joseph was at this moment in high dispute with all his generals upon those very points.

Napoleon had directed the king to enlarge and strengthen the works of Burgos, and form magazines there and at Santoña for the armies in the field. At this time no magazines had been formed at either place, and although a commencement had been made to strengthen Burgos, it was not capable of sustaining four hours' bombardment and offered no support for the armies.

Napoleon had desired a more secure and shorter line of correspondence than that by Zaragoza should be established with Suchet; for his plan embraced, though it did not prescribe, the march of that general upon Zaragoza, and he had repeatedly warned the king how dangerous it would be to have Suchet isolated and unconnected with the northern operations. Nevertheless the line of correspondence remained the same, and the allies could excise Suchet's army from the north.

Napoleon had long and earnestly urged the king to put down the northern insurrection in time to make head against the allies on the Tormes. Now, when the English general was ready to act, that insurrection was in full activity; and all the army of the north and great part of the army of Portugal were employed to suppress it instead of being on the lower Duero.

Napoleon had clearly explained to the king the necessity of keeping his troops concentrated towards the Tormes in an offensive position, and desired him to hold Madrid so as that it could be abandoned in a moment. The campaign was now being opened, the French armies were scattered, Leval was encumbered at Madrid with a part of the civil administration, with large stores, parcs of artillery and the care of families attached to Joseph's court; while the other generals were stretching their imaginations to devise which of the several projects open to him Wellington would adopt. Would he force the passage of the Tormes and the Duero with his whole army and thus turn the French right? Would he march straight upon Madrid either by the district of Avila or by the valley of the Tagus or by both; and would he then operate against the north or upon Zaragoza, or towards the south in co-operation with the Anglo Sicilians? Everything was vague, uncertain, confused.

All the generals complained that the king's conduct was not military, and Napoleon told him if he would command an army he must give himself up entirely to it, thinking of nothing else; but Joseph was always demanding gold when he should have trusted to iron. His skill was unequal to the arrangements and combinations for taking an initiatory and offensive position, and he could neither discover nor force his adversary to show his real design. The French being thrown upon a timid defensive system, every movement of the allies produced alarm and the dislocation of troops without an object. It was at this moment that Wellington entered upon what has been in England called, not very appropriately, the march to Vitoria, that march being but one portion of the action. The concentration of the army on the banks of the Duero was the commencement, the movement towards the Ebro and the passage of that river was the middle, the battle of Vitoria was the catastrophe, and the crowning of the Pyrenees the end of the splendid drama.

The British cavalry of the left wing, which had wintered about the Mondego, crossed the Duero, some at Oporto, some near Lamego, and entered the Tras os Montes. About the middle of May the cavalry were followed by many divisions of infantry and by the pontoon equipage, thus forming with the horsemen and artillery a mass of more than forty thousand men under Graham. The infantry and guns, rapidly placed on the right of the Duero by means of large boats assembled between Lamego and Castello de Alva, marched in several columns towards the lower Esla, one column however having with it two brigades of cavalry went by Braganza. One the 20th Hill came to Bejar, and the 22nd, Graham being well advanced, Wellington quitted Freneda and put his right wing in motion towards the Tormes. It consisted of five divisions of Anglo-Portuguese and Spanish infantry, five brigades of cavalry, including Julian Sanchez' horsemen, presenting with the artillery a mass of thirty thousand men. Being divided, one part under Hill moved from Bejar upon Alba de Tormes, the other under Wellington upon Salamanca.

On the 27th and 28th the left of the allies approached Zamora, the right approached Toro; the latter thus covered the line of Rodrigo, the former neared the point of the Duero where a bridge of communication was to be thrown. Wellington then left Hill in command and went off suddenly, being disquieted for his combination on the Esla. The 29th he passed the Duero at Miranda in a basket slung on a rope stretched from rock to rock, the river foaming hundreds of feet below – the 30th he reached Carvajales, and joined Graham who had overcome many obstacles in his passage through the Tras os Montes. His troops, extended from Carvajales to Tabara, were on the left in communication with the Galicians, but the operations were disarranged by the difficulty of crossing the Esla. That river should have been passed the 29th, at which time the right wing should have been close to Zamora and the passage of the Duero insured; the French would thus have been surprised, separated and beaten in detail. They were indeed still ignorant that an army was on the Esla; but that river was guarded by their piquets, the stream was full and rapid, the banks steep, the fords hard to find, deep and with stony footing, and the alarm had spread from the Tormes through all the cantonments.

At daybreak on the 31st, English hussars, having infantry holding by their stirrups, entered the stream at the ford of Almendra and Graham approached the right bank with all his forces. A French piquet of thirty men was surprised in the village of Villa Perdrices by the hussars, the pontoons were immediately laid down, and the columns commenced passing, but several men even of the cavalry had been drowned at the fords. Next day the head of the allies entered Zamora, which the French evacuated after destroying the bridge.

The right wing passed the Duero, the artillery and baggage by a ford, the infantry at the bridge of Toro, ingeniously repaired by the lieutenant of engineers Pringle, who dropped ladders at each side of the broken arch and laid planks across just above the water level. Thus the line of the Duero was mastered, and those who understand war may say if it was an effort worthy of the man and his army. Trace the combinations, follow Graham's columns, some of which marched a hundred and fifty, some two hundred and fifty miles through the wild Tras os Montes. Through those regions held to be nearly impracticable even for small corps, forty thousand men, infantry, cavalry, artillery and pontoons, had been carried and placed as if by a superantural power upon the Esla before the enemy knew even that they were in movement!

But if Napoleon's instructions had been worked out by the king during the winter, this great movement could not have succeeded; for the insurrection in the north would have been crushed, or so far quelled that sixty thousand French infantry and ten thousand cavalry with one hundred and twenty pieces of artillery would have been disposable. Such a force held in an offensive position on the Tormes would have compelled Wellington to adopt a different plan of campaign. If concentrated between the Duero and the Esla it would have baffled him on those rivers, because operations effectual against thirty-five thousand infantry would have been powerless against sixty thousand. Joseph said he could not put down the insurrection, he could not feed such large armies; a thousand obstacles arose on every side which he could not overcome; in fine, he could not execute his brother's instructions. They could have been executed notwithstanding. Activity, the taking time by the forelock, would have quelled the insurrection; and for the feeding of the troops, the boundless Tierras de Campos where the armies were now operating were covered with the ripening harvest; the only difficulty was to subsist the French who were not engaged in the northern provinces during the winter. Joseph could not find the means though Soult told him they were at hand, because difficulties overpowered him; they would not have overpowered Napoleon; but the difference between a common general and a great captain is immense; the one is victorious when the other is defeated.

The king had now fifty-five thousand fighting men, exclusive of his Spanish division which was escorting the convoys and baggage; but he did not judge the Carrion a good position and retired behind the upper Pisuerga, desiring if possible to give battle there. He sent Jourdan to examine the state of Burgos, and expedited fresh letters, for he had already written from Valladolid on the 27th and 30th of May, to Foy, Sarrut and Clausel, calling them towards the plains of Burgos. Suchet also he directed to march upon Zaragoza, hoping he was already on his way; but Suchet was then engaged in Catalonia, Clausel's troops were on the borders of Aragon, Foy and Palombini's Italians were on the coast of Guipuzcoa, and Sarrut's division was pursuing Longa in the Montaña.

Higher than seventy or eighty thousand Joseph did not estimate the allied forces, and he was desirous of fighting them on the elevated plains of Burgos. But more than one hundred thousand men were before and around him. For all the partidas of the Asturias and the Montaña were drawing together on his right, Julian Sanchez and the partidas of Castile were closing on his left, Abispal with the reserve and Freyre's cavalry had passed the Gredos mountains and was making for Valladolid. Nevertheless Joseph was sanguine of success if he could rally Clausel's and Foy's divisions, and his despatches to the former were frequent and urgent. Come with the infantry of the army of Portugal! Come with the army of the north and we shall drive the allies over the Duero! Such was his cry to Clausel, and again he urged his political schemes upon his brother; but he was not a statesman to advise Napoleon, nor a general to contend with Wellington; his was not the military genius, nor were his the arrangements that could recover the initiatory movement at such a crisis and against such an adversary. While still on the Pisuerga he received Jourdan's report. Burgos was untenable, there were no provisions, the new works were unfinished, they commanded the old which were unable to hold out a day: of Clausel's and Foy's divisions nothing had been heard. It was then resolved to retire beyond the Ebro. All the French outposts in the Bureba and Montaña were immediately withdrawn, and the great dépôt of Burgos was evacuated upon Vitoria, which was thus encumbered with the artillery dépôts of Madrid, of Valladolid and of Burgos, and with the baggage and stores of so many armies and so many fugitive families; and at this moment also arrived from France a convoy of treasure which had long waited for escort at Bayonne.

The castle of Burgos was mined, but from hurry, or negligence or want of skill, the explosion was outwards at the moment a column of infantry was defiling beneath. Several streets were laid in ruins, thousands of shells and other combustibles left in the place were ignited and driven upwards with a horrible crash, the hills rocked above the devoted column, and a shower of iron, timber and stony fragments falling on it in an instant destroyed more than three hundred men! Fewer deaths might have sufficed to determine the crisis of a great battle!

But such an art is war! So fearful is the consequence of error, so terrible the responsibility of a general. Strongly and wisely did Napoleon speak when he told Joseph he must give himself up entirely to the business, labouring day and night, thinking of nothing else. Here was a noble army driven like sheep before prowling wolves, yet in every action the inferior generals had been prompt and skilful, the soldiers brave, ready and daring, firm and obedient in the most trying circumstances of battle. Infantry, artillery and cavalry, all were excellent and numerous, and the country strong and favourable for defence; but that soul of armies, the mind of a great commander, was wanting, and the Esla, the Tormes, the Duero, the Carrion, the Pisuerga, the Arlanzan, seemed to be dried up, the rocks, the mountains, the deep ravines to be levelled; Clausel's strong positions, Dubreton's thundering castle had disappeared like a dream, and sixty thousand veteran soldiers, though willing to fight at every step, were hurried with all the tumult and confusion of defeat across the Ebro. Nor was that barrier found of more avail to mitigate the rushing violence of their formidable enemy.

*   *   *

While the echoes of the explosion at Burgos were still ringing in the hills, Wellington was in motion by his left towards the sources of the Ebro. The centre of the army followed on the 15th of June and the same day the right wing under Hill marched through the Bureba and crossed at the Puente Arenas. This general movement was masked by the cavalry and the Spanish irregulars, who infested the French rear on the roads to Briviesca and Domingo Calçada; the allies were thus suddenly placed between the sources of the Ebro and the great mountains of Reynosa, and cut the French entirely off from the sea-coast. All the ports, except Santoña and Bilbao were immediately evacuated by the enemy; Santoña was invested by Mendizabal, Porlier, Barcena and Campillo; and

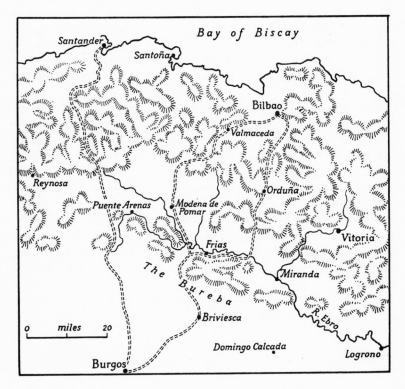

MOVEMENTS ALONG THE RIVER EBRO

English vessels entered Santander, where a dépôt and hospital station were established, because the royal road from thence through Reynosa to Burgos furnished a free communication with the forces. This single blow severed the long connexion of the English troops with Portugal, which was thus cast off by the army as a heavy tender is cast from its towing rope: all the British military establishments were broken up and transferred by sea to the coast of Biscay.

Now the English general could march bodily down the left bank of the Ebro, and fall upon the enemy wherever he met with them; or, still turning the king's right, place the army in Guipuzcoa on the great communication with France, while the fleet, keeping pace with this movement, furnished fresh dépôts at Bilbao and other ports. The first plan was a delicate and uncertain operation, because narrow and dangerous defiles were to be passed; the second, scarcely to be contravened, was secure even if the first should fail; both were compatible to a certain point, inasmuch as to gain the great road leading from Burgos by Orduña to Bilbao was a good step for either; and failing in that, the road leading by Valmaceda to Bilbao was still in reserve. Wherefore, with an eagle's sweep, Wellington brought his left wing round and, pouring his numerous columns through all the deep valleys and defiles, descended towards the great road of Bilbao between Frias and Orduña. At Modina de Pomar, a central point, he left the sixth division to guard his stores and supplies, but the march of the other divisions was unmitigated; neither the winter gullies nor the ravines, nor the precipitate passes amongst the rocks, retarded even the march of the artillery; where horses could not draw, men hauled, when the wheels would not roll, the guns were let down or lifted up with ropes; and strongly did the rough veteran infantry work their way through those wild but beautiful regions; six days they toiled unceasingly; on the seventh, swelled by the junction of Longa's division and all the smaller bands which came trickling from the mountains, they burst like raging streams from every defile and went foaming into the basin of Vitoria.

XVI

Vitoria

THE BASIN into which all the French troops, parcs, convoys
and encumbrances were thus poured, was about eight miles
broad by ten in length, Vitoria being at the further end. The river
Zadora, narrow and with rugged banks, after passing very near
that town, runs towards the Ebro with many windings and divides
the basin unequally, the largest portion being on the right bank.
A traveller coming from Miranda by the royal Madrid road, would
enter the basin by the pass of Puebla, through which the Zadora
flows between two very high and rough mountain ridges, the one
on his right called the heights of Puebla, that on his left the heights
of Morillas. The road leads up the left bank of the Zadora, and on
emerging from the pass, six miles to the left would be seen the
village of Subijana de Morillas, furnishing that opening into the
basin which Reille defended while the other armies passed the defile
of Puebla. The spires of Vitoria would appear eight miles distant;
and from that town the road to Logroño goes off on the right hand,
the road to Bilbao by Murgia and Orduña on the left hand, crossing
the Zadora at a bridge near the village of Ariaga; further on, the
roads to Estella and to Pamplona branch off on the right, a road to
Durango on the left; and between them the royal causeway leads
over the great Arlaban ridge into the mountains of Guipuzcoa by the
formidable defiles of Salinas. But of all these roads, though several
were practicable for guns, especially that to Pamplona, the royal
causeway alone could suffice for the retreat of such an encumbered
army. And as the allies were behind the hills edging the basin on
the right of the Zadora, their line was parallel to the great causeway, and by prolonging their left they could infallibly cut off the
French from that route.

The long-expected battle was now at hand, and on neither side
were the numbers and courage of the troops of mean account. The
allies had lost two hundred killed and wounded in the previous
operations; the sixth division, six thousand five hundred strong,
was left at Medina de Pomar; and only sixty thousand Anglo-
Portuguese sabres and bayonets with ninety pieces of cannon, were

actually in the field. The Spanish auxiliaries were above twenty thousand, and the whole army, including sergeants and artillery-men, exceeded eighty thousand combatants. The French muster-roll of troops was lost with the battle and an approximation to their strength must suffice. The number killed and taken in different combats was about two thousand men, and some five thousand had marched to France with the two convoys; but Sarrut's division, the garrison of Vitoria, and many smaller posts had joined, and hence, by comparison with former returns about seventy thousand men were present. Wherefore deducting the officers, artillerymen, sappers, miners and non-combatants, always borne on the French muster-rolls, the sabres and bayonets would scarcely reach sixty thousand, but in the number and size of their guns the French had the advantage.

All the defects in the king's position were apparent. His best line of retreat was on the prolongation of his right flank, which being at Gamara Mayor was too distant to be supported by the main body of the army; yet the safety of the latter depended upon that point. Many thousand carriages and impediments of all kinds were heaped about Vitoria, blocking all the roads and creating con-fusion amongst the artillery parcs; and Maransin, placed on the Puebla mountain, was isolated and weak to hold that ground. The centre indeed occupied an easy range of hills, its front was open with a slope to the river, and powerful batteries seemed to bar all access by the bridges; but many of the guns, being pushed with an advanced post into a deep loop of the Zadora, were within musket-shot of a wood on the right bank which was steep and rugged, giving the allies good cover close to the river. There were seven bridges within the scheme of the operations, namely the bridge of La Puebla on the French left beyond the defile, the bridge of Nan-clares facing Subijana de Alava and the French end of the defile of Puebla, and three other bridges placed around the deep loop before mentioned opened upon the right of the French centre, that of Mendoza being highest up the stream, Vellodas lowest, Tres Puentes in the centre: lastly the bridges of Gamara Mayor and Ariaga on the upper Zadora, guarded by Reille, completed the number, and none of the seven were either broken or entrenched.

Wellington observing these things formed his army for three distinct battles. Graham, advancing from Murguia by the Bilbao road, was to fall on Reille and attempt the passage at Gamara Mayor and Ariaga; by this movement the French would be completely turned and great part shut up between the Puebla mountain on one

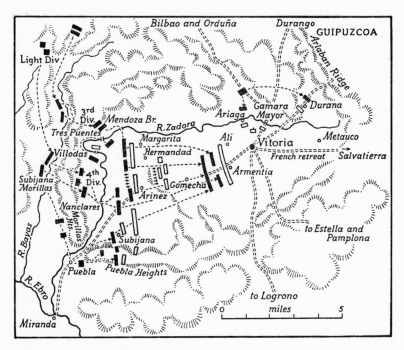

THE BATTLE OF VITORIA

side and the Zadora on the other. The first and fifth Anglo-
Portuguese divisions, Bradford's and Pack's independent Portuguese brigades, Longa's Spanish division and Anson's and Bock's
cavalry, in all twenty thousand men with eighteen pieces of cannon,
were destined for this attack, and Giron's Galicians came up by a
forced march in support.

    Hill was to attack the enemy's left. His corps, twenty thousand
strong, was composed of Morillo's Spaniards, Silveira's Portuguese
and the second British division, with some cavalry and guns.
Collected on the southern slope of the Morillas between the Bayas
and lower Zadora, and pointing to the village of Puebla, it was
destined to force a passage at that point, to assail Maransin, thread
the defile of La Puebla and so enter the basin of Vitoria, turning
and menacing all the French left and securing the passage of the
Zadora at the bridge of Nanclares.

    In the centre Wellington personally directed the third, fourth,
seventh and light divisions of infantry, the great mass of the artillery,
the heavy cavalry and d'Urban's Portuguese horsemen, in all thirty
thousand combatants. Encamped along the Bayas from Subijana

Morillas to Ulivarre, they had only to march across the ridges which formed the basin of Vitoria on that side, to come down to their different points of attack on the Zadora at the bridges of Mendoza, Tres Puentes, Villodas and Nanclares. But so rugged was the country and the communications between the different columns so difficult, that no exact concert could be expected and each general of division was in some degree master of his movements.

At daybreak the 21st of June, the weather being rainy with a thick vapour, the troops moved from their camps on the Bayas, and the centre of the army advancing by columns from the right and left of the line passed the ridges in front and slowly approached the Zadora. The left column pointed to Mendoza, the right column skirted the Morillas ridge, on the other side of which Hill was marching. That general seized the village of Puebla about ten o'clock and commenced the passage. Morillo leading with his first brigade on a bye-way assailed the mountain of La Puebla, where the ascent was so steep the soldiers seemed to climb rather than walk, and the second brigade, being to connect the first with the British troops below, only ascended half way. No opposition was made until the first brigade was near the summit, but then a sharp skirmishing commenced, Morillo was wounded, his second brigade joined, and the French feeling the importance of the height reinforced Maransin with a fresh regiment. Hill succoured Morillo with the seventy-first regiment and a battalion of light infantry, both under Colonel Cadogan; yet the fight was doubtful, for though the British secured the summit and gained ground along the side of the mountain, Cadogan, a brave officer and of high promise, fell, and Gazan sent Villatte's division to succour his side. Strongly did these troops fight and the battle remained stationary, the allies being scarcely able to hold their ground. Hill however sent fresh troops, and with the remainder of his corps, threading the long defile of Puebla, fiercely issued forth on the other side and won the village of Subijana de Alava in front of Gazan's line: he thus connected his own right with the troops on the mountain, and maintained this forward position in despite of the enemy.

Wellington had meanwhile brought the fourth and light divisions, the heavy cavalry, the hussars and d'Urban's Portuguese horsemen, from Subijana Morillas and Montevite, down by Olabarre to the Zadora. The fourth division was placed opposite the bridge of Nanclares, the light division opposite that of Villodas; both were covered by rugged ground and woods, and the light

THE BATTLE OF VITORIA

division was so close to the water that their skirmishers could with
ease have killed the French gunners in the loop of the river at
Villodas. The day was now clear and, when Hill's battle began, the
riflemen of the light division spread along the bank and exchanged
a biting fire with the enemy's skirmishers. No serious effort was at
first made, because the third and seventh divisions having rough
ground to traverse were not up; and to have pushed the fourth
division and the cavalry over the bridge of Nanclares, would have
imprudently crowded the space in front of the Puebla defile before
the other divisions were ready to attack. But while thus waiting, a
Spanish peasant told Wellington the bridge of Tres Puentes on the
left of the light division was unguarded, and offered to guide the
troops over it. Kempt's brigade was instantly directed towards this
point, and being concealed by some rocks from the French and well led
by the brave peasant, they passed the narrow bridge at a running
pace, mounted a steep curving rise of ground and halted close under
the crest on the enemy's side of the river, being then actually behind
the king's advanced post and within a few hundred yards of his line
of battle. Some French cavalry now approached and two round
shots were fired by the enemy, one of which killed the poor peasant
to whose courage and intelligence the allies were so much indebted; but as no movement of attack was made, Kempt called the
fifteenth hussars over the river; and they came at a gallop, crossing
the narrow bridge one by one, horseman after horseman, yet still
the French remained torpid: there was an army there, but no
general.

It was now one o'clock, Hill's assault on the village of Subijana
de Alava was developed, and a curling smoke, faintly seen far up
the Zadora on the enemy's extreme right and followed by the dull
sound of distant guns, showed that Graham was at work. Then
the king, finding his flanks in danger, caused the reserve about
Gomecha to file off towards Vitoria, and gave Gazan orders to retire
by successive masses. But at that moment, the third and seventh
divisions being descried in rapid movement towards the bridge of
Mendoza, the French guns opened upon them, a body of cavalry
drew near the bridge, and the numerous light troops commenced a
vigorous musketry. Some British guns replied to the French cannon
from the opposite bank, and the value of Kempt's forward position
was instantly made manifest; for Andrew Barnard, springing forward, led the riflemen of the light division in the most daring
manner between the French cavalry and the river, taking their light
troops and gunners in flank, and engaging them so closely that the

English artillery-men, thinking his darkly clothed troops were enemies, played upon both alike. This singular attack enabled a brigade of the third division to pass the bridge of Mendoza without opposition; the other brigade forded the river higher up, and the seventh division and Vandeleur's brigade of the light division followed; the French then abandoned the ground in front of Villodas, and the battle which had before somewhat slackened revived with extreme violence. Hill pressed the enemy harder, the fourth division passed the bridge of Nanclares, the smoke and sound of Graham's attack became more distinct, and the banks of the Zadora presented a continuous line of fire. The French, weakened in the centre by the absence of Villatte and dispirited by the order to retreat, were perplexed, and no regular retrograde movement could be made, the allies were too close.

Now also the seventh division and Colville's brigade of the third division forded the river on the left, and were immediately and severely engaged with the French right in front of Margarita and Hermandad; and almost at the same time Wellington, seeing the hill in front of Arinez nearly denuded of troops by the withdrawal of Villatte's troops, carried Picton and the rest of the third division in close columns of regiments at a running pace diagonally across the front of both armies towards that central point. This attack was headed by Barnard's riflemen and followed by the remainder of Kempt's brigade and the hussars, but the other brigade of the light division acted in support of the seventh division. Cole advanced from the bridge of Nanclares, and the heavy cavalry, a splendid body, passing the river, galloped up, squadron after squadron, into the plain ground between Cole's right and Hill's left. The French thus caught in the midst of their dispositions for retreat, threw out a prodigious number of skirmishers, while fifty pieces of artillery played with astonishing activity; this fire was answered by many British guns, and both sides were shrouded by a dense cloud of smoke and dust, under cover of which the French retired by degrees to the range of heights in front of Gomecha on which their reserve had been posted. They however continued to hold the village of Arinez on the main road, and Picton's troops, still headed by Barnard's riflemen, plunged into the streets amidst a heavy fire; in an instant three guns were captured, but the post was important, more French troops came in, and for a time the smoke and dust and clamour, the flashing of fire-arms and the shouts and cries of the combatants mixed with the thundering of the guns were terrible; yet finally the British troops issued forth victorious on the further

side. During this conflict the seventh division, reinforced by Vandeleur's brigade, was heavily raked by a battery at the village of
Margarita, until the fifty-second regiment, led by Colonel Gibbs,
with an impetuous charge drove the French guns away and carried
the village: at the same time the eighty-seventh under Colonel
Gough won the village of Hermandad. Then all on Picton's left
advanced fighting, and on his right the fourth division also made
way, though more slowly because of the rugged ground.

When Picton and Kempt's brigades had carried the village of
Arinez and gained the main road, the French troops near Subijana
de Alava were turned; and being hard-pressed on their front and
left flank by Hill and the troops on the Puebla mountain, fell back
for two miles in a disordered mass, striving to regain the great line
of retreat to Vitoria. Some cavalry launched at the moment would
have totally disorganized the French battle and secured several
thousand prisoners, but it was not tried, and the confused multitude
shot ahead of the British lines and recovered order. The ground was
exceedingly diversified, in some places wooded, in others open,
here covered with high corn, there broken by ditches, vineyards and
hamlets, and the action resolved itself into a running fight and
cannonade for six miles, the dust and smoke and tumult of which
filled all the basin, passing onwards towards Vitoria as the allies
advanced taking gun after gun in their victorious progress.

At six o'clock the French reached the last defensible height one
mile in front of Vitoria. Behind them was the plain in which the
city stood, and beyond the city thousands of carriages and animals
and non-combatants, men, women and children, were crowding
together in all the madness of terror; and as the English shot went
booming over head the vast crowd started and swerved with a convulsive movement while a dull and horrid sound of distress arose,
but there was no hope, no stay for army or multitude; it was the
wreck of a nation! Still the courage of the French soldier was un-
quelled. Reille, on whom everything now depended, maintained the
upper Zadora, and the armies of the south and centre drawing up
on their last heights, between the villages of Ali and Armentia,
made their muskets flash like lightning, while more than eighty
pieces of artillery, massed together, pealed with such a horrid up-
roar that the hills laboured and shook and streamed with fire and
smoke, amidst which the dark figures of the French gunners were
seen bounding with frantic energy. This terrible cannonade and
musketry kept the allies in check, and scarcely could the third division, which bore the brunt of this storm, maintain its advanced

position. Again the battle became stationary, and the French endeavoured to draw off their infantry in succession from the right wing; but suddenly the fourth division, rushing forward, carried a hill on their left and the heights were at once abandoned. Joseph, finding the royal road so completely blocked by carriages that the artillery could not pass, then indicated the road of Salvatierra as the line of retreat, and the army went off in a confused yet compact body on that side, leaving Vitoria on its left; the British infantry followed hard, and the light cavalry galloped through the town to intercept the new line of retreat which was through a marsh and the road also was choked with carriages and fugitive people, while on each side there were deep drains. Thus all became disorder and mischief, the guns were left on the edge of the marsh, the artillerymen and drivers fled with the horses, and the vanquished infantry, breaking through the miserable multitude, went off by Metauco towards Salvatierra: the cavalry however still covered the retreat, and many of the generous horsemen were seen taking up children and women to carry off from the dreadful scene.

Vehemently and closely did the British pursue, and neither the resolute demeanour of the French cavalry, which was strengthened on the flanks by light troops and made several vigorous charges, nor the night, which now fell, could stop their victorious career until the flying masses of the enemy had cleared all obstacles and passing Metauco got beyond the reach of further injury. Then the battle ended. The French escaped with comparatively little loss of men; but to use Gazan's words, 'they lost all their equipages, all their guns, all their treasure, all their stores, all their papers; so that no man could prove even how much pay was due to him; generals and subordinate officers alike were reduced to the clothes on their backs, and most of them were barefooted'.

Never was an army more hardly used by its commander, for the soldiers were not half beaten, and yet never was a victory more complete. The trophies were innumerable. The French carried off but two pieces of artillery from the battle. Jourdan's baton of command, a stand of colours, one hundred and forty-three brass pieces, two-thirds of which had been used in the fight, all the parcs and dépôts from Madrid, Valladolid and Burgos, carriages, ammunition, treasure, everything fell into the hands of the victors. The loss in men did not however exceed six thousand, including some hundreds of prisoners; the loss of the allies was nearly as great, the gross numbers being five thousand one hundred and seventy-six killed wounded and missing. Of these, one thousand and fifty-nine

Boney receiving an account of the Battle of Vittoria — or; the Little Emperor in a Great Passion.

were Portuguese and five hundred and fifty Spanish; hence the loss of the English was more than double that of the Portuguese and Spaniards together; and yet both fought well, and especially the Portuguese, but British troops are the soldiers of battle. The spoil was immense, and to such extent was plunder carried, principally by the followers and non-combatants, for with some exceptions the fighting troops may be said to have marched upon gold and silver without stooping to pick it up, that of five millions and a half of dollars indicated by the French accounts to be in the money-chests, a fiftieth part only came to the public. Wellington sent fifteen officers with power to stop and examine all loaded animals passing the Ebro and the Duero in hopes to recover the sums so shamefully carried off; and this disgraceful conduct was not confined to ignorant and vulgar people, some officers were seen mixed up with the mob contending for the disgraceful gain.

Pakenham with the sixth division came up from Medina Pomar, and the remainder of the army followed Joseph towards Pamplona, for he had continued his retreat up the Borundia and Araquil valleys all night. The weather was rainy, the roads heavy, and the French rear-guard, unable to destroy the bridges, set fire to the villages behind them to delay the pursuit.

Joseph having reached Pamplona the 24th, the army bivouacked on the glacis of the fortress in such a state of destitution and insubordination that the governor would not suffer them to enter the town; for his magazines were reduced by Mina's long blockade, and some writers say it was proposed to blow up the works and abandon the place: however, by great exertions, additional provisions were obtained from the vicinity, the garrison was augmented to three thousand, and the army marched towards France.

The whole line of the Spanish frontier, from Roncevalles to the mouth of the Bidassoa river, was thus occupied by the victorious allies, and Pamplona and San Sebastian were invested. Joseph's reign was over, the crown had fallen from his head, and after years of toils and combats which had been rather admired than understood, the English general, emerging from the chaos of the Peninsula struggle, stood on the summit of the Pyrenees a recognized conqueror. From those lofty pinnacles, the clangour of his trumpets pealed clear and loud, and the splendour of his genius appeared as a flaming beacon to warring nations.

XVII

The Pyrenees

TEN DAYS AFTER the battle of Vitoria, Marshal Soult, under a decree issued from Dresden, succeeded the king as lieutenant to Napoleon, who thus showed how little he had been biased by Joseph's accusations. Travelling with surprising expedition, he was enabled on the 12th of July to assume the command of the three beaten armies, now re-organized in one under the title of the *'army of Spain'*, and he had secret orders to put Joseph forcibly aside if necessary, but that monarch willingly retired. At this period General Paris was still at Jaca, but Clausel had entered France, and Soult, reinforced from the interior, had nine divisions of infantry, a reserve, and two divisions of cavalry besides light horsemen attached to the infantry. Including garrisons, and twelve Italian and Spanish battalions not included in the organization, he had one hundred and fourteen thousand men; and, as the armies of Aragon and Catalonia had above sixty-six thousand, one hundred and eighty thousand men and twenty-six thousand horses were still menacing Spain. One hundred and fifty-six thousand were present under arms: and in Germany and Poland seven hundred thousand French troops were employed!

Such masses directed by Napoleon seemed sufficient to defy the world; but moral power, defined by himself as three-fourths of military strength, that power which puny essayists, declaiming for their hour against the genius of warriors, are unable to comprehend although the most important part of the art they decry, was wanting. One-half of this force, organized in peace and setting forth in hope at the beginning of a war, would have enabled Napoleon to conquer; now, near the close of a terrible struggle, with a declining fate and the national confidence shaken, although his genius was never more surpassingly displayed, his military power was a vast but unsound machine. The public mind was bewildered by combinations the full scope of which he alone could see clearly; generals and ministers doubted and feared when they should have supported him, neglecting their duty or coldly executing when their zeal should have redoubled. The unity of impulse so essential to success was thus lost, and the numerous armies carried not with them proportionate strength. To have struggled with hope under such astounding difficulties was scarcely to be expected from the greatest minds. But like the emperor to calculate and combine the most stupendous efforts with calmness and accuracy; to seize every favourable chance with unerring rapidity; to sustain every reverse with undisturbed constancy; never urged to rashness by despair yet enterprising to the utmost verge of daring consistent with reason, was a display of intellectual greatness so surpassing, that it is not without justice Napoleon has been called, in reference as well to past ages as to the present, the foremost of mankind.

Sudden and wide was the destruction caused by the snows of Russia; it shattered the emperor's military and political system, and the fragments of the former were useless until he could again bind them together. To effect that, he rushed with a raw army into the midst of Germany; for his hope was to obtain by celerity a rallying point for those veterans who, having survived the Russian winter and the succeeding pestilence, were dispersed all over the continent. His first effort was successful, but without good cavalry victory cannot be pushed far, and the practised horsemen of France had nearly disappeared: their successors, badly mounted and less skilful, were too few and too weak, and thus extraordinary exertion was required from soldiers whose youth and inexperience rendered them unfit even for the ordinary hardships of war. The measure of Wellington's campaign is thus attained; for if Joseph had opposed him with only moderate ability, and avoided a great battle, not less than fifty thousand veterans could have reinforced the young soldiers in Germany. On the side of Spain those veterans were still numerous; but the military spirit of the French people, previously almost worn out by victory was now abashed by defeat; and even the generals who had acquired grandeur and riches beyond their hopes were, with few exceptions, averse to further toil. Napoleon's astonishing firmness of mind was understood by few in high stations, shared by fewer; and many were the traitors to him and to France, and to the glories of both. However his power was still enormous, and where-ever he led in person his brave and faithful soldiers, fighting with the true instinct of patriotism, conquered. Where he was not their iron hardihood abated.

Soult was one of the few whose indefatigable energy rendered them worthy lieutenants of the emperor; and with singular zeal and ability he now served. His troops, nominally above one hundred thousand men, ninety-seven thousand being present under arms with eighty-six pieces of artillery, were not all available for field operations. Pamplona, San Sebastian, Santoña, Bayonne and the foreign battalions had seventeen thousand men; but most of those battalions had orders to regain their own countries with a view to form the new levies. The permanent '*army of Spain*' furnished therefore only seventy-seven thousand five hundred men present under arms, seven thousand of which were cavalry. Its condition was not satisfactory. The people on the frontier were flying from the allies, the military administration was disorganized, the recent disasters had discouraged the soldiers and deteriorated their discipline. Soult was therefore desirous of some delay to secure his base and restore order ere he attempted to regain the offensive, but his instructions on that point were imperatively adverse.

Napoleon's system was perfectly adapted for great efforts, civil or military; yet so rapid had been Wellington's advance, so decided his operations, that the resources of France were in a certain degree paralysed, and the army still reeled and rocked from the blows it had received. Bayonne, a fortress of no great strength in itself, had been quite neglected; it was now being armed and provisioned; and the restoration of an entrenched camp, originally traced by Vauban to cover Bayonne, followed. Then the enforcement of discipline, the removal of the immense train of Spanish families, civil administrators and other wasteful followers of Joseph's court, the arrangement of a general system for supply of money and provisions, aided by judicious efforts to stimulate the civil authorities and excite the national spirit, indicated that a great commander was in the field. The soldiers' confidence soon revived, and some leading merchants of Bayonne zealously seconded the general; but the people of the south were more inclined to avoid the burthen of defending their country than to answer appeals to their patriotism.

*   *   *

On the 23rd, Soult issued an order of the day remarkable for its force and frankness. Tracing with a rapid pen the leading events of the past campaign, he said the disasters had sprung from the incapacity of the king, not from the weakness of the soldiers, whose military virtue he justly extolled, inflaming their haughty courage by allusions to former glories. This address has been by writers, who disgrace English literature with unfounded aspersions of a courageous enemy, treated as unseemly boasting as to his intended operations; but the calumny is refuted by the following passage from his despatch to the minister at war. '*I shall move directly upon*

Pamplona; if I succeed in relieving it, I will operate towards my right to embarrass the enemy's troops in Guipuzcoa, Biscay and Alava, and to enable the reserve to join me, which will relieve San Sebastian and Santoña. If this should happen I will then consider what is to be done, either to push my own attack or to help the army of Aragon, but to look so far ahead would now be temerity.' Here he puts every point hypothetically, and though conscious of superior abilities he did not suppress the sentiment of his own worth as a commander and was too proud to depreciate brave adversaries on the eve of battle. *'Let us not,'* he said, *'defraud the enemy of the praise which is due to him. The dispositions of the general have been prompt, skilful and consecutive; the valour and steadiness of his troops have been praiseworthy.'* Having thus stimulated the ardour of his troops he put himself at the head of Clausel's divisions at daylight the 25th.

Picton having assumed command in the Val Zubiri the 26th, retired before dawn the 27th and without the hope or intention of covering Pamplona. Soult followed in the morning, having first sent scouts towards the ridges where Campbell's troops had appeared the evening before. Reille marched by the left bank of the Guy river, Clausel by the right bank, the cavalry and artillery closed the rear, the whole in compact order: the narrow valley was thus gorged with troops, a hasty bicker of musketry alone marking the separation of the hostile forces. The garrison of Pamplona made a sally, and O'Donnel in great alarm spiked some of his guns, destroyed his magazines, and would have suffered a disaster if Carlos d'España had not fortunately arrived at that moment and checked the garrison. Great now was the danger. Cole, first emerging from the valley of Zubiri, had passed Villalba, three miles from Pamplona, in retreat; Picton was at Huarte, and O'Donnel's Spaniards were in confusion; in fine Soult was all but successful, when Picton suddenly turned on some steep ridges which, under the names of San Miguel, Mont Escava and San Christoval, crossed the mouths of the Zubiri and Lanz valleys and screened Pamplona.

Posting his own division on the right of Huarte, he prolonged his line to the left with Morillo's Spaniards, called upon O'Donnel to support him, and directed Cole to occupy some heights between Oricain and Arletta. But that general having with a surer eye observed a salient hill near Zabaldica, one mile in advance and commanding the road to Huarte, demanded and obtained permission to occupy it instead of the heights first appointed. Two Spanish regiments of the blockading troops were still there, and towards them Cole directed his course. Soult had also marked this hill. A

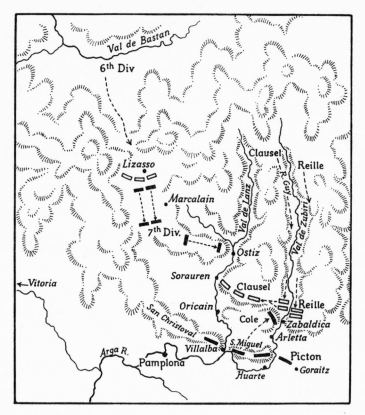

PAMPLONA

detachment issuing from the mouth of the Val de Zubiri was in full
career to seize it, and the hostile masses were rapidly approaching
the summit on either side when the Spaniards, seeing the British so
close, vindicated their own post by a sudden charge. This was for
Soult the stroke of fate. His double columns, just then emerging
exultant from the narrow valley, were suddenly stopped by ten
thousand men under Cole, who crowned the summit of the mountain in his front; and two miles further back stood Picton with a
greater number, for O'Donnel had now taken post on Morillo's
left. To advance by Villalba and Huarte was impossible, to stand
still was dangerous; the army, contracted to a span in front and
cleft in its whole length by the river Guy, was compressed on each
side by the mountains, which in that part narrowed the valley to a
quarter of a mile. It was a moment of difficulty, but Soult, like a

great and ready commander, instantly shot the head of Clausel's columns to his right across the ridge separating the Val de Zubiri from the Val de Lanz; and at the same time threw one of Reille's divisions of infantry and a body of cavalry across the mountains on his left, beyond the Guy river as far as the village of Elcano, to menace Picton's right at Huarte. His remaining divisions were established at Zabaldica in the Val de Zubiri, close under Cole's right, and Clausel seized Sorauren close under that general's left.

While Soult was thus forming his line of battle, Wellington, who had quitted Hill's quarters in the Bastan early on the 27th, was descending the valley of Lanz, unable to learn anything of Picton's movements or position; and in this state of uncertainty he reached Ostiz a few miles from Sorauren, where he found Long with the light cavalry which had furnished the posts of correspondence in the mountains. There learning that Picton had abandoned Linzoain and was moving on Huarte, he left his quarter-master-general with instructions to stop all the troops coming down the valley of Lanz until the state of affairs at Huarte should be ascertained. But at racing speed he made for Sorauren himself, and entering that village saw Clausel coming along the crest of the mountain, and knew the allied troops in the valley of Lanz were intercepted. Pulling up his horse he wrote on the parapet of the bridge of Sorauren fresh instructions to turn everything from that valley on to a road which, through Lizasso and Marcalain, led behind the hills to Oricain in rear of Cole's position: Lord Fitzroy Somerset, the only staff-officer who had kept up with him, galloped with these orders out of Sorauren by one road, the French light cavalry dashed in by another, and the English general rode alone up the mountain to reach his troops. One of Campbell's Portuguese battalions first descried him and raised a joyful cry; then the shrill clamour, caught up by the next regiments, soon swelled as it ran along the line into that stern appalling shout which the British soldier is wont to give upon the edge of battle, and which no enemy ever heard unmoved. Suddenly he stopped at a conspicuous point, for he desired both armies should know he was there, and a double spy who was present pointed out Soult, who was so near that his features could be distinguished. Attentively Wellington fixed his eyes upon that formidable man, and as if speaking to himself said, '*Yonder is a great commander, but he is cautious, and will delay his attack to ascertain the cause of these cheers; that will give time for the sixth division to arrive and I shall beat him.*' And the French general made no serious attack that day!

This front of battle being less than two miles was well filled. The Lanz and Guy torrents washed the flanks, and two miles further down broke through the crossing ridges of San Miguel and Christoval to meet behind them and form the Arga river; on the ridges thus cleft Picton's line was formed, nearly parallel to Cole's but on a more extended front. His left was at Huarte, his right, strengthened with a battery, stretched to the village of Goraitz, covering more than a mile of ground on that flank; Morillo prolonged his left along the crest of San Miguel to Villalba, and O'Donnel continued the line to San Christoval. Carlos d'España's division maintained the blockade, and the British cavalry under Cotton, coming up from Tafalla and Olite, took post, the heavy brigades on some open ground behind Picton, the hussar brigade on his right: this second line entirely barred the openings of the two valleys leading down to Pamplona. Soult's position was also a mountain filling the space between the two rivers. It was even more rugged than the allies' mountain, and they were only separated by a narrow valley.

The first battle of Sorauren was fought on the fourth anniversary

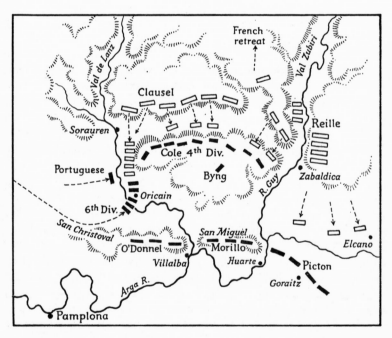

THE BATTLE OF SORAUREN

of the battle of Talavera. About mid-day the French gathered at the foot of the position, and their skirmishers spread over the face of the mountain working upward like a conflagration; but the columns of attack were not all prepared when Clausel's division, too impatient to await the general signal of battle, threw out its flankers on the ridge beyond the river and pushed down the valley of Lanz in one mass. With a rapid pace it turned Cole's left, and was preparing to wheel up on his rear, when a Portuguese brigade of the sixth division, suddenly appearing on the ridge beyond the river, drove the French flankers back and instantly descended with a rattling fire upon the right and rear of the column in the valley. Nearly at the same instant, the main body of the sixth division, emerging from behind the same ridge near the village of Oricain, formed in order of battle across the front. It was the counter-stroke of Salamanca! The French, while striving to encompass the left of the allies, were themselves encompassed; for two brigades of the fourth division turned and smote them on their left, the Portuguese smote them on their right; and while thus scathed on both flanks with fire they were violently shocked and pushed back with a mighty force by the sixth division – not in flight however, but fighting fiercely and strewing the ground with their enemies' bodies as well as with their own.

Clausel's second division, seeing this dire conflict, with a hurried movement assailed the chapel height to draw off the fire from the troops in the valley, and gallantly did the French soldiers throng up the craggy steep; but the general unity of the attack was ruined; neither their third division nor Reille's brigades had yet received the signal, and the attacks which should have been simultaneous were made in succession, running from right to left as the necessity of giving aid became apparent. It was however a terrible battle and well fought. One column darting out of the village of Sorauren silently, sternly, without firing a shot, worked up to the chapel under a tempest of bullets which swept away whole ranks without abating the speed and power of the mass. The seventh *caçadores* shrunk abashed and that part of the position was won; but soon they rallied on Ross's brigade, and the whole mass charging the French with a loud shout dashed them down the hill. Heavily stricken they were, yet undismayed, for re-forming below they again ascended to be again broken and cast down. But the other columns of attack were now bearing upwards through the smoke and flame with which the skirmishers had covered the face of the mountain, and the tenth Portuguese regiment, fighting on the right of Ross's brigade

yielded to their fury. Thus a column crowned the heights and
wheeling against the exposed flank of Ross forced that gallant
officer also to go back, and his ground was instantly occupied by
those with whom he had been engaged in front. The fight then
raged close and desperate on the crest of the position, charge succeeded charge, and each side yielded and rallied by terms; yet this
astounding effort of French valour availed not. Wellington brought
Byng's brigade forward at a running pace, and sent the twenty-
seventh and forty-eighth British, of Anson's brigade, from the
higher ground in the centre against the crowded masses, rolling
them backward in disorder and throwing them one after the other
violently down the mountain side; and with no child's play, for the
two British regiments fell upon the enemy three separate times with
the bayonet, and lost more than half their own numbers.

During this battle on the mountain-top, the British brigades of
the sixth division, strengthened by a battery of guns, gained ground
in the valley of Lanz and arrived on the same front with the left of
the victorious troops about the chapel. Wellington, seeing the momentary disorder of the enemy, then ordered Madden's Portuguese
brigade, which had never ceased its fire against the right flank of
the French column, to assail the village of Sorauren in the rear; but
the state of the action in other parts and the exhaustion of the troops
soon induced him to countermand this movement. Meanwhile
Reille's brigades, connecting their right with the left of Clausel's
third division, had environed the Spanish hill, had ascended it
unchecked, and at the moment the fourth division was so hardly
pressed, made the regiment of El Pravia give way on the left of
the fortieth. A Portuguese battalion rushing forward covered the
flank of that invincible regiment, which waited in stern silence until
the French set their feet upon the broad summit; but then when
their glittering arms appeared over the brow of the mountain the
charging cry was heard, the crowded mass was broken to pieces,
and a tempest of bullets followed its flight. Four times this assault
was renewed, and the French officers were seen to pull up their
tired men by the belts, so fierce and resolute they were to win; yet
it was the labour of Sisyphus, the vehement shout and shock of the
British soldier always prevailed; and at last, with thinned ranks,
tired limbs, hearts fainting and hopeless from repeated failures, they
were so abashed that three British companies sufficed to bear down
a whole brigade. And while the battle was thus being fought on the
mountain, the French cavalry beyond the Guy river passed a rivulet
and with a fire of carbines forced the tenth hussars to yield some

rocky ground on Picton's right; yet the eighteenth hussars, having better fire-arms than the tenth, renewed the combat, killed two officers and drove the French over the rivulet again.

Such were the leading events of this sanguinary struggle, which Wellington, fresh from the fight, with homely emphasis called *'bludgeon work'*. Two generals and eighteen hundred men had been killed or wounded on the French side, following their official reports; a number far below the estimate made at the time by the allies, whose loss amounted to two thousand six hundred. But these discrepancies between hostile calculations ever occur, and there is little wisdom in disputing where proof is unattainable; but the numbers actually engaged were of French twenty-five thousand, of the allies twelve thousand; and if the strength of the latter's position did not save them from the greater loss their steadfast courage is to be the more admired.

Wellington now occupied the hills through which the roads lead from Elizondo to San Estevan, and was full of hope to strike a terrible blow; for Soult, after passing Doña Maria, had halted in San Estevan. He was in a deep narrow valley – three British and one Spanish division were behind the mountains overlooking the town – the seventh division was at Doña Maria, the light division and Graham's Spaniards were marching to block the Vera and Echallar exits from the valley, Byng was at Maya, Hill was moving by Almandoz. A few hours gained and the French must surrender or disperse. Wellington gave strict orders to prevent the lighting of fires, the straggling of soldiers, or any other indication of the presence of troops; and he placed himself amongst some rocks at a commanding point from whence he could observe every movement of the enemy. Soult seemed tranquil and four of his gens d'armes were seen to ride up the valley in a careless manner. Some of the staff proposed to cut them off; the English general, anxious to hide his own presence, forbad this, but the next moment three marauding English soldiers entered the valley and were instantly carried off by the gens d'armes; half an hour afterwards the French drums beat to arms and their columns began to move out of San Estevan towards Sumvilla. Thus the disobedience of three plundering knaves, unworthy of the name of soldiers, deprived one consummate commander of the most splendid success, and saved another from the most terrible disaster.

Soult walked from the prison, but his chains still hung about him. The way was narrow, wounded men borne on their comrades' shoulders and followed by baggage, filed in long procession;

Clausel had the rear-guard, but on the morning of the 1st he was still near San Estevan when Cole's skirmishers and O'Donnel's Spaniards, thronging on the heights along his flank, opened a fire which he could not return. Then troops and baggage got intermingled, many men fled up the hills, and the commanding energy of Soult, whose personal exertions were conspicuous, could scarcely prevent a general dispersion; baggage fell at every step into the hands of the pursuers, the boldest were dismayed, and worse would have awaited them in front if Wellington had been on other points well seconded by his generals.

Instead of taking the first road leading from Sumbilla to Echallar, the head of the French passed onward towards that leading from the bridge near Yanzi; the valley narrowed to a mere cleft in the rocks as they advanced, the Bidassoa was on their left, there was a tributary torrent to cross, and the bridge was defended by a Spanish *caçadore* battalion, detached from the heights of Vera by General Barceñas. The front was thus as much disordered as the rear, and had Longa or Barceñas reinforced the *caçadores*, those only of the French who being near Sumbilla could take the road to Echallar would have escaped; but the Spanish generals kept aloof and d'Erlon won the defile. Reille's divisions were still to pass, and when they came up a new enemy had appeared. This was the light division. The order to intercept the French being received the evening of the 31st, Alten, repassing the defiles of Zubieta, again descended into the deep valley of Lerins and reached Elgoriaga about mid-day the 1st of August. He had then marched twenty-four miles, was little more than a league from Estevan, about the same distance from Sumbilla, and the French movement along the Bidassoa was discovered; but instead of marching on Sumbilla he clambered up the great mountain of Santa Cruz and made for the bridge of Yanzi. Very sultry was the weather, the mountain steep and hard to overcome, many men fell and died convulsed and frothing at the mouth, while others, whose spirit and strength had never before been quelled, leaned on their muskets and muttered in sullen tones that they yielded for the first time.

Towards evening, after marching nineteen consecutive hours and over forty miles of mountain roads, the head of the column reached the edge of a precipice near the bridge of Yanzi. Below, within pistol-shot, Reille's divisions were seen hurrying forward along the horrid defile and a fire of musketry commenced, slightly from the British on the high rock, more vigorously from some low ground near the bridge of Yanzi, where the riflemen had ensconced themselves in the brushwood; but the scene which followed shall be described by an eye-witness. 'We overlooked the enemy at stone's throw, and from the summit of a tremendous precipice. The river separated us, but the French were wedged in a narrow road with inaccessible rocks on one side and the river on the other. Confusion impossible to describe followed, the wounded were thrown down in the rush and trampled upon, the cavalry drew their swords and endeavoured to charge up the pass of Echallar, but the infantry beat them back, and several, horses and all, were precipitated into the river; some fired vertically at us while the wounded called out for quarter, and others pointed to them, supported as they were on branches of trees, on which were suspended great coats clotted with gore and blood-stained sheets taken from different habitations to aid the sufferers.'

On these miserable supplicants brave men could not fire; and so piteous was the spectacle that it was with averted aim the British soldier shot at the sound men; although the latter rapidly plied their muskets in passing, and some in their veteran hardihood even dashed across the bridge of Yanzi to make a counter-attack! It was a soldier-like but a vain effort, the night found the British in possession of the bridge; and though the great body of the French escaped by the road to Echallar, their baggage was all cut off with many prisoners by the troops hanging on the rear in pursuit from San Estevan.

The light division held the road running from the bridge of Yanzi to Echallar until relieved by the fourth division, and then marched by Lesaca to Santa Barbara, thus turning Clausel's right. The fourth division marched from Yanzi upon Echallar to attack his front; the seventh moved from Sumbilla against his left; but Barnes's brigade, contrary to Wellington's intention, arrived unsupported before the fourth and light divisions were either seen or felt, and without awaiting the arrival of more troops assailed Clausel's strong position. The fire became vehement, yet neither the steepness of the mountain nor the overshadowing multitude of the enemy, clustered above in support of their skirmishers, could arrest the assailants; and then was seen the astonishing spectacle of fifteen hundred men driving by sheer valour and force of arms six thousand good troops from a position so rugged that there would have been little to boast of if the numbers had been reversed and the defence made good. The fourth division arrived indeed towards the end of the action, and the French, who had fulfilled their mission as a rear-guard, were worn with fatigue and ill-provided with ammunition, having exhausted all their reserve stores during the retreat: but their inferiority here belongs to the highest part of war. The British soldiers, their natural fierceness stimulated by the remarkable personal daring of their General, Barnes, were excited by success; the French were those who had failed in attack the 28th, had been utterly defeated the 30th, and had suffered so severely the day before about Sumbilla. Such then is the preponderance of moral power. The men who had assailed the terrible rocks above Sorauren with a force and energy that all the valour of the hardiest British veterans scarcely sufficed to repel, were now, only five days afterwards, unable to sustain the shock of one-fourth of their own numbers. And at this very time, eighty British soldiers, the comrades and equals of those who achieved this wonderful exploit, being surprised while plundering, surrendered to some French peasants who, as Wellington truly observed, *'they would under other circumstances have eat up!'* What gross ignorance of human nature then do those declaimers display, who assert that the employing of brute force is the highest qualification of a general!

This day's fighting cost the British four hundred men, and Wellington narrowly escaped the enemy's hands. He had carried with him towards Echallar half a company of the forty-third as an escort, and placed a sergeant named Blood with a party to watch in front while he examined his maps. The French being close at hand sent a detachment to cut the party off; and such was the nature of the ground that their troops, rushing on at speed, would infallibly have fallen upon Wellington, if Blood, a young intelligent man, seeing the danger, had not with surprising activity, leaping rather than running down the precipitous rocks, given him notice: yet the French arrived in time to send a volley of shot after him as he galloped away.

Wellington had on the 1st directed Graham to move up with pontoons and cross the Bidassoa, but now abandoned this design; the two armies therefore rested quiet in their respective positions, after nine days of continual movement during which they had fought ten serious actions. Of the allies, including the Spaniards, seven thousand three hundred officers and soldiers had been killed, wounded or taken, and many were dispersed from fatigue or to plunder. On the French side the loss was terrible, and their disorder rendered the official returns inaccurate. Wellington at first called it twelve thousand, but hearing that the French officers admitted more he raised his estimate to fifteen thousand. The engineer, Belmas, in his *Journals of Sieges*, compiled from official documents by order of the French government, sets down above thirteen thousand. Soult, in his despatches at the time, stated fifteen hundred as the loss at Maya, four hundred at Roncevalles, two hundred on the 27th, and eighteen hundred on the 28th, after which he speaks no more of losses by battle. There remains therefore to be added the killed and wounded at the combats of Linzoain on the 26th, the double battles of Sorauren and Buenza on the 30th, the combats of the 31st, and those of the 1st and 2nd of August; finally, four thousand unwounded prisoners. Let this suffice. It is not needful to sound the stream of blood in all its horrid depths.

XVIII

Toulouse

1814

The War of the Peninsula was over. The invasion of France had begun. The fortresses of San Sebastian and Pamplona were reduced and although Marshal Suchet retained his hold on Catalonia until the end, he was pinned down by the threat from the sea and unable to affect the main confrontation between Wellington and Soult, two commanders at the height of their professional skill.

Napoleon was waging his last astonishing campaign in northern France against the badly co-ordinated armies of Prussia, Russia and Austria. He also suddenly bethought himself of the captive Ferdinand, and signed the Treaty of Valençay to restore him to his Spanish throne, hoping thereby to ruin Wellington's alliance. The Spanish junta handsomely rejected its conditions.

Soult was determined to hold Wellington in the south and prevent him from threatening Paris. Wellington, further perturbed by the ill success of the eastern powers, feared that peace or an armistice might bring Napoleon in person down on him. He was also obliged to return most of his Spanish troops home as their plundering and disorder threatened to turn the quiescent local population against him. Investing Bayonne, he attacked Soult over the river lines of the Nivelle, the Nive and the Adour, while the French marshal, his left flank anchored on the impenetrable Pyrenees, drew his adversary eastwards. Their highly professional manoeuvrings culminated in the last battles of Toulouse and Bayonne, fought after Napoleon had abdicated at Fontainebleau.

WELLINGTON'S difficulties were great. Those of his adversary were even more embarrassing, because the evil was at the root; it was not misapplication of power but the want of power itself which paralysed Soult's operations. Napoleon trusted much to the effect of his treaty with Ferdinand, but the intrigues to retard his journey continued; and though the emperor, after the refusal of the treaty by the Spanish government, permitted him to return without conditions, as thinking his presence would alone em-

THE PASSAGE OF THE BIDASSOA

barrass and perhaps break the English alliance with Spain, he did not arrive until March. How Napoleon's views were frustrated by his secret enemies is one of the obscure parts of French history which time may possibly clear, but probably only with a feeble and uncertain light; for truth can never be expected in the memoirs, if any should appear, of such men as Talleyrand, Fouché and other politicians of their stamp, whose plots rendered his supernatural efforts to rescue France from her invaders abortive: meanwhile there is nothing to check or expose the political and literary empirics who never fail on such occasions to poison the sources of history.

Relying on Ferdinand's journey, and pressed by the necessity of augmenting his own weak army, Napoleon now told Soult he must ultimately take from him two divisions of infantry and one of cavalry. The undecided nature of his first battle at Brienne caused him to enforce this notice in the beginning of February; but he had previously sent imperial commissaries to the different departments of France, with instructions to hasten the new conscription, to form national and urban guards, to draw forth the resources of the country and aid the operations of the armies by the action of the people. These measures failed generally in the south. The urban cohorts were readily formed as a means of police, and the conscription was successful, but the people remained sullen and apathetic; and the civil commissaries are said to have been, with some exceptions, pompous, declamatory and affecting great state and dignity without energy and activity. Ill-will was also produced by the vexatious and corrupt conduct of the subordinate government agents who, seeing in the general distress and confusion a good opportunity to forward their personal interests, oppressed the people for their own profit. This was easy to do, because the extreme want of money rendered requisitions unavoidable; and under the confused direction of civilians, partly ignorant and unused to difficult times, partly corrupt and partly disaffected to the emperor, the abuses inevitably attendant upon such a system were numerous and to the people so offensive that numbers, to avoid them, passed with their carts and utensils into the lines of the allies. An official letter written from Bayonne at this period run thus: 'The English general's policy and the good discipline he maintains does us more harm than ten battles; every peasant wishes to be under his protection.'

Another source of anger was Soult's works near Bayonne, where the richer inhabitants could not bear to have their country villas and gardens destroyed by the engineer, he who spares not for beauty or for pleasure. The merchants, a class nearly alike in all nations, with whom profit stands for country, had been with a few exceptions long averse to Napoleon's policy, which from necessity interfered with their commerce. And this feeling must have been very strong in Bayonne and Bordeaux; for one Batbedat, a banker of the former place, having obtained leave to go to St Jean de Luz under pretence of settling the accounts of English officers, prisoners of war, to whom he had advanced money, offered Wellington to supply his army with various commodities and even provide money for bills on the English treasury. In return he demanded licences for twenty vessels to go from Bordeaux, Rochelle and Mantes to St Jean de Luz; and they were given on condition that he should not carry back colonial produce; but as the English navy would not respect them, the banker and his coadjutors hesitated and thus saved their ships, for the English ministers refused to sanction the licences and rebuked Wellington!

During these events the partisans of the Bourbons, coming from Brittany and La Vendée, spread themselves all over the south of France, and one of the heroic family of La Roche Jacquelin arrived at head-quarters. Bernadotte also sent an agent to those parts, and the Count of Grammont, a captain in the British cavalry, was at the desire of the Marquis de Mailhos, another of the malcontents, sent to England to call the princes of the house of Bourbon forward. Finally the Duke of Angoulême arrived at head-quarters and was received with respect in private, though not suffered to attend the army. The English general indeed, persuaded that the great body of the French people, especially in the south, were inimical to Napoleon's government, was sanguine as to the utility of encouraging a Bourbon party; yet he held his judgment in abeyance, sagaciously observing he could not come to a safe conclusion merely from the feelings of some people in one corner of France. And as the allied sovereigns seemed backward to take the matter in hand unless some positive general movement in favour of the Bourbons was made, and there were negotiations for peace actually going on, it would be, he said, unwise and ungenerous to precipitate the partisans of the fallen house into a premature outbreak and then leave them to the vengeance of the enemy.

That Wellington should think public opinion was against Napoleon is not surprising, it seemed to be so, and a very strong Bourbon party, and one still stronger, averse to the continuation of war, existed: but nothing is more dangerous, more deceitful, than the outward show and declarations on such occasions. The great mass of men are only endowed with moderate capacity and spirit;

their thoughts are for the preservation of their families and property, they bend to circumstances; fear and suspicion, ignorance, baseness and good feeling, all combine to urge men in troubled times to put on the mask of enthusiasm, for the most powerful and selfish knaves ever shout with the loudest. Let the scene change and the multitude will turn with the facility of a weathercock. Wellington soon discovered that Viel Chastel, Bernadotte's agent, while pretending to aid the Bourbons, was playing a double part. And one year after this period Napoleon returned from Elba, when neither the presence of the Duke of Angoulême, nor the energy of the Duchess, nor all the activity of their partisans, could raise in this very country more than the semblance of an opposition to him – the tricolor was everywhere hoisted and the Bourbon party vanished. This was the true test of national feeling. For in 1814 the white colours were supported by foreign armies, and misfortune had bowed the great democratic chief to the earth; but when rising again in his wondrous might he came back alone from Elba, the poorer people, with whom only patriotism is ever really to be found, and that because they are poor and therefore unsophisticated, crowded to meet and hail him as a father. Not because they held him entirely blameless. Who born of woman is? They demanded redress of grievances even while they clung instinctively to him as their stay and protection against the locust tyranny of aristocracy.

There was however at this period in France enough of discontent, of passion and intrigue, enough of treason and enough of grovelling spirit in adversity, added to the natural desire of escaping the ravages of war, a desire carefully fostered by the admirable policy of the English general, to render the French general's position extremely dangerous. Nor is it the least remarkable circumstance of this remarkable period, that while Soult expected relief from Spanish aversion to the English alliance, Wellington received from the French secret and earnest warnings to beware of some great act of treachery meditated by the Spaniards. It was at this period also that the Spanish generals encouraged their soldiers' licentiousness, and displayed their own ill-will by sullen discontent and captious complaints, while the civil authorities disturbed the communications and made war in their fashion against the hospitals and magazines.

Wellington's apprehensions are plainly to be traced in his correspondence. He observes that the Spanish military people about himself desired peace with Napoleon according to the treaty of Valençay, that they all had some notion of what had occurred and yet had been quite silent about it; that he had repeated intelligence from the French of some act of treachery meditated by the Spaniards; that several persons of that nation had come from Bayonne to circulate reports of peace, and charges against the British which he knew would be well received on that frontier; that he had arrested a man calling himself an agent of and actually bearing a letter of credence from Ferdinand. But the most striking proof of alarm was his great satisfaction at the conduct of the Spanish government in rejecting the treaty. Sacrificing all his former great and just resentment, he changed at once from an enemy to a friend of the regency, supported the members of it against the serviles, spoke of the matter as the most important that had engaged his attention, and when O'Donnel proposed some violent and decided action of hostility against the regency, which a few weeks before would have been received with pleasure, he checked and softened him, saying the conduct of that body about the treaty should content every Spaniard: it was not possible to act with more frankness and loyalty, and they had procured honour for themselves and for their nation not only in England but all over Europe. Such is the light mode in which words are applied by public men, even by the noblest and greatest, when their wishes are fulfilled. This glorious and honourable conduct of the regency was simply a resolution to uphold their personal power and that of their faction, both of which would have been destroyed by the arrival of the king.

Napoleon, hoping much from the effect of these machinations, not only intimated to Soult that he would require ten thousand of his infantry immediately, but that twice that number with a division of cavalry would be called away if the Spaniards fell off from the English alliance. The Duke of Dalmatia then foreseeing the ultimate result of his own operations against Wellington, conceived a vast general plan of action which evinced his capacity to treat the greatest questions of military power.

'I propose then to form a great army in front of Paris by a union of all the disposable troops on the different frontiers, and to spread what remains as partisans wherever the enemy threatens to penetrate. All the marshals of France, the generals and other officers, in activity or in retirement, who shall not be attached to the great central army, should organize the partisan corps and bring those not actively useful as such up to the great point of union; and they should have military power to make all men able to bear arms find them at their own expense.' – 'This measure is revolutionary but will produce important results, while none or a very feeble effect will be caused by the majority of the imperial commissioners already sent to the military divisions. They are grand persons, they temporize, make proclamations and treat everything as civilians instead of acting with vigour to obtain promptly a result which would astonish the world; for notwithstanding the cry to the contrary the resources of France are not exhausted – what is wanted is to make those who possess resources use them for the defence of the throne and the emperor.' Having thus explained his views, he requested to serve near the emperor, but declared himself ready to obey any order and serve in any manner; all he demanded was clear instructions with reference to the events that might occur. 1°. What he should do if the treaty with Ferdinand had no effect and the Spanish troops remained with Wellington. 2°. If those troops retired and the British, seeing the French weakened by detachments, should alone penetrate into France. 3°. If the changes in Spain should cause the allies to retire altogether.

This great project was not adopted and the emperor's reasons for neglecting it have not been made known. Nor can the workings of that capacious mind be judged of without a knowledge of all the objects and conditions of his combinations. Yet it is probable that at this period he did not despair of rejecting the allies beyond the Rhine either by force of arms, by negotiation, or by working upon the family pride of the Emperor of Austria. With this hope he would be averse to risk civil war by placing France under martial law; averse to revive the devouring fire of revolution which it had been his object for so many years to quell – and it seems nearly certain that one of his reasons for replacing Ferdinand on the Spanish throne was his fear lest the republican doctrines which had gained ground in Spain should spread to France. Was he wrong? The fierce democrat will answer yes! Those who think real liberty was never attained under a single unmixed form of government giving no natural vent to the swelling pride of honour, birth or riches – those who measure the weakness of pure republicanism by the miserable state of France at home and abroad when Napoleon first assumed power to save her; those who saw America with her militia and licentious liberty, unable to prevent three thousand British soldiers from passing three thousand miles of ocean and burning their capital – those persons will hesitate to condemn him. And this without detriment to the democratic principle which in substance may and should always govern under judicious forms. Napoleon early judged, and the event has proved he judged truly, that the democratic spirit of France was then unable to overbear the aristocratic and monarchic tendencies of Europe; wisely therefore, while he preserved the essence of the first by fostering equality, he endeavoured to blend it with the other two; thus satisfying as far as human institutions would permit the conditions of the great problem he had undertaken to solve. His object was the reconstruction of the social fabric which had been shattered by the French revolution, mixing with the new materials what remained of the old sufficiently unbroken to build with again; if he failed to render his structure stable it was because his design was misunderstood, and the terrible passions let loose by the previous stupendous explosion were too mighty even for him to compress.

To have accepted Soult's project would have been to save himself at the expense of his system, and probably to plunge France into the anarchy from which he had with so much care and labour drawn her. But Napoleon's ambition was for the greatness and prosperity of France, for the regeneration of Europe, for the stability of the system which he had formed with that end, never for himself personally. Hence it is that multitudes of many nations instinctively revere his memory; and neither the monarch nor the aristocrat, dominant though they be by his fall, feel themselves so easy in their high places as to rejoice much in their victory.

Soult's project was not adopted, and in February two divisions of infantry and Treilhard's cavalry, with many batteries, were withdrawn; two thousand of the best soldiers were also selected to join the imperial guards, and all the gens d'armes were sent to the interior. The total number of old soldiers left did not, including the division of Paris, exceed forty thousand exclusive of the garrison of Bayonne and other posts; the conscripts, beardless youths, were generally unfit to enter the line, nor were there enough of muskets to arm them. It is remarkable also, as showing how easily military operations may be affected by distant combinations, that Soult expected and dreaded at this time the descent of a great English army upon the coast of La Vendée, led thereto by hearing of an expedition, preparing in England under Graham, really to aid the Dutch revolt.

While his power was thus diminishing, Wellington's situation was as suddenly ameliorated. First by the arrival of reinforcements, next by the security he felt from the rejection of the treaty of Valençay; lastly by the approach of better weather and the acquisition of a very large sum in gold which enabled him to put his Anglo-Portuguese in activity and to bring the Spaniards again into line with less danger of their plundering the country. During the cessation of operations, he had prepared the means to enter France with power and security, sending before him the fame of a just discipline and a wise consideration for the people who were likely to fall under his power; for there was nothing he so much dreaded as the partisan and insurgent warfare proposed by Soult. The peasants of Baygorry and Bidarray had done him more mischief than the French army, and his terrible menace of destroying their villages and hanging all the population he could lay his hands upon if they ceased not their hostility, marks his apprehensions in the strongest manner. Yet he left all the local authorities free to carry on the internal government, to draw their salaries and raise the necessary taxes in the same mode and with as much tranquillity as if perfect peace prevailed. He opened the ports also and drew a large commerce, which served to support his own army and engage the mercantile interests in his favour; he established many sure channels for intelligence, political and military, and would have extended his policy further and to more advantage if the English ministers had not so ignorantly interfered with his proceedings. Finally, foreseeing that the money he might receive would, being in foreign coin, create embarrassment, he adopted an expedient which he had before practised in India.

Knowing that in a British army a wonderful variety of knowledge and vocations, good and bad, may be found, he secretly caused the coiners and die-sinkers amongst the soldiers to be sought out; and once assured that no mischief was intended them, it was not difficult to persuade them to acknowledge their peculiar talents. With these men he established a secret mint and coined gold Napoleons, marking them with a private stamp and carefully preserving their just fineness and weight to enable the French government when peace should be established to call them in again. He thus avoided all the difficulties of exchange, and removed a fruitful graft of quarrels and ill-will between the troops and the shopkeepers; for the latter are always fastidious in taking and desirous of abating the current worth of strange coin, and the former attribute to fraud any declination from the value at which they receive their money. This sudden increase of the current coin tended also to diminish the pressure necessarily attendant upon troubled times.

Nor was his provident sagacity less manifest in purely military matters than in administrative and political operations. During the bad weather he had formed large magazines at the ports, examined the course of the Adour, and carefully meditated upon his future plans. To enter France and rally a great Bourbon party was his wish.

This last point depended upon the political proceedings and successes of the allied sovereigns; yet the military operations most suitable at the moment did not clash with it; to drive the French from Bayonne and blockade or besiege that place was the first step in either case. But this required extensive and daring combinations.

He thought Soult would readily abandon the care of the lower Adour to defend the rivers beyond the Nive if his left was attacked, and thus the lower Adour would be laid open for his enterprise. Nor did he fear that the French marshal, in retiring before the troops destined to force the rivers near the roots of the Pyrenees, would gain the boundary road and come down on the investing force at Bayonne; because to do so he must enter the sandy wilderness of the Landes, and might be prevented from getting out again.

While the English general was secretly arranging this great offensive operation, Soult was diligently increasing his defensive means and fortified all the principal passages of the rivers crossing the main roads leading against his left; but the diminution of his force in January compelled him to withdraw his outposts from Anglet in front of Bayonne, which enabled Wellington closely to examine the lower Adour and prepare with more certainty for the passage. Soult however, in pursuance of Napoleon's maxim of covering physical weakness by moral audacity, concentrated troops on his left, renewing the partisan warfare against the allies' right, and endeavoured to keep them entirely on the defensive.

On the side of the lower Pyrenees he improved the works of Navarrens and designed an entrenched camp in front of it; the castle of Lourdes in the high Pyrenees was already defensible, and he gave orders to fortify the castle of Pau; thus providing supporting points for the retreat which he foresaw. At Mauleon he put on foot some partisan corps, and the imperial commissary Caffarelli gave him hopes of a reserve of seven or eight thousand national guards, gens d'armes and artillerymen at Tarbes. Dax, containing his principal dépôts, was being fortified, and the communication with it was maintained across the rivers by fortified bridges at Port de Landes, Hastingues, Pereyhorade and Sauveterre; but the floods in the beginning of February carried away his permanent bridge at the Port de Landes, and the communication between Bayonne and the left of the army was thus interrupted.

All these preparations were made in the supposition that Wellington had one hundred and twenty thousand infantry and fifteen thousand cavalry, for Soult knew not of the political and financial crosses which had reduced that general's power. The twenty thousand British and Portuguese reinforcements promised, had not arrived, Clinton's army was still in Catalonia; and though the exact numbers of the Spaniards cannot be stated, their forces available, and that only partially and with great caution on account of their licentious conduct, did not exceed the following approximation.

Freyre had, including España's division, twelve thousand men, Morillo four thousand, O'Donnel six thousand, and the Prince of Anglona eight thousand. The Anglo-Portuguese present under arms were by the morning states on the day the advance commenced, seventy thousand of all arms, ten thousand being cavalry. The whole force, exclusive of Mina's bands which were spread from Navarre to the borders of Catalonia, was therefore one hundred thousand with one hundred guns, ninety-five being Anglo-Portuguese. The French numbers opposed it is difficult to fix with precision because the imperial muster-rolls, owing to the troubled state of the emperor's affairs, were not continued beyond December 1813 or have been lost. But from Soult's correspondence and other documents it would appear that, exclusive of his garrisons, his reserves, and detachments at Bordeaux and in the department of the high Pyrenees, exclusive also of the conscripts of the second levy which were now beginning to arrive, he could place in line thirty-five thousand soldiers of all arms, three thousand being cavalry, with forty pieces of artillery. But Bayonne alone, without reckoning the fortresses of St Jean Pied de Port and Navarrens, occupied twenty-eight thousand of the allies; and by this and other drains Wellington's superiority in the field was so reduced that his penetrating into France, the France which had made all Europe tremble at her arms, must be viewed as a surprising example of courage and fine conduct.

*   *   *

One of Hill's posts near the confluence of the Aran with the Adour was surprised by some French, who remained until fresh troops forced them to repass the river again. This was in retaliation for the surprise of a French post a few days before by the sixth division, which was attended with circumstances repugnant to the friendly habits long established between the French and British troops at the outposts. The value of such a generous intercourse old soldiers well understand, and some illustrations of it at this period may be quoted. The forty-third was assembled on an open space within twenty yards of the enemy's out-sentry; yet the latter continued to walk his beat for an hour, relying so confidently on the customary system that he placed his knapsack on the ground to ease his shoulders. When the order to advance was given, one of the soldiers having told him to go away helped him to replace his pack, and the firing then commenced. Next morning the French in like manner warned a forty-third sentry to retire. A more remarkable instance happened however, when Wellington, desirous of getting to the top of a hill occupied by the enemy near Bayonne, ordered some riflemen to drive the French away; seeing them stealing up too close as he thought, he called out to fire; but with a loud voice one of those old soldiers replied, *'no firing!'* and holding up the butt of his rifle tapped it in a peculiar way. At the well-understood signal, which meaned *'we must have the hill for a short time'*, the French, who though they could not maintain, would not have relinquished the post without a fight if they had been fired upon, quietly retired. And this signal would never have been made if the post had been one capable of a permanent defence, so well do veterans understand war and its proprieties.

*   *   *

[During the preliminary battles in the south of France] from some oversight the despatches did but scant and tardy justice to the light division. Acting alone, that division, only four thousand seven hundred strong, first carried the smaller Rhune defended by Barbot, and then beat Taupin from the main position, thus driving superior numbers from the strongest works; and being less than one-sixth of the whole force directed against Clausel, those matchless veterans defeated one-third of his corps. Many brave men they lost, and of two who fell I will speak.

The first, low in rank for he was but a lieutenant, rich in honour for he bore many scars, was young of days – he was only nineteen and had seen more combats and sieges than he could count years. So slight in person and of such surpassing and delicate beauty that the Spaniards often thought him a girl disguised in man's clothing, he was yet so vigorous, so active, so brave, that the most daring and experienced veterans watched his looks on the field of battle and, implicitly following where he led, would like children obey his slightest sign in the most difficult situations. His education was incomplete, yet were his natural powers so happy that the keenest and best-furnished intellects shrunk from an encounter of wit; and every thought and aspiration was proud and noble, indicating future greatness if destiny had so willed it. Such was Edward Freer of the forty-third. The night before the battle he had that strange anticipation of coming death so often felt by military men; he was struck with three balls at the first storming of the Rhune rocks, and the sternest soldiers wept even in the middle of the fight when they saw him fall.

On the same day and at the same hour was killed Colonel Thomas Lloyd. He likewise had been a long time in the forty-third. Under him Freer had learned the rudiments of his profession; but in the course of the war, promotion placed Lloyd at the head of the ninety-fourth, and it was leading that regiment he fell. In him also were combined mental and bodily powers of no ordinary kind. Graceful symmetry, herculean strength, and a countenance frank and majestic, gave the true index of his nature; for his capacity was great and commanding, and his military knowledge extensive both from experience and study. Of his mirth and wit, well known in the army, it only need be said that he used the latter without offence, yet so as to increase his ascendancy over those with whom he held intercourse; for though gentle he was ambitious, valiant and conscious of fitness for great exploits. And he, like Freer, was prescient of and predicted his own fall, but with no abatement of courage; for when he received the mortal wound, a most painful one, he would not suffer himself to be moved and remained to watch the battle, making observations upon its changes until death came. It was thus at the age of thirty that the good, the brave, the generous Lloyd died. Tributes to his merit have been published by Wellington and by one of his own poor soldiers; by the highest and by the lowest! To their testimony I add mine: let those who served on equal terms with him say whether in aught it has exaggerated his deserts.

*　　*　　*

On the 10th of April at two o'clock in the morning the light division passed the Garonne by the bridge at Seilh, and at six o'clock the whole army moved forwards in the order assigned for the different columns. Picton and Alten, on the right, drove the French advanced posts behind the works of the bridges on the canal. Freyre, marching along the Alby road, was cannonaded by St Pol with two guns until he passed a small stream by the help of some temporary bridges, when the French general following his instructions retired to the horn-work on Calvinet. Freyre was thus established on the Pugade, from whence Major Arentschild's Portuguese guns opened a heavy cannonade. Beresford, preceded by the hussars, marched from Croix d'Orade in three columns abreast; passing behind the Pugade, through the village of Montblanc, he entered the marshy ground between the Ers river and Mont Rave, but left his artillery at

Montblanc, fearing to engage it in that deep and difficult country under the fire of the enemy. Beyond the Ers on his left, Vivian's cavalry, now under Colonel Arentschild, drove Berton's horsemen with loss over the bridge of Bordes, which the French destroyed with difficulty at the last moment. However the hussars gained the bridge of Montaudran higher up, though it was barricaded and defended by a detachment of cavalry sent there by Berton, who remained himself in position near the bridge of Bordes, looking down the left of the Ers.

While these operations were in progress, Freyre, who had asked as a favour to lead the battle at Calvinet, either from error or impatience assailed the horn-work on that platform while Beresford was still in march. His Spaniards, nine thousand strong, advanced with great resolution at first, throwing forwards their flanks so as to embrace the end of the Calvinet hill, and though the French musketry and great guns thinned the ranks at every step, they still

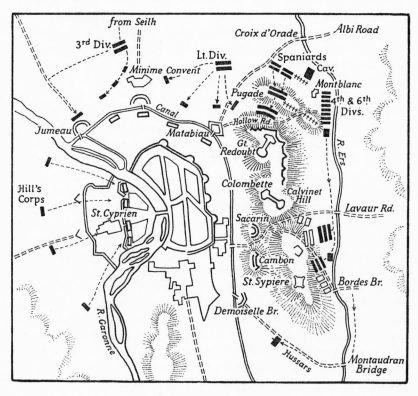

THE BATTLE OF TOULOUSE

ascended the hill; but the formidable fire they were exposed to increased in violence; and their right wing, which was raked from the bridge of Matabiau, unable to endure the torment, wavered, and the leading ranks rushing madly onwards jumped for shelter into a hollow road, twenty-five feet deep in parts, which covered this front of the French entrenchments. The left wing and the second line run back in disorder, the Cantabrian fusiliers under Colonel Leon de Sicilia alone maintaining their ground under cover of a bank which sheltered them. Then the French came leaping out of their works with loud cries and, lining the edge of the hollow road, poured an incessant stream of shot upon the helpless crowds entangled in the gulph below; while the battery from Matabiau, constructed to rake this hollow, sent its bullets from flank to flank hissing through the quivering mass of flesh and bones.

Rallying their fugitive troops, the Spanish generals led them back again to the brink of the fatal hollow, but the frightful carnage below, and the unmitigated fire in front filled them with horror. Again they fled, and again the French bounding from their trenches pursued, while several battalions sallying from the bridge of Matabiau and from behind the Calvinet followed hard along the road of Alby. The country was now covered with fugitives whose headlong flight could not be restrained, and with pursuers whose numbers and vehemence increased, until Wellington covered the panic-stricken troops with Ponsonby's cavalry and the reserve artillery, which opened with great vigour. Meanwhile the Portuguese guns on the Pugade never ceased firing, and a brigade of the light division, wheeling to its left, also menaced the flank of the victorious French who retired to their entrenchments on Calvinet: but more than fifteen hundred Spaniards had been killed or wounded and their defeat was not the only misfortune.

Picton, regardless of his orders, which, his temper on such occasions being known, were given to him verbally and in writing, had turned his false attack into a real one against the bridge of Jumeaux; but the enemy, fighting from a work too high to be forced without ladders and approachable only along an open flat, repulsed him with a loss of nearly four hundred men and officers: amongst the latter Colonel Forbes of the forty-fifth was killed, and General Brisbane who commanded the brigade was wounded. Thus from the hill of the Pugade to the Garonne the French had completely vindicated their position; the allies had suffered enormously; and beyond the Garonne, although Hill had now forced the first line of entrenchments covering St Cyprien and was menacing the second line, the latter, more contracted and very strongly fortified, could not be stormed. The musketry battle therefore subsided for a time, yet a prodigious cannonade was kept up along the whole of the French line, and on the allies' side from St Cyprien to Mont-blanc, where the artillery left by Beresford, acting in conjunction with the Portuguese guns on the Pugade, poured its shot incessantly against the Calvinet; injudiciously however, because the ammunition thus used for a secondary object was afterwards wanted when a vital advantage might have been gained.

It was now evident that the victory must be won or lost by Beresford, and yet, from Picton's error, Wellington had no reserves to enforce the decision; for the light division and the heavy cavalry only remained in hand, and these troops were necessarily retained to cover the rallying of the Spaniards and protect the artillery. The crisis therefore approached with all happy promise to the French general. For the repulse of Picton, the dispersion of the Spaniards, the strength of the second line at St Cyprien, enabled him to draw, first Taupin's whole division, and then one of Maransin's brigades from that quarter to reinforce his battle on the Mont Rave. Thus three divisions and his cavalry, nearly fifteen thousand combatants, were disposable for an offensive movement, without in any manner weakening the defence of his works on Mont Rave or on the canal. With this mass he might have fallen upon Beresford, whose force, originally less than thirteen thousand bayonets, was cruelly reduced as it made slow and difficult way for two miles through a deep marshy country crossed and tangled with water-courses. Sometimes moving in mass, sometimes filing under the French musketry, always under the fire of their artillery from the Mont Rave without a gun to reply, the length of the column had augmented so much at every step, from the difficulty of the way, that frequent halts were necessary to close up the ranks.

Between the river and the heights the miry ground became narrower and deeper as the troops advanced, Berton's cavalry was ahead, an impassable river was on the left, three French divisions supported by artillery and horsemen overshadowed the right flank! But Fortune rules in war! Soult, always eyeing their march, had, when the Spaniards were defeated, carried Taupin's division to St Sypiere and, supporting it with a brigade of d'Armagnac's division, disposed the whole about the redoubts; from thence after a short hortative to act vigorously he ordered Taupin to fall on with the utmost fury, at the same time directing a regiment of Vial's cavalry to descend the heights by the Lavaur road and intercept the line of retreat, while Berton's horsemen assailed the other flank from the side of the bridge of Bordes. This was not half of the force which he might have employed, and Taupin's artillery, retarded in its march, was still in the streets of Toulouse: that general also, instead of attacking at once, took ground to his right, giving Beresford full time to complete his flank march and wheel into lines at the foot of the heights.

Taupin's infantry, unskilfully arranged for action it is said, at last poured down the hill; but some rockets discharged in good time ravaged the ranks, and with their noise and terrible appearance, unknown before, dismayed the French soldiers; then the British skirmishers running forwards plied them with a biting fire; and Lambert's brigade of the sixth division, aided by Anson's and some provisional battalions of the fourth division – for it is an error to say the sixth division alone repulsed this attack – rushed forwards with a terrible shout, and the French fled back to the upper ground. Vial's horsemen, trotting down the Lavaur road, now charged on the right flank, but the seventy-ninth regiment being thrown into square repulsed them; and on the other flank Cole had been so sudden in his advance up the heights that Berton's cavalry had no opportunity to charge. Lambert, following hard upon the beaten infantry in his front, killed Taupin, wounded a general of brigade, and without a check won the summit of the platform, his skirmishers even descended in pursuit on the reverse slope. And at the St Sypiere redoubt a French regiment, seeing its commanding officer killed by a soldier of the sixty-first regiment, fled in a panic. Cole then established himself on the summit, and so great was the rout that the two forts were abandoned, and the French sought shelter at Sacarin and Cambon.

Soult, astonished at this weakness in troops from whom he had expected so much, and who had but just before given him assurances of their resolution and confidence, was in fear that Beresford, push-ing his success, would seize the bridge of the Demoiselles on the canal. Wherefore, covering the flight as he could with the remainder of Vial's cavalry, he hastily led d'Armagnac's reserve brigade to the works of Sacarin, and thus checking the foremost British skir-mishers, rallied the fugitives; Taupin's guns arrived from the town at the same moment, and the mischief being stayed, a part of Travot's reserve moved to defend the bridge of the Demoiselles. A fresh order of battle was thus organized; yet the indomitable courage of the British soldiers had decided the first great crisis of the fight.

Lambert's brigade now wheeled to its right across the platform

on the line of the Lavaur road, menacing the flank of the French on
the Calvinet, while Pack's Scotch brigade and Douglas's Portuguese,
composing the second and third lines of the sixth division, were
disposed on the right with a view to march against the Colombette
redoubts on the original front of the enemy. And now also the
eighteenth and German hussars, having forced the bridge of Montaudran on the Ers river, came round the south end of the Mont
Rave, where, in conjunction with the skirmishers of the fourth division, they menaced the bridge of the Demoiselles, from whence and
from the works of Cambon and Sacarin the enemy's guns played
incessantly. The aspect and form of the battle were thus changed,
and the French were thrown entirely on the defensive, occupying
three sides of a square; their right, extending from the works of
Sacarin to the redoubts of Calvinet and Colombette, was closely
menaced by Lambert, who was solidly posted on the platform of
St Sypiere, while the redoubts themselves were menaced by Pack
and Douglas. The French left, thrown back to the bridge-head of
Matabiau awaited a renewed attack by the Spaniards and the position was strong, not exceeding a thousand yards on each side; the
angles were defended by formidable works, the canal and city walls
and entrenched suburbs offered a sure refuge in case of disaster,
and the Matabiau on one side, Sacarin and Cambon on the other,
insured retreat.

In this contracted space were concentrated Vial's cavalry, the
whole of Villatte's division, one brigade of Maransin's, another of
d'Armagnac's; and, with exception of the regiment driven from the
St Sypiere redoubt, the whole of Harispe's division. On the allies'
side, therefore, defeat had been staved off, but victory was still to
be contended for; and with apparently inadequate means; for Picton,
successfully opposed by Daricau, was paralysed; the Spaniards,
rallying slowly, were not to be depended upon for another attack;
there remained only the heavy cavalry and the light division, which
Wellington dared not thrust into action under pain of being left
without any reserve in the event of a repulse. The final stroke
therefore was still to be made on the left, and with a very small
force, seeing that Lambert and Cole had to keep in check the French
at the bridge of the Demoiselles, at Cambon and Sacarin. This heavy
mass, comprising one brigade of Travot's reserve, half of d'Armagnac's division, and all Taupin's together with Harispe's regiment
which had abandoned the fort of St Sypiere, was under Clausel, and
he disposed the greater part in advance of the entrenchments as if
to retake the offensive.

Such was the state of affairs about half-past two o'clock when Beresford renewed the action with Pack's Scotch brigade, and the Portuguese of the sixth division under Douglas. These troops, ensconced in the hollow Lavaur road on Lambert's right, had been hitherto well protected from the fire of the French works; and now scrambling up the steep banks of that road, they wheeled to their left by wings of regiments as they could get out. Ascending the heights by the slope facing the Ers, under a wasting fire of cannon and musketry, they carried all the French breast-works, and the forty-second and seventy-ninth took the Colombette and Calvinet redoubts; it was a surprising action when the loose disorderly nature of the attack imposed by the difficulty of the ground is considered; but the French, although they yielded at first to the thronging rush of the British troops, soon rallied and came back with a reflux; their cannonade was incessant, their reserves strong, and the struggle became terrible. Harispe, who commanded in person at this part, and under him the French seemed always to fight with redoubled vigour, brought up fresh men, and surrounding the two redoubts with a surging multitude, recovered the Calvinet by storm, with great slaughter of the forty-second, which fell back in disorder on the seventy-ninth forcing that regiment to abandon the Colombette also. Still the whole clung to the brow of the hill with wonderful obstinacy, though they were reduced to a thin line of skirmishers. Some British horsemen now rode up from the low ground to their aid, but were stopped by a hollow road, and some of the foremost tumbling in, perished. The French had then the best of the fight; but when two fresh British regiments, the eleventh and ninety-first, came up, when two generals, Harispe and Baurot, had been carried off dangerously wounded, the battle turned, and the French abandoned the platform, falling back on their right to Sacarin, and on their left towards Matabiau and the houses on the canal.

It was now four o'clock, the Spaniards had once more partially attacked, and were again put to flight, and the French remained masters of their entrenchments in that quarter; for the sixth division had been hardly handled, and Beresford halted to reform his order of battle and receive his artillery: it came to him indeed about this time, yet with great difficulty and with little ammunition, in consequence of the heavy cannonade it had previously furnished from Montblanc. However Soult, seeing the Spaniards, supported by the light division, had rallied a fourth time, that Picton still menaced the bridge of Jumeaux and the Minime convent, while Beresford, master of three-fourths of Mont Rave, was now advancing along the summit, deemed farther resistance useless; he relinquished the northern end of the Calvinet platform also, and about five o'clock withdrew his whole army behind the canal, still holding Sacarin and Cambon: Wellington then established the Spaniards in the abandoned works, and so became master of the Mont Rave in all its extent. The French had five generals and perhaps three thousand men killed or wounded, and they lost one piece of artillery. The allies lost four generals and four thousand six hundred and fifty-nine men and officers, of which two thousand were Spaniards. A lamentable spilling of blood, and a useless, for before this period Napoleon had abdicated the throne of France and a provisional government was constituted at Paris.

During the night Soult, defeated but undismayed, replaced the ammunition expended in the action, re-organized and augmented his field artillery from the arsenal of Toulouse, and made dispositions for fighting the next morning behind the canal. Yet looking to the final necessity of a retreat he wrote to Suchet to inform him of the result of the contest, and proposed a combined plan of operations illustrative of the firmness and pertinacity of his temper. 'March', said he, 'with the whole of your forces by Quillan upon Carcassonne, I will meet you there with my army; we can then retake the initiatory movement, transfer the seat of war to the upper Garonne, and, holding on by the mountains, compel the enemy to recall his troops from Bordeaux, which will enable Decaen to recover that city and make a diversion in our favour.'

On the morning of the 11th he was again ready to fight, but the English general was not. The French position, within musket-shot of the walls, was still inexpugnable on the northern and eastern fronts. The possession of Mont Rave was only a preliminary step to the passage of the canal at the bridge of the Demoiselles, and other points above the works of Sacarin and Cambon; for Wellington still meaned to throw his army as originally designed to the south of the town: but that was a great affair requiring fresh dispositions and a fresh supply of ammunition, only to be obtained from the parc on the other side of the Garonne. Wherefore, to accelerate the preparations, ascertain Hill's state, and give that general further instructions, Wellington repaired on the 11th to St Cyprien; but though he had shortened his communications by removing the pontoon-bridge from Grenade to Seilh, the day was spent before the ammunition arrived and the final arrangements for the passage of the canal could be completed. The attack was therefore deferred until daylight on the 12th.

Meanwhile all the light cavalry were sent up the canal, to interrupt the communications with Suchet and menace Soult's retreat by the road leading to Carcassonne. The appearance of these horsemen on the heights of St Martyn, above Baziege, together with the preparations in his front, taught Soult that he could no longer delay if he would not be shut up in Toulouse; wherefore, having terminated all his arrangements, he left eight pieces of heavy artillery, two generals, the gallant Harispe being one, and sixteen hundred men whose wounds were severe, to the humanity of the conquerors; then filing out of the city with surprising order and ability, he made a forced march of twenty-two miles, cut the bridges over the canal and the upper Ers, and the 12th established his army at Villefranche. On the same day Hill's troops were pushed close to Baziege in pursuit, and the light cavalry, acting on the side of Montlaur, beat the French with the loss of twenty-five men, and cut off a like number of gens d'armes on the side of Revel.

Wellington entered Toulouse in triumph, the white flag was displayed and, as at Bordeaux, a great crowd of persons adopted the Bourbon colours; but the mayor, faithful to his sovereign, had retired with the French army. The British general, true to his honest line of policy, did not fail to warn the Bourbonists that their revolutionary movement must be at their own risk. But in the afternoon two officers, the English Colonel Cooke, and the French Colonel St Simon, arrived from Paris, charged to make known to the armies the abdication of Napoleon. They had been detained near Blois by the officiousness of the police attending the court of the Empress Louise and the blood of eight thousand brave men had overflowed the Mont Rave in consequence: nor did their arrival immediately put an end to the war. When St Simon, in pursuance of his mission, reached Soult's quarters on the 13th, that marshal, not without just cause, demurred to his authority, and proposed to suspend hostilities until authentic information could be obtained from the ministers of the emperor; then sending all his encumbrances by the canal to Carcassonne, he took a position of observation at Castelnaudary and awaited the progress of events. Wellington refused to accede to his proposal, and as General Loverdo, commanding at Montauban, had acknowledged the authority of the provisional government and readily concluded an armistice, he judged Soult designed to make a civil war and therefore marched against him. The 17th the outposts were on the point of engaging, when the Duke of Dalmatia, who had now received official information from the chief of the emperor's staff, notified his adhesion to the new state of affairs in France – and with this honourable distinction that he had faithfully sustained the cause of his great monarch until the very last moment.

A convention which included Suchet's army was immediately agreed upon; but that marshal had previously adopted the white colours of his own motion, and Wellington instantly transmitted the intelligence to Clinton in Catalonia and to the troops at Bayonne. Too late it came for both and useless battles were fought; at Bayonne misfortune and suffering had fallen upon one of the brightest soldiers of the British army.

*   *   *

During the progress of the main army in the interior, Hope conducted the investment of Bayonne with the unremitting vigilance and activity which the operation required. He had gathered stores of gabions and fascines and platforms, and was ready to attack the citadel when rumours of the events at Paris reached him; yet indirectly, and without any official character to warrant a formal communication to the garrison without Wellington's authority. These rumours were however made known at the outposts, and perhaps lulled the vigilance of the besiegers; but to such irregular communications, which might be intended to deceive, the governor naturally paid little attention.

The piquets and fortified posts at St Etienne were at this time furnished by a brigade of the fifth division; from thence to the extreme right the guards had charge of the line, and they had also one company in St Etienne itself. Hinuber's German brigade was encamped as a support to the left, the remainder of the first division was encamped in the rear, towards Boucaut. In this state, about one o'clock in the morning of the 14th, a deserter coming over to General Hay, who commanded the outposts that night, gave an exact account of the projected sally; the general, unable to speak French, sent him to Hinuber, who immediately interpreted the man's story to Hay, assembled his own troops under arms, and transmitted the intelligence to Hope. It would appear that Hay, perhaps disbelieving the man's story, took no additional precautions: and it is probable that neither the German brigade nor the reserves of the guards would have been put under arms but for the activity of Hinuber. However at three o'clock the French, commencing with a false attack on the left of the Adour as a blind, poured suddenly out of the citadel to the number of three thousand combatants; they surprised the piquets, and with loud shouts breaking through the chain of posts at various points, carried with one rush the church and the whole of the village of St Etienne with exception of a fortified house which was defended by Captain Forster of the thirty-eighth regiment. Masters of every other part and overthrowing all who stood before them, they drove the piquets and supports in heaps along the Peyrehorade road, killed General Hay, took Colonel Townsend of the guards prisoner, divided the wings of the investing troops, and passing in rear of the right threw the whole line into confusion. Then Hinuber, having his Germans well in hand moved up on the side of St Etienne, rallied some of the fifth division and, being joined by a battalion of Bradford's Portuguese from the side of St Esprit, bravely gave the counter-stroke to the enemy and regained the village and church.

On the right the combat was at first even more disastrous than in the centre, neither the piquets nor the reserves were able to sustain the fury of the assault, and the battle was most confused and terrible; for on both sides the troops, broken into small bodies by the enclosures and unable to recover their order, came dashing together in the darkness, fighting often with the bayonet, and sometimes friends encountered, sometimes foes: all was tumult and horror. The guns of the citadel, vaguely guided by the flashes of the musketry, sent their shot and shells booming at random through the lines of fight; and the gun-boats, dropping down the river, opened their fire upon the flank of the supporting columns, which being put in motion by Hope on the first alarm were now coming up from the side of Boucaut. Thus nearly one hundred pieces of artillery were in full play at once, and the shells having set fire to the fascine dépôts and to several houses, the flames cast a horrid glare over the striving masses.

Amidst this confusion Hope suddenly disappeared, none knew how or wherefore at the time; but it afterwards appeared, that having brought up the reserves on the right to stem the torrent in that quarter, he pushed for St Etienne by a hollow road which led close behind the line of piquets, one of which had been improperly withdrawn by an officer of the guards, and the French thus lined both banks. A shot struck him in the arm, and his horse, a large one as was necessary to sustain the gigantic warrior, received eight bullets and fell upon his leg; his followers had by this time escaped from the defile; yet two of them, Captain Herries and Mr Moore, a nephew of Sir John Moore, seeing his helpless state turned back, and endeavoured amidst the heavy fire of the enemy to draw him from beneath the horse. While thus engaged they were both struck down with dangerous wounds, the French carried them all off, and Hope was again severely hurt in the foot by an English bullet before they gained the citadel.

Day now broke and the allies were enabled to act with more unity and effect. The Germans were in possession of St Etienne, and the reserve brigades of the guards, being properly disposed by Howard, who had succeeded to the command, suddenly raised a loud shout and running in upon the French drove them back into the works with such slaughter that their own writers admit a loss of one general and more than nine hundred men: on the British side General Stopford was wounded, and the whole loss was eight hundred and thirty men and officers. More than two hundred were taken, besides the commander-in-chief; and it is generally acknowledged that Forster's firm defence of the fortified house first, and next the readiness and gallantry with which Hinuber retook St Etienne, saved the allies from a very terrible disaster.

A few days after this piteous event the convention made with Soult became known and hostilities ceased.

All the French troops in the south were now re-organized in one body under the command of Suchet; but they were so little inclined to acquiesce in the revolution, that Prince Polignac, acting for the Duke of Angoulême, applied to the British commissary-general, Kennedy, for a sum of money to quiet them. The Portuguese returned to Portugal. The Spaniards to Spain, the generals being it is said inclined at first to declare for the Cortes against the king, but they were diverted from their purpose by the influence and authority of Lord Wellington. The British infantry embarked at Bordeaux, some for America, some for England, and the cavalry marching through France took shipping at Boulogne.

Thus the war terminated, and with it all remembrance of the veteran's services.

Envoi

PLACE AN ATTAINABLE object of war before the French soldier and he will make supernatural efforts to gain it, but failing he becomes proportionately discouraged; let some new chance be opened, some fresh stimulus applied to his ardent sensitive temper, and he will rush forward again with unbounded energy; the fear of death never checks him, he will attempt anything: but the unrelenting vigour of the British infantry in resistance wears his fury out. It was so proved in the Peninsula, where the sudden deafening shout, rolling over a field of battle with a more full and terrible sound than that of any other nation, and always followed by the strong unwavering charge, startled and appalled those French columns before whose fierce and vehement assault all other troops had given way.

Napoleon's system of war was admirably adapted to draw forth and augment the military excellence and to strengthen the weakness of the national character. His discipline, severe, but appealing to the feelings of hope and honour, wrought the quick temperament of the French soldiers to patience under hardships, and strong endurance under fire; he taught the generals to rely on their own talents, to look to the country wherein they made war for resources, and to dare everything even with the smallest numbers, that the impetuous valour of France might have full play: hence the violence of their attacks. But he also taught them to combine all arms together, and to keep strong reserves that sudden disorders might be repaired and the discouraged troops have time to rally and recover their pristine spirit; certain that they would then renew the battle with the same confidence as before. He thus made his troops, not invincible indeed, nature had put a bar to that in the character of the British soldier, yet so terrible and sure in war that the number and greatness of their exploits surpassed those of all other nations, the Romans not excepted if regard be had to the shortness of the period, nor the Macedonians if the quality of their opponents be considered.

Look at their amazing toils in the Peninsular war alone, which though so great and important was but an episode in their military history. *'In Spain large armies will starve and small armies will be beaten'*, was the saying of Henry IV of France, and it was not the light phrase of an indolent king, but the profound conclusion of a sagacious general. Yet Napoleon's enormous armies were so wonderfully organized that they existed and fought in Spain for six years, and without cessation; for to them winters and summers were alike; they endured incredible toils and privations, yet were not starved out, nor were their small armies beaten by the Spaniards. And for their daring and resource a single fact recorded by Wellington will suffice. They captured more than one strong place in Spain without any provision of bullets save those fired at them by their enemies, having trusted to that chance when they formed the siege! Before the British troops they fell; but how terrible was the struggle, how many defeats they recovered from, how many brave men they slew; what changes and interpositions of fortune occurred before they could be rolled back upon their own frontiers! And this is the glory of England, that her soldiers and hers only were capable of overthrowing them in equal battle. I seek not to defraud the Portuguese of his well-earned fame, nor to deny the Spaniard the merit of his constancy; but what battle except Baylen did the Peninsulars win? What fortress did they take by siege? What place defend? Sir Arthur Wellesley twice delivered Portugal. Sir John Moore's march to Sahagun saved Andalusia and Lisbon from invasion at a critical moment. Sir Arthur's march to Talavera delivered Galicia. Wellington recaptured Ciudad and Badajoz, rescued Andalusia from Soult, and Valencia from Suchet. England indeed could not alone have triumphed in the struggle, but for her share let this brief summary speak.

She expended more than one hundred millions sterling on her own operations, she subsidized both Spain and Portugal, and with her supplies of clothing, arms and ammunition maintained the armies of each even to the guerrillas. From thirty up to seventy thousand British troops were employed by her; and while her naval squadrons harassed the French with descents upon the coasts, and supplied the Spaniards with arms and stores and money after every defeat, her land forces fought and won nineteen pitched battles and innumerable combats, made or sustained ten sieges, took four great fortresses, twice expelled the French from Portugal, preserved Alicante, Carthagena, Tarifa, Cadiz, Lisbon; they killed, wounded and took two hundred thousand enemies, and the bones of forty thousand British soldiers lie scattered on the plains and mountains of the Peninsula. For Portugal she re-organized a native army and supplied officers who led it to victory; and to the whole Peninsula she gave a general whose like has seldom gone forth to conquer. And all this and more was necessary to redeem that land from France!

Wellington's campaigns furnish lessons for generals of all nations, but they must always be especial models for British commanders in future continental wars because he modified and reconciled the great principles of art with the peculiar difficulties which attend generals controlled by politicians who prefer parliamentary intrigue to national interests. An English commander must not trust his fortune. He dare not risk much, however conscious he may be of personal resources, when one disaster will be his ruin at home; his measures must be subordinate to this primary consideration. Wellington's caution, springing from that source, has led friends and foes alike into wrong conclusions as to his system of war; the French call it want of enterprise, timidity; the English have denominated it the Fabian system. These are mere phrases. His system was the same as that of all great generals. He held his army in hand, keeping it with unmitigated labour always in a fit state to march or to fight, and acted indifferently as occasion offered on the offensive or defensive, displaying in both a complete mastery of his art. Sometimes he was indebted to fortune, sometimes to his natural genius, always to his untiring industry, for he was emphatically a painstaking man.

That he was less vast in his designs, less daring in execution, neither so rapid nor so original a commander as Napoleon, must be admitted; and being later in the field of glory, it is to be presumed he learned something of the art from that greatest of all masters. Yet something besides the difference of genius must be allowed for the difference of situation; Napoleon was never, even in his first campaign of Italy, so harassed by the French as Wellington was by the English, Spanish and Portuguese governments: their systems of war were however alike in principle, their operations being only modified by their different political positions. Great bodily exertion, unceasing watchfulness, exact combinations to protect their flanks and communications without scattering their forces; these were common to both; in defence firm, cool, enduring, in attack fierce and obstinate; daring when daring was politic, yet always operating by the flanks in preference to the front; in these things they were alike: in following up a victory the English general fell short of the French emperor. The battle of Wellington was the stroke of a battering-ram, down went the wall in ruins; the battle of Napoleon was the swell and dash of a mighty wave before which the barrier yielded and the roaring flood poured onwards covering all.

But there was nothing of timidity or natural want of enterprise to be discerned in the English general's campaigns. Neither was he of the Fabian school. He recommended that commander's system to the Spaniards, he did not follow it himself; his military policy more resembled that of Scipio Africanus. Fabius, dreading Hanni-bal's veterans, red with the blood of four consular armies, hovered on the mountains, refused battle, and to the unmatched skill and valour of the great Carthaginian opposed the almost inexhaustible military resources of Rome. Wellington was never loath to fight when there was any equality of numbers; he landed in Portugal with only nine thousand men, with intent to attack Junot who had twenty-four thousand; at Roriça he was the assailant; at Vimeiro he was assailed, but he would have changed to the offensive during the battle if others had not interfered. At Oporto he was again the daring and successful assailant; in the Talavera campaign he took the initiatory movements, although in the battle itself he sustained the shock. His campaign of 1810 in Portugal was entirely defensive, because the Portuguese army was young and untried; but his pur-suit of Masséna in 1811 was entirely aggressive although cautiously so, as well knowing that in mountain warfare those who attack labour at a disadvantage. The operations of the following campaign, including the battles of Fuentes de Oñoro and Albuera, were of a mixed character; so was the campaign of Salamanca; but the cam-paign of Vitoria and that in the south of France were entirely and eminently offensive.

Slight therefore is the resemblance to the Fabian warfare. And for the Englishman's hardiness and enterprise, bear witness the passage of the Douro at Oporto, the capture of Ciudad Rodrigo, the storming of Badajoz, the march to Vitoria, the passage of the Bidassoa, the crowning battle of Toulouse! To say that he committed faults is only to say that he made war; to deny him the qualities of a great commander is to rail against the clear mid-day sun for want of light. How few of his combinations failed. How many battles he fought, victorious in all! Iron hardihood of body, a quick and sure vision, a grasping mind, untiring power of thought, and the habit of laborious minute investigation and arrangement; all these qualities he possessed, and with them that most rare faculty of coming to prompt and sure conclusions on sudden emergencies.

This is the certain mark of a master-spirit in war; without it a commander may be distinguished, he may be a great man, he cannot be a great captain: where troops nearly alike in arms and knowledge are opposed, the battle generally turns upon the decision of the moment.

At the Somosierra, Napoleon sent the Polish cavalry successfully charging up the mountain when more studied arrangements with ten times that force might have failed. At Talavera, if Joseph had not yielded to the imprudent heat of Victor, the fate of the allies would have been sealed. At Bussaco, Masséna would not suffer Ney to attack the first day, and thus lost the only favourable opportunity for assailing that formidable position. At Fuentes de Oñoro, the same Masséna suddenly suspended his attack when a powerful effort would probably have been decisive. At Albuera, Soult's column of attack, instead of pushing forward, halted to fire from the first height they had gained on Beresford's right, which saved that general from an early and total defeat; again, at a later period of that battle, the unpremeditated attack of the fusileers decided the contest. At El Bodon, Marmont failed to seize the most favourable opportunity which occurred during the whole war for crushing the allies. At Orthes, Soult let slip two opportunities of falling upon the allies with advantage, and at Toulouse he failed to crush Beresford.

At Vimeiro, Wellington was debarred by Burrard from giving a signal illustration of this intuitive generalship; but at Bussaco and the heights of San Christoval, near Salamanca, he suffered Masséna and Marmont to commit glaring faults unpunished. On the other hand he has furnished many examples of that successful improvisation in which Napoleon seems to have surpassed all mankind. His sudden retreat from Oropesa across the Tagus by the bridge of Arzobispo; his passage of the Douro in 1809, his halt at Guinaldo in the face of Marmont's overwhelming numbers; the battle of Salamanca, his sudden rush with the third division to seize the hill of Arinez at Vitoria, his counter-stroke with the sixth division at Sorauren; his battle of the 30th two days afterwards; his sudden passage of the Gave below Orthes. Add to these his wonderful battle of Assaye, and the proofs are complete that he possesses in an eminent degree that intuitive perception which distinguishes the greatest generals.

Fortune however always asserts her supremacy in war, and often from a slight mistake such disastrous consequences flow, that in every age and every nation the uncertainty of arms has been proverbial. Napoleon's march upon Madrid in 1808 before he knew the exact situation of the British army is an example. By that march he lent his flank to his enemy, Sir John Moore seized the advantage, and though the French emperor repaired the error for the moment by his astonishing march from Madrid to Astorga, the fate of the Peninsula was then decided. If he had not been forced to turn against Moore, Lisbon would have fallen, Portugal could not have been organized for resistance, and the jealousy of the Spaniards would never have suffered Wellington to establish a solid base at Cadiz: that general's after-successes would then have been with the things that are unborn. It was not so ordained, Wellington was victorious, the great conqueror was overthrown, England stood the most triumphant nation of the world. But with an enormous debt, a dissatisfied people, gaining peace without tranquillity, greatness without intrinsic strength, the present time uneasy, the future dark and threatening. Yet she rejoices in the glory of her arms! And it is a stirring sound! War is the condition of this world. From man to the smallest insect all are at strife, and the glory of arms, which cannot be obtained without the exercise of honour, fortitude, courage, obedience, modesty and temperance, excites the brave man's patriotism and is a chastening corrective for the rich man's pride. It is yet no security for power. Napoleon, the greatest man of whom history makes mention – Napoleon, the most wonderful commander, the most sagacious politician, the most profound statesman, lost by arms, Poland, Germany, Italy, Portugal, Spain and France. Fortune, that name for the unknown combinations of infinite power, was wanting to him, and without her aid the designs of man are as bubbles on a troubled ocean.

Index

SET IN 11 POINT BELL LEADED 1 POINT
WITH BELL AND GRESHAM TYPES FOR DISPLAY.
MAPS DRAWN BY K. C. JORDAN, FRGS.
TEXT AND LITHO ILLUSTRATIONS
PRINTED BY W AND J MACKAY LIMITED, CHATHAM
ON GUARD BRIDGE SMOOTH LAID PAPER.
BOUND BY W AND J MACKAY LIMITED, IN BUCKRAM
BLOCKED WITH A DESIGN TAKEN FROM
A SPANISH BINDING OF 1819.